Study Guide to Acc

Essentials of Psychology
Exploration and Application
Sixth Edition

Dennis Coon

Santa Barbara City College

Prepared by

Tom Bond

Thomas Nelson Community College

Bill Cunningham

Thomas Nelson Community College

West Publishing Company

Minneapolis/St. Paul   New York   Los Angeles   San Francisco

WEST'S COMMITMENT TO THE ENVIRONMENT

In 1906, West Publishing Company began recycling materials left over from the production of books. This began a tradition of efficient and responsible use of resources. Today, up to 95% of our legal books and 70% of our college texts and school texts are printed on recycled, acid-free stock. West also recycles nearly 22 million pounds of scrap paper annually—the equivalent of 181,717 trees. Since the 1960s, West has devised ways to capture and recycle waste inks, solvents, oils, and vapors created in the printing process. We also recycle plastics of all kinds, wood, glass, corrugated cardboard, and batteries, and have eliminated the use of Styrofoam book packaging. We at West are proud of the longevity and the scope of our commitment to the environment.

Production, Prepress, Printing and Binding by West Publishing Company.

 TEXT IS PRINTED ON 10% POST CONSUMER RECYCLED PAPER  PRINTED WITH SOY INK

table of contents

acknowledgements

First of all, we would like to extend our appreciation to all of the students who have provided feedback since the last edition of this *Study Guide*. Second, we would like to thank Dennis Rallings, our editor at West Publishing, for his patience, understanding, encouragement, and willingness to help us solve problems. Finally, without the initial encouragement and friendship of Clyde Perlee, Editor in Chief at West Publishing, none of this would have been possible.

We could not have put together this *Study Guide* nor would we have wanted to without the fantastic Coon text. Dennis and Sevren Coon have been a continuing source of warmth and support. We wish each of you could get to know them personally.

Tom Bond
Bill Cunningham

to the student

GENERAL INTRODUCTION

This *Study Guide* is essentially self-explanatory. It is designed to help you learn as much as possible about the interesting field of psychology. At the same time we want you to have every opportunity to succeed in your efforts. If you use this *Study Guide* in the way we have intended for you to, you will probably achieve both of these goals and enjoy the process.

ABOUT THIS *STUDY GUIDE*

If you turn to any chapter in this *Guide* you will quickly see the general structure. Each chapter is divided into six sections:

KEY TERMS, CONCEPTS, AND INDIVIDUALS — This is just a list of the main terms, ideas, and individuals contained in the material in the chapter. These terms and ideas will be tested and reinforced in the other sections.

LEARNING OBJECTIVES — Each learning objective relates to the essential information in the text. Knowledge of all of the learning objectives will ensure that you know the chapter well. Write in the spaces provided. This gives you practice in mastering the material. Be sure to do all of the objectives before proceeding to the self-quizzes.

DO YOU KNOW THE INFORMATION? — This section contains different kinds of self-quizzes (multiple choice, true-false, and/or matching) to give you feedback regarding your basic knowledge of the material.

CAN YOU APPLY THE INFORMATION? — This section contains more self-quizzes, but these quizzes require that you apply the concepts. We have tried to make the questions challenging, but fun. We hope you will find an item every once in a while that will tickle your fancy.

CHAPTER REVIEW — This section is a fill-in-the-blank review to be used shortly before a test. It will give you a good review by focusing on the key terms and concepts presented in each chapter.

ANSWER KEYS — These keys give you the correct answer, the objective being tested, and the corresponding page in the text. Use the answer keys wisely. Don't cheat yourself by looking up the answer ahead of time.

USING THIS *STUDY GUIDE*

While no one study technique works equally well for each student, our best students from over the years have related the following method which has proved most successful for them. First, one should read quickly through the objectives in this *Study Guide*. Then with the *Guide* open beside the textbook, read the chapter while noting either by underlining or highlighting the material which relates to each objective. Next, write the answers to the objectives in the *Study Guide*. Then use the self-quizzes to test your knowledge of the concepts. Finally, use the Chapter Review shortly before a test.

LET US HEAR FROM YOU

This *Study Guide* is written for you. We are interested in your comments and suggestions. This in not just lipservice. Please let us hear from you. It need not be a formal letter; just drop me a note. Only through your critical comments can the *Study Guide* really be improved. The best revision comes from the input of the users.

Tom Bond and Bill Cunningham
Department of Psychology
Thomas Nelson Community College
P.O. Box 9407
Hampton, Virginia 23670

chapter one

Psychology and Psychologists

KEY TERMS, CONCEPTS, AND INDIVIDUALS

definition of psychology X
behavior √
    overt vs. covert √
empirical evidence
    data
the young science
comparative psychologists
    anthropomorphic fallacy
goals of psychology
Wundt & introspection
Titchener & structuralism
William James & functionalism
    Darwin & natural selection
John Watson & behaviorism
    Ivan Pavlov, B.F. Skinner
women in psychology
    Mary Washburn
Max Wertheimer & gestalt psychology
Freud & psychoanalytic psychology
    unconscious, behavior is determined,
    psychoanalysis
    Jung & neo-Freudians

Rogers & Maslow: humanism
    free will, self-actualization
eclectic
cognitive and biological perspectives
types of mental health workers
    psychiatrist, psychologist,
    psychoanalyst, counselor
    psychiatric social worker,
    clinical versus counseling psychologist
APA professional code
basic versus applied research
psychologists:
    developmental, learning,
    personality, sensation and perceptual,
    physiological, social, cross-cultural
the fallacy of common sense
scientific method
    hypothesis & operational definition
naturalistic observation
    observer effects & observer bias
correlational study

coefficient of correlation
experiment (causal relationship)
    independent, dependent &
    extraneous variables
    experimental vs. control groups
    random assignment
    placebo effect
    single vs. double blind
    experimenter effect & self-fulfilling
prophecy
    ethics of research
clinical method (case study)
survey method
    representative sample, courtesy bias
pseudo-psychologies:
    palmistry, phrenology,
    graphology, astrology
uncritical acceptance
fallacy of positive instances
P.T. Barnum Effect
critical reading of the popular press

LEARNING OBJECTIVES

To demonstrate mastery of this chapter you should be able to:

1. List two reasons for studying psychology.

    a.

    b.

2. Define psychology.

3. Describe what behavior is and differentiate overt from covert behavior.

 4. Explain what empirical evidence is and give an example of it.

 5. Identify the point at which psychology became a science.

 6. Explain why psychology is referred to as a "young science" and give three reasons to support your answer.

    a.

    b.

    c.

7. Explain what the anthropomorphic fallacy is and how it can lead to problems in psychological research.

 8. List and/or explain each goal of psychology including its ultimate goal. Explain why the word "control" has a special meaning for psychologists which is distinct from the everyday meaning of the word.

    a.

    b.

    c.

    d.

9.   Explain the sentence "Psychology has a long past but a short history."

10. Describe the school of psychology known as structuralism including:

   a.   where and when it was established

   b.   who established it (the "father" of psychology)

   c.   the focus of its study

   d.   research method and its drawback

   e.   goal

11. Describe the functionalist school of psychology including:

   a.   its founder

   b.   its goal

   c.   major interests

   d.   impact on modern psychology

12. Describe behaviorism (S-R psychology) including:

   a.   its founder

   b.   why its founder could not accept structuralism or functionalism

   c.   its emphasis

   d.   Skinner's contribution and his concept of a "designed culture"

   e.   therapeutic outgrowth

13.   Describe the Gestalt school of psychology including:

    a.   what the word Gestalt means

    b.   who founded it

    c.   goal

    d.   slogan

    e.   areas of interest

14.   Describe the psychoanalytic school of psychology including:

    a.   who founded it

    b.   point of departure

    c.   four contributions to psychology

    d.   method of psychotherapy

15.   Characterize the representation of the sexes in early psychology and explain the reason for the discrepancy. State the ratio of the sexes receiving doctorates in psychology today. Name the first woman to receive her doctorate in psychology.

16.   List the three "forces" in psychology.

    a.   b.   c.

17.   Describe the humanistic school of psychology including:

    a.   how its approach differs from psychoanalytic and behavioristic thought

    b.   who its major representatives are

    c.   position on "free will" (as contrasted with determinism)

    d.   psychological needs

    e.   interest in a scientific approach

    f.   subjective factors

    g.   concept of self-actualization

18. Describe the eclectic approach.

19. List and briefly describe the 5 major perspectives in modern psychology.

    a.

    b.

    c.

    d.

    e.

20. Briefly describe cognitive psychology.

21. Characterize the differences in training, emphasis and/or expertise among psychologists, psychiatrists, psychoanalysts, counselors, and psychiatric social workers.

22. List the three points in the professional code for psychologists established by the APA.

    a.

    b.

    c.

23. Identify the largest areas of specialization among psychologists. Name the major source of employment for psychologists.

24. Differentiate basic from applied research.

25. Write a brief summary of each of the following areas of specialization in psychology:

    a. clinical and counseling

    b. developmental

c.   learning

d.   personality

e.   sensation and perception

f.   comparative

g.   biopsychology

h.   social

i.   cross-cultural

j.   industrial

k.   school

l.   experimental

26.   Explain the problem with using common sense as a source of information.

27.   List the five steps of the scientific method.

a.

b.

c.

d.

e.

28.   Define the term "hypothesis" and be able to identify one. Explain what an operational definition is.

29. Explain the purpose of theory formulation.

30. Describe the technique of naturalistic observation including both the advantages and limitations of this method.

31. Describe what a correlational study is and list three advantages and disadvantages of this a method. Explain what a correlation coefficient is, how it is expressed, what it means, and how it is related to causation.

advantages   *disadvantages*

a.   a.

b.   b.

c.   c.

32. List and describe the three essential variables of the experimental method.

    a.

    b.

    c.

33. Explain the nature and the purpose of the control group and the experimental group in an experiment.

34. Explain the purpose of randomly assigning subjects to either the control or the experimental group.

35. Identify three advantages and two disadvantages of the experimental method.

    advantages   *disadvantages*

    a.   a.

    b.   b.

    c.

36. Explain what a placebo is, how effective it is, how it probably works, and what its purpose in an experiment is.

37. Explain what single-blind and double-blind experimental arrangements are.

38. Explain the nature of the experimenter effect and how it is related to the self-fulfilling prophecy.

39. List and describe the three areas of ethical concern in psychological experiments, and explain the position of the APA in terms of ethical guidelines.

    a.

    b.

    c.

40. Briefly describe the clinical method of research including two advantages and three disadvantages. Give an example of a case in which the clinical method would be used.

41. Briefly describe the survey method of investigation including the importance of a representative sample, and an advantage and a disadvantage of the method. Define the term "courtesy bias."

42. Define the term "critical thinking." Describe each of the four principles which form the foundation of critical thinking.

a.

b.

c.

d.

43. Indicate the foundations and fallacies of each of the following pseudo-psychologies:

a. palmistry

b.. phrenology

c. graphology

d. astrology

44.   List and explain the three reasons why pseudo-psychologies continue to thrive even though they have no scientific basis.

    a.

    b.

    c.

The following objectives are related to the material in the "Applications" section of your text.

45.   List eight suggestions that your author gives to help you become a more critical reader of psychological information in the popular press.

    a.

    b.

    c.

    d.

    e.

    f.

    g.

    h.

─────────────────── SELF-QUIZZES ───────────────────

Do You Know the Information?

Multiple Choice

1.   Your author states that psychology should be studied because
    (a) a person can hardly be considered "educated" without knowing something about the field of psychology.
    (b) we are in the midst of a psychological revolution.
    (c) it helps us better serve as informal therapists.
    (d) it allows us to become one with the universe.

2.   Psychology is
    (a) the study of the behavior of animals.
    (b) the study of the mind of man.
    (c) the scientific study of human and animal behavior.
    (d) the scientific study of organisms.

3.   Which of the following is an example of *covert* behavior?
    (a) talking   (b) thinking   (c) glaring   (d) laughing

4.   Empirical evidence is evidence that
    (a) relies on authority for its veracity.
    (b) is as good as a professional psychologist's opinion.
    (c) is gained through direct observation and measurement.
    (d) is not described by any of the above answers..

5. Psychology became a science when
   (a) psychologists began performing experiments.
   (b) the first psychological laboratory was built.
   (c) behaviorism became the major school of psychology.
   (d) philosophy was downgraded to an art.

6. Psychology has been described as a "young science" because
   (a) it has not had a long enough past.
   (b) it has not yet sufficiently differentiated itself from philosophy.
   (c) scientific study of some topics is not yet possible.
   (d) other sciences use different experimental methods.

7. Some questions about behavior go unanswered because
   (a) ethical standards may be violated in conducting the research.
   (b) a suitable method is lacking.
   (c) social attitudes may limit that research.
   (d) all of the above are true.

8. The temptation to attribute human thoughts, feelings, and motives to animals is called the
   (a) fallacy of overgeneralization.
   (b) anthropomorphic fallacy.
   (c) rattomorphic view.
   (d) cynical veterinarian syndrome.

9. Which of the following is *not* a goal of psychology (immediate or ultimate)?
   (a) predict
   (b) control
   (c) understand
   (d) describe
   (e) judge
   (f) gather knowledge to benefit humanity

10. Probably the most misunderstood goal of psychology is
    (a) control.
    (b) prediction.
    (c) understanding.
    (d) description.

11. Psychology is said to have a long past but a short history because
    (a) the experimental techniques used by psychologists were developed by philosophers.
    (b) introspection was not an accepted method of investigation until the early 20th century.
    (c) psychology's past includes philosophy which is hundreds of years old, whereas psychology's history is only about 100 years old.
    (d) the word "past" is more ambiguous in its meaning than "history."

12. In the history of psychology very few women were credited with accomplishments or even mentioned because
    (a) there were very few female psychologists, about one in every 100.
    (b) there were no women who were awarded doctorates.
    (c) men dominated the academic life in the late 1800s.
    (d) there were really no well-known female psychologists.

13. A person who blends ideas and perspectives from different schools of thought could be called
    (a) Freudian.
    (b) clinical.
    (c) eclectic.
    (d) philosophical.

14. Which of the following *are not* considered to be one of the five major perspectives in modern psychology?
    (a) structuralism
    (b) functionalism
    (c) behaviorism
    (d) Gestalt
    (e) psychodynamic
    (f) humanism
    (g) cognitive
    (h) psychobiological

15. The APA professional code for psychologists does *not* stress
    (a) performing only recognized psychoanalytic therapy.
    (b) confidentiality in professional endeavors.
    (c) accurate representation of professional qualifications.
    (d) protection of the client's welfare.

16. The largest area of specialization in psychology is
    (a) counseling.
    (b) school and educational.
    (c) clinical.
    (d) industrial.

17. Most psychologists
    (a) are in private practice.
    (b) do psychotherapy.
    (c) work in hospital settings.
    (d) are employed by educational institutions.

18. Common sense is often a very poor source of information because
    (a) most of the pseudo-psychologies rely on it.
    (b) it was the very reason for the beginning of the scientific revolution.
    (c) it can prevent people from seeking better information or seeing the truth.
    (d) of all of the above reasons.

19. Which of the following is *not* one of the steps of the scientific method?
    (a) experimentation   (b) inference   (c) hypothesizing   (d) defining the problem

20. A hypothesis
    (a) is a guess that has been tested.
    (b) is like a theory.
    (c) proves or disproves a correlation.
    (d) is a tentative explanation of an event.

21. Without theory formulation
    (a) hypotheses would be useless.
    (b) experiments could not be conducted.
    (c) research would yield a mass of disconnected facts.
    (d) experiments would be useless.

22. If a researcher is taking copious notes while watching her subject behave in its own environment the researcher is probably engaged in
    (a) a survey.
    (b) the experimental method.
    (c) computing a correlation coefficient.
    (d) naturalistic observation.

23. An advantage of the naturalistic observation method of study is
    (a) the causes of an observed behavior can be determined.
    (b) the subject is studied in its customary environment.
    (c) powerful controlled observations can be made.
    (d) information regarding large numbers of subjects can be gathered.

24. A coefficient of correlation is a number which
    (a) expresses the degree and nature of the relationship between two events.
    (b) shows the degree to which one event causes another.
    (c) indicates the extent of control in the experimental method.
    (d) is frequently used when doing a case study.

25. In the experimental method the variable which is manipulated is the
    (a) dependent variable.
    (b) variable that is "tried" on the control group.
    (c) independent variable.
    (d) extraneous variable.

26. Outside variables which can contaminate an experiment and which the researcher wishes to remove are called
    (a) controlled.   (b) random.   (c) extraneous.   (d) artificial.

27. The purpose of the control group in the experimental method is to
    (a) be subjected to the independent variable.
    (b) serve as a point of reference to which to compare the experimental group.
    (c) be manipulated by receiving the dependent variable.
    (d) allow surveys to be taken.

28. In order to eliminate differences in personal characteristics of subjects in the control and experimental groups that could influence the outcome of the experiment
    (a) all of the relevant characteristics of the subjects are controlled by testing and then the subjects are divided equally into the two groups by characteristics.
    (b) the researcher hand picks each subject and uses very large groups.
    (c) more than one experimental group is used.
    (d) subjects are randomly assigned to each group.

29. The experimental method may be criticized as a research technique because it
    (a) involves too many variables.
    (b) often appears artificial.
    (c) may involve observation.
    (d) is subject to all of the above.

30. In an experiment to test the effects of a drug, the control group is given a placebo
    (a) so that each group will be exactly alike except for the drug.
    (b) because the experimental group has been given a placebo plus the drug.
    (c) to test the effect of the dependent variable.
    (d) to control for a single-blind design.

31. A double-blind research design is used to
    (a) control for the experimenter effect.
    (b) insure that the experimenter does not influence the subjects.
    (c) control for the placebo effect.
    (d) take care of all of the above.

32. If subjects in a psychological experiment respond to subtle cues from the experimenter about what is expected of them, this is called
    (a) cue-dependent submission.   (b) experimental expectation.   (c) the experimenter effect.   (d) cheating.

33. Ethical or moral questions raised by certain psychological research
    (a) have largely gone unanswered.
    (b) have produced a spate of laws sponsored by the Department of Health, Education and Welfare.
    (c) prompted the APA to adopt research guidelines.
    (d) have been deemed to be irrelevant because of the pursuit of knowledge.

34. In order to take advantage of situations where important information can be gathered about topics that could not be studied any other way, which method of investigation would be employed?
    (a) clinical   (b) naturalistic observation   (c) survey   (d) experimental

35. The research methods in which little control is possible are
    (a) survey, naturalistic observation, and clinical.
    (b) correlational, experimental, and survey.
    (c) naturalistic observation, correlational, and survey.
    (d) correlational, clinical, and naturalistic observation.

36. The method of investigation which is designed for the gathering of information from large numbers of people is
    (a) the experimental method.   (b) naturalistic observation.   (c) the survey method.   (d) the clinical method.

37. Which of the following is *not* one of the four basic principles of critical thinking?
    (a) Few "truths" transcend the need for empirical testing.
    (b) Evidence varies in quality.
    (c) The expertise of an authority makes an idea true.
    (d) Critcal thinking requires an open mind.

38. Which of the following pseudo-psychologies analyzes a person's personality by studying his or her handwriting?
    (a) phrenology   (b) palmistry   (c) graphology   (d) astrology

39. Which of the following is *not* a reason why pseudo-psychologies continue to thrive even though they have no scientific basis?
    (a) the P.T. Barnum Effect
    (b) the fallacy of positive instances
    (c) uncritical acceptance
    (d) they make good philosophical points

40. In order to be able to distinguish the difference between wishful thinking and science, an informed reader should
    (a) discriminate between inference and observation.
    (b) look for errors in distinguishing between correlation and causation.
    (c) be skeptical.
    (d) be concerned with all of the above.

41. A key element in the scientific pursuit of truth is the
    (a) random assignment of variables.
    (b) ability to make critical judgments.
    (c) correlational method combined with observations.
    (d) ability to replicate observations or experiments.

Matching *(Each will have more than one answer. Use the letters on the right only once.)*

_____ 1. behaviorism
_____ 2. functionalism
_____ 3. Gestalt
_____ 4. humanism
_____ 5. psychoanalytic
_____ 6. structuralism
_____ 7. cognitive

A Freud
B. pseudo-science
C. study of conscious experience
D. functions of consciousness
E. whole is greater than the sum of its parts
F. behavior modification
G. goal was to develop a sort of "mental chemistry"
H. free will
I. shouldn't analyze psychological phenomena; study wholes
J. third force psychology
K. founder wanted to make psychology more scientific
L. centers on thinking, language, problem-solving, creativity
M. goal – to learn how thought, perception, habits, and emotions aid human adaptation
N. unconscious
O. love, self-esteem, belonging, self-actualization
P. importance of childhood for later personality
Q. emphasized S-R relationships
R. introspection
S. has refocused attention on internal processes, such as consciousness
T. spurred the development of industrial psychology
U. experimental self-observation

Can you differentiate psychologists from psychiatrists, psychoanalysts and counselors? Place an "x" in the appropriate column(s).

	1	2	3	4	5	6	7	8	9
psychologist									
psychiatrist									
psychoanalyst									
counselor									

1. first undergoes analysis before treating others
2. must have a medical degree (M.D.)
3. may teach, do research, act as a consultant to business or industry
4. has either a Ph.D. or an M.D.
5. may do psychotherapy
6. may prescribe drugs
7. trained in Freudian theory
8. looks for physical causes of psychological difficulties
9. at one time limited practice to less serious adjustment problems

Fill in the Blank

1. "I am interested in behavior and how people grow and change from conception through death. I am a(n) _____ psychologist."

2. "I do psychotherapy to try to help people with emotional or behavioral disorders. I am a(n) _____ psychologist."

3. "I am interested in racism, conformity, attitudes, and in the behavior of people in groups. I am a(n) _____ psychologist."

4. "I used to study the bumps on a person's head to discover aspects of their personality. I was a _____."

5.   "I am interested in improving learning and motivation in the classroom. I am a(n) _____ psychologist."

6.   "I read the lines on your hand to foretell your future and evaluate your personality. I am engaged in _____."

7.   "I am interested in all aspects of a person's job and work environment. I am a(n) _____ psychologist."

8.   "I am interested in how your brain and nervous system affect your behavior. I am a(n) _____ psychologist."

9.   "I learn about you and your personality by analyzing your handwriting. I am a _____.

10.   "I am interested in questions about animal behavior. I am a(n) _____ psychologist."

11.   "How do we come to know the world? I am interested in information processing. I am interested in _____ and _____."

12.   "I apply scientific research methods to study human and animal behavior. I am a(n) _____ psychologist."

13.   "I am interested in how a person's culture influences their behavior especially with regard to comparisons of the different influences of different cultures. I am a(n) _____-_____ psychologist.

True-False

_____ 1. Cognitive behavorism combines thinking and environmental control to explain behavior.

_____ 2. Psychiatric social workers emphasize the use of social science principles to solve individual mental health problems.

_____ 3. Operational definitions allow abstract concepts to be tested in real-world terms.

_____ 4. The accuracy of any naturalistic observation may be diminished because the observer may report biased observations.

_____ 5. Coefficients of correlation vary between 0 and +1.

_____ 6. A correlational study is one that determines the degree of correlation between two traits or behaviors.

_____ 7. Correlation does not prove causation because by its very nature correlation can only show that two events are related.

_____ 8. One advantage of the experimental method is that causal relationships can be identified.

_____ 9. Many researchers feel that a major disadvantage of the experimental method is that there are too many controls.

_____10. A placebo is a substance which has no direct chemical effect itself.

_____11. Research indicates that placebos do nothing physically; the effect of the placebo is imaginary.

_____12. The way a sample is chosen can either make or break a survey.

_____13. Since most surveys primarily measure attitudes, it is essential that the information gathered be truthful.

Can You Apply the Information?

1.   Which of the following is an acceptable example of behavior?
     (a) looking   (b) daydreaming   (c) thinking   (d) all of these are acceptable

2.   Which of the following is an example of empirical evidence?
     (a) The results of a controlled experiment reveal that children who are reinforced for aggressive behavior act more aggressively.
     (b) The Methodist minister said, "After 30 years of religious study I am convinced that there is life after death."
     (c) A person argues that a seven-month-old fetus has better chance of survival if born than an eight-month-old fetus.
     (d) none of the above

3.   The United States and the Soviet Union are planning a joint mission to the planet Mars, with humans, sometime after the year 2000. Besides the physical challenges to overcome, no one knows what the psychological effects will be on the people involved living in cramped quarters, with no gravity, unable to leave, and with the same people for three years. Even though that information is vital to the completion of the mission, it is not currently obtainable. The reason for that is probably because
     (a) of the ethical restrictions that would be placed on the research.
     (b) the social attitudes of the two countries involved would limit the research.
     (c) there is currently no suitable method to test those conditions.
     (d) of the money involved in doing long term research.

4.   The statement "our dog is jealous of our new baby" reflects
     (a) the views of the functionalist school.   (c) a philosophical inquiry.
     (b) the anthropomorphic fallacy.   (d) a lack of humanistic concern.

5.   The woman did not receive help when she was attacked because there were many potential helpers standing around. This statement best exemplifies which of the four goals of psychology?
     (a) prediction   (b) control   (c) understanding   (d) description

6.   You are the inventor of the first time machine. As the initial test, you decide to go back in time and meet some of the founders of the historical schools of psychology. When you disembark, the first person you meet greets you by saying, "A rose is a rose is a rose." You have just met
     (a) Wilhelm Wundt   (b) John B. Watson   (c) William James   (d) Edward B. Titchener

7.   The school of psychology that would probably have the *least* interest in the study of a person's experiences after being declared clinically dead would be
     (a) psychoanalytic psychology. (b) behaviorism.   (c) structuralism.   (d) humanism.

8.   "I believe that a person can be motivated by unconscious forces but also that one strives for self-actualization. I am using behavior modification to help a student who suffers from overwhelming test anxiety. I see myself as _____."
     (a) a humanist   (b) psychoanalytically oriented (c) a behaviorist   (d) eclectic

9.   The psychotherapist *most* likely to be interested in the repressed aspects of your toilet training would be a
     (a) psychologist.   (b) psychiatrist.   (c) psychoanalyst.   (d) gestalt therapist.

10. Which of the following is the *best* example of "basic" research?
     (a) a study of the aerodynamic characteristics of a car being designed for maximum gas mileage
     (b) the effects of differing levels of high density lipoproteins on the recurrence of heart attacks
     (c) the effect of immediate versus delayed feedback of test results on student performance
     (d) the effect of lysergic acid diethylamide (LSD) on the Asiatic elephant

11. George's dog Gus wandered away from home. This disturbed George so he decided to try to find a way to teach Gus a lesson. The next time Gus wandered away George called and called his name. Finally Gus came to George who was waiting with a rolled up newspaper. George smacked Gus a couple of times and said, "That'll teach you not to wander away again!" The next time Gus got out and wandered away George could not coax him home by calling but had to go out and find him. The dog no longer responded to George's calling. (Smart dog!) George's plan was an example of
     (a) using naturalistic observation.   (c) using common sense.
     (b) problem solving by correlation.   (d) reverse psychology.

12. George pondered, "I'll bet if I reward instead of punish Gus when he responds to my call, he'll begin to respond faster and more often." George's statement is an example of
(a) an observation. (b) a theory. (c) defining the problem. (d) a hypothesis.

13. You are a psychologist and have been conducting research on aggression in children. Your studies have focused on modeling and aggression, the effects of TV on aggression, and the effects of punishment on aggression. You have performed many studies and have collected much data but you feel as if there is no unifying idea in all your data. You can't see the proverbial forest because of the trees. According to the scientific method your next step would probably be to
(a) develop a theory. (c) conduct research on one specific idea.
(b) propose a different, totally new hypothesis. (d) give up and have a good cry.

For questions 14-18, choose the letter of the research technique from the list below which would most effectively give you answers to each question.

(a) naturalistic observation (c) experimental method (e) survey method
(b) correlational method (d) clinical method

_____14. You are a doctor interested in the gastrointestinal tract. You have the opportunity to observe a person whose surgeon did a poor job repairing a gunshot wound to the stomach. The patient was left with a fistula (a hole from a hollow organ to the surface of the body). What does the process of human digestion in the stomach really look like?

_____15. Is there any relationship between unemployment and the number of admissions to psychiatric hospitals?

_____16. What kinds of breakfasts are eaten by lower, middle, and upper income families?

_____17. Does eating breakfast enable children to do better in school?

_____18. If a person is lying on a sidewalk in front of a bank, dressed in a suit, and moaning about needing money to eat, how many people will stop and try to help?

19. This is your first trip with the Lewis and Clark expedition to explore and map portions of the U.S. One day your party hears thunder and you overhear the person next to you say, "Ugh! I hate rain. Rain causes mos-quitoes. Whenever it rains we start getting more mosquitoes." You laugh to yourself because
(a) the person obviously has used the clinical method instead of observation.
(b) this is an example of confusing causation and correlation.
(c) there are too many extraneous variables to draw a valid conclusion.
(d) his observation was caused by the self-fulfilling prophecy.

20. A researcher notes that the amount of ice cream consumed and the number of drownings are correlated +.66. The researcher may conclude that
(a) as the amount of ice cream consumed decreases, the number of drownings also decreases.
(b) ice cream causes people to drown.
(c) as the amount of ice cream consumed increases, the number of drownings decreases.
(d) there is very little relationship between ice cream and drownings.

21. For a person on a diet, the correlation between the number of calories consumed and the number of pounds lost would be
(a) positive. (c) nonexistent.
(b) negative. (d) unknown without more information.

22. In an experiment involving the effects of certain kinds of practice on the acquisition of piano-playing skill, the researcher is worried that one student may have certain advantages over another. To control for some of these advantages (such as age, sex, previous musical training, manual dexterity, and pitch discrimination) the researcher has each student fill out a detailed question-naire so that each group can be made roughly comparable to the others. The researcher
(a) appears to have thought of most of the important extraneous variables.
(b) can't do this type of research on this problem.
(c) should use naturalistic observation.
(d) needs to use random assignment of groups instead.

23.   You are a physician and have a patient with chronic, intractable pain. The patient is rapidly becoming addicted to the morphine derivative that you have prescribed. Which of the following statements is most applicable?
   (a) The pain is most likely psychosomatic.   (c) A fourth surgical procedure is definitely indicated.
   (b) Send the patient to a psychotherapist.   (d) This might be a good time to try a placebo.

For questions 24-32, use the following paragraph as a basis.

   Children who watch an aggressive program on television are more aggressive in free play than children who do not watch the aggressive program. In this experiment twenty 6-year-old children are randomly assigned to two groups. One group watches a 30 minute program that has been previously rated as aggressive. The other group watches a 30 minute program that has been previously rated as unaggressive. Both groups of children are then observed through a one-way mirror in a lab for 15 minutes of free play. The number of aggressive acts (which have been previously operationally defined) is counted.

Using the above paragraph place the correct letter from the following in the appropriate blank.

   (a) experimental group   (c) hypothesis   (e) control group
   (b) dependent variable   (d) independent variable   (f) extraneous variable

_____24. number of observed aggressive acts

_____25. watched unaggressive television program

_____26. aggressive TV program

_____27. Children who view aggressive TV are more aggressive than children who view unaggressive TV.

_____28. viewed aggressive TV show

_____29. amount of time the TV is watched

30.   This is an example of
   (a) a field experiment.   (b) a controlled experiment.   (c) naturalistic observation.   (d) a clinical study.

31.   If the researcher knew which children had seen the aggressive TV program, this could serve as the basis for
   (a) the experimenter effect.   (b) a negative correlation.   (c) the placebo effect.   (d) the dependent measure.

32.   In order to minimize bias
   (a) the person observing the children should administer the independent variable.
   (b) one group of children should listen to taped violence.
   (c) the observer measuring the dependent variable should not know which group each child was in.
   (d) the children should understand the hypothesis.

Chapter Review

1.   One reason for studying psychology is that you can hardly consider yourself _____ without knowing something about the field. Another reason is so we can know _____ better.

2.   _____ is the scientific study of human and animal behavior. Running, thinking, laughing, and learning are all examples of _____. Hidden behaviors are called _____, and visible behaviors are called _____.

3.   Evidence gained by direct observation and measurement is said to be _____.

4.   Psychology became a science when psychologists began to perform _____, make _____, and seek _____.

5. Psychology is sometimes described as a "_____ _____" because scientific study of some topics is not yet possible. Many psychological questions may remain unanswered because of _____ or _____ concerns. More frequently, there is just the lack of a suitable_____.

6. _____ psychologists attempt to study the similarities and differences in the behavior of different species. One problem (the _____ _____) is the tendency to attribute human thoughts, feelings, and motives to animals. This is an important concern because animals sometimes serve as _____ that provide the only information available on a subject of interest.

7. Psychology's goals are to _____, _____, _____, and _____ behavior. Its ultimate goal is to gather _____ for the benefit of _____. The goal of understanding behavior is satisfied when we explain _____ a phenomenon occurs.

8. _____, another goal, is the ability to accurately forecast behavior. This goal is especially important in _____ where specialists use tests to forecast behavior such as success in school or work.

9. _____ is the goal of psychology that is frequently questioned and misunderstood probably because it sounds like a threat to personal _____. To most psychologists, it simply means altering _____ that influence behavior in predictable ways.

10. Psychology's past is long because it includes _____ which is centuries old. Psychology's history is short. It began in the year _____ in _____, Germany. There _____ established the first psychological laboratory. He is considered the "father of psychology." He wanted to study _____ _____ by analyzing it into basic elements. To do this he developed an investigative method known as _____. His approach to the study of consciousness combined _____ introspection with objective measurement of various _____ (an appoach Wundt termed _____ _____-_____). The method unfortunately could not answer psychological questions if two people disagreed. His ideas eventually served as the basis of the school of psychology known as _____.

11. James is associated with the _____ school of psychology. He was interested in how the mind _____ to adapt us to changing demands. The functionalists sought to learn the ways in which thought, perception, habits, and emotions aid human _____. This was because the functionalists were strongly influenced by Darwin's principle of _____ _____. Functionalism had a direct impact on the development of _____ and _____ psychology.

12. Watson is associated with the _____ school of psychology. He considered introspection _____. He placed much importance on the relationship between _____ and an organism's _____. As a means of explaining most behavior, Watson adopted Pavlov's concept, the _____ _____.

13. One of the most widely known and influential modern behaviorists is _____. He emphasizes stimulus-response relationships and ignores _____ and _____ experience. He believes that behavior is shaped and maintained by its _____. A particularly valuable product of behaviorism is a form of therapy called _____ _____ which is based on learning principles. Skinner also promoted the idea of a "_____ _____" where positive reinforcement could encourage desirable behavior.

14. The German word _____ means form, pattern or whole. This school of psychology, founded by _____, sought to study experience as _____. These psychologists differed from the structuralists who sought to analyze or break down conscious experience. This viewpoint is particularly influential in the areas of _____ and _____.

15. _____ psychology was established by Freud. According to him, many areas of thoughts, conflicts, and desires are unknown to us and are termed _____. He also maintained that personality development was greatly influenced by a person's _____. The method of psychotherapy that he developed was called _____. His fourth major contribution was his insistence that all actions are _____.

16. There were few women in psychology in its early years largely because men _____ academic life in the late 1800s. Today for every 100 doctorates awarded in psychology, roughly _____ will be awarded to women. The first woman to be awarded a doctorate in psychology was Margaret _____.

17. The "third force" in psychology is known as _____. The other two forces are _____ and _____ _____.

18. The school of psychology that was developed to counter the negativity of behaviorism and psychoanalysis was _____. Two of its major proponents have been _____ and _____. This school of psychology rejects the Freudian idea of the _____ and the behavioristic idea that people are controlled by the _____. This school emphasizes the human ability to make choices, the concept of _____ _____. This concept is the opposite of _____ which holds that behavior is largely determined by forces beyond our control. It is not overly concerned with psychology trying to be _____. According to this school all humans have a need for _____ - _____, the need to develop to our fullest _____.

19. If a psychologist is not loyal to just one theoretical viewpoint but draws from many theories, he or she can be called _____. The five major perspectives evident in psychology today are the _____, _____, _____, _____, and _____ views.

20. _____ believe that all behavior will eventually be explained in terms of physical mechanisms. _____ psychologists study thoughts, language, consciousness, etc.

21. The label "_____" refers to a person who has master's degree or a doctorate in his or her specific discipline. A _____ must have a medical degree. If both of these people are providing psychotherapy, the former is probably a _____ _____. The latter is trained to look for the _____ causes of psychological disorders.

22. A _____ has to have either an M.D. or a Ph.D. and has been extensively trained in _____ theories. To be a _____, a person must typically have a _____ degree. At one time these professionals handled _____ problems that did not involve serious mental disorder. Today however, the distinctions between them and _____ psychologists is becoming blurred because they are both doing psychotherapy. A _____ _____ _____ usually joins other psychologists/psychiatrists as part of a team. Their training emphasizes the use of _____ _____ principles to solve social problems.

23. The professional code for psychologists established by the APA stresses accurate representation of one's _____ _____, _____ in professional work and _____ of the client's welfare.

24. The largest subareas of specialization in the field of psychology are _____ and _____/ _____, but most psychologists are employed by _____ institutions.

25. Research that is performed just for the sake of knowledge is termed _____. However, if the information gained from the research is to be put to immediate use the research is called _____.

26. A(n) _____ or a(n) _____ psychologist does psychotherapy. Psychologists who are interested in basic questions about animal behavior are called _____ psychologists. Investigating how people grow and change over time would make a person a(n) _____ psychologist.

27.   If you believe that all other areas of psychology will ultimately be explained by reference to the action of nerve cells or parts of the brain you are probably a(n) _____ .

28.   _____ psychologists are interested in people in a group setting. A(n) _____ psychologist would be interested in the improvement of the work environment and in the selection, evaluation, and training of job applicants.

29.   "I am interested in detecting and treating learning disabilities, counseling students with vocational or emotional concerns, and improving learning and motivation in the classroom. I am a(n) _____ psychologist."

30.   A(n) _____ psychologist applies scientific research methods to study human and animal behavior.

31.   A(n) _____ - _____ psychologist is interested in the different cultural forces that shape human behavior.

32.   We can be prevented from seeking better information or seeing the truth by a set of blinders called _____ _____. As an alternative to this and to avoid faulty observations, many scientists make use of the _____ _____. This method ideally includes the following steps:
      (a) _____
      (b) _____ _____ _____
      (c) _____ _____ _____
      (d) _____
      (e) _____ _____

33.   A _____ is a description or explanation of an event or observation that is tentative because it has not yet been adequately tested. An _____ definition gives the exact procedures used to represent a concept.

34.   In order to summarize a large number of observations in a way that accounts for existing data, predicts new observations, and guides further research, psychologists formulate _____.

35.   _____ _____ involves studying subjects in their customary environment. One of the advantages of this research method is that the behavior of the subject is observed in a _____ _____. One disadvantage is that the presence of an _____ may change the behavior of the _____. In addition, the observer may be _____ , and it is difficult to determine the _____ of the observed events.

36.   A _____ study is one that determines the degree of relationship between two traits, behaviors, or events. This type of study can be done in the _____ or in the _____ _____ and it allows for _____. On the negative side, little or no _____ is possible, relationships may be _____, and a researcher cannot confirm _____-_____ relationships.

37.   Coefficients of correlation vary between _____ and _____. If the number is _____ or close to it, there is a weak or nonexistent relationship. A positive correlation would be a number above _____ and indicates that _____ in one measure are matched by _____ in the other. In a negative correlation, _____ in the first measure are associated with _____ in the second, and vice versa. Correlational studies help us discover _____, but correlation do not demonstrate _____.

38.   To identify cause-effect relationships an _____ must be conducted. The three essential elements are _____ variables, _____ variables, and _____ variables. The variable which is manipulated, applied or changed by the experimenter is the _____ variable. Measures of the outcome of the experiment are called _____ variables. _____ variables are not allowed to affect the outcome of the experiment by making the conditions the same for both groups.

39. In the simplest psychological experiment there are two groups of subjects. The _____ group and the _____ group are treated exactly alike except for the _____ variable. The _____ group is exposed to this variable and the _____ group is used to establish a point of reference to which to compare the other group. Subjects are assigned to each group _____ so that each subject has an equal chance of being a member of either group.

40. The experimental method is advantageous because it allows you to establish _____ and because everything but the independent variable is _____. Also, there is no need to wait for the _____ event to occur. On the negative side, the experimental method is somewhat _____. Some _____ behavior is not easily studied in the lab.

41. A substance which is basically inert but has a tremendous psychological impact is called a _____. Its effects are not imaginary because experiments have shown that pain-killing, opiate-like drugs called _____ are released in the _____. A _____ is used in an experiment to insure that both groups are treated exactly alike except for the _____ variable.

42. A psychologist is doing research on a drug that is usually given in injection form. To control for the effect of the injection itself (the _____ effect) all subjects would be given an _____. This experimental technique is known as a _____-_____ arrangement and it controls for the _____ effect. Thus the subjects do not know who received the drug. The control group would be given the _____ and the experimental group would be given the _____. Thus the subjects would all be _____ as to who actually received the drug. If the experimenter is also _____ as to who actually received the drug, this would be a _____-_____ arrangement. This arrangement prevents the experimenter from consciously or unconsciously influencing the subjects' reactions which is called the _____ effect.

43. There are three areas of ethical concern that anyone conducting psychological research should be sensitive to: the use of _____, invasion of _____, and lasting _____ to participants. In response to these concerns the American Psychological Association has adopted guidelines which stress _____ for the people who participate and concern for their _____ and _____.

44. If a clinical psychologist conducts an in-depth interview with a person to learn as much as possible about the person's background, the psychologist is using the _____ method of investigation. One problem with this research method is that there is little possibility of _____. Another problem is that the researcher may not make _____ interpretations.

45. A researcher interested in how large segments of the general population feel about the issue of abortion would be likely to use the _____ method of investigation. It is very important when using this method to make sure that the sample of people questioned is _____. Sometimes this method may not be very _____. An example of this is when people show a _____ bias, the tendency to give answers which are agreeable and socially acceptable.

46. _____ _____ refers to an ability to evaluate, compare, analyze, critique, and synthesize information. Critical thinkers are willing to challenge _____ _____. To the critical thinker _____ _____ is built on thinking skills that allow us to continuously revise and enlarge our understanding of the world. It is built upon four basic principles:
(1) few "truths" transcend the need for _____ _____;
(2) evidence varies in _____;
(3) _____ expertise does not automatically make an idea true; and,
(4) critical thinking requires an open _____.

47. _____-_____ are dubious and unfounded systems superficially resembling psychology. _____ claims that lines in the hand are indicators of personality and a person's future.

48. _____ is the theory of personality based upon the location of bumps on the _____. Brain research revealed that many areas listed as controlling one characteristic were actually responsible for something drastically different.

49. Despite the fact that it scores close to zero on tests of accuracy in rating personality, handwriting analysis or _____ is used in this country to evaluate job applicants by over 500 companies.

50. _____ is based on the assumption that the position of the stars and planets at the moment of a person's birth determines personality characteristics. It has been repeatedly shown to have no scientific _____.

51. Pseudo-psychologies continue to survive and be popular because of _____ _____ by people, the fallacy of _____ _____, and the _____ _____ _____ Effect.

52. The _____ ____ _____ _____ occurs when a person tends to remember or notice things that confirm his or her expectations and to forget the rest.

53. The ____ ____ _____ _____ is a personality description written in such vague generalities that everybody can find something in it to believe.

54. There is much that can be learned from the popular press about psychology. However, much is written that is not scientific, and appears to be based on wishful thinking. One way to discriminate science from half-truths in the popular press is to be a(n) _____ reader. One should also consider the _____ of the information. If an experiment was discussed, a wise reader should be sure to look for a _____ group.

55. Two more suggestions for being a more critical reader of the popular press are look for errors in distinguishing between _____ and causation, and be sure to distinguish between observation and _____. It is also important for the informed reader to be aware of _____ and to remember that the phrase "_____ _____" is no guarantee of proof. A key element in the scientific pursuit of truth is the ability to _____ observations or experiments.

ANSWER KEYS

Do You Know the Information?

Multiple Choice

1. (a) obj. 1, p. 1
2. (c) obj. 2, p. 2
3. (b) obj. 3, p. 2
4. (c) obj. 4, p. 2
5. (a) obj. 5, p. 4
6. (c) obj. 6, p. 4
7. (d) obj. 6, p. 4
8. (b) obj. 7, p. 5
9. (e) obj. 8, p. 6
10. (a) obj. 8, p. 6
11. (c) obj. 9, p. 7
12. (c) obj. 13, p. 12
13. (c) obj. 18, p. 14
14. (a,b,d) obj. 19, p. 14
15. (a) obj. 22, p. 17
16. (c) obj. 23, p. 17, Fig. 1-17
17. (d) obj. 23, p. 17, Fig. 1-17
18. (c) obj. 26, p. 20
19. (b) obj. 27, p. 20
20. (d) obj. 28, p. 21
21. (a) obj. 29, p. 22
22. (d) obj. 30, p. 23

23. (b) obj. 30, pp. 24, 33
24. (a) obj. 31, p. 24
25. (c) obj. 32, p. 26
26. (c) objs. 32,34 pp. 25-27
27. (b) obj. 33, p. 26
28. (d) obj. 34, p. 27
29. (b) obj. 35, p. 33
30. (a) obj. 36, p. 29
31. (d) obj. 37, p. 29
32. (c) obj. 38, pp. 29-30
33. (c) obj. 39, p. 30
34. (a) obj. 40, p. 31
35. (d) objs. 30,31,40, p. 31
36. (c) obj. 41, p. 32
37. (c) obj. 42, p. 34
38. (c) obj. 43, p. 35
39. (d) obj. 44, pp. 36-37
40. (d) obj. 45, pp. 38-40
41. (d) obj. 45, p. 40

Matching

1. F,K,Q; obj. 12, p. 9
2. D,M,T; obj. 11, p. 8
3. E,I; obj. 13, p. 11
4. H,J,O; objs. 16-17, p. 13
5. A,N,P; obj. 14, pp. 11-12
6. C,G,R,U; obj. 10, pp. 8-9
7. L,S; obj. 20, pp. 15

True-False

1. T, obj. 12, p. 9
2. F, obj. 21, p. 16
3. T, obj. 28, p. 21
4. T, obj. 30, p. 23
5. F, obj. 31, p. 24
6. T, obj. 31, p. 24
7. T, obj. 31, p. 24
8. T, obj. 35, p. 26
9. F, obj. 35, p. 26
10. T, obj. 36, p. 29
11. F, obj. 36, p. 29
12. T, obj. 41, pp. 31-32
13. F, obj. 41, p. 32

	1	2	3	4	5	6	7	8	9
psychologist			X		X				
psychiatrist		X	X		X	X		X	
psychoanalyst	X		X	X	X	X			
counselor			X		X				X

Ans.: obj. 21, pp. 15-16

Can You Apply the Information?

1. (d) obj. 3, p. 2
2. (a) obj. 4, p. 2
3. (c) obj. 6, p. 4
4. (b) obj. 7, p. 5
5. (c) obj. 8, p. 6
6. (a) objs. 10-12, pp. 7-8
7. (b) objs. 10-14, 16-17, p. 9
8. (d) obj. 18, p. 14

9. (c) obj. 21, p. 15
10. (d) obj. 24, p. 17
11. (c) obj. 26, p. 20
13. (a) objs. 27,29, pp. 20-22
12. (d) obj. 28, p. 21
14. (d) obj. 40, p. 31
15. (b) obj. 31, p. 24
16. (e) obj. 41, pp. 31-32
17. (c) objs. 32-33, p. 26
18. (a) obj. 30, pp. 23-24
19. (b) obj. 31, p. 24
20. (a) obj. 31, p. 24
21. (b) obj. 31, p. 24
22. (d) obj. 34, p. 27
23. (d) obj. 36, p. 29
24. (b) objs. 32-33, p. 26
25. (e) obj. 33, p. 26
26. (d) obj. 32, p. 26
27. (c) obj. 28, p. 21
28. (a) obj. 32, p. 26
29. (f) obj. 32, p. 26
30. (b) objs. 32-33, p. 26
31. (a) obj. 38, pp. 29-30
32. (c) objs. 37-38, pp. 29-30

Fill in the Blank

1. developmental; obj. 25, p. 17
2. counseling or clinical; obj. 25, p. 18
3. social; obj. 25, p. 19
4. phrenologist; obj. 43, p. 35
5. school or educational; obj. 25, p. 18
6. palmistry; obj. 43, p. 35
7. industrial; obj. 25, p. 18
8. biopsychology; obj. 25, p. 19
9. graphologist; obj. 43, p. 35
10. comparative; obj. 25, p. 19
11. sensation, perception; obj. 25, p. 19
12. experimental; obj. 25, p. 18
13. cross-cultural; obj. 25, p. 19

Chapter Review

1. educated, ourselves (p. 1)
2. Psychology, behavior, covert, overt (p. 2)
3. empirical (p. 2)
4. experiments, observations, evidence (p. 4)
5. young science, ethical, practical; method (p. 4)
6. comparative, anthropomorphic fallacy; models (p. 5)
7. describe, understand, predict, control, knowledge, humanity, why (p. 6)
8. Prediction (p. 6); psychometrics (p. 6)
9. Control, freedom, conditions, (p. 6)
10. philosophy; 1879, Leipzig, Wundt, conscious experience, introspection, trained, stimuli, experimental self-observation, structuralism (p. 7)
11. functionalist, functions; adaptation, natural selections, educational, industrial (p. 8)
12. behaviorist, unscientific, stimuli, responses, conditioned response (p. 9)
13. Skinner, thought, subjective, consequences, behavior modification (p. 9); "designed culture" (p. 10)
14. Gestalt, Wertheimer; wholes, perception, personality (p. 11)
15. Psychoanalytic, unconscious, (p. 11); childhood, psychoanalysis, determined (p. 12)
16. dominated, 50, Washburn (p. 12)
17. humanism, behaviorism, psychodynamic psychology (p. 13)
18. humanism, Maslow, Rogers, unconscious, environment, free will, determinism, scientific, self-actualization, potential (p. 13)
19. eclectic, behavioristic, humanistic, psychodynamic, cognitive, biological (p. 14)
20. Psychobiologists, Cognitive (p. 14)
21. psychologist (p. 15); psychiatrist (p. 16); clinical (counseling) psychologist (p. 15); physical (p. 16)
22. psychoanalyst, Freudian, counselor (p. 16); master's, adjustment, clinical (p. 15); psychiatric social worker, social science (p. 16)
23. professional qualifications, confidentiality, protection (p. 16)
24. clinical, school/educational, educational (p. 17)
25. basic, applied (p. 17)
26. clinical, counseling (p. 16); comparative (p. 19); developmental (p. 17)
27. biopsychology (p. 19)

28. Social (p. 19); industrial (p. 18)
29. school (p. 18)
30. experimental (p. 18)
31. cross-cultural (p. 19)
32. common sense, scientific method, observation, defining a problem (p. 19); formulating a hypothesis, experimentation, theory formulation (p. 20)
33. hypothesis, operational (p. 21)
34. theories (p. 22)
35. Naturalistic observation, natural setting, observer (p. 23); observed, biased (p. 24); causes (p. 33)
36. correlational, lab, natural environment (p. 24); prediction, control, coincidental, cause-effect (p. 33)
37. +1, -1, 0, 0, increases (decreases), increases (decreases), increases, decreases (p. 24); relationships, causation (p. 25)
38. experiment, independent, dependent, extraneous, independent, dependent, Extraneous (p. 26)
39. experimental, control, independent, experimental (p. 26); control, randomly (p. 27)
40. causation, controlled (p. 28); natural, artificial, natural (p. 33)
41. placebo (p. 29); endorphins, brain, placebo (p. 29)
42. placebo, injection, single-blind, placebo, placebo, drug, blind, blind, double-blind, experimenter (p. 29)
43. deception, privacy, harm, respect, dignity, welfare (p. 30)
44. clinical (case study) (p. 31); control, objective (p. 33)
45. survey, representative (p. 32); accurate, courtesy (p. 33)
46. Critical thinking, conventional wisdom (p. 33); true knowledge, empirical testing, quality, claimed, mind (p. 34)
47. Pseudo-psychologies, Palmistry (p. 35)
48. Phrenology, skull (p. 35)
49. graphology (p. 35)
50. Astrology, validity (p. 36)
51. uncritical acceptance, positive instances (p. 36); P.T. Barnum (p. 37)
52. fallacy of positive instances (p. 37)
53. P.T. Barnum Effect (p. 37)
54. skeptical (informed), source (p. 38); control (p. 39)
55. correlation, inference (p. 39); oversimplifications, for example, replicate (p. 40)

chapter two

The Brain, Biology, and Behavior

LEARNING OBJECTIVES

To demonstrate mastery of this unit you should be able to:

1. Define biopsychology.

2. Name the basic unit of the nervous system, state what it is specifically designed to do, and list and describe its four parts.

  a.   c.

  b.   d.

3.   Explain how a nerve impulse (action potential) occurs and how it is an all-or-nothing event.

4.   Describe the difference between the nature of a nerve impulse and the nature of the communication between neurons.

5.   Explain how nerve impulses are carried from one neuron to another.

6.   Explain what determines whether a neuron will have an action potential triggered.

7.   Explain the function of neuropeptides.

8.   Differentiate a nerve from a neuron.

9.   Describe the effect of myelin on the speed of the nerve impulse.

10.   Explain what determines whether or not a neuron or a nerve will regenerate. Explain how in some cases brain damage can be somewhat alleviated and briefly describe the progress in generating regrowth of brain and spinal cord neurons.

11. Chart the various subparts of the human nervous system and generally explain their functions.

12. Differentiate between the two branches of the autonomic nervous system.

13. Explain the mechanism of the reflex arc.

14. List and describe five techniques for studying the brain. Briefly describe how electroencephalography works.

    a.

    b.

    c.

    d.

    e.

15. Describe each of the three scanning techniques for studying the entire brain as it functions.

    a.

    b.

    c.

16. Describe the main difference between the brains of lower and higher animals. Name what appears to be the foundation of human intellectual superiority.

17. Complete the following sentence: The cortex is composed of two sides, or _____ which are connected by the _____ _____. Describe the problem known as spatial neglect.

18. Explain how and why a brain is "split" and describe what the resulting effects are.

19. Differentiate the abilities of the two hemispheres of the cerebral cortex. Describe what is known about their working together as well as how they process information.

20. Describe the function(s) of each of the following:

    a. occipital lobes

    b. parietal lobes (include the somatosensory areas)

    c. temporal lobes

    d. frontal lobes

    e. associative areas (include Broca's and Wernicke's areas)

21. Explain the relationship between the size of the various parts of the somatosensory and motor areas of the cortex and the degree of sensitivity or importance of the corresponding body parts.

22. Describe the cause and effect of the two disorders aphasia and agnosia.

    aphasia   *agnosia*

23. List and be able to recognize the three areas of the subcortex.

    a.   b.   c.

24. Explain the function of each of the following parts of two of the three areas of the subcortex:

    a. Hindbrain (brainstem)

       1. medulla

       2. cerebellum

       3. reticular formation

    b. Forebrain

       1. thalamus

       2. hypothalamus

25. Name the structures that comprise the limbic system and explain its function (include a description of the function of the hippocampus). Briefly describe the significance of "pleasure" and "aversive" areas in the limbic system.

26. List five basic functions of the brain and associate them respectively to the actions of appropriate brain divisions.

   a.

   b.

   c.

   d.

   e.

27. Briefly explain the purpose of the endocrine system and name the mechanism by which this system carries out its function.

28. Describe the effect that the following glands have on the body and behavior:

   a. pituitary (include a description of giantism, hypopituitary dwarfism, and acromegaly)

   b. thyroid

   c. adrenal medulla

   d. adrenal cortex (include a description of virilism, premature puberty, and the problems of anabolic steroids)

The following objectives are related to the material in the "Applications" section of your text.

29. Describe the relationship among handedness, brain dominance, and speech. Describe what about handedness is inherited.

30. Explain how a person can determine which hemisphere is dominant.

31. State the incidence of left-handedness and discuss the relative advantages and/or disadvantages of being right-handed versus left-handed.

SELF-QUIZZES

Do You Know the Information?

Multiple Choice

1. Biopsychology is the study of
    (a) the mind.
    (b) the way our behavior is affected by the spinal cord.
    (c) how the brain and nervous system relate to behavior.
    (d) the neuron and the mechanism of nerve transmission.

2. Impulses are triggered and travel down the
    (a) soma.   (b) dendrite.   (c) axon.   (d) synapse.

3. An action potential is started when
    (a) charged particles move in and out of the cell.
    (b) the neurotransmitters charge the axon.
    (c) the synapse is crossed.
    (d) the cell's voltage drops below its resting potential.

4. Which of the following statements *best* characterizes the difference between axonal and synaptic transmission?
    (a) Synaptic transmission (communication between neurons) is primarily a molecular event.
    (b) The nerve impulse (axonal transmission) is basically a chemical event.
    (c) Axonal transmission may vary in strength.
    (d) Synaptic transmission is basically an electrical event.

5. A nerve impulse crosses the synapse by
    (a) jumping the gap like a spark.
    (b) releasing neurotransmitters.
    (c) stimulating the resting potential.
    (d) moving potassium and sodium ions across a membrane.

6. If enough excitatory messages arrive at a neuron at the same time or in quick succession a neuron's _____ is reached and an action potential is triggered.
    (a) potential   (b) level of inhibition   (c) resting potential   (d) threshold

7. Neuropeptides
    (a) aid in the regeneration of neurons.
    (b) regulate basic processes such as memory, pain, emotion, and pleasure.
    (c) lower the threshold for an action potential.
    (d) are found in the parasympathetic system.

8. Myelin is a layer of insulation around an axon that
   (a) speeds up the action potential.
   (b) aids in axonal regeneration.
   (c) protects the nerve.
   (d) both a and c above.

9. The structure found on many nerve fibers outside the CNS which aids in regeneration is the
   (a) telodendria.
   (b) neurilemma.
   (c) myelin sheath.
   (d) somatos.

10. The peripheral nervous system is divided into two parts, the
    (a) autonomic and the parasympathetic systems.
    (b) spinal cord and the parasympathetic systems.
    (c) somatic and the sympathetic systems.
    (d) autonomic and the somatic systems.

11. Which of the following statements is *correct* concerning the differing functions of the two branches of the autonomic nervous system?
    (a) The parasympathetic system prepares the body for "fight or flight."
    (b) The sympathetic system responds during times of arousal or emotional upheaval.
    (c) The sympathetic system is the "status quo" system.
    (d) All of the above are correct.

12. Indicate (by circling) which of the following are necessary for a reflex arc.
    (a) connector neuron
    (c) motor neuron
    (e) spinal cord
    (g) sensory neuron
    (b) brain
    (d) subcortex
    (f) motor cortex
    (h) effector cells

13. _____ is a research method whereby target areas within the brain are destroyed.
    (a) Ablation
    (b) Deep lesioning
    (c) ESB
    (d) Electroencephalography

14. _____ scans allow scientists to peer into the brain as if it were transparent.
    (a) EEG
    (b) CT
    (c) MRI
    (d) PET

15. Human intellectual superiority appears to be related to
    (a) the size and weight of the brain.
    (b) the ratio of the mass of brain compared to the mass of the spinal cord.
    (c) the increase in the size and wrinkling of the cortex.
    (d) the proportion of the frontal lobes.

16. The cortex is composed of two sides or _____, which are connected by the _____ _____.
    (a) lobes; limbic system.
    (b) lobes; parasympathetic system.
    (c) hemispheres; sympathetic system.
    (d) hemispheres; corpus callosum.

17. A split-brain individual has a circle flashed to her left brain and a square to her right brain. Which of the following statements describes the results?
    (a) Both sides of the brain are aware of the square and the circle.
    (c) She will draw a square with her right hand.
    (b) She will draw a circle with her left hand.
    (d) She will draw a square with her left hand.

18. Place an "R" in the blank for right hemisphere functions and an "L" for the left as they apply to the "typical" person:
    _____ (a) judges time and rhythm
    _____ (c) performs math computations
    _____ (e) recognizes melodies
    _____ (b) little speech present
    _____ (d) good at perceptual skills
    _____ (f) expresses emotion

19. Bodily sensations are channeled to and are registered on the
    (a) parietal lobes.
    (b) frontal lobes.
    (c) temporal lobes.
    (d) occipital lobes.

20. A map of bodily sensations on the somatosensory cortex would correspond to a map of bodily motor functions on the motor cortex in the following way:
    (a) the sensitivity or importance of the body area, respectively, is more important than its size.
    (b) the size of the body part is more important on the somatosensory map than on the motor map.
    (c) the size of the body part is more importnat on the motor map than on the somatosensory map.
    (d) both maps are useless in terms of understanding the functioning of the somatosensory and motor areas of the cortex.

21. Which of the following is *not* one of the three areas of the subcortex?
    (a) midbrain   (b) brainstem   (c) forebrain   (d) spinal cord

22. The part of the brain responsible for posture, muscle tone, and coordination is the
    (a) thalamus.   (b) limbic system.   (c) cerebellum.   (d) medulla.

23. The hypothalamus
    (a) acts as the final sensory switching system.
    (b) controls heart rate and respiration.
    (c) receives and processes visual information.
    (d) affects behavior such as sex, rage, eating, and drinking.

24. The limbic system is important for
    (a) the production of emotion and motivated behavior.
    (b) the regulation of salt balance in the body.
    (c) the processing and interpreting of auditory information.
    (d) direct control of voluntary muscles.

25. The rewarding properties of commonly abused drugs arise from
    (a) their ability to activate pleasure pathways.
    (b) their ability to activate the hippocampus.
    (c) their ability to deactivate the thalamus.
    (d) their ability to turn on the entire limbic system without destruction of major neurotransmitters.

26. The endocrine system "communicates" with the rest of the body by means of chemicals called _____ which are secreted directly into the blood stream.
    (a) endocrines   (b) corticoids   (c) hormones   (d) phermones

27. Which of the following glands is very important for the regulation of the salt balance in the body and the body's ability to withstand stress?
    (a) adrenal cortex   (b) thyroid   (c) adrenal medulla   (d) pituitary

28. Anabolic steroids are synthetic versions of
    (a) corticoids.   (b) growth hormones.   (c) adrenaline   (d) testosterone

29. Which of the following statements is *incorrect*?
    (a) Almost all right-handers process speech in the left hemisphere.
    (b) Left-handed people who write with a hooked hand are right-brain dominant.
    (c) About 15% of left-handers use both sides of the brain for language.
    (d) In the left-handed person, the left hemisphere controls the right hand.

True-False

_____ 1. Neurons are designed to carry information.

_____ 2. The soma collects and combines incoming information.

_____ 3. A nerve cell fires with differing intensities.

_____ 4. Neurons (which can also be called nerves) are the basic unit of the nervous system.

_____ 5. Sometimes damage to the brain can be partially alleviated by cutting out the damaged portion and allowing healthy new tissue to regenerate in its place.

_____ 6. The reflex arc is the simplest behavior sequence and can occur without any direct participation of the brain.

_____ 7. Results of PET scan research indicate that the smarter the person the less energy their brain requires.

_____ 8. The most important difference in the brains of man and lower animals is the proportion of brain tissue devoted to connecting the brain to the body.

_____ 9. The hemispheres of the brain are "split" by severing the spinal cord.

_____ 10. With right hemisphere damage a person could understand what was said, but would not recognize whether it was said in an angry or humorous way.

_____ 11. With careful training it is possible to be totally right- or left-brain thinking.

_____ 12. Voluntary muscle movements are controlled by the frontal lobes.

_____ 13. The larger the size of the part of the somatosensory area on the parietal lobe, the more sensitive the corresponding body part.

_____ 14. With aphasia a person has an impaired ability to use language.

_____ 15. The medulla controls vital life functions such as heart rate, swallowing, and respiration.

_____ 16. The reticular formation is responsible for alertness and wakefulness.

_____ 17. The hypothalamus and the reticular formation are parts of the limbic system.

_____ 18. One of the five basic functions of the brain is to control responses such as reflexes.

_____ 19. The success of growth hormone therapy is best measured by increased emotional well-being.

_____ 20. One of the benefits of being left-handed is that typically brain injuries aren't as damaging because there is less lateralization.

Matching (use the letters on the right only once)

_____ 1. dendrites
_____ 2. neuron
_____ 3. neurotransmitters
_____ 4. action potential occurs
_____ 5. nerve
_____ 6. central nervous system
_____ 7. corpus callosum
_____ 8. left hemisphere
_____ 9. Wernicke's area damage
_____ 10. occipital lobes
_____ 11. temporal lobes
_____ 12. hands
_____ 13. aphasia
_____ 14. thyroid
_____ 15. pituitary
_____ 16. acromegaly
_____ 17. effector cell
_____ 18. electroencephalography

A. problem with language
B. problems with the meaning of words
C. connects hemispheres
D. auditory area
E. balance and coordination
F. aids process of reorganization and recovery after injury
G. directly regulates metabolism
H. regulates salt balance
I. collect information
J. if threshold is reached
K. brain and spinal cord
L. basic unit of nervous system
M. recognizes melodies
N. bundle of axons and dendrites
O. visual area
P. measures brain's electrical activity
Q. secretion of too much growth hormone by pituitary late in the growth period
R. carry impulses from one neuron to another
S. large area on motor cortex
T. comprehends language in 95% of people
U. regulates functions of other glands
V. muscle fibers which contract

Can You Apply the Information?

1. You stimulate a neuron with a brick. Then you stimulate the same neuron with a feather. The feather stimulates a weaker action potential from the neuron than does the brick.
    (a) True   (b) False

2. You are the first to arrive at the scene of a horrible accident. One of the victims has her arm severed midway between the wrist and the elbow. There are a few very small whitish looking strands protruding from the severed limb. These are most likely
    (a) neurons.   (b) telodendria.   (c) cell bodies.   (d) nerves.

3. If the victim in question 2 had her arm reattached she would likely soon begin to experience some sensation because of the
    (a) soma.   (b) myelin sheath.   (c) neurilemma.   (d) reinnervation phenomenon.

4. As you sit reading this question the _____ branch of your autonomic nervous system is probably the more active branch.
    (a) peripheral   (b) parasympathetic   (c) somatic   (d) sympathetic

5. It is possible (but not very likely) that Marie Antoinette who was beheaded during the French Revolution could have had a knee jerk reflex elicited *immediately* after her death.
    (a) True   (b) False

6. You are in an automobile accident and suffer a cracked skull. A dime-sized portion of your cortex is inadvertently removed by the broken bone. Over time your behavior changes significantly and doctors attribute the changes to the loss of tissue. Although you did not plan this, your accident most resembles which research technique?
    (a) deep lesioning   (b) ESB   (c) clinical studies   (d) ablation

7. If you were a mad scientist and wanted to operate on the human brain to produce the closest thing to a two-headed person, which brain structure should be cut?
    (a) optic chiasm   (b) cerebellum   (c) somatosensory area   (d) none of the above

8. Mary, a 68-year-old widow, had a stroke in her right hemisphere. Although her speech center was undamaged, she never brushes her hair on the left side of her head, and she forgets to wear makeup on the left side of her face. She even forgets to put her left arm through the sleeve of her blouse. What is Mary's condition called?
    (a) contralateral unconsciousness   (c) spatial neglect
    (b) hemispheric nondominance   (d) peripheral atrophy

9. A right-handed man who has had a split-brain operation is driving down a divided highway in his Honda automatic transmission car. He is staring straight ahead. A car from the other side of the highway (to his left) begins to skid across the median strip toward him. Which of the following statements best reflects what the split-brained man will probably be able to do?
    (a) push on the car's accelerator with his right foot to avoid an accident
    (b) yell "Damn! I'm going to die!"
    (c) steer out of the way of the oncoming car
    (d) push on the brake to avoid an accident

10. You whisper "sweet nothings" lovingly into your husband's ear. You angrily yell at your husband. In each case he gets your literal meaning but he just doesn't seem to emotionally respond to the tone of your messages. It is likely that his problem is
    (a) damage to his Broca's area.   (c) damage to the right hemisphere.   (c) that he is as dumb as an onion.
    (b) lack of sufficient neurotransmitters.   (d) damage to the left hemisphere.

11. Bob has recovered from a car accident in which he suffered extensive damage to his left hemisphere. He hasn't had problems at work. It is likely that Bob is
    (a) a graphic artist.   (c) a mathematician.   (e) President of the U.S.
    (b) an English teacher.   (d) a free-lance writer.

12. One reason people probably enjoy kissing so much is that
    (a) the neurons from the lips transmit impulses slightly faster than from most other body parts.
    (b) the temporal lobes are especially sensitive to the processing of sensory information from the facial region.
    (c) there are no myelin sheaths to interfere with the transmission of action potentials to the CNS.
    (d) there is a larger area on the parietal lobe for the reception of information from the lips.

13. If a child is hit in the head in the area of the frontal region and aphasia results, the child will most likely have
    (a) difficulty with complex motor skills.   (c) a lower than average I.Q.
    (b) difficulty speaking.   (d) vivid memories produced.

14. If you *had* to lose one structure in your brain and you were vitally concerned that your body at least stay alive, which brain structure would be the *last* one that you would want to lose?
    (a) cerebellum   (b) reticular formation   (c) medulla   (d) corpus callosum

15. Thermal stimulation of a certain part of the brain can make a rat in a 120° cage shiver. Which structure must be stimulated to produce this effect?
    (a) limbic system   (b) hypothalamus   (c) cerebellum   (d) occipital lobes

16. A patient complains to his doctor about being tired all of the time and feeling sleepy. The doctor also notes that the patient is 20 pounds overweight and decides to run some tests. The doctor is probably looking for signs of
    (a) damage to the hippocampus   (c) an adrenal problem
    (b) a thyroid condition   (d) acromegaly

Chapter Review

1. _____ _____ is the study of how the brain and nervous system relate to behavior.

2. The basic unit of the nervous system is the _____. It is designed to carry _____. The four basic parts of this unit of the nervous system are the _____, _____, _____, and _____ _____.

3. A nerve impulse or _____ _____ occurs when a brief flow of electrical current is caused by movement of charged molecules called _____ in and out of the cell. A neuron will only carry an impulse if the _____ is reached. This makes the nerve impulse an _____ - _____ - _____ event.

4. The nerve impulse is primarily a(n) _____ event. In contrast, transmission between neurons is _____. The impulse is carried from one neuron to another by means of _____. Some _____ may excite the next neuron or inhibit it. The neuron will carry an _____ _____ if a number of excitatory messages arrive close enough together to reach the _____.

5. Recent research has revealed a new class of neurotransmitters called _____. These important chemicals seem to serve as _____ of memory, pain, emotion, and other basic processes.

6. Nerve impulses are faster when _____ surrounds the axon. Nerves are not the same as _____ but are bundles of _____ and _____. Most nerves outside the brain and spinal cord also have a thin layer of living cells called the _____ wrapped around them which aid regeneration. Recently, damage to the brain has also been repaired through _____ of healthy _____ cells.

7. The _____ and the _____ _____ comprise the central nervous system. The _____ nervous system consists of nerves which carry information to and from the _____ nervous system.

8. The peripheral nervous system (PNS) is divided into two subparts: the _____ system and the _____ system. The latter system can also be further divided into the _____ and _____ branches. The _____ branch operates during periods of low arousal, while the _____ branch operates during times of arousal or emotional upheaval.

9. The cable system of the body that connects the brain to the rest of the body is called the _____ _____. It is responsible for the simplest behavioral sequence that can occur without direct participation of the brain. This behavior sequence is called a _____ _____. There are several mechanisms involved. The incoming stimulus is detected by a _____ neuron and carried to the _____ _____ where the _____ neuron is activated. This neuron communicates information to a _____ neuron which leads back to muscle fibers composed of _____ cells.

10. Many functions of the brain are learned through _____ _____ of changes caused by brain illness or injury. A related technique (_____) is the surgical removal of specific brain parts. An alternate approach to removal is to electrically stimulate, or "_____ _____" a site by touching the surface of the cortex with an _____. An electrode can be inserted into the brain to remove (_____ _____) or to stimulate (_____ _____ of the _____) target areas. Finally, _____-_____ can be used to record the activity of single neurons.

11. There are different methods to record the functioning of the brain as a whole. _____ measures the waves of electrical activity produced by the brain. A CT scan is a specialized type of ____-_____ which can image the brain. ____ ____ ____ scans use magnetic fields and allow scientists to view the brain as if it were _____. A PET scan detects _____ emitted by radioactive _____ as it is consumed by the brain. Since the brain runs on _____, PET scans show which areas of the brain are using _____.

12. As we move up the phylogenetic scale towards man there is an ever-increasing proportion of brain tissue devoted to the _____. Human intellectual superiority appears to be related to _____, the increase in size and wrinkling of this portion of the brain.

13. The cortex is composed of two sides or _____ which are connected by the _____ _____. Each hemisphere controls the _____ side of the body. Therefore, damage to the right hemisphere will result in paralysis or loss of _____ to the _____ side of the body. _____ _____ is where patients with _____ hemisphere damage pay no attention to the _____ side of _____ space.

14. If the corpus callosum is surgically cut, the brain is referred to as "_____." This procedure is typically done to lessen the severity of the seizures associated with _____. After the surgery is performed, it is almost like having two _____ in one body.

15. The left hemisphere is usually responsible for _____, _____, and comprehending _____. In addition, the left hemisphere is better at _____, judging _____ and _____, and at coordinating complex _____. In contrast, the right hemisphere can only respond to very simple _____ and cannot speak. However, the right hemisphere is better than the left at recognizing visual patterns, _____ and _____, and it is involved in the recognition and expression of _____.

16. The occipital lobes, which are located at the back of the brain, are responsible for _____. The area of the brain to which bodily sensations are channeled is the _____ lobe. The temporal lobes are responsible for _____. For most people, this lobe also contains a _____ center. The frontal lobes contain areas which direct the body's _____ responses and receive information for the sense of _____. All other areas of the cerebral cortex (including parts of the lobes just described) are called the _____ cortex. When stimulated, it yields responses more complex than simple sensations or movements. When people have trouble with their speaking or writing, the _____ area may have been damaged. When they have trouble understanding the meaning of words, their _____ area may have been damaged.

17. The larger the area on the somatosensory portions of the _____ lobes, the greater the _____ of the corresponding body part. Similarly, the larger the area on the motor cortex of the _____ lobes, the more _____ the corresponding body part.

18. Injury to either Broca's area or Wernicke's area may result in _____, an impaired ability to use _____. Other injuries to the brain may cause a person to be unable to identify seen objects, a condition known as _____.

19. The subcortex can be divided into three general areas called the _____ or _____, the _____, and the _____. The first area can be further divided into three areas: the _____, the _____, and the _____ _____. The structure that contains centers important for the reflex control of vital life functions is the _____. The _____ functions primarily to regulate posture, muscle tone, and coordination. Among many activities, the _____ _____ is responsible for alertness and wakefulness.

20. The forebrain is composed of the _____ _____, the _____, and the _____. The _____ acts as a final switching station for sensory information. The _____ has been implicated in the control of behaviors such as sex, temperature control, eating, and drinking. These two structures along with several others comprise the _____ system. This system is important in the production of _____ and _____ behavior. When lasting memories are stored, the _____ is involved.

21. The brain controls _____ _____ _____, keeps track of the _____ world, issues commands to the _____ and _____, generates _____ in the light of current needs, creates _____, and _____ its own behavior.

22. The _____ system is the chemical communication system in the body. The chemicals are called _____. The _____ regulates bodily growth and is one of the structures in this system. If too little growth _____ is released, a person may remain far smaller than average, a condition called _____ _____. If too much is released, _____ may result. If too much is released toward the end of the growth period, there may be excessive growth of the extremities—a condition called _____.

23. Metabolism is regulated by the _____ gland. The _____ glands are located on top of the kidneys. The _____ _____ is the source of adrenaline and noradrenaline. The _____ _____ secretes a _____ which regulates the salt balance in the body. Oversecretion of adrenal sex hormones may cause _____ in adults and _____ _____ in children.

24. Almost all right-handers and about 68% of left-handers produce speech from the _____ hemisphere. Right-handed individuals who write with a straight hand, and lefties who write with a hooked hand, are _____-brain dominant for _____. The prevalence of right-handedness in humans probably reflects the left brain's specialization for _____. Left-handed people have less brain _____ than righties.

| ANSWER KEYS |

Do You Know the Information?

Multiple Choice

1. (c) obj. 1, p. 44
2. (c) obj. 2, p. 44
3. (a) obj. 3, p. 44

4. (a) obj. 4, pp. 45-47
5. (b) obj. 5, p. 47
6. (d) obj. 6, p. 47
7. (b) obj. 7, p. 47
8. (a) obj. 9, p. 48

9. (b) obj. 10, p. 48
10. (d) obj. 11, p. 50
11. (b) obj. 12, p. 50
12. (a,c,e,g,h) obj. 13, p. 51
13. (b) obj. 14, p. 52

Multiple Choice *(continued)*

14. (c) obj. 15, pp. 53-54
15. (c) obj. 14, p. 56
16. (d) obj. 15, p. 56
17. (d) obj. 16, p. 58
18. (a) L, (b) R, (c) L, (d) R,
    (e) R, (f) R obj. 19, pp. 58-60
19. (a) obj. 20, p. 60
20. (a) obj. 21, pp. 61-62
21. (d) obj. 23, p. 63
22. (c) obj. 24, pp. 63-64
23. (d) obj. 24, p. 65
24. (a) obj. 25, p. 65
25. (a) obj. 25, pp. 65-66
26. (c) obj. 27, p. 66
27. (a) obj. 28, p. 68
27. (d) obj. 28, p. 68
28. (d) obj. 28, p. 68
29. (b) objs. 29-30, pp. 70-73

True-False

1. T, obj. 2, p. 44
2. T, obj. 2, p. 44
3. F, obj. 3, p. 45
4. F, obj. 8, p. 44

5. F, obj. 10, p. 48
6. T, obj. 13, p. 50
7. T, obj. 15, p. 56
8. F, obj. 16, p. 56
9. F, obj. 18, p. 57
10. T, obj. 19, p. 59
11. F, obj. 19, p. 60
12. T, obj. 20, p. 61
13. T, obj. 21, p. 61
14. T, obj. 22, p. 61
15. T, obj. 24, p. 63
16. T, obj. 24, p. 64
17. F, obj. 25, p. 65
18. F, obj. 26, p. 66
19. T, obj. 28, p. 69
20. T, obj. 31, p. 73

Matching

1. I, obj. 2, p. 44
2. L, obj. 2, p. 44
3. R, obj. 5, p. 47
4. J, obj. 6, p. 47
5. N, obj. 8, p. 48
6. K, obj. 11, p. 48
7. C, obj. 17, p. 56
8. T, obj. 19, p. 58

9. B, obj. 20, p .61
10. O, obj. 20, p. 60
11. D, obj. 20, p. 61
12. S, obj. 21, pp. 61-62
13. A, obj. 22, p. 61
14. G, obj. 28, p. 67
15. U, obj. 28, p. 67
16. Q, obj. 28, p. 67
17. V, obj. 13, p. 51
18. P, obj. 14, p. 52

Can You Apply the Information?

1. (b) obj. 3, p. 45
2. (d) obj. 8, p. 48
3. (c) obj. 10, p. 48
4. (b) obj. 12, p. 50
5. (a) obj. 13, p. 51
6. (d) obj. 15, p. 56
7. (c) obj. 17, p. 56
8. (d) objs. 18-19, pp. 57-59
9. (c) obj. 19, pp. 58-59
10. (a) obj. 19, pp. 58-59
11. (d) obj. 21, p. 62
12. (b) obj. 22, p. 61
13. (c) obj. 24, pp. 63-64
14. (b) obj. 24, p. 64
15. (b) obj. 25, p. 69

Chapter Review

1. Biopsychology (p. 44)
2. neuron, information, dendrites, soma, axon, axon terminals (p. 44)
3. action potential, ions, threshold, all-or-nothing (p. 45)
4. electrical (p. 46); chemical, neurotransmitters, neurotransmitters, action potential, threshold (p. 47)
5. neuropeptides, regulators (p. 47)
6. myelin, neurons, axons, dendrites, neurilemma, grafts, brain (p. 47)
7. brain, spinal cord (p. 48); peripheral, central (p. 50)
8. somatic, autonomic, sympathetic, parasympathetic, parasympathetic, sympathetic (p. 50)
9. spinal cord, reflex arc (p. 50); sensory, spinal cord, connector, motor, effector (p. 51)
10. clinical studies, ablation, "turn on," electrode, deep-lesioning, electrical stimulation, brain, micro-electrodes (p. 52)
11. Electroencephalography (p. 52); X-ray, MRI, transparent (p. 53); positrons, glucose, glucose, energy (p. 54)
12. cerebrum (p. 55); corticalization (p. 56)
13. hemispheres, corpus callosum, opposite, sensation, left, Spatial neglect, right, left, visual (p. 56)
14. split, epilepsy, brains (p. 57)
15. speaking, writing, language, math, time, rhythm, movements, language (p. 58); faces, melodies, emotion (p. 59)
16. vision, parietal (p. 60); hearing, language, motor, smell, association , Broca's, Wernicke's (p. 61)
17. parietal, sensitivity, frontal, important (p. 61)
18. aphasia, language, agnosia (p. 61)
19. brainstem, hindbrain, midbrain, forebrain, medulla, cerebellum (p. 63); reticular formation (p. 64); medulla, cerebellum (p. 63); reticular formation (p. 64)
20. cerebral cortex (p. 63); thalamus, hypothalamus, thalamus, hypothalamus, limbic, emotion, motivated (p. 65); hippocampus (p. 66)
21. vital bodily functions, external, muscles, glands, responses, consciousness, regulates (p. 66)
22. endocrine, hormones (p. 66); pituitary, hormone; hypopituitary dwarfism (p. 69); giantism, acromegaly (p. 67)
23. thyroid (p. 67); adrenal, adrenal medulla, adrenal cortex, hormone, virilism, premature puberty (p. 68)
24. left (p. 71); left, language, language (p. 72); lateralization (p. 73)

chapter three

Child Development

| LEARNING OBJECTIVES |

To demonstrate mastery of this chapter you should be able to:

1.   Define developmental psychology and name its principal focus.

2.   Name and describe four adaptive reflexes of a neonate.

     a.

     b.

     c.

     d.

3.   Describe the intellectual capabilities and the sensory preferences of a neonate.

4.   Discuss the concept of maturation.

5.   With respect to maturation, describe the course of emotional development.

6.   Explain how there is an interplay between the emotions of infants and adults.

7.   Discuss the concept of readiness (principle of motor primacy). Include in your answer the relationship between practice (training) and readiness.

8. Explain what is meant by the nature-nurture controversy and give supporting evidence for each position. Discuss the outcome of this debate.

9. Define or describe each of the following terms:

    a. chromosome

    b. gene

    c. polygenetic

    d. dominant gene

    e. recessive gene

10. Characterize the three types of children according to temperament and explain how these temperamental differences influence development.

    a.

    b.

    c.

11. List the three factors which combine to determine a person's developmental level.

    a.

    b.

    c.

12. Distinguish between congenital and genetic problems.

13. Describe the relationship between the blood supplies of the mother and her developing child. Discuss the effect of drugs, alcohol (include a description of fetal alcohol syndrome), and tobacco on an unborn child.

14. Describe genetic counseling and genetic screening. Differentiate amniocentesis from chorionic villi sampling.

15. Briefly differentiate conventional deliveries from prepared childbirth in terms of methods and effects. Evaluate how important it is for the father to be present at the time of birth.

16. Differentiate maternity blues and postpartum depression. Describe what may predict the occurrence of the latter and the best way to treat it.

17. Describe the extremes of the maternal caretaking styles and their results.

18. Discuss the importance of paternal influences in child development. Compare these influences to maternal ones.

19. Explain the concepts of social awareness and social referencing.

20. Discuss the concepts of critical periods and imprinting.

21. Discuss the importance of emotional attachment including the concept of separation anxiety. Include in your answer a differentiation of Ainsworth's attachment types as well as the key to secure attachments.

22. Review the debate concerning mother-infant "bonding" and describe the current position regarding early contact.

23. Discuss the effects of daycare on attachment.

24. Describe Harlow's "motherless monkey" research and explain the importance of meeting a child's affectional needs.

25. List and briefly describe the five stages of language acquisition.

     a. Controlled crying, used as attn. getting device—Communicating a need or needs to parents

     b. Cooing (repetition of vowel sounds-ú "oo" "ah"

     c. babbling— Formation of consonant sounds, producing an outpouring (continuous) of repeated sounds

     d. single word stage —1st use of single words

     e. telegraphic speech— Formation of simple two word sentences that "telegraph" a communicate ideas

26. Describe what the "language dance" is and explain why children probably do it.

the movement of infants arms & legs in sync. to the rhythms of human speech — its source (hearing ear)
language recognition is innate/ humans are biologically pre disposed to develop language (chomsky cu)

27. Define the term <u>psycholinguist</u>. Describe the role of learning in the acquisition of language.

a specialist in the psychology of language. —〉 Imitation of adults-rewards for correct
usage of words - are part of language learning.

28. Explain how parents communicate with infants before the infants can talk. Include the ideas of signals, turn taking, and parentese.

parental efforts at evoking baby's smile & vocalization
parental change in actions in obtaining infants attn.

use of care giver speech .
or parentese

29. Explain how a child's intelligence and thinking differ from an adult's. Explain the concept of transformations.

child's thinking is less abstract than an adult's/ children use fewer generalizations
Their (children's) understanding of the world is based on particular examples - sensations -
Transformations - [mental ability to change the shape or form of a substance (like clay or water) & to perceive that its volume remains the same.] -

30. List (in order) and briefly describe Piaget's four stages of cognitive development. Include an explanation of assimilation and accommodation.

a. Sensorimotor Stage (0→ age 2) non-verbal intellectual development/ child learns to coordinate purposeful movements → via information from senses; conceptions become more stable; world becomes more orderly & predictable

b. Preoperational Stage (2-7 yrs) child develops ability to think in terms of symbols - to use language - child is egocentric

c. Concrete-operational Stage (7-11 yrs) - concept of conservation learned in this stage - ask concept learned rolling a ball of clay into a snake - doesn't increase the clay's volume; concept of time, space & # develops belief in Santa disappears - reversability of thought develops - ak: 4+2=6 2x4 also =8

d. Formal Operation Stage (11 yrs→) abstract thinking begins - children become less egocentric
Assimilation = application of existing mental patterns to new situations
Accommodation - modification of existing mental patterns to fit new demands ie - mental schemes changed to accommodate new information & experiences

31. Describe the research which indicates that Piaget may have underestimated infant cognitive abilities.

Psychologist Baillargeon (1991) little "magic shows" for infants - (possible & impossible events are staged with toys or other objects - Some 3 month old infants act surprised& look longer at impossible events - ej-solid objects appearing to pass through each other - By the time they're 8 months old babies can remember where objects are [etc] - full adult ability

32. Evaluate the usefulness of Piaget's theory of cognitive development. - its a valuable "road map" for understanding how children think.

33. Briefly describe each of Kohlberg's three levels of moral development as well as their respective stages.

a. Level 1: Preconventional; moral thinking is based on the consequences of actions - ie punishment, reward & exchange of favors
   1. Stage 1: Punishment orientation - actions evaluated in terms of possible punishment (not in goodness or badness) & obedience to authority) "He shouldn't steal (the drug) because he might get caught& sent to jail
   2. Stage 2: Pleasure seeking Orientation "Right" action based on one's needs
   EX "It won't do him any good to steal (the drugs) because his wife will die before his jail term ends
b. Level 2: Conventional - actions are guided by a desire to conform to others' expectation or be accepted rules & values
   1. Stage 3: Good boy/girl orientation Good behavior is that which pleases others in immediate group emphas- being nice. EX He shouldn't steal (drug) because others will think he's a thief
   2. Stage 4: Authority orientation - emphasis - upholding the law, order, doing one's duty (continued on page 48)
   EX "Although his wife needs the drug, he shouldn't break the law to get it!

c. Level 3: Post conventional—advanced moral development. Behavior at this level is guided by self-accepted moral principles

    1. Stage 5: Social contract orientation; support of laws & rules based on rational analysis & mutual agreement. Example—He should not steal the drugs

    2. Stage 6: Morality of Individual Principles—Behavior is directed by self-chosen ethical principles— high value on justice, dignity, equality. example

He should steal the drug & then inform the authorities— He'll face penalty—but he'll have saved a human life.

34. Describe how Kohlberg's moral development levels are distributed among the population.

Preconventional stages (of moral development) are typical of young children & delinquents. Conventional group-oriented morality stages 3 & 4 are characteristic of older children & most adult population. Post conventional morality—(self-direction & higher principles) is achieved by only about 20% of the adult population.

35. Explain Gilligan's argument against Kohlberg's system of moral development. Describe the current status of the argument.

Kohlberg Kohlberg's concern is mainly with justice.—there is also an ethic of caring & responsibility to others. Caring is also a major element of moral development.

36. Give examples of the effects of deprivation on development. Define the term hospitalism.

Children (ages 5-6) 1st years of life spent in closets, attics & other restricted environments— these children—mute, retarded, emotionally damaged. dwarfism (stunted growth associated with isolation, rejection, & gnl deprivation in home area—

Hospitalism—pattern of deep depression observed in institutionalized infants—marked by weeping & sadness & a lack of normal responsiveness to other humans.

37. List and describe the two factors or elements in early deprivation.

a. Loss of attachment—absence of loving mother—

b. Lack of perceptual stimulation—(they're isolated—in an atmosphere where "nothing is happening"

38. Describe Harlow's experiment dealing with contact comfort, and state the results of the experiment. Relate his findings to the merits of breast and bottle feeding. Harlow separated rhesus monkeys from their mothers

at birth— replacing mothers with surrogate (dummies) of monkeys— Some dummies were of cold wire / others covered with soft, terry cloth.— Infants given the choice between the two mothers—they chose the terry cloth dummie mother— QED— the importance of contact comfort in early development / simulation.

The contact comfort of breast feeding was development

39. Review the research demonstrating the benefits of enriched environments. *—Infant rat research; —Infant rats ÷'d into 2 groups (group A - raised in stimulus free environment) (group B - raised in rat wonderland) —upon adulthood—both groups, tested.— the rats of "rat wonderworld"- ability to read learn mazes superior to non stimulated rats — stimulated rat brains prove superior! Same experiment with infants = same results*

The following objectives are related to the material in the "Applications" section of your text.

40. Describe White's practical advice on effective parenting for each of the following areas:

    a. attachment *—touch, hold & handle infants frequently; attend promptly to baby's cries as often as possible; respond promptly to baby's signs of discomfort;*

    b. overindulgence *From age 2 on— parents invite trouble if they do everything & buy everything they can for the child. Set limits & guidelines for acceptable behavior - at appropriate age levels*

    c. the outside world *in encouraging infant's-world exploration - minimize use of restrictive devices — When child crawls-walks-" child proof" house - Avoid use of too many "No No"—*

    d. respecting individual variation (include a differentiation between the statistical child and the particulare child) *be aware of normal pattern of emerging skills — facilitate their emergence — be aware that individual differences in maturation rates—are the rule — Child's uniqueness should be recognized*

    e. enrichment *—baby should be surrounded by colors, music, people —things to see, taste, smell & touch — take babies outside, hang mobiles over their crib, — place mirrors - rearrange rooms periodically - talk to infants. Respond to baby's coos, gurgles & other vocalizations - By age 2, be on guard for possible hearing loss*

    f. responsiveness *experiences—allowing children to see cause & effect results from their own behavior are especially effective. The most expensive toys are the least responsive. — One of most responsive toys is a $1.00 rubber ball.*

    g. forced teaching *—flooding an infant with stimuli, flash cards, & exercise is not enriching - forced teaching bores a oppresses a child; is expensive & unnecessary. these are "hot house" exercises like trying to force a plant to grow pre maturely!*

41. Describe the methods of encouraging intellectual development in children in each of Piaget's cognitive stages.

    Sensorimotor stage (0-2) active play with child—encourage exploration in touching, smelling, & manipulating objects. Peekaboo is a good way to establish objects' permanence

    Preoperational stage (2-7) touching & seeing things will continue to be more helpful than verbal explanations. Concrete examples preferable to ginlizations; encourage child to classify things, —concept of conservation learned via demos. involving liquids, beads, clay et al

    Concrete operational stage (7-11) ~~explain things verbally or symbolically to child, help child to master gint rules~~ children begin to use generalization - children still require specific examples to grasp ideas.

    Formal operations stage (11-adult) its now more realistic to explain things verbally or symbolically to child. — Help child to master gint rules & principles - Encourage child to create hypothesis & imagine how things can be

Do You Know the Information?

Multiple Choice

1. Developmental psychology is the study of
    (a) the role of maturation in the unfolding of human potential.
    (b) the stages of life and the important tasks of each.
    (c) the language, personality, and emotions of children and adolescents.
    (d) progressive changes in behavior and abilities from conception to death.

2. When startled by a loud sound, an infant makes movements similar to an embrace. This is called a _____ reflex.
    (a) Moro   (b) rooting   (c) grasping   (d) sucking

3. If you touch an infant's cheek, he or she will turn toward you. This reflex is known as the _____ reflex.
    (a) Moro   (b) rooting   (c) grasping   (d) sucking

4. Which of the following statements is *false*?
    (a) The easiest way to describe an infant is as a bundle of reflexes.
    (b) Children as young as 3- to 8-weeks-old show signs of understanding that a person's voice and body are connected.
    (c) Infants as young as 20-days-old can imitate adult facial features.
    (d) Infants as young as 3-days-old demonstrate a preference for complex visual patterns, such as checkerboards, over simple colored rectangles.

5. Which of the following *most* accurately describes the course of human development?
    (a) The sequence of development differs from culture to culture. (c) Each individual displays a unique order of development.
    (b) It is totally unlike the development of nonhumans.   (d) It follows an identifiable order but can vary in rate.

6. The only emotional response(s) newborn infants clearly express is
    (a) fear, joy, and sadness.   (b) anger.   (c) general excitement.   (d) unpleasantness.

7. "Until the necessary physical structures are mature, no amount of practice will be sufficient to establish a skill." This is a statement of the principle of
    (a) motor primacy.   (b) maturation.   (c) accommodation.   (d) motor learning.

8. Which of the following statements concerning the nature-nurture controversy is *false*?
    (a) A person's chromosomes affect the sequence of growth, the timing of puberty, and the course of aging.
    (b) The outcome of the controversy is that there is a constant interaction between the forces of nature and nurture.
    (c) The broad outlines of the human growth sequence are greatly influenced by the environment and are therefore universal.
    (d) The differences in environment are largely responsible for children making greater use of their native capacities today than they did 30,000 years ago.

9. Which of the following statements is *false*?
    (a) Chromosomes are smaller areas on genes.
    (b) Each sperm cell and each ovum contain the same number of chromosomes.
    (c) Recessive traits are only expressed when two recessive genes are paired.
    (d) A polygenetic trait is determined by many genes working in combination.

10. "Difficult" infants
    (a) tend to under-react to stimulation.   (c) will try most new foods easily.
    (b) are not prone to tantrums.   (d) are moody and easily angered.

11. Congenital problems
    (a) may be caused by poor maternal nutrition.   (c) are different from genetic problems.
    (b) are sometimes called "birth defects."   (d) include all of the above.

12. The placenta provides a connection between the bloodstreams of the mother and the developing child. Which of the following statements accurately describes the nature of this connection?
    (a) The blood supplies intermingle freely.
    (b) In the sixth month, some of the mother's blood flows into the fetus as the first installment of its blood supply.
    (c) The placenta lets nutrients pass to the embryo but all harmful entities are prevented from passing through.
    (d) The mother's blood never mixes with that of the unborn child.

13. Babies can be born addicted to drugs. This is possible because
    (a) the fetal blood has a high degree of affinity for narcotics.
    (b) there are critical periods in development.
    (c) there is an exchange of materials between the two bloodstreams.
    (d) narcotics affect the mother's genes.

14. Characteristics of children who suffer from fetal alcohol syndrome include
    (a) prematurity.
    (b) low birth weight.
    (c) bodily defects and deformities.
    (d) all of the above.

15. Amniocentesis is a test that
    (a) is conducted during genetic counseling.
    (b) involves taking a sample of maternal blood.
    (c) can detect many genetic defects.
    (d) can be done between 6 and 8 weeks of pregnancy

16. Which of the following statements about childbirth is *false*?
    (a) Some form of painkiller is used in almost all deliveries in the United States.
    (b) Prepared childbirth typically shortens labor but results in more pain for the mother.
    (c) Fathers who want to be present at the birth of their children are more likely to help care for them later.
    (d) General anesthesia during birth has major drawbacks.

17. Postpartum depression appears to
    (a) be related to the occurrence of the maternity blues.
    (b) involve perceptions of husbands as being unsupportive.
    (c) occur in as many as 20 percent of all women who give birth.
    (d) be all of the above.

18. With regard to maternal influences, research has demonstrated that
    (a) proactive maternal involvement is related to a lack of behavioral problems in 4-year-olds.
    (b) the "super mother" caregiving style produces unusually competent, or "C" type, children.
    (c) the "zoo-keeper mother" caregiving style produces unusually incompetent, or "A" type, children.
    (d) a mother's responsiveness loses its influence on a child's intellectual abilities after the age of 4.

19. Whereas mothers typically emphasize _____ functions with children, fathers tend to have an important role as a _____ for the infant.
    (a) comforting, model   (b) caretaker, disciplinarian   (c) emotional, model   (d) caretaker, playmate

20. Which of the following statements regarding social development is *incorrect*?
    (a) Self-awareness depends upon maturation of the nervous system.
    (b) Social referencing occurs when babies glance at their caregiver.
    (c) By the end of their first year, infants seek guidance from the facial expressions of adults.
    (d) The real core of social development is found in how fast the child begins social referencing.

21. The period of time during which environmental influences have their greatest impact is called the
    (a) deterministic period.   (b) critical period.   (c) imprinting period.   (d) period of maximal impact.

22. Which of the following statements regarding emotional attachment in humans is *incorrect*?
    (a) The occurrence of separation anxiety signals the formation of an emotional bond between infants and their caregivers.
    (b) A mother's acceptance and sensitivity to her baby's signals and rhythms is a key ingredient for secure attachment.
    (c) Babies born by cesarean section have a harder time developing affectionate bonds with their mothers.
    (d) Cross-cultural studies suggest that Ainsworth's attachment types are universal.

23. Which of the following is *not* likely to promote insecurity in a child in a daycare setting?
    (a) his/her mother working full-time
    (b) his/her father helps little in child care
    (c) the child is over 1 year of age
    (d) the parent's marriage is in trouble

24. In monkeys (and perhaps humans) inadequate affection and touching during infancy can lead to
    (a) autism.
    (b) abnormal development of perceptual abilities.
    (c) the lack of the development of normal sexual behaviors and parenting skills.
    (d) all of the above.
    (e) the growth of hair all over your body.

25. Telegraphic speech refers to
    (a) simple two-word sentences characteristic of early speech.
    (b) the continuous outpouring of repeated language sounds.
    (c) the seemingly meaningless babble of young infants.
    (d) children using one word to express an entire thought.

26. Language dance refers to
    (a) the early communication pattern between parent and child where the baby smiles and the parent smiles back.
    (b) infants moving their arms and legs in synchrony to the rhythms of human speech.
    (c) the biological predisposition to form vowels before consonants.
    (d) a funky new wave dance from San Francisco.

27. One possible reason why all children do the language dance and why they use a limited number of patterns in their first sentences is that
    (a) children learn language from adults.
    (b) language recognition is innate.
    (c) infants have a readiness to interact socially with parents.
    (d) all of the above.

28. Which of the following statements about language development is *incorrect*?
    (a) Imitation and reinforcement play important roles in language learning.
    (b) A psycholinguist is a specialist in the psychology of language.
    (c) Language is automatically switched on in infants by exposure to adult language.
    (d) Parents and children begin to communicate long before the child can speak.

29. Generally speaking, a child's thinking
    (a) is more abstract than an adult's.
    (b) shows the ability to make transformations.
    (c) is more concrete than an adult's.
    (d) is exemplified by answers b and c.

30. Which of the following statements concerning cognitive development is *incorrect*?
    (a) During the preoperational stage a child begins to think symbolically.
    (b) Assimilation and accommodation are the processes through which intellectual growth occurs.
    (c) A child's conceptions during the sensorimotor stage become more stable..
    (d) It is during the formal operations stage that most children begin to realize that the Tooth Fairy is a fantasy.

31. Assimilation refers to
    (a) the nonverbal use of objects.
    (b) using existing patterns in new situations.
    (c) modifying existing ideas to fit new requirements.
    (d) passing through a series of stages in intellectual growth.

32. According to Piaget, the development of the concept of object permanence takes place during the
    (a) sensorimotor stage.   (b) preoperational stage.   (c) concrete operational stage.   (d) formal operations stage.

33. Mastery of the concept of conservation usually occurs during the
    (a) sensorimotor stage.   (b) preoperational stage.   (c) concrete operational stage.   (d) formal operations stage.

34. During the formal operations stage, children begin to
    (a) accurately use concepts of time, space, and number.
    (b) think in terms of abstract principles and hypothetical possibilities.
    (c) make more purposeful movements.
    (d) think primarily about concrete objects or situations.

35. Current research on infant cognition has demonstrated that
    (a) Piaget was correct about the timing of most cognitive abilities in infants.
    (b) Piaget probably thought the limited physical skills of infants represented mental incompetence.
    (c) infants under the age of 1 year cannot think.
    (d) newer more sensitive tests are validating Piaget's observations.

36. At present
    (a) researchers have found cycles of brain growth that correspond to the times of Piaget's stages.
    (b) some research indicates that intellectual growth is not as age-and-stage-related as Piaget said.
    (c) Piaget's findings run counter to the findings of learning theorists.
    (d) all of the above are correct.

37. Morality based on trying to please others is typical of which level of moral development?
    (a) postconventional   (b) conventional   (c) preconventional   (d) none of these

38. According to Gilligan and her critique of Kohlberg's system of moral development,
    (a) women's concerns with relationships appears to be a moral weakness rather than a strength.
    (b) stage 5 postconventional morality only applies to women.
    (c) the moral maturity of women needs to be judged on the basis of justice and autonomy.
    (d) there is no difference in the moral reasoning abilities of men and women.

39. A pattern of depression marked by weeping, sadness, and long periods of immobility in institutionalized infants is termed
    (a) perceptual understimulation. (b) hospitalism.   (c) perceptual hunger.   (d) anaclitic depression.

40. The two major elements in early deprivation are
    (a) lack of attachment and lack of perceptual stimulation.   (c) hospitalism and poor maturational timetable.
    (b) lack of exercise and lack of correct diet.   (d) lack of stimulation and poor diet.

41. Harlow found that infant monkeys separated from their mothers at birth
    (a) spent more time clinging to the terry cloth mother.
    (b) spent more time with the wire mother because she was the source of food.
    (c) roamed freely and only ran to the terry cloth mother when frightened.
    (d) suffered from perceptual problems as adults.

42. Harlow's contact comfort experiments suggest that
    (a) all mothers should breast feed their children.
    (b) children will benefit more from being breast fed than bottle fed.
    (c) touching and cuddling are the important factors in feeding and can be provided with any type of feeding.
    (d) bottle feeding can provide the best combination of the right nutrients for maximum development of the child.

43. Research with stimulus-rich environments has demonstrated
    (a) a greater effect on rats than on humans.
    (b) a positive relationship between stimulation and improvements in various abilities.
    (c) no lasting improvements in school performance.
    (d) no speed-up of visually directed reaching as compared to those raised in stimulus-poor environments.

44. Among the things that parents can do to provide varied sensory experiences during infancy include
    (a) spending increased time interacting with an infant to help develop language and thinking abilities.
    (b) surrounding the infant with things to see, smell, taste, and touch.
    (c) rearranging the infant's room occasionally.
    (d) all of the above.

45. According to Piaget the experiences most likely to encourage intellectual development are those which are
    (a) very different from the child's present level of ability.   (c) related to visual or motor stimulation.
    (b) mildly frustrating so as to challenge the child.   (d) slightly novel or unusual.

True-False

_____ 1. Infants will spend more time looking at a human face than at a scrambled face or a same-size oval.

_____ 2. Maturation refers to the growth and development of the body.

_____ 3. Early emotional development appears closely related to maturation of the brain.

_____ 4. If parents feel annoyed or irritated when they hear a baby cry, then they are not likely to attend to the baby's needs.

_____ 5. It is not possible for brown-eyed parents to have blue-eyed children because brown genes are always dominant over blue genes.

_____ 6. The temperament of an infant can affect his or her behavior which in turn affects the types of responses that the parent gives.

_____ 7. The factors which determine a person's developmental level are heredity, environment, and the person's own behavior.

_____ 8. Congenital problems are those which result from the transmission of abnormal genes at conception.

_____ 9. A mother who smokes heavily is more likely to miscarry than non-smokers.

_____10. A "crack" baby's behavior at birth (excitable or sluggish) will depend on how recently the mother used cocaine.

_____11. The Lamaze method of natural childbirth is partly designed to reduce the fears and anxiety concerning childbirth.

_____12. The risk of postpartum depression is increased by high levels of anxiety during pregnancy and negative attitudes toward childrearing.

_____13. Mental competence in early adolescence is nourished by a mother's responsiveness during childhood.

_____14. A child's sex role development is significantly influenced by his or her maternal and paternal caregiving styles.

_____15. Awareness of self develops about 3 months ahead of social referencing of mothers and fathers.

_____16. Imprinting is an instinctive, innate ability that can take place at any time.

_____17. Extended contact (for about three hours) immediately after birth is necessary for the mother-infant bond.

_____18. Children who are in day-care are usually slightly less attached to their mothers than are children who are reared at home.

_____19. Conversational "turn-taking" refers to how children learn the "language dance."

_____20. Kohlberg found that preconventional stages of morality are most typical of young children and delinquents.

_____21. Studies of developmental dwarfism suggest that only the first six months is a relatively critical period in development.

_____22. Rats raised in a stimulus-enriched environment out-performed other rats in maze tests and had heavier, larger brains with a thicker cortex.

_____23. In most cases a child can be considered abnormal if he or she has not demonstrated a certain ability during the developmental norm for this ability.

_____24. The child who is told *not* to explore or investigate the world may become passive and intellectually dulled.

Can You Apply the Information?

1. Lindsey is holding her two-month-old son when her 5-year-old daughter comes in the back door. Slam! goes the door. Her son jumps and throws his arms out in an embrace. Which reflex has her son just exhibited?
    (a) rooting   (b) grasping   (c) Moro   (d) Babinski

2. Olaf and Sven are both 2 years old. When their mothers take them to an art museum, Olaf is interested in looking at abstract pictures where facial features and body parts are out of place. Sven, on the other hand, spends more time looking at very traditional paintings where all body parts are where they should be. This apparent difference between the two children is probably because
    (a) Olaf is maturing at a faster rate than Sven.
    (b) the order of maturation for the two children is different.
    (c) Olaf has had more experience with three-dimensional objects.
    (d) Sven was never exposed to complex patterns as he was growing up.

3. Practice will
    (a) accelerate a child's locomotor abilities.
    (b) accelerate a child's developmental rate for the skill being practiced but slow down other skills.
    (c) have little effect on the child's ability if the ability is maturationally controlled.
    (d) will have a demonstrable effect on the skill before it develops but will have little effect on the skill as it is being perfected.

4. Most experts now conclude that
    (a) heredity is most important during infancy and childhood, and environment is most important during adolescence and adulthood.
    (b) heredity and environment are inseparable, interacting factors in development.
    (c) environment is the most important factor in development since it can override the effects of heredity.
    (d) heredity is important for only a few psychological traits such as intelligence and temperament.

5. At her son's birthday party Jennifer observes a child who does not interact with the other children and appears rather unexpressive. How would this child probably be classified according to temperament?
    (a) slow-to-warm-up   (b) difficult   (c) easy   (d) doesn't fit into one category

6. Hemophilia is a blood clotting disorder which can be passed through generations of a family. It is a congenital disorder that can therefore be quite serious for a neonate.
    (a) True   (b) False

7. Murray and Rebecca were about to have a baby when Murray, who is in the Navy, was deployed on a six-month cruise to the Mediterranean. He had taken Lamaze training with Rebecca and was looking forward to helping in the birth process even to the point of taking pictures for their memories of a joyous time. Now they are worried that his not being at the birth may negatively influence Murray's relationship with his child. Your advice to them is to
    (a) be careful of his reaction when the child angers him because bonding has not taken place.
    (b) not worry because Murray's attitude toward the birth may be more important than his actually being there.
    (c) remember and use the breathing techniques they learned in Lamaze class when he has difficulty with the child.
    (d) try to obtain a hardship leave from the Navy for the birth under the grounds that Murray's not being there will negatively influence the child's first months of life.

8. Given the above situation with Murray and Rebecca, the likelihood of Rebecca experiencing postpartum depression is
    (a) high.   (b) low.

9. Your friend has two children. She seems to interact with them very little, but their physical needs are taken care of. Your friend
    (a) will raise A children.   (c) will have children who are slow in language development.
    (b) is a super mother.   (d) is a zoo-keeper mother.

10. Parents who take swimming classes with their very young children are told that if the child goes underwater and comes up sputtering with a frightened look on his/her face to smile at the child and make it look as if it is the greatest fun in the whole world. This is a good example of the concept of
    (a) maturation.   (b) a paternal influence.   (c) turn taking.   (d) social referencing.

11. You are sitting in a doctor's waiting room with your one-year-old son. A nurse calls your name and since you know the visit will take only about 30 seconds, you leave your son behind. He starts crying. It is likely that he is suffering from
    (a) attachment deprivation.   (b) stranger anxiety.   (c) attachment anxiety.   (d) separation anxiety.

12. As a researcher interested in Ainsworth's types of attachment, you are observing the reactions of children in a daycare facility as their mothers pick them up at the end of the day. One child sits on the floor playing with blocks even after her mother repeatedly calls for her to get her coat and leave. You determine that this child has a(n) _____ attachment because
    (a) secure; the child is not upset and knows that everything will be fine when she gets home.
    (b) insecure-avoidant; the child shows no interest in reuniting with her mother after the day's separation.
    (c) insecure-ambivalent; the child is resisting contact now but will seek it later.
    (d) separation-anxiety; earlier in the day the child was upset at being left with strangers.

13. Joan's father died before she was born and her mother died in childbirth. She is now 1 month old and has been in two different foster homes waiting for adoption. She is going to be adopted by a couple who are infertile but have always wanted a child and will make every effort to meet all of her affectional needs. It is most likely that
    (a) Joan's lack of attachment at birth will result in antisocial behavior as an adult.
    (b) she has been experiencing separation anxiety from birth, but that it can be overcome with the proper care.
    (c) Joan will develop normal affectionate bonds with her new parents.
    (d) Joan's development will appear normal until such time, as an adult, she decides to have children.

14. Any subject can be taught to a child at any age if it is taught in an intellectually honest form. Piaget would likely
    (a) agree with the statement.
    (b) agree with the statement provided the child is beyond the sensorimotor stage.
    (c) disagree with the statement because there are some concepts that absolutely cannot be mastered until a certain stage of development is reached.
    (d) disagree with the statement because the child may not be emotionally ready to master the concept.

15. "I won't steal that bicycle because I might get caught." This statement is an example of the _____ level of moral reasoning.
    (a) conventional   (b) postconventional   (c) preconventional   (d) pleasure-seeking

16. Most children begin walking around the age of one year. Your child begins walking at six months of age. In this regard your child is a good example of
    (a) the effects of practice.
    (b) the statistical child.
    (c) the effects on an enriched environment.
    (d) the particular child.

17. Which of the following is the best example of the concept of responsiveness for a two-year-old child?
    (a) a chalkboard and a box of multicolored chalk
    (b) a box that unfolds and refolds itself completely automatically
    (c) a doll that walks, talks, wets, etc.
    (d) a videotape player

Chapter Review

1. The study of _____ is the heart of developmental psychology. However, developmental psychology is more accurately defined as the study of progressive changes in _____ and abilities from _____ to _____.

2. The human _____ (newborn) possesses a number of reflexes which improve its chances for survival. For example, an object pressed to its palm will be grasped tightly. This reflex is appropriately called the_____ reflex.

3. The _____ reflex occurs when a neonate is touched on its cheek and turns its head in that direction. When a nipple touches the neonate's mouth, the _____ reflex helps the baby obtain food. The _____ reflex involves a baby's making movements similar to an _____ when his or her head is dropped.

4. Neonates are probably much smarter than people think. Research indicates that newborns are able to _____ another person's facial expressions. Tests of infant vision indicate that the neonate prefers _____ patterns and human _____, especially _____ ones. The preference for familiarity _____ at about age two.

5. _____ refers to growth and development of the body. It underlies the orderly _____ observed in the unfolding of many basic responses. Its _____ varies from child to child, but its _____ is virtually universal.

6. Early _____ development follows a pattern closely tied to maturation. The basic reactions of _____, _____, and _____ take time to develop with general _____ the only emotional response newborn infants clearly express.

7. Development of the ability to express emotion is probably related to _____ of the _____ since children of all cultures show a _____ pattern.

8. The principle of _____ _____ states: "Until the necessary physical structures are mature, no amount of _____ will be sufficient to establish a skill." In this way maturation creates a condition of _____ for learning.

9. The nature-nurture controversy refers to the relative contributions to development of _____ (nature) and _____ (nurture).

10. Hereditary instructions are carried by the _____. Smaller areas on these are called _____. When many of these latter units work in combination, a characteristic is called _____.

11. Genes may either be _____ or _____. The latter must be paired with a similar gene in order for its characteristic to be expressed.

12. The broad outlines of the human _____ _____ are universal and extend from conception to _____. In actuality, heredity and environment are _____, _____ factors. The extent to which _____ tendencies are fully developed depends on the quality of the _____ in which a child lives.

13. Children can be classified into three different temperamental categories: _____ children, _____ children, and _____-_____-_____-_____ children. A person's developmental level is determined by _____, _____, and the individual's own _____.

14. Damage that occurs to an unborn child because of environmental influences is referred to as a _____ problem. These problems are sometimes referred to as _____ _____. Problems that are inherited are called _____ problems.

15. Many drugs may pass through the mother and reach the fetus. Evidence for this comes from the fact that if the mother is addicted to a drug, the infant may be born with a drug _____. Mothers who use cocaine during the pregnancy will have babies who will have _____ when they start school. Repeated heavy drinking by a pregnant woman can produce a pattern known as _____ _____ syndrome which can produce _____ and physical deformities.

16. Heavy smokers run a higher risk of _____ birth and tend to give birth to babies who are _____.

17. Prospective parents who suspect that they may have a genetic disorder may seek _____
_____. Genetic screening can also be done during pregnancy and may include a test called
_____ which is usually done at about the _____ week of pregnancy.
An alternative procedure, _____ _____ _____, can be done between 6 and 8
weeks of pregancy.

18. Some form of _____ is used in 95% of all deliveries in the U.S even though drugs reduce
_____ flow to the fetus and can cause the infant to be born partially _____.
Many women and men are now going through _____ childbirth using such methods as the
_____ method. This typically shortens labor and reduces pain. Having the father present can make a
difference in his willingness to later _____ for the child.

19. A temporary disturbance in mood after childbirth is called _____ _____. A more
serious disorder called _____ _____ involves mood swings,
despondency, and feelings of inadequacy. It appears related to high levels of _____ during pregnancy. The
amount of _____ support a person receives seems to be related to the problem.

20. Differing maternal styles have been related to whether a child is unusually competent (A) or possesses little competence (C).
_____ mothers produce A children and go out of their way to provide educational experiences for the child. The
_____-_____ mother produces C or lower children and interacts with them very little but provides for their physical needs. In addition, proactive _____ involvement has been found strongly
related to an absence of _____ problems in 4-year-olds, and a mother's _____
during infancy can predict a child's intellectual abilities at age 12.

21. Fathers contribute significantly to an infant's social and intellectual growth. Whereas mothers typically emphasize
_____, fathers tend to function as a _____ for the infant.

22. Two important areas of social development are _____-_____ and
_____ _____. The former depends upon _____ of
the nervous system and begins to form the core of social development. It increases as the child develops. When a child
glances at its parent in order to decide how to respond to something, this is called _____
_____.

23. A _____ period is a time when susceptibility to environmental influences is increased. The rapid and
relatively permanent establishment of a behavior pattern is called _____. Even this behavior pattern is
subject to a _____ period.

24. Emotional _____ of human infants to their caretaker is a very important event. There is a
_____ period during which this must occur for healthy development, but it is not essential that this occur
within the first few _____ after birth.

25. Around 8 to 12 months babies display _____ _____ when their parents leave them
which demonstrates that an _____ _____ has been formed. The quality of the attachment is
revealed by how _____ act when their _____ return after a brief separation:
_____ _____ infants seek to be near their mothers when they return;
_____-_____ turn away when their mothers return;
_____-_____ infants both seek to be near and yet resist contact with their
mothers. The key to a _____ attachment is a mother who is accepting and sensitive to her baby's signals
and rhythms.

26. According to Klaus and Kennel, mother-child pairs who spend extra time together after birth form a stronger
_____ _____. However, because _____ children,
_____ babies and those born by cesarean section all develop normal bonds with their mothers, it is
unlikely that emotional attachments depend _____ on the first few hours of life. In any event, meeting a
baby's _____ _____ is every bit as important as meeting more obvious needs for food, water,
and physical care.

27. High quality _____-_____ care does not appear to have _____ effects on preschoolers unless it exceeds _____ hours per week. Signs of insecurity are likely if the child is under ____ year(s) of age, if the _____ works full-time, if the _____ helps little in child care, and if the parent's marriage is _____.

28. Harlow has found that monkeys raised without a _____ and in _____ never develop normal _____ behaviors, and they make poor _____ if mated. On the human side, some psychologists believe that similar types of antisocial behavior may result from a lack of _____ in infancy.

29. The first stage of language acquisition is _____. Babies do this from the moment of _____. Around six to eight weeks babies begin repeating certain vowel sounds. This is called _____. Next the child begins to _____. The child then begins to form _____ _____. Last, simple two-word sentences called _____ speech are formed.

30. Infants move their arms and legs in synchrony to the rhythms of human_____. This is called a _____ _____. Chomsky believes that language recognition is _____, and that humans have a _____ _____ to develop language.

31. Other specialists in the psychology of language (called _____) have recently shown that _____ and _____ are an important part of language learning.

32. Before infants can talk, parents and infants create a system of shared _____ which helps to establish a pattern of "conversational" _____-_____. The more time parents spend _____ with children the faster they learn to talk. Parents also help through the use of _____ or _____ speech. Specifically, it uses _____ sentences, repeated with a _____ rate of speaking and a distinct _____ quality.

33. A child's thinking is less _____ than that of an adult. Piaget believed that the growth of intellect proceeds through fixed _____. There are two processes which help the intellect grow. _____ refers to using existing patterns in new situations. In _____, existing ideas are modified to fit new requirements.

34. The first stage is the _____ stage. During this time the infant's movements become _____ and the concept of _____ _____ begins to emerge. The second stage is the _____ stage and is marked by development of the ability to think _____ and to use _____. The child's thinking is still _____ and the child is quite _____.

35. The next stage is the _____ _____ stage and is marked by the mastery of the concepts of _____ and _____. The last stage is called the _____ _____ stage. Now thinking is based more on _____ principles, and the child can consider _____ possibilities.

36. Contrary to Piaget, new research shows that babies as young as _____ months know that objects are _____ and do not disappear when out of view. Likely, Piaget mistook babies' limited _____ skills for _____ incompetence. However, babies appear to be born with the capacity to _____ _____ about the world.

37. Some research suggests that cognitive development is not as strictly _____-and-_____-related as Piaget claimed. Many psychologists are convinced that he gave too little credit to _____. Conversely, researchers have recently found evidence for cycles of _____ growth at times that correspond with Piaget's stages. On the whole Piaget's _____ have held up well, but his _____ for the growth of thinking abilities are still debated.

38. To study moral development, Kohlberg posed _____ _____ to children of different ages. Kohlberg identified three levels and six stages of moral development. In the first level, the _____ level, moral development is determined by the _____ of actions (i.e., punishment, reward, or exchange of favors).

39. In the second or _____ level of morality, actions are directed by a desire to _____ to the expectations of others or to uphold socially accepted _____ and _____. The third or _____ level represents advanced moral develop- ment. Behavior is directed by _____-_____ moral principles.

40. According to Kohlberg, the preconventional stages of morality are most typical of young children and _____; the conventional stages are typical of older children and most of the _____ population; and, postconventional morality is achieved by only about _____ percent of the adult population.

41. Gilligan has pointed out that Kohlberg's system is concerned with the ethics of _____. However, morality should also include an ethic of _____ and _____ to others.

42. Early perceptual and emotional deprivation may seriously retard development. The resulting condition may be called _____. Lack of _____ and lack of perceptual _____ are two major factors in _____.

43. Harlow's research with monkeys confirms the effects of a lack of stimulation in infancy. Monkeys separated from their mothers preferred _____ mothers with a soft terry cloth surface. Harlow concluded from this that an important dimension of early stimulation is _____ _____ supplied by touching, holding, and stroking an infant.

44. On the other hand, _____ of the environment has been found to have a beneficial effect on a child's develop- ment. Rats raised in _____ environments have been found to have larger _____ with thicker _____ than rats raised in _____ environments. Likewise, early education programs with children show a _____ relationship between early stimulation and _____ in various "intellectual" abilities.

45. Because parents want to see their children's _____ develop fully, some practical advice for effective parenting is as follows:
    (1) give an infant a feeling of being _____ which will help build a _____ mother-infant bond;
    (2) avoid _____ by giving age-appropriate limits and guidelines for acceptable behavior;
    (3) encourage a child to _____ the outside world;
    (4) remember that developmental norms are based on _____ (the concept of the _____ child) and that there is always a wide range of variation around each average which may encompass individual differ- ences (the concept of the _____ child);
    (5) provide an _____ environment for the child;
    (6) create a world that _____ to the infant not one that bombards the infant with _____; and finally,
    (7) keep in mind that _____ _____ can bore a child.

46. Piaget suggests that in order to promote intellectual development, experiences should be provided that are only _____ novel or challenging. Experiences that are too unfamiliar may cause _____ and withdrawal.

47. Parents should encourage _____ growth by encouraging a child's _____ of the world.

| ANSWER KEYS |

Do You Know the Information?

Multiple Choice

1. (d) obj. 1, p. 76
2. (a) obj. 2, p. 77
3. (b) obj. 2, p. 77
4. (a) obj. 3, pp. 78-79
5. (d) obj. 4, p. 79
6. (c) obj. 5, p. 80
7. (a) obj. 7, p. 80
8. (c) obj. 8, p. 83
9. (a) obj. 9, p. 82
10. (d) obj. 10, pp. 84-85
11. (d) obj. 12, p. 85
12. (d) obj. 13, p. 86
13. (c) obj. 13, p. 86
14. (d) obj. 13, p. 86
15. (c) obj. 14, p. 86
16. (b) obj. 15, p. 87
17. (d) obj. 16, p. 88
18. (a) obj. 17, p. 88
19. (d) obj. 18, pp. 89-90
20. (d) obj. 19, p. 91
22. (c) objs. 21-22, pp. 92-93
23. (c) obj. 23, p. 93
24. (c) obj. 23, pp. 93-94
25. (a) obj. 25, p. 95
26. (b) obj. 26, p. 95
27. (b) obj. 26, p. 95
28. (c) objs. 27-28, pp. 95-97
29. (c) obj. 29, p. 98
30. (d) obj. 30, p. 99

31. (b) obj. 30, p. 99
32. (a) obj. 30, p. 99
33. (c) obj. 30, p. 99
34. (b) obj. 30, p. 100
35. (b) obj. 31, p. 101
36. (d) obj. 32, p. 102
37. (b) obj. 33, p. 103
38. (a) obj. 35, pp. 104-105
39. (b) obj. 36, pp. 105-106
40. (a) obj. 37, p. 106
41. (a) obj. 38, p. 106
42. (c) obj. 38, pp. 106-107
43. (b) obj. 39, p. 108
44. (d) obj. 40, p. 111
45. (d) obj. 41, p. 111

True-False

1. T, obj. 3, p. 78
2. T, obj. 4, p. 79
3. T, obj. 5, p. 80
4. F, obj. 6, p. 80
5. F, objs. 8-9, p. 82
6. T, obj. 10, p. 84
7. T, obj. 11, p. 85
8. F, obj. 12, p. 85
9. T, obj. 13, p. 86
10. T, obj. 13, p. 86
11. T, obj. 15, p. 87
12. T, obj. 16, p. 88
13. T, obj. 17, p. 88

14. T, obj. 18, p. 90
15. F, obj. 19, p. 91
16. F, obj. 20, p. 91
17. F, obj. 22, p. 93
18. F, obj. 23, p. 93
19. F, objs. 25, 27, pp. 95-97
20. T, obj. 32, p. 104
21. F. obj. 36, p. 105
22. T, obj. 39, p. 108
23. F, obj. 40, p. 110
24. T, obj. 41, p. 111

Can You Apply the Information?

1. (c) obj. 2, p. 77
2. (a) objs. 3-4, pp. 78-79
3. (c) obj. 7, p. 80
4. (b) obj. 8, p. 83
5. (a) obj. 10, p. 85
6. (b) obj. 12, p. 85
7. (b) obj. 15, p. 87
8. (b) obj. 16, p. 89
9. (d) obj. 17, p. 89
10. (d) obj. 19, p. 91
11. (d) obj. 21, p. 92
12. (b) obj. 21, p. 92
13. (c) objs. 21, 22, 24, pp. 92-94
14. (c) objs. 29-30, pp. 98-102
15. (c) obj. 33, p. 103
16. (d) obj. 40, p. 110
17. (a) obj. 40, p. 111

Chapter Review

1. children, behavior, conception, death (p. 76)
2. neonate, grasping (p. 77)
3. rooting, sucking, Moro, embrace (p. 77)
4. imitate, complex, faces, familiar, reverses (p. 78)
5. Maturation, sequence, rate, order (p. 79)
6. emotional, anger, fear, joy, excitement (p. 80)
7. maturation, brain, similar (p. 80)
8. motor primacy, practice, readiness (p. 80)
9. heredity (p. 82); environment (p. 83)
10. chromosomes, genes, polygenetic (p. 82)
11. dominant, recessive (p. 82)
12. growth sequence, senescence, inseparable, interacting, hereditary (p. 83); environment (p. 84)
13. easy, difficult (p. 84); slow-to-warm-up, heredity, environment, behavior (p. 85)
14. congenital, birth defects, genetic (p. 85)
15. addiction, tremors (hyperactivity, listlessness, etc.), fetal alcohol, miscarriages (prematurity) (p. 86)
16. premature, underweight (p. 86)

17. genetic counseling, amniocentesis, fifteenth, chorionic villus sampling (p. 86)
18. painkiller, oxygen, anesthetized, prepared, Lamaze, care (p. 87)
19. maternity blues, postpartum depression, stress, social (p. 88)
20. Super, zoo-keeper, maternal, behavioral, responsiveness (p. 88)
21. caretaking, playmate (p. 89)
22. self-awareness (p. 90); social referencing, maturation, social referencing (p. 91)
23. critical, imprinting, critical (p. 91)
24. attachment, critical (p. 92); hours (p. 93)
25. separation anxiety, emotional attachment (emotional bond), infants (babies), mothers, securely attached, insecure-avoidant, insecure-ambivalent, secure (p. 92.)
26. emotional bond, adopted, premature, solely, affectional, needs (p. 93.)
27. day-care, harmful, 20, 1, mother, father, troubled (p. 93)
28. mother, isolation, sexual, mothers, attachment (p. 93)
29. crying, birth (p. 94); cooing, babble, single words, telegraphic (p. 95)
30. speech, language dance, innate, biological predisposition, (p. 95)
31. psycholinguists, imitation, rewards (p. 95)
32. signals, turn-taking, interacting, parentese, caretake (caregiver), short (simple), slow (p. 96); musical (p. 97)
33. abstract, stages (p. 98); Assimilation, accommodation (p. 99)
34. sensorimotor, purposeful, object permanence, preoperational, symbolically, language, intuitive, egocentric (p. 99)
35. concrete operational, conservation (p. 99); reversibility, formal operations, abstract, hypothetical (p. 100)
36. 3, solid, physical, mental, form concepts (p. 101)
37. age, stage, learning, brain, observations, explanations (p. 102)
38. moral dilemmas, preconventional, consequences (p. 103)
39. conventional, conform, rules, values, postconventional, self-accepted (p. 103)
40. delinquents, adult, 20 (p. 104)
41. justice, caring, responsibility (p. 104)
42. hospitalism (p. 105); attachment, stimulation, deprivation (p. 106)
43. surrogate (substitute), contact comfort (p. 106)
44. enrichment, enriched, brains, cortexes, impoverished, positive, improvements (p. 108)
45. potential (p. 109); loved, secure, overindulgence, explore, averages, statistical, particular (p. 110); enriched, responds, stimuli, forced teaching (p. 111)
46. slightly, frustration (p. 111)
47. intellectual, investigation (exploration) (p. 110)

chapter four

From Birth to Death: Life-Span Development

KEY TERMS, CONCEPTS, AND INDIVIDUALS

life stage
developmental task
Erik Erikson
psychosocial dilemmas
   trust vs. mistrust
   autonomy vs. shame and doubt
   initiative vs. guilt
   industry vs. inferiority
   identity vs. role confusion
   intimacy vs. isolation
   generativity vs. stagnation
   integrity vs. despair
styles of parenting
   authoritarian
   overly permissive
   authoritative
stress – a normal childhood process
overprotection
normal childhood problems
significant childhood problems

enuresis, encopresis
overeating, anorexia, pica
delayed speech, stuttering
learning disabilities, dyslexia
ADHD, autism
stimulant drugs
behavior modification
child abuse
   characteristics of abusers
   preventing child abuse
adolescence vs. puberty
peak growth spurt
early and late maturation
   hurried childhood development
imaginary audience
parent/teenager conflict
phases of career development
   fantasy, tentative, and realistic stages
   vocational counseling
Gould's adult challenges

midlife crisis
menopause vs. climacteric
biological aging
   fluid vs. crystallized abilities
activity vs. disengagement theories
maximum life span vs. life expectancy
ageism
   myths about aging
living wills
fears of death
   reactions to impending death
hospices
bereavement and grief
parenting – two key areas
techniques of discipline
   power assertion, withdrawal of love
   child management (self-esteem)
guidelines for punishment
ingredients for (+) parent-child relationship
"I" message

LEARNING OBJECTIVES

To demonstrate mastery of this chapter you should be able to:

1. Describe the term "psychosocial dilemma" and explain, according to Erikson, how the resolution of the psychosocial dilemmas affects a person's adjustment to life.

2. State the nature of the psychosocial crisis and the nature of an adequate or inadequate outcome for each of Erikson's eight life stages. Match each crisis with the corresponding age.

    a.

    b.

    c,

    d.

    e.

    f.

    g.

    h.

3. Compare and contrast the following three parenting styles and their effects on children:

    a. authoritarian

    b. overly permissive

    c. authoritative

4. Discuss the positive and negative aspects of stress on a developing child.

5. List and describe (where applicable) nine "normal" childhood problems.

   a.   f.

   b.   g.

   c.   h.

   d.   i.

   e.

6. Give a brief description of the following childhood disorders and their possible causes:

   a. enuresis

   b. encopresis

   c. overeating

   d. anorexia nervosa

   e. pica

   f. delayed speech

   g. stuttering

7. Describe what the label "learning disability" includes. Briefly describe dyslexia including its possible cause.

8.   Describe the following disorders in terms of symptoms, causes, and treatments.

    a.   hyperactivity

    b.   autism

9.   Describe the characteristics of abusive parents and the conditions likely to foster abusive behavior.

10.   Describe what can be done to prevent child abuse.

11.   Define and differentiate the terms adolescence and puberty.

12.   Discuss the advantages and disadvantages of early and late puberty for males and females.

males	*females*

13.   Discuss the importance of imaginary audiences to adolescents.

14.   Explain why Elkind believes that our society is rushing adolescents and what he feels the net effect will be.

15. Describe the interactions between an adolescent and his/her parents and peers as identity formation occurs.

16. List and describe the four broad phases of career development.
    a.   c.

    b.   d.

17. Describe the two steps which aid a person in selecting a realistic and rewarding vocation.
    a.   b.

18. Generally describe the pattern of adult life stages proposed by Roger Gould.

19. Describe what a midlife crisis is and how it can be both a danger and an opportunity.

20. Distinguish menopause from the male climacteric and describe the typical reactions to each.

21. Describe what is meant by the term "biological aging." Include the concepts of fluid and crystallized abilities in your answer.

22. Describe the disengagement theory and the activity theory of aging.

23. Differentiate the concepts maximum life span and life expectancy. List six suggestions for increasing life expectancy.

a   d.

b.   e.

c.   f.

24. Outline the characteristics of ageism. List five significant myths of aging, and relate them to the concept of ageism.

25. Explain the purpose or intent of a living will.

26. Explain how fears about death might be expressed as a denial of death.

27. List and briefly characterize the five emotional reactions typically experienced by people facing death.

a.   d.

b.   e.

c.

28.   Explain how knowledge of the reactions to coping with death is important.

29.   Describe the purpose of a hospice.

30.   Discuss the general characteristics of the process of bereavement. Explain how suppression of the grieving process is related to later problems.

The following objectives are related to the material in the "Applications" section of your text.

31.   Name the two most important areas of effective parent-child relationships.

32.   Discuss the considerations to be aware of in using discipline in childrearing.

33.   Give a brief description of each of the following childrearing techniques and describe their effects on children:

a.   power assertion

b.   withdrawal of love

c.   child management (include the concept of self-esteem)

34. List six guidelines that should be followed if physical punishment is used in disciplining children.

    a.

    b.

    c.

    d.

    e.

    f.

35. List the four basic ingredients (Dinkmeyer & McKay) of a positive parent-child relationship.

    a.

    b.

    c.

    d.

36. Describe what Dr. Thomas Gordon calls an "I" message.

| SELF-QUIZZES |

Do You Know the Information?

Multiple Choice

1. According to Erikson, successfully resolving the psychosocial dilemmas at each stage of life results in
   (a) a heightened sense of oneness with the universe.
   (b) a balance between a person's integrity and his or her selfhood.
   (c) healthy development and a satisfying life.
   (d) a reduction of a person's need to self-actualize.

2. During the first year of life, a favorable outcome to the life crisis discussed by Erikson would be
   (a) faith in the environment and others.
   (b) ability to begin one's own activities.
   (c) feelings of self-control and adequacy.
   (d) ability to form bonds of love and friendship with others.

3. According to Erikson, a major conflict in the first year of life is between
   (a) trust vs mistrust.
   (b) initiative vs guilt.
   (c) autonomy vs shame and doubt.
   (d) relatedness vs isolation.

4. Which psychosocial stage is the one in which a person's feelings of adequacy are shaped by his or her successes or failures in learning skills valued by society?
   (a) initiative vs guilt
   (b) industry vs inferiority
   (c) identity vs role confusion
   (d) autonomy vs shame and doubt

5. A favorable outcome to the life crisis of adolescence would include
   (a) an ability to feel intimate.
   (b) concern for family, society, and future generations.
   (c) an integrated image of oneself as a unique person.
   (d) confidence in productive skills, learning how to work.

6. According to Erikson, the need to develop a sense of identity is the principal task of
   (a) middle childhood.   (b) later adulthood.   (c) early adulthood.   (d) adolescence.

7. If the psychosocial dilemma of middle adulthood is favorably resolved, the outcome is a(n)
   (a) concern for family, society, and future generations.
   (b) confidence in productive skills, learning how to work.
   (c) feelings of self-control and adequacy.
   (d) ability to form bonds of love and friendship with others.

8. Which of the following would be *most* characteristic of authoritative parents?
   (a) The child usually gets his or her own way.
   (b) The parents tend to demand strict adherence to rules.
   (c) Discipline is firm and consistent but not rigid and harsh.
   (d) The children are usually obedient and self-controlled but they are also emotionally stiff, withdrawn, and apprehensive.

9. Which of the following statements regarding stress is *false*?
   (a) Confronting some problems can prepare a child to later tackle the demands of life.
   (b) Most children will do a good job of keeping stress at a comfortable level in activities they initiate.
   (c) Overprotection is generally viewed as slightly more damaging to a child than too much stress.
   (d) Too much stress can result in certain childhood problems.

10. Of the following, which are considered *normal* reactions to the unavoidable stress of growing up?
    (a) sleep disturbances   (e) clinging   (h) hyperactivity
    (b) sibling rivalry   (f) enuresis   (i) reversals to more infantile behaviors
    (c) autism   (g) rebellion   (j) general dissatisfaction
    (d) specific fears of the dark, school, etc.

11. Lack of bowel control is called
    (a) bulimia.   (b) MBD.   (c) encopresis.   (d) enuresis.

12. Anorexia nervosa may be caused by
    (a) conflicts about sexual maturation.
    (b) compensation for a parent's showering with "love" in the form of food.
    (c) consuming inedible substances.
    (d) all of the above.

13. Which of the following is a type of eating disorder in which inedible objects are chewed or eaten?
    (a) pica   (b) bulimia   (c) overeating   (d) compulsion

14. Most researchers now believe that stuttering is due to
    (a) psychological factors.
    (b) dominant, demanding parents.
    (c) anxiety.
    (d) physical problems.

15. Which of the following statements is *true*?
    (a) Learning disabilities include such things as problems with language, attention, and activity level.
    (b) Dyslexia is an inability to understand certain kinds of spoken language.
    (c) Dyslexia is best treated with Ritalin.
    (d) Dyslexia is probably caused by right hemispheric dominance for language.

16. The most widely accepted theory of ADHD states that it is the result of
    (a) poor diet.
    (b) parental detachment.
    (c) a brain condition present at birth.
    (d) too many stimulating drugs.

17. Which of the following does *not* characterize childhood autism?
    (a) language deficiencies
    (b) difficulties in forming social relationships
    (c) inability to sit still, encopresis, and overeating
    (d) violent temper tantrums and repetitive actions

18. Which of the following is a behavior in which spoken words are simply repeated in parroting, stereotyped manner?
    (a) encopresis
    (b) stuttering
    (c) echolalia
    (d) idioglossia

19. A therapy which has been an effective form of treatment for both ADHD and autism is
    (a) drug therapy.
    (b) withdrawal of love.
    (c) restraint or seclusion.
    (d) behavior modification.

20. Which of the following statements about child abuse is *incorrect*?
    (a) Abusive parents often have a high level of stress and frustration in their lives.
    (b) Most abused children are between the ages of three and eight.
    (c) Abusive parents are typically under 30 and from lower income levels.
    (d) Abusive mothers are likely to believe that their children are acting intentionally to annoy them.

21. With regards to preventing child abuse, which of the following is *not* a good idea?
    (a) finding a legal "cure" for this problem
    (b) attending a self-help group staffed by former child abusers
    (c) changing the attitudes of people so that physical punishment is less accepted
    (d) specific training to help parents curb violent impulses

22. Which of the following statements about puberty and adolescence is *false*?
    (a) Puberty refers to rapid physical growth and hormonal changes.
    (b) Adolescence refers to a period of time when we move from childhood to acceptance as adults.
    (c) For boys, early maturation is generally beneficial because it enhances their self-image.
    (d) Girls who are developmentally advanced in elementary school tend to have more prestige among their peers.

23. Which of the following statements about adolescence is *false*?
    (a) The conflicts between adolescents and their parents are usually over issues such as morals, religion, marriage, etc.
    (b) Elkind feels that our society is hurrying adolescents into adulthood and that the net effect is that they are left without sufficient guidance to make a healthy transition into adulthood.
    (c) Conformity to peer values peaks in early adolescence.
    (d) Many teenagers feel that they have an imaginary audience that is constantly evaluating them.

24. According to Elkind and his overview of the social markers of our society,
    (a) it has become easier for adolescents to make the transition into adulthood.
    (b) children are being hurried into adulthood resulting in serious stress symptoms.
    (c) violence and youth crime have now become two of the new social markers.
    (d) teenagers are given adequate guidance today, more so than in times past.

25. In the _____ phase of career development productivity and acceptance by co-workers would probably be at their highest.
    (a) midcareer
    (b) establishment
    (c) later career
    (d) exploration

26. According to Gould, adults are striving for accomplishment during the _____ challenge.
    (a) crisis of questions
    (b) building a workable life
    (c) crisis of urgency
    (d) leaving the family

27. The midlife crisis may take the form of
    (a) breaking out of a seriously flawed life structure.
    (b) a serious midlife decline due to failure or poor earlier choices.
    (c) a last-chance effort to achieve goals.
    (d) all of the above.

28. Concerning menopause and the climacteric
    (a) during the latter men suffer decreases in male hormone which produces many significant and varied physical symptoms.
    (b) most menopausal women report that the experience was worse than they expected because of the anxiety over not knowing what was going to happen.
    (c) most men suffer a decrease in fertility when their level of hormones drops.
    (d) none of the above statements are true.

29. Which of the following statements concerning aging is (are) *correct?*
    (a) IQ scores do not begin a rapid decline until a person is 80-85 years of age.
    (b) Biological aging begins in midlife or after.
    (c) The prime for most abilities occurs around ages 30-35.
    (d) Most older people prefer to live apart from their children.
    (e) Most elderly people eventually show signs of senility.

30. Which of the following postulates that people who remain psychologically, physically, and socially involved are better able to adjust to the aging process?
    (a) activation-arousal theory   (b) engagement theory   (c) disengagement theory   (d) activity theory

31. Which of the following statements is *true*?
    (a) Life expectancy refers to the boundary that limits the length of our lives.
    (b) It is important to remain socially and economically active in retirement.
    (c) It is possible to extend the human life span by following certain principles.
    (d) The actual number of years a person lives is called the maximum life span.

32. In studies with adults concerning their fears about death,
    (a) 1/4 showed evidence of directly fearing their own death.
    (b) young and old alike feared the circumstances of their own death.
    (c) their responses reflected a deeply ingrained denial of death.
    (d) young and old alike feared the occurrence of their own death.

33. The first emotional reaction in dealing with death is usually
    (a) anger.   (b) depression.   (c) bargaining.   (d) denial.

34. Which of the following statements regarding coping with death and dying is *incorrect?*
    (a) Knowing about the reactions to coping with death can help one deal with a dying person who may need to share feelings.
    (b) In general, one's approach to dying will be similar to the way the person handled other major problems in life.
    (c) The desire for silent companionship is indicative of depression in either the dying individual or a relative.
    (d) Knowledge of the stages of death and dying can help the survivors deal with the denial.

35. Regarding the process of bereavement, which of the following statements is *correct?*
    (a) A period of shock occurs when the survivor accepts the reality of their loss.
    (b) Signs of apathy in normal life may continue for months following the death of a friend or relative.
    (c) Pangs of grief occur with intense shock or numbness.
    (d) Suppressing grief leads to more severe and lasting depression.

36. The two most important areas of parent-child relationships are
    (a) discipline and communication.   (c) communication and autonomy.
    (b) discipline and autonomy.   (d) love and attention.

37. When rearing children, it is important to remember that
    (a) discipline can be as important as love.   (c) it is important to recognize a child's psychological needs.
    (b) the goal is to socialize a child without undue frustration.   (d) all of the above statements are true.

38. Withdrawal of love as a technique of discipline tends to produce children who are all of the following *except*
    (a) self-disciplined.   (c) defiant and rebellious.
    (b) anxious and insecure.   (d) dependent upon adult approval.

39.   High self-esteem is related to the use of which style of discipline?
       (a) management techniques   (b) withdrawal of love   (c) physical punishment   (d) guilt-oriented approaches

40.   For punishment to be effective,
       (a) the act should be disapproved, not the child.
       (b) the use of physical punishment should be minimized before age 2 and after age 5.
       (c) it should be administered immediately after the misdeed.
       (d) all of the above must happen.

41.   An "I" message is one which
       (a) tells children what effect their behavior has had on you   (c) tell children what is wrong with them
       (b) sometimes takes the form of threats   (d) includes all of the above

True-False

_____ 1. Pretend play during Erikson's stage 3 helps children practice identity achievement.

_____ 2. Most children do a good job of keeping stress at comfortable levels when they initiate an activity.

_____ 3. Evidence for stuttering being hereditary is the fact that it is 4 times more common in females than in males.

_____ 4. Puberty tends to dramatically increase body awareness and concerns about physical appearance.

_____ 5. Conformity to peer values peaks in late adolescence.

_____ 6. To find out beforehand what an occupation is like, it is best to consult with a vocational counselor.

_____ 7. Even though adult development is complex, Erikson's, Gould's, and Levinson's stages of development fit for nearly all people.

_____ 8. Although fluid abilities may decline with age, crystallized abilities appear to improve at least into the 70's.

_____ 9. Positive stereotypes of the elderly can be as much of a problem as negative ones.

_____ 10. Living wills are designed to allow death with dignity and are made out when the person is still healthy.

_____ 11. At present, hospices are rarely found in large cities because hospitals there can provide those services.

Can You Apply the Information?

1.   Ralph decides to give up his high-paying job to join VISTA (Volunteers in Service to America). He is probably in which of Erikson's psychosocial crises?
      (a) generativity versus stagnation   (c) integrity versus despair
      (b) intimacy versus isolation   (d) autonomy versus shame and doubt

2.   Mary is 85 years old and is trying to justify why she never went to work when she wanted to early in her marriage. She is also struggling with her atheistic views. She is probably
      (a) in Erikson's stage of initiative versus guilt.   (c) becoming senile.
      (b) in Erikson's stage of integrity versus despair.   (d) suffering from ageism.

3.   As a 23-year-old, Robert is very shy and has very few friends. He is socially withdrawn whenever he goes out, which in itself is rare. At work, he does what he is told even if he doesn't like it and always keeps his emotions in check. His unemotional nature has meant that he has never had a long-term relationship. His current personality may be a by-product of having had _____ parents.
      (a) authoritarian   (b) permissive   (c) authoritative   (d) effective

4. Your 4-year-old has recently started asking for a light to be left on in her room at night because she is scared. You are concerned that this could be the beginning of either a bad habit or an all-consuming fear of the dark. What is your pediatrician *most likely* to tell you about this situation when you ask?
    (a) Specific fears are very common and you should not worry unless it lasts for a long time or worsens.
    (b) The next problem that will surface will be an excessive amount of clinging.
    (c) This is a sign of regression to more infantile behavior.
    (d) If you let her have her way she will start showing a defiance of all adult authority.

5. Gail is 13 years old and is in the 8th grade. She is constantly on a diet and worried about her figure. She weighs 70 pounds and is 5 feet tall. Gail's problem is
    (a) a normal reaction of adolescence.
    (b) pica.
    (c) anorexia nervosa.
    (d) related to her dislike of school which is considered a normal reaction of childhood.

6. Paul reads the word "stop" as "tsog." Paul is probably suffering from
    (a) autism.   (b) delayed speech.   (c) bulimia.   (d) dyslexia.

7. Roberta and Robert are both 11 years old and both of them just started puberty. Therefore, we could expect
    (a) Roberta to be taller than Robert.   (c) Roberta to have better relationships than Robert.
    (b) Robert to have a better self-image than Roberta.   (d) Robert to be less poised and dominant than Roberta.

8. Shannon is a 13 year old adolescent. Her mother buys her a pair of jeans from a discount store. When she wears these jeans, she is sure that everyone knows they are cheap. Shannon is preoccupied with
    (a) social markers.   (c) her social network.
    (b) her imaginary audience.   (d) growth of her separate identity.

9. Bill and Christine have been married for a number of years and they have no children. They used to feel that togetherness was most important but are now starting to be unsure. In fact, both of them are secretly considering reaching out to others in an extramarital sort of way. Gould would describe them as
    (a) trying to build a workable life.   (c) being in a crisis of urgency.
    (b) being in a crisis of questions.   (d) failing to attain stability.

10. Stuart is 60 years old and worried about the inevitable overall decline in all abilities during old age. Which of the following statements apply?
    (a) He will probably become senile by age 90 as do most 90-year-olds.
    (b) Although his psychological functioning will decline his physical abilities need not change substantially if he stays physically fit.
    (c) His physical abilities will steadily decline as will his intellectual functioning.
    (d) none of the above

11. Harriet is 70 year old and has been forced to retire from her job of 30 years where her performance was beginning to decline. According to the disengagement theory she will probably
    (a) be depressed.   (c) adapt reasonably well to the new situation.
    (b) go out and get another job.   (d) do none of the above.

12. About 2 months ago Charles discovered that he has inoperable cancer and only a short time left. At this point, he envies his wife for her good health and is trying to make life miserable for her. He is probably in the _____ emotional reaction.
    (a) denial   (b) anger   (c) bargaining   (d) depression

13. Anne, a 38 year old mother of two, has terminal breast cancer which has metastasized to her brain. She has always been viewed as an extroverted person, the life of the party. Her impending death has been hard to accept for her family and close friends. What might be an important consideration in her situation?
    (a) that her friends and family will overcompensate and upset her by wanting to talk too much about her impending death
    (b) that expressing anger over the situation will have no real effect and serve no purpose for either her or the family
    (c) that the family help her through the five stages of emotional reaction to her impending death in the correct order
    (d) that people close to her will have a great deal of difficulty with the idea of her death and will end up making her feel isolated and alone

14. You receive a call from your daughter's third grade teacher. She is concerned about an incident that just occurred on the playground in which your daughter struck another girl. What is the *best* thing to do?
    (a) Spank your daughter when she comes home from school and take away her privileges.
    (b) Tell the teacher to spank your daughter since punishment should be immediate to be effective.
    (c) Tell your daughter what a bad girl she has been.
    (d) Tell your daughter that her behavior makes you feel ashamed and embarrassed.

Chapter Review

1. Personality theorist Erik Erikson suggests that we face a specific _____ dilemma at each stage of life. A dilemma is a conflict between _____ _____ and the _____ world that affects development. Resolving these crises creates a new _____ between a person and the social world. An unfavorable outcome throws one off balance and makes it harder to deal with later _____.

2. During the first year of life, Erikson believes that a basic attitude of _____ or _____ is formed. A favorable outcome of this stage is faith in the _____.

3. During stage two (1-3 years), the life crisis involves _____ vs. _____ and _____. Successful resolution of this stage would include the development of feelings of _____-_____ and _____.

4. During stage three (3-5 years), the child moves from simple self-control to an ability to take initiative. Thus, this stage involves the conflict of _____ vs _____. During stage three, parents can reinforce _____ by giving freedom to play, to ask questions, to use imagination, and to choose activities.

5. During stage four (6-12 years) the major crisis involves the development of _____ vs _____. If a child develops confidence in _____ skills, this stage has been resolved successfully.

6. During stage five, Erikson believes that _____ vs _____ _____ is the major developmental task facing the individual. A child should complete this stage with an _____ sense of self.

7. Stage six involves the psychosocial crisis of developing _____ or _____. The person should be able to form bonds of _____ or _____ with others if this stage has a favorable outcome.

8. During stage seven, _____ vs _____ is the major conflict. This period involves broadening one's concern and energies to include the welfare of others and society as a whole.

9. During the final life phase, old age, Erikson sees _____ vs _____ as the psychological crisis that must be resolved. A person should leave this stage with a sense of _____ and _____.

10. Parents who view children as having few rights but adultlike responsibilities and who demand strict adherence to rules are called _____. In contrast overly _____ parents view children as having few responsibilities but rights similar to adults. _____ parents are those who balance their rights with those of their children. They tend to encourage the child to act _____.

11. Although too much _____ may be _____, too little may also be _____. Parents should not be too _____. Most children do a good job of keeping _____ at comfortable levels when they initiate activities.

12. There are several childhood problems which can be considered a normal part of growing up. One of these, _____ disturbances, is a common problem. All children experience occasional wakefulness, frightening dreams, or a desire to get into the parents' bed.

13. Specific _____ of the dark, dogs, school, or of a particular room or person are also common childhood problems. Most children will be overly _____ at times, allowing themselves to be bullied by other children. There may also be temporary periods of general _____ when nothing pleases the child. Children also normally display periods of general _____ marked by tantrums or refusal to do anything requested.

14. Another normal problem is _____, in which the child refuses to leave his or her mother's side. Development does not always advance smoothly. Every child will show occasional _____ or _____ to more infantile behavior. Two additional problems common to the elementary school years are _____ _____ (not getting along with brothers and sisters) and _____ against rules and limitations of the adult world.

15. Severe emotional disturbances do affect children. Emotional difficulties may develop during _____- _____ or over bowel and bladder habits. The two most common problems are _____ (lack of bladder control) and _____ (lack of bowel control). Both problems can be a means of expressing pent-up _____.

16. Feeding disturbances is another area of emotional difficulty. _____ may be encouraged by a parent who compensates for feeling unloved by showering the child with "love" in the form of food.

17. Serious cases of undereating are called _____ _____ (nervous loss of appetite). Most people who suffer such disorders are usually adolescent _____. The disorders may represent conflicts about _____ maturity.

18. Another childhood problem associated with eating difficulties is a condition called _____, during which children go through a period of intense appetite and eat or chew on all sorts of inedible substances.

19. Two common speech problems are _____ _____ and _____. A child may fail to learn language because of a general lack of _____. Stuttering was once held to be primarily a psychological disturbance; it is now believed to be more _____ in origin.

20. Learning disabilities include problems with _____, _____, _____, _____, or _____ levels. An inability to read with understanding is called _____. Researchers suspect that the latter disorder is related to a malformation of the _____ processing areas on the _____ side of the brain.

21. A child may experience barriers to learning for many reasons. One of the most significant problems is _____, a condition in which the child is constantly in motion and cannot concentrate. The most widely accepted theory of this condition states that it is the result of a _____ condition at birth. Medical authorities advocate the use of _____ drugs. However, a number of psychologists have objected to the blanket use of these drugs and instead advocate the use of _____ for behavioral and emotional problems.

22. _____ is one of the most severe childhood problems. In addition to extreme _____, the child may throw gigantic _____ _____ including self-destructive behavior. Language learning is usually so retarded that the child is mute. If these children speak at all, they often parrot back everything said, a reaction known as _____.

23. Experts used to blame parents for autism. It is now recognized that autism is caused by _____ defects in the _____ _____. The therapy which has had the greatest success in treating autism is _____ _____.

24. Abusive parents are usually under _____ years of age and are from _____ income levels. They often have a high level of _____ and _____ in their lives. The typical abused child is generally under _____ years of age. Abusive mothers are more likely to believe that their children are acting _____ to annoy them.

25. There are _____ cures for child abuse including _____ homes and court _____ for the _____ while living with their _____. Also, there are _____ - _____ groups. A third way of helping is through changing the _____ of our society toward _____ _____.

26. The period during which we move from childhood to acceptance as an adult is called _____. _____ is a biological event. The growth spurt occurs roughly two years earlier for _____ than it does for _____. For boys, early maturation is generally _____. For girls in elementary school, those who are developmentally _____ seem to have less prestige among peers, but this is reversed by junior high school.

27. Elkind feels that we are _____ teenagers too much and that they will be left without sufficient _____ to make a healthy transition to adulthood. According to Elkind, the traditional _____ _____ of adolescence have all but disappeared.

28. Many teenagers believe that everyone seems to be watching everything he or she does. This is called their _____ _____. Therefore, adolescents become very concerned with controlling the _____ they make on others.

29. The adolescent search for identity often results in increased _____ with parents, but usually only in _____ areas of importance.

30. Increased identification with _____ _____ is quite common during adolescence. Membership in such groups gives a measure of _____ apart from the family and practice in belonging to a social _____. It is important to remember, however, that conformity to peer values peaks in _____ adolescence and remains strong at least through _____ _____.

31. Career development tends to go through four phases: (1) the _____ phase during which an initial search for a career possibilities is made; (2) the _____ phase when the person settles in; (3) the _____ phase which is the time of highest productivity and acceptance by co-workers; and (4) the _____ _____ phase when the person may serve as a respected expert.

32. Since most people choose their vocations during the _____ phase, there is a recognizable series of stages that are progressed through: (1) the _____ stage where children under 10 imagine what they want to be when they grow up; (2) the _____ stage where adolescents form more realistic ideas about what they want to do; and (3) the _____ stage where work is used to find out what a person is good at and what holds their interest.

33. To make sure your vocational choice will be realistic and personally rewarding, you must: (1) gain an accurate _____ of various occupations and (2) get a clear picture of your own _____, _____, and _____.

34. The easiest way to improve occupational choice is to consult a _____ counselor. If one is not available, most libraries carry the _____ _____ Handbook which includes job descriptions, requirements, and earnings for most jobs available in the marketplace. Another option is to talk to people in that line of work and _____ people in an occupation that interests you.

35. Certain relatively consistent events, according to Roger Gould, mark adult development in our society. These range from escaping _____ _____ in the late teens to a noticeable acceptance of one's _____ in the late forties. Some research indicates that a _____ _____ affects many people in the 37-41 age range.

36.   Adjustment to later middle age may be complicated for women by _____ and for men by a _____. For women, the level of the hormone _____ drops. Males do not undergo such dramatic physical changes. Decreases in male _____ output may cause _____ symptoms similar to a woman's. Many of a male's symptoms are probably due to _____-_____.

37.   _____ _____ is a gradual process that begins early in life. Peak functioning in most physical capacities reaches a maximum by about _____ to _____ years of age and then gradually declines. For those who are still young, the prospect of physical aging may be the largest threat of old age. However, only about _____ percent of the elderly are in nursing homes.

38.   _____ (those who study aging) believe that only about _____ percent of the disability of old people is medically based. For example, regarding intelligence, _____ abilities (those requiring speed) may decline with age, yet _____ abilities (such as vocabulary) seem to improve with age.

39.   The _____ theory of aging assumes that it is normal and desirable for people to withdraw from society as they age. The second view, the _____ theory, predicts that people who remain active physically, mentally, and socially will adjust better to aging.

40.   The length of our lives is limited by a boundary called the _____ _____ _____. For most people, _____ _____ (the actual number of years the average person lives) is shorter.

41.   Discrimination or prejudice on the basis of age is called _____. It tends to have a _____ impact on older individuals by expressing _____ of the elderly. Ageism can also include _____ of the elderly. Studies of the elderly generally contradict most of the misconceptions about them. Studies show them to be _____, _____, and _____ healthy.

42.   In a poll of 1500 adults, only about _____ percent showed evidence of directly fearing their own death. Those fears that do exist apparently change with age such that _____ individuals fear the occurrence of death, whereas _____ individuals fear the circumstances of death. It is impetus of this last group that has prompted the development of the _____ _____ in order to allow death with dignity.

43.   An indication of the emotional response to death comes from the work of Elisabeth Kubler-Ross, a _____ or one who studies death. She has found that the dying person tends to go through five basic emotional reactions in order to prepare for death. The reactions are _____, _____, _____, _____, and _____.

44.   Not all terminally ill individuals display these reactions, and they may not occur in this _____. Knowledge of these reactions is important because it can help both the dying individual and the survivors cope with the emotional upheaval. It is also important to note that a dying person may need to share _____ and talk about _____ openly. Someone who does not have all of these reactions is not somehow _____.

45.   A _____ is basically a hospital for the terminally ill with the goal of improving the quality of life in a person's final days.

46.   Bereavement and grief generally begins with _____. This is followed by pangs of _____. This gradually gives way to weeks or months of _____, _____, and _____. Eventually the bereaved person accepts what cannot be changed and makes a new beginning (a period of _____).

47.   It is important to note that suppressing grief does not necessarily lead to more severe and lasting _____. Bereaved persons should work through their grief at their own pace.

48. As a single problem area in development, the question of how to be a good parent has probably attracted more attention than any other. Much of the answer can be found in _____ and _____. The goal should be to socialize a child without undue _____ or destroying the bond of _____ and _____ between parent and child. Therefore, many experts advocate a style of child rearing that recognizes a child's _____ needs.

49. Parents tend to base discipline on one or more of the following techniques: _____ _____, _____ of _____, or _____ _____.

50. Power-oriented techniques are associated with _____ and _____ of parents, and a lack of spontaneity and warmth. Severely punished children also tend to be _____, _____, and _____.

51. Withdrawal of love produces children who tend to be _____-_____. As a side-effect they are also frequently _____, _____, and _____ on adults for approval.

52. High _____-_____ was related to management techniques which emphasized strict and consistent discipline coupled with high parental interest and concern for the child.

53. If punishment is to be used parents should separate disapproval of the _____ from disapproval of the _____. Punishment should never be _____ or _____ to a child. Punishment is most effective if it is delivered _____. Physical punishment is not particularly effective before age _____ or after age _____. Reserve _____ punishment for situations that pose danger for the child. Remember that it is usually more effective to _____ good behavior.

54. Dinkmeyer and McKay believe that mutual _____, shared _____, _____, and _____ are the four key ingredients in a positive parent-child relationship. Dr. Thomas Gordon, who has developed a program called Parent Effectiveness Training (PET), believes that parents should send _____ messages instead of _____ messages.

ANSWER KEYS

Do You Know the Information?

Multiple Choice

1. (c) obj. 1, p. 116
2. (a) obj. 2, pp. 116-117
3. (a) obj. 2, pp. 116-117
4. (b) obj. 2, pp. 116-117
5. (c) obj. 2, p. 118
6. (d) obj. 2, p. 118
7. (a) obj. 2, p. 118
8. (c) obj. 3, p. 121
9. (c) obj. 4, pp. 121-122
10. (a,b,d,e,g,i,j) obj. 5, pp. 122-123
11. (c) obj. 6, p. 123
12. (a) obj. 6, p. 124
13. (a) obj. 6, p. 124
14. (d) obj. 6, p. 124
15. (a) obj. 7, p. 124
16. (c) obj. 8, p. 125

17. (c) obj. 8, pp. 125-126
18. (c) obj. 8, p. 126
19. (d) obj. 8, pp. 125-126
20. (b) obj. 9, p. 127
21. (a) obj. 10, p. 127
22. (d) objs. 11-12, pp. 129-130
23. (a) objs. 13-15, pp. 131-132
24. (b) obj. 14, p. 131
25. (a) obj. 16, p. 134
26. (b) obj. 18, p. 136
27. (d) obj. 19, p. 137
28. (d) obj. 20, p. 138
29. (d) objs. 21, 24 pp. 138-142
30. (d) obj. 22, p. 141
31. (b) obj. 23, p. 140
32. (c) obj. 26, p. 143
33. (d) obj. 27, p. 143
34. (c) objs. 27-28, pp. 144-145

35. (b) obj. 30, p. 146
36. (a) obj. 31, p. 147
37. (d) obj. 32, pp. 148-149
38. (c) obj. 33, p. 148
39. (a) obj. 33, p. 149
40. (d) obj. 34, p. 149
41. (a) obj. 36, p. 150

True-False

1. F, obj. 2, p. 117
2. T, obj. 4, p. 121
3. F, obj. 6, p. 124
4. T, obj. 11, p. 130
5. F, obj. 15, p. 132
6. F, obj. 17, p. 135
7. F, obj. 18, p. 135
8. T, obj. 21, p. 139

True-False (continued)

9. T, obj. 24, p. 141
10. T, obj. 25, p. 144
11. F, obj. 29, p. 145

Can You Apply the Information?

1. (a) obj. 2, p. 118
2. (b) obj. 2, p. 118
3. (a) obj. 3, p. 121
4. (a) obj. 5, p. 122
5. (c) obj. 6, p. 123
6. (d) obj. 7, p. 124

7. (b) objs. 11-12, pp. 130-131
8. (b) obj. 13, p. 132
9. (b) obj. 18, p. 136
10. (d) objs. 21, 24, pp. 138-141
11. (c) obj. 22, p. 140
12. (b) obj. 27, p. 144
13. (d) objs. 27-28, p. 145
14. (d) objs. 34, 36, pp. 148-150

Chapter Review

1. psychosocial, personal impulses, social, balance, crises (p. 116)
2. trust, mistrust (p. 117); environment (p. 120)
3. autonomy, shame, doubt (p. 117); self-control, adequacy (p. 120)
4. initiative, guilt, initiative (p. 117)
5. industry, inferiority (p. 117); productive (p. 120)
6. identity, role confusion (p. 118); integrated (p. 120)
7. intimacy, isolation, love, friendship (p. 118)
8. generativity, stagnation (p. 118)
9. integrity, despair (p. 118); dignity, fulfillment (p. 120)
10. authoritarian (p. 120); permissive (p. 121); Authoritative, responsibly (p. 121)
11. stress, harmful (damaging), harmful (damaging), overprotective, stress (p. 121)
12. sleep (p. 122)
13. fears, timid, dissatisfaction, negativism (p. 122)
14. clinging (p. 122); reversals, regressions, sibling rivalry, rebellion (p. 123)
15. toilet-training, enuresis, encopresis, frustration (hostility) (p. 123)
16. Overeating (p. 123)
17. anorexia nervosa, females, sexual, (p. 124)
18. pica (p. 124)
19. delayed speech, stuttering, stimulation, physical (p. 124)
20. thinking, perception, language, attention, activity, dyslexia, language, left (p. 124)
21. ADHD (p. 124); brain, stimulant, therapy (p. 125)
22. Autism (p. 125); isolation, temper tantrums, echolalia (p. 126)
23. congenital, nervous system, behavior modification (p. 126)
24. 30, lower, stress, frustration, three, intentionally (p. 127)
25. legal, foster, supervision, children, parents, self-help (p. 127); attitudes, physical punishment (p. 128)
26. adolescence, Puberty, girls, boys (p. 129); beneficial, advanced (p. 130)
27. hurrying, guidance (direction, support), social markers (p. 131)
28. imaginary audience, impressions (p. 132)
29. conflict, superficial (p. 132)
30. peer groups, security (identity), network, early, high school (p. 132)
31. exploration, establishment, midcareer, later career (p. 134)
32. exploration, fantasy, tentative, realistic (p. 134)
33. understanding, interests, needs, goals (p. 135)
34. vocational, Occupational Outlook, observe (p. 135)
35. parental dominance (p. 136); fate, midlife crisis (p. 137)
36. menopause, climacteric, estrogen, hormone, psychological, self-doubt (p. 138)
37. Biological aging, 25, 30 (p. 138); 5 (p. 139)
38. Gerontologists, 25 (p. 139); fluid, crystallized (p. 140)
39. disengagement (p. 140); activity (p. 141)
40. maximum life span, life expectancy (p. 140)
41. ageism, negative, aversion (hatred, rejection), stereotyping (p. 141); integrated, active, psychologically (p. 142)
42. 4, younger, older, living will (p. 143)
43. thanatologist, denial (isolation) (p. 143); anger, bargaining, depression, acceptance (p. 144)
44. order, feelings, death, deviant (immature) (p. 144)

45. hospice (p. 145)
46. shock, grief (p. 145); apathy, dejection, depression, resolution (p. 146)
47. depression (p. 146)
48. communication, discipline (p. 147); frustration, love, trust, psychological (p. 148)
49. power assertion, withdrawal, love, child management (p. 148)
50. fear, hatred, defiant, rebellious, aggressive (p. 148)
51. self-disciplined, anxious, insecure, dependent (p. 149)
52. self-esteem (p. 149)
53. act, child, harsh, injurious, immediately, two, five, physical, reinforce (p. 149)
54. respect, enjoyment, love, encouragement (p. 149); I, you (p. 150)

chapter five

Sensation and Reality

LEARNING OBJECTIVES

To demonstrate mastery of this chapter you should be able to:

1. Explain how our senses act as a data reduction system by selecting, analyzing, and coding incoming information.

2. Explain how sensory receptors act as biological transducers.

3. Explain the concept of localization of function including the idea behind the statement "Seeing does not take place in the eyes."

4. Define sensation.

5. Explain the approach of psychophysics.

6. Define the terms "absolute threshold" and "difference threshold" (JND), and explain Weber's law.

7. Explain the process of perceptual defense.

8. Define limen and describe subliminal perception including its effectiveness.

9. Describe hue, saturation, and brightness in terms of their representation in the visual spectrum.

10. Briefly compare the structure of the eye to a camera and explain the process of accommodation.

11. Describe the following four conditions:
   a. hyperopia

   b. myopia

   c. astigmatism

   d. presbyopia

12. Describe the location and explain the functions. of the following parts of the eye:
   a. cornea

   b. lens

   c. iris

   d. pupil

   e. rods (very sensitive to what?)

   f. cones

   g. blind spot

   h. fovea

   i. retina

13. Describe the research of Hubel and Wiesel.

14. Discuss peripheral vision. Include the structures responsible for it and how this type of vision affects night vision.

15. Discuss the applications that have been made of the differing maximum color sensitivity of the rods and cones.

16. Discuss the following theories of color vision:

    a. trichromatic theory

    b. opponent-process theory (include a description of afterimage)

17. Describe color blindness and color weakness.

18. Explain the purpose of the Ishihara test.

19. Briefly describe the process of dark adaptation including the function of rhodopsin in night vision and night blindness.

20. Explain how dark adaptation can be speeded up.

21.   Describe the process by which sound travels and what psychological dimensions correspond to the physical ones.

22.   Describe the location and explain the function(s) of the following parts of the ear:

    a.   eardrum (tympanic membrane)

    b.   auditory ossicles

    c.   oval window

    d.   cochlea

    e.   hair cells

23.   Briefly explain how the sense of hearing works by tracing an incoming stimulus from the time it strikes the tympanic membrane until it is transduced and sent to the temporal lobes.

24.   Describe the frequency and the place theories of hearing.

25.   List and describe the three general types of deafness.
    a.

    b.

    c.

26. Describe the factors that determine whether hearing loss will occur from stimulation deafness. Discuss how temporary threshold shift and tinnitus are related to stimulation deafness.

27. Describe how cochlear implants can help overcome deafness.

28. Describe the sense of smell (olfaction) including:

    a. its nature

    b. how it works

    c. a description of the condition anosmia

    d. a description of the lock and key theory

29. Describe the sense of taste (gustation) including:

    a. its nature

    b. the four basic taste sensations

    c. the tastes to which humans are most and least sensitive

    d. how the vast number of flavors is explained

    e. how it works

30. List the three somesthetic senses and be able to describe the function of each.

    a.

    b.

    c.

31. Name and describe the functions of the structures responsible for the vestibular sense.

32. Explain how the sensory conflict theory explains motion sickness.

33. List and be able to recognize the five different sensations produced by the skin receptors.

    a.   d.

    b.   e.

    c.

34. Explain why certain areas of the body are more sensitive to touch than other areas.

35. Name the most frequently found receptor in the skin.

36. Name and describe the two different pain systems in the body.

    a.

    b.

37. List and discuss the three reasons many sensory events never reach conscious awareness.

    a.

    b.

    c.

38. Name the process that prevents visual sensory adaptation.

39. Describe gate control theory.

40. Discuss how endorphins explain some of the feelings associated with running, acupuncture, ESB, masochism, and childbirth.

The following objective is related to the material in the "Applications" section of your text.

41. Discuss four techniques that can be used to reduce the amount of pain perceived.

42. Discuss how the four pain reduction techniques can be applied in:

   a. prepared childbirth training.

   b. distraction and reinterpretation.

   c. counterirritation.

SELF-QUIZZES

Do You Know the Information?

Multiple Choice

1. The senses can be said to serve as a data reduction system because
   (a) each sense only responds to one type of stimulation.
   (b) many receptors break down information before sending it to the brain.
   (c) each sensation is directly affected by the area of the brain where it terminates.
   (d) all of the above are true.

2. When the photoreceptors in the eye convert photons of light into nerve impulses, the photoreceptors have functioned as
    (a) transformers.   (b) translocutors.   (c) adaptors.   (d) transducers.

3. Localization of function means that
    (a) each area of the body is capable of receiving a single specific type of stimulation.
    (b) the type of sensation experienced depends ultimately on the type of nerve pathway on which it travels.
    (c) specific brain areas receive messages from each of the senses.
    (d) "hearing" takes place in the ears.

4. Sensation may be defined as
    (a) the incoming flow of information.   (c) feelings made up of the somesthetic senses.
    (b) the organization of incoming information by the brain.   (d) the transduction of the internal world.

5. The absolute threshold is
    (a) the minimum amount of stimulus change necessary to detect a noticeable difference in the stimulus.
    (b) the minimum amount of stimulus necessary to raise a threshold.
    (c) the difference between physical stimuli and psychological responses.
    (d) the least amount of stimulation necessary for sensation to occur.

6. The difference threshold is
    (a) the minimum amount of stimulus change necessary to detect a noticeable difference in the stimulus.
    (b) the minimum amount of stimulus necessary to raise a threshold.
    (c) the difference between physical stimuli and psychological responses.
    (d) the least amount of stimulation necessary for sensation to occur.

7. A visual stimulus that is subliminal is
    (a) basically weak.   (c) below the normal threshold for that particular sense.
    (b) rather ineffective as an advertising medium.   (d) all of the above.

8. The dimension of vision known as brightness corresponds to which characteristic of light waves?
    (a) amplitude   (c) wavelength
    (b) the narrowness of the band of wavelengths   (d) purity

9. The process whereby the lens of the eye is stretched or thickened to focus the incoming image is called
    (a) facilitation.   (b) accommodation.   (c) adaptation.   (d) acuity.

10. Hyperopia is the condition that exists when
    (a) the length of the eye is too short.   (c) farsightedness exists because of old age.
    (b) a person cannot focus distant subjects.   (d) a person can see subjects close to the eye.

11. The mechanism of the eye that controls the amount of light entering is the
    (a) lens.   (b) aperture.   (c) iris.   (d) diaphragm.

12. The visual receptor primarily responsible for color vision is the
    (a) cone.   (b) fovea.   (c) rod.   (d) pupil.

13. The best night vision is obtained when
    (a) looking at the center of an object.
    (b) a moving object is detected at the center of the visual field.
    (c) the incoming image is focused on the fovea.
    (d) looking slightly to one side or the other of an object.

14. The opponent-process theory of color vision holds that
    (a) afterimages are caused by the fatigue of one of the three types of rods.
    (b) there are three paired receptors and while one of the pair is "on" the other is "off."
    (c) there are three types of cones.
    (d) none of the above are true.

15. A person who has color weakness
   (a) sees the world much like the view presented on a black and white TV.
   (b) has partial color blindness such as red-green color blindness.
   (c) has a rare condition.
   (d) probably also suffers from presbyopia.

16. The increase in sensitivity to light that occurs when one spends time in the dark is called
   (a) light enhancement.   (b) dark facilitation.   (c) light sensitizing.   (d) dark adaptation.

17. The frequency of sound waves corresponds to the perceived _____ of a sound.
   (a) pitch   (b) rarefaction   (c) amplitude   (d) loudness

18. The structures actually responsible for transduction in the ear are the
   (a) ossicles.   (b) hair cells.   (c) tympanic membranes.   (d) stapes.

19. The oval window is connected to the
   (a) eardrum.   (b) round window.   (c) hair cells.   (d) ossicles.

20. The frequency theory of hearing holds that
   (a) tones of differing frequencies register on different places on the cochlea.
   (b) pitch is signaled by the area of the cochlea most strongly activated.
   (c) as pitch rises, nerve impulses of the same frequency are fed into the auditory nerve.
   (d) "Hunter's notch" is a result of very low frequency sound waves.

21. The type of deafness that occurs when auditory messages do not reach the brain because the eardrum or the auditory ossicles are immobilized is called
   (a) nerve deafness.   (b) stimulation deafness.   (c) brain deafness.   (d) conduction deafness.

22. Whether or not a person will suffer a hearing loss due to stimulation deafness depends upon
   (a) the loudness of the sound.   (c) the length of exposure to the sound.
   (b) the presence of damage to the hair cells.   (d) all of the above.

23. The lock and key theory is based on the idea that
   (a) scents are identified by the location of activated receptors in the nose.
   (b) our specific patterns of genetic inheritance hold the keys that will in time unlock our sensitivities to certain tastes.
   (c) there are holes on the odor receptors that match the shape of the various odor molecules.
   (d) the number of activated receptors tells the brain how strong an odor is.

24. Which of the following statements concerning taste is *incorrect*?
   (a) The taste buds are not equally distributed on the tongue.
   (b) Humans are most sensitive to sour and least sensitive to salt.
   (c) The sense of taste is chemical in nature.
   (d) Subjective flavor is probably one-half smell.

25. Which of the following is considered to be a somesthetic sense?
   (a) the kinesthetic sense   (b) the skin senses   (c) the vestibular senses   (d) all of the above

26. The sensory conflict theory explains the occurrence of nausea as when sensations from the _____ fail to match information from the eyes and body.
   (a) otolith organs   (b) semicircular canals   (c) ampulla   (d) all of the above

27. Which of the following is *not* one of the sensations which has its own receptors?
   (a) cold   (b) pressure   (c) hot   (d) pain

28. The body's _____ system for pain utilizes large nerve fibers.
   (a) warning   (b) reminder   (c) somesthetic   (d) kinesthetic

29. The decrease in sensory response that accompanies a constant or unchanging stimulus is called
    (a) sensory adaptation.   (b) selective attention.   (c) sensory habituation.   (d) response decrement.

30. Our ability to tune in on any one of many sensory messages while excluding others is known as
    (a) sensory selection.   (b) sensory adaptation.   (c) selective attention.   (d) selective sensation.

31. Physiological nystagmus is the process in which
    (a) the eye makes involuntary movements to move the visual image off of the inoperative fovea.
    (b) the tiny muscle movements made by the eye shift the visual image from one receptor to another and prevent adaptation.
    (c) the eye counteracts negative afterimages.
    (d) the eye selectively attends to only important stimuli.

32. Using the concept of sensory gating, Wall and Melzack explain the phenomenon of acupuncture as
    (a) a patient's subjective response to the placebo effect.
    (b) a subtle hypnotic suggestion.
    (c) one pain message closing the "gate" to pain transmitted by another fiber.
    (d) due to the release of endorphins in the brain.

33. One possible explanation for the phenomenon known as the runner's "high" is
    (a) a well functioning vestibular system.   (c) sensory adaptation to the pain from running.
    (b) selective attention of pleasure signals from the muscles.   (d) the release of endorphins in the brain.

34. Which of the following can be used to reduce a person's perception of pain?
    (a) Apply a brief, mildly painful stimulus to another part of the body.
    (b) Shift the focus of attention away from the painful stimulus.
    (c) Seek some degree of control over the stimulus.
    (d) All of the above are true.

True-False

_____ 1. The reason why seeing does not occur only in the eyes is that what we call vision involves structures and processes from the eyes all the way to the brain.

_____ 2. In psychophysics, physical sensations are measured and related to psychological stimuli.

_____ 3. Perceptual defense occurs when the absolute threshold is lowered.

_____ 4. White light is that way because it is saturated white hue.

_____ 5. If the cornea or the lens is misshapen, the resulting condition is a partially focused field and is called astigmatism.

_____ 6. The fovea is packed with rods.

_____ 7. The rods are mainly responsible for our ability to see in dim light.

_____ 8. Cells in the brain seem to first analyze incoming visual information into basic features of what is being observed.

_____ 9. Because rods are most sensitive to blue-green lights, many police cars have blue emergency lights for use at night.

_____ 10. The presence of afterimages proves the opponent-process theory to be the best explanation for how color vision works.

_____ 11. The Ishihara test is a test for nystagmus.

_____ 12. If a room is illuminated with red light, the process of dark adaptation is speeded up because the rods do not respond well to this wavelength of light.

_____ 13. The occurrence of tinnitus is a sure sign of conduction deafness.

_____ 14. Anosmia is a "smell blindness" for only one type of odor.

_____ 15. The sense that signals balance is called the kinesthetic sense.

_____ 16. The ampulla contain tiny crystals in a soft, gelatin-like mass.

_____ 17. The sensitivity of a certain area of the skin roughly corresponds to the number of receptors in that area.

_____ 18. The most frequently found receptor in the skin is for temperature.

_____ 19. In terms of pain, the reminding system is carried on small nerve fibers and the pain is slow, nagging, aching, and widespread.

_____ 20. Receptor sites for endorphins are found in large numbers in brain areas associated with hunger and thirst.

Matching *(use the letters on the right only once)*

_____ 1. nerve deafness
_____ 2. myopia
_____ 3. olfaction and gustation
_____ 4. cochlear implant
_____ 5. Weber's Law
_____ 6. cochlea
_____ 7. counterirritation
_____ 8. kinesthesis
_____ 9. hue
_____ 10. ossicle damage
_____ 11. endorphins
_____ 12. limen
_____ 13. Vitamin A
_____ 14. feature detectors
_____ 15. sensory gating
_____ 16. pupils
_____ 17. tunnel vision

A. phosphenes
B. corresponds to wavelength
C. subliminal
D. basic elements of a stimulus pattern
E. conduction deafness
F. masking one pain with another under your control
G. nearsightedness
H. contains the ultimate receptors for hearing
I. constant proportion of the original stimulus intensity
J. chemical senses
K. hearing aid cannot help
L. stimulates the auditory nerve directly
M. necessary for the production of rhodopsin
N. related to a central biasing system
O. defined as threshold or limit
P. relays information on body position and movement
Q. released during pain and stress
R. warmth
S. dilate in dim light; constrict in bright light
T. loss of peripheral vision

Can You Apply the Information?

1. In which of the following locations does transduction take place?
   (a) auditory ossicles   (b) lens   (c) blind spot   (d) cochlea

2. The fact that a person reports hearing music when the auditory area of the brain is stimulated exemplifies the principle of
   (a) localization of function.   (c) temporal location.
   (b) reduction of sensory information.   (d) sensory gating.

3. You are riding along in your car listening to the radio. You find that the very least you can turn your radio dial is 1/10 of a turn to be able to detect a change in the volume. You are experiencing
   (a) JNDs.   (b) Weber's law.   (c) difference thresholds.   (d) all of the above.

4. Betty has long had a keen sense of smell. She used to help her mother cook by telling her when it "smelled right." However, since the sudden death of her mother, which left Betty distraught, she seems to have lost her sense of smell for foods. This loss could be explained by the concept of
   (a) absolute thresholds.   (b) perceptual defense.   (c) subliminal perception.   (d) difference thresholds.

5. As the president of Knock-M-Dead Exterminators, you have to decide how to spend your advertising dollars most efficiently. Your marketing director is trying to convince you to do some subliminal advertising over radio and television. If you follow that recommendation, you can realistically expect
   (a) between an 18% to 57% increase in extermination jobs.
   (b) only an increase in the number of people calling asking for estimates.
   (c) only that the company name will be recognized easier.
   (d) that you will be making an absolute waste of your money.

6. If your tattooist was in the middle of doing a tattoo of "Rambo" on your left buttock and he stepped on his glasses and broke them, which of the following visual defects would you hope he had?
   (a) hyperopia   (c) presbyopia
   (b) myopia   (d) "Who cares, I'd rather him do it by feel anyway."

7. You've had a freak accident with a marshmallow and lost the sight in one eye. With your good eye, you are looking at a bright, multicolored object. The light from the object is being projected onto the retina at the point where the optic nerve leaves the eye. It is likely that you will be
   (a) able to see the object as black, white, or a shade of gray
   (b) able to see the colors of the object, although they may appear dull
   (c) able to partially focus the object
   (d) unable to see the object because of a lack of photoreceptors at this point

8. If it is true that cones are concentrated in the fovea, why do we see color in images that fall outside the fovea?
   (a) The fovea has no distinct boundaries. It covers a large area of the retina.
   (b) Rods can simulate the illusion of color.
   (c) There are some cones in the periphery of the retina.
   (d) Movement is often experienced as color.

9. Barbara has partial color blindness. Which of the following explain(s) how she acquired this defect? (You may choose more than one answer.)
   (a) Her mother and father are both color blind.
   (b) Her mother carries one defective gene and her father is not color blind.
   (c) Her mother carries one defective gene and her father is color blind.
   (d) Her mother does not carry any defective genes and her father is color blind.

10. Your friend LuAnn claims she was abducted by aliens. While a prisoner, she observed an intergalactic battle between the Goodums and the Evildoers. This battle took place in space outside the orbit of Pluto. She claims the sounds of exploding star cruisers could be heard all over that section of space. You know that she's a little goofy because
    (a) sound waves can't be carried by metal.
    (b) sound waves do not travel in a vacuum.
    (c) the distance from the object producing the sound would be too great.
    (d) compression can't happen in space because there are too many molecules.

11. You are a surgeon and have been asked to insert a prosthesis to replace a portion of a person's auditory system that has become fused and no longer functions properly. This portion was the crucial part that dealt with bone conduction. What portion will you be replacing?
    (a) cochlea   (b) eardrum   (c) tibia   (d) auditory ossicles

12. As a young child, Toby suffered many severe middle ear infections. When Toby turned two, his pediatrician recommended that he be taken to an ear, nose, and throat specialist. The specialist would probably be looking for symptoms of what disorder?
    (a) conduction deafness   (b) nerve deafness   (c) stimulation deafness   (d) tone deafness

13.   Bill likes to work in his shop at night after work. He frequently uses a power saw which is very loud, and afterwards he suffers from tinnitus. It is likely that in the future Bill may suffer from
(a) conduction deafness.   (b) nerve deafness.   (c) stimulation deafness.   (d) all of the above.

14.   George has a rare medical problem which will be fatal unless he has immediate surgery. The by-product of the surgery is that he will lose one of his chemical senses. He, however, has a choice as to which one to lose. Which of the following would be appropriate recommendations on your part? (You may choose more than one.)
(a) Eliminate the sense of smell because his sense of taste will remain intact to help protect him from bad food.
(b) Eliminate the sense of smell because it has little purpose beside enhancing the flavor of food.
(c) Eliminate the sense of taste because he would lose his subjective flavor of food if his sense of smell was removed.
(d) Eliminate the sense of taste because his sense of smell will remain intact to help protect him from bad food.

15.   When a person is tested for allergies, a commonly used method is the "scratch test." In this procedure many small, very shallow incisions or "scratches" are made on the back and substances are painted on the scratches to test the body's reaction. Doctors have made a wise choice of the back for this test because
(a) the pollen-containing substances will have less effect on overall physiological functioning when introduced through the back.
(b) the back does not scar as easily as other areas of the skin and so there is less permanent disfiguration.
(c) there are fewer receptors on the back and hence less sensitivity.
(d) there is less of a problem of sensory adaptation.

16.   You walk in the front door from work and detect that your husband has burned the fish dinner. The odor is enough to drive you out of the house. After a while the smell has greatly diminished. At this time you take out the trash. When you re-enter the house you again smell the odor of burned fish. Why did the odor seem less offensive after you had been in the house for a while?
(a) because of the process known as sensory adaptation
(b) because you habituated to the smell
(c) because the degree of sensitivity of the gustatory sense diminished
(d) because of the process known as counterirritation
(e) because your husband finally broke down and took a bath

17.   If you are asked to think about your hair, you can, but you probably do not usually pay much attention to the way that your hair feels on your head. The reason that you do not is that
(a) you have accommodated to the feel of your hair.
(b) you are selectively attending to only important stimuli.
(c) there are few touch receptors on your head.
(d) you have been deprived of a sufficient amount of this type of stimulus previously.

Chapter Review

1.   Our senses act as a _____ _____ system. Only certain kinds of energy are _____ for conversion to nerve impulses because of the _____ of the receptors. Many sensory systems _____ the environment into important features before sending nerve impulses to the brain. Also, sensory systems _____ these important features into usable messages for the brain.

2.   Sensory receptors act as biological _____ by converting one form of energy into _____ _____.

3.   Localization of function means that the sensation you experience depends upon the specific area of the _____ which receives the message from the sense organs.

4.   "Seeing" ultimately takes place in the _____. Thus, the senses do not send back xerox-like pictures of the world, but instead they collect, analyze, and transmit _____ to the _____. This process is called _____.

5.   _____ is the branch of psychology that attempts to understand the relationship between changes in physical stimuli and psychological sensation. The smallest amount of stimulation necessary for sensation to occur is the _____ _____.

6. The _____ threshold is the amount of change in a stimulus necessary to produce a just noticeable difference. This is also referred to as the study of ____ ____ ____s. According to Weber's Law, the amount of change in a stimulus necessary to produce a JND is a constant _____ of the original stimulus intensity.

7. A stimulus that causes anxiety or embarrassment may be sensed long before it is perceived because of _____ _____ when the threshold is raised.

8. A threshold or limit is called the _____. Any time information is processed below the normal _____, awareness for it is said to be _____. Studies have shown that such stimuli experienced below the level of conscious awareness are basically _____.

9. As a physical property of light, wavelength corresponds to the psychological experience of _____, or the specific color of a stimulus, Colors are narrow bands of the visible spectrum. Colors produced by a very narrow band of wavelengths are said to be pure or _____. Brightness corresponds roughly to the _____ of light waves.

10. The _____ focuses the incoming image on the layer of light-sensitive cells at the back of the eye called the _____. The focusing of the incoming image is called _____. The clear covering on the front of the eye is the _____.

11. If the eye is too short, _____ objects cannot be focused, but _____ objects are clear. This is farsightedness or _____. If the eyeball is too long, _____ objects cannot be focused, and nearsightedness or _____ results. When either the cornea or the lens is misshapen, some of the visual field will be partially focused or fuzzy. This condition is called _____. If the lens becomes less resilient because of age and cannot accommodate as easily, the resulting condition is called _____.

12. The _____ is a colored circular muscle that controls the amount of light that enters the eye through the _____. There are two types of receptors on the retina. The _____ function in bright light and produce _____ sensations and pick up _____ details. By contrast, the _____ are incapable of picking up _____. They are much more sensitive to _____ than the _____. Therefore _____ are mainly responsible for our ability to see in very dim light.

13. Each eye has a place where there are no receptors because the optic nerve exits at the back of the eyeball. This place is called the _____ _____. The cones are concentrated in the _____. This is the place where an image is focused for greatest _____. The number of cones _____ rapidly as we move away from the _____.

14. The _____ reach their greatest numbers about 20 degrees to each side of the _____, so much _____ vision is _____ vision. Fortunately, the rods are quite sensitive to _____. In addition, since _____ are especially sensitive to dim light, the best night vision occurs when looking slightly to the _____ of an object. _____ _____ occurs when a person has lost peripheral vision,

15. Rods and cones have differing maximal color sensitivities. The cones are most sensitive to wavelengths in the _____-_____ region of the spectrum. You may have seen some emergency vehicles this color. Remember, rods do not produce _____, but some colored dim lights will appear brighter than others. At night and under conditions of dim light when rod vision predominates, the brightest-colored light will be _____ or _____-_____. Many emergency vehicles now have _____ emergency lights for nighttime work.

16. The _____ (or three-color) theory of color vision holds that there are three types of cones, each with a heightened sensitivity to a specific color: _____, _____, or _____. Other colors are assumed to result from a combination of these. A basic problem with this theory is that four colors seem to be psychologically primary: the original three and _____.

17. The _____-_____ theory was developed to explain why you can't have a reddish-green or a yellowish-blue. According to this theory the visual system can produce messages for either red or green, yellow or blue, black or white. Coding one color in a pair seems to _____ the opposite message color. Fatigue caused by making one response causes an _____ of the opposite color as the system recovers.

18. In reality, both theories may be correct at a particular level in the visual system. The trichromatic theory seems to apply at the level of the _____, while the opponent-process theory applies to events recorded in the _____ _____ after information leaves the retina.

19. The person who has total _____ _____ sees the world as if it were a black and white movie.

20. More common than total color blindness is partial color blindness, or _____ _____. Red-green color blindness is a fairly common form of partial color blindness and is usually found in _____.

21. Both of the above conditions (color blindness and color weakness) can be detected by a common test for color blindness called the _____ test.

22. The eyes become more sensitive to light at night due to a process called _____ _____. Most of the eye's increased sensitivity comes from the _____ which contain a pigment called visual purple or _____. Increased concentrations of this pigment correspond directly to improved _____ _____. This process, _____ _____, can be speeded up by being exposed to only _____ light. Night _____ may occur if a person has a _____ _____ deficiency because _____ production declines.

23. Sound travels as invisible waves of _____ and _____ in the air. Basically any vibrating object will produce sound waves by setting _____ molecules in motion. The _____ of sound waves corresponds to perceived pitch, just as the _____ corresponds to sensed loudness.

24. Sound waves collide with the _____ which causes the three bones of the middle ear, called the _____ _____, to vibrate. The third bone is attached to a second membrane called the _____ _____. This membrane moves back and forth and sets up waves in the canals of the _____. When these waves stimulate tiny _____ _____, nerve impulses are sent to the temporal lobes of the brain.

25. The _____ theory of hearing states that as pitch rises, nerve impulses of the same frequency are fed into the auditory nerve. The _____ theory states that pitch is signaled by the area of the cochlea most strongly activated.

26. When the eardrums or auditory ossicles are immobilized by disease or injury, the resulting condition is called _____ deafness. This type of deafness can often be overcome by making sounds _____. _____ deafness is a hearing loss resulting from damage to the auditory nerve. Not much can be done to remedy this type of deafness. Exposure to very loud noise can result in _____ deafness. _____ implants can help overcome deafness by stimulating the auditory nerve directly and bypassing the hair cells.

27. The danger of hearing loss depends on both the _____ of sound and the _____ of the exposure. Any activity that causes a temporary loss of hearing (temporary _____ _____) or a whistling or ringing sensation (_____) in the ears may cause _____ deafness.

28. Both gustation and olfaction are _____ in nature. As air enters the nose, it passes over millions of _____ _____ in the lining of the upper nasal passages. This is the point where _____ occurs and nerve signals are sent to the brain. If a person develops a sort of "smell blindness" for one type of odor this is called _____.

29. It is currently believed that different odors correspond to different shaped _____ which fit into the "holes" of the odor receptors. This is called the _____ and _____ theory.

30. The four basic taste sensations are _____, _____, _____, and _____. We are most sensitive to the taste of _____ and least sensitive to _____. We experience the sense of taste when food is dissolved and enters a _____ _____ where _____ takes place and a nerve impulse is sent to the brain. The sense of taste is particularly influenced by _____.

31. The somesthetic senses include the _____ senses (touch, pressure, pain, etc.), the _____ senses (body position and movement), and the _____ senses (balance).

32. Motion sickness occurs when sensory information from the _____ organs, the ampulla, and the _____ canals (all of the vestibular system) fails to match the information received from the eyes and the body. This is called the _____ _____ theory.

33. The skin receptors produce at least five different sensations: _____ _____, _____, _____, _____, and _____. Some areas of the body are more sensitive than others because they contain a greater concentration of _____. The most frequently found _____ in the skin is for _____.

34. There are two kinds of pain. The _____ system consists of pain carried by _____ nerve fibers. This pain is sharp and is associated with specific body areas. The _____ system is carried by _____ nerve fibers and is nagging and widespread.

35. Many sensory events never reach conscious awareness. There are three reasons for this. A decrease in sensory response that accompanies a constant or unchanging stimulus is called _____ _____. This does not occur in the eye because of tiny tremors (called _____ _____) in the eye muscles which shift visual images from one receptor to another.

36. Another reason why some sensory events never reach conscious awareness is because humans have the ability to "tune in on" some incoming information while ignoring others. This is called _____ _____. The ability is probably based on a _____ - _____ process of selecting sensory messages.

37. The third reason probably explains why acupuncture works. This process is known as _____ _____ and occurs when the acupuncturist's needles activate small pain fibers which relay through a central biasing system to close the _____ to intense or chronic pain.

38. Both acupuncture and electrical stimulation cause a build up of _____ in the brain. There are a large number of receptors for this chemical in the _____ system and brain areas associated with pleasure, pain and emotion. This chemical is similar to _____ and may explain the "high" or euphoria associated with childbirth, masochism, acupuncture, and other similar painful or stressful events.

39. There are four factors that can be used to influence the amount of pain experienced. These are _____, _____, _____, and _____. High levels of _____ increase pain so if the _____ can be lowered, less pain will be experienced.

40. If a person can shift _____ away from the pain by being _____, this can help alleviate pain. If the painful stimulus can be _____ differently, pain can be reduced. Finally, a person might gain some degree of _____ over the painful stimulus by being able to terminate it when it gets too intense or by applying another mildly painful stimulus. This last process is called _____.

ANSWER KEYS

Do You Know the Information?

Multiple Choice

1. (b) obj. 1, p. 155
2. (d) obj. 2, p. 155
3. (c) obj. 3, p. 156
4. (a) obj. 4, p. 156
5. (d) obj. 6, p. 157
6. (a) obj. 6, p. 157
7. (d) obj. 8, pp. 158-159
8. (a) obj. 9, p. 160
9. (b) obj. 10, p. 161
10. (a) obj. 11, p. 161
11. (c) obj. 12, p. 162
12. (a) obj. 12, p. 162
13. (d) obj. 14, p. 165
14. (b) obj. 16, p. 166
15. (b) obj. 17, p. 167
16. (d) obj. 19, p. 168
17. (a) obj. 21, p. 172
18. (b) obj. 22, p. 172
19. (d) obj. 23, p. 172
20. (c) obj. 24, p. 172
21. (d) obj. 25, p. 172
22. (d) objs. 25-26, p. 174
23. (c) obj. 28, p. 176
24. (b) obj. 29, p. 177
25. (d) obj. 30, pp. 177-178
26. (d) objs. 31-32, p. 178
27. (c) obj. 33, p. 178
28. (a) obj. 36, p. 180
29. (a) obj. 37, p. 180
30. (c) obj. 37, p. 181
32. (c) obj. 39, p. 182

31. (b) obj. 38, p. 180
33. (d) obj. 40, p. 183
34. (d) objs. 41-42, pp. 184-185

True-False

1. T, obj. 3, p. 156
2. F, obj. 5, p. 157
3. F, obj. 7, p. 158
4. F, obj. 9, p. 160
5. T, obj. 11, p. 161
6. F, obj. 12, p. 162
7. T, obj. 12, p. 162
8. T, obj. 13, p. 163
9. T, obj. 15, p. 166
10. F, obj. 16, p. 166
11. F, obj. 18, p. 168
12. T, obj. 20, p. 170
13. F, obj. 26, p. 175
14. T, obj. 28, p. 176
15. F, obj. 30, p. 178
16. F, obj. 31, p. 178
17. T, obj. 34, p. 178
18. F, obj. 35, p. 179
19. T, obj. 36, p. 180
20. F, obj. 40, p. 183

Matching

1. K, obj. 25, p. 167
2. G, obj. 11, p. 154
3. J, objs. 28-29, p. 167
4. L, obj. 27, p. 167

5. I, obj. 6, p. 150
6. H, obj. 22, p. 165
7. F, obj. 42, p. 179
8. P, obj. 30, p. 170
9. B, obj. 9, p. 152
10. E, obj. 25, p. 165
11. Q, obj. 40, p. 176
12. O, obj. 8, p. 150
13. M, obj. 19, p. 163
14. D, obj. 2, p. 147
15. N, obj. 39, p. 175
16. S, obj. 12, p. 155
17. T, obj. 14, p. 157

Can You Apply the Information?

1. (d) objs. 2,22, pp. 155, 172
2. (a) obj. 3, p. 156
3. (d) obj. 6, pp. 157-158
4. (b) obj. 7, p. 158
5. (c) obj. 8, pp. 158-159
6. (b) obj. 11, p. 161
7. (d) obj. 12, p. 162
8. (c) objs. 12,14, pp. 162-163
9. (a,c) obj. 17, p. 167
10. (b) obj. 21, pp. 171-172
11. (d) obj. 22, p. 172
12. (a) obj. 25, p. 172
13. (c) objs. 25-26, pp. 174-175
14. (c,d) objs. 28-29, pp. 175-177
15. (c) obj. 34, pp. 178-179
16. (a) obj. 37, p. 180
17. (b) obj. 37, p. 181

Chapter Review

1. data reduction, selected, sensitivity, analyze (p. 155); code (p. 156)
2. transducers, nerve impulses (p. 155)
3. brain (p. 156)
4. brain, information (data), brain, sensation (p. 156)
5. Psychophysics, absolute threshold (p. 157)
6. difference (p. 157); JND, proportion (p. 158)
7. perceptual defense (p. 158)
8. limen, limen, subliminal (p. 158); weak (p. 159)
9. hue, saturated, amplitude (p. 160)
10. lens, retina, accommodation, cornea (p. 161)
11. nearby, distant, hyperopia, distant, myopia, astigmatism, presbyopia (p. 161)
12. iris, pupil, cones, color, fine, rods, color, light, cones, rods (p. 162)
13. blind spot, fovea (p. 163); acuity, decreases, fovea (p. 163)
14. rods, fovea, peripheral, rod, movement (p. 163); rods, side, tunnel vision (p. 165)

15. yellowish-green (p. 165); color, blue, blue-green, blue (p. 166)
16. trichromatic, red, green, blue, yellow (p. 166)
17. opponent-process, block, afterimage (p. 166)
18. retina, optic pathways (p. 166)
19. color blindness (p. 167)
20. color weakness, males (p. 167)
21. Ishihara (p. 168)
22. dark adaptation, rods, rhodopsin, night vision (p. 168); dark adaptation, red (p. 170); blindness, vitamin A, rhodopsin (p. 171)
23. compression, rarefaction, air (p. 171); frequency, amplitude (p. 172)
24. eardrum, auditory ossicles, oval window, cochlea, hair cells (p. 172)
25. frequency, place (p. 172)
26. conduction, louder, Nerve (p. 172); stimulation, Cochlear, (p. 174)
27. loudness, length, threshold shift (p. 174); tinnitus, stimulation (p. 175)
28. chemical, nerve fibers, transduction (p.175); anosmia (p. 176)
29. molecules, lock, key (p. 176)
30. sweet, salt, sour, bitter, bitter, sweet, taste bud, transduction, smell (p. 177)
31. skin, kinesthetic (p. 177); vestibular (p. 178)
32. otolith, semicircular, sensory conflict (p. 178)
33. light touch, pressure, pain, cold, warmth, receptors (p. 178); receptor, pain (p. 179)
34. warning, large, reminding, small (p. 180)
35. sensory adaptation, physiological nystagmus (p. 180)
36. selective attention, brain (p. 181)
37. sensory gating (p. 181); gates (p. 182)
38. endorphins, limbic, morphine (p. 183)
39. anxiety, attention, control, interpretation, anxiety, anxiety (p. 184)
40. attention, distracted, interpreted (p. 184); control, counterirritation (p. 185)

chapter six

Perceiving the World

perception
size, shape, and brightness constancy
reversible figure
perceptual organizing principles
   figure-ground, nearness, similarity
   continuation, closure, contiguity
engineering psychologist
perceptual hypothesis
   ambiguous stimulus
depth perception
   visual cliff
monocular and binocular cues
   accommodation, convergence
   retinal disparity, stereoscopic vision
pictorial depth cues
   linear perspective, relative size, light

and shadow, overlap, texture gradient,
   aerial perspective, relative motion
moon illusion
   apparent distance hypothesis
perceptual habit & perceptual features
   inverted vision
adaptation level
   context
   frame of reference
illusion versus hallucination
Muller-Lyer illusion
size distance invariance
attention
   selective, divided
adaptation
habituation

orientation response
boiled frog syndrome
perceptual processing
   bottom-up, top-down
perceptual expectancy
parapsychology
   clairvoyance, telepathy
   precognition, psychokinesis
coincidence
Zener cards
other interpretations of ESP
perceptions as reconstructions
accuracy of eyewitnesses
weapon focus
reality testing
dishabituation

To demonstrate mastery of this chapter you should be able to:

1.   Define perception.

2.   Describe the visual abilities of a person who has just had his or her sight restored.

3.   Describe the following constancies:

   a.   size

   b.   shape

   c.   brightness

4. Give examples of the following as they relate to the organization of perception:

    a. figure-ground

    b. nearness

    c. similarity

    d. continuation

    e. closure

    f. contiguity

5. Describe the activities of an engineering psychologist. Include a discussion of the two components of effective design. (Highlight 6-1)

6. Explain what a perceptual hypothesis is.

7. Define and give an example of an ambiguous stimulus.

8. Define depth perception and discuss the nativistic and empirical view of it. Describe two techniques for investigating depth perception, and describe the end results of studies with each technique.

9. Describe the following cues for depth perception and indicate in each case whether the cue is monocular or binocular:

   a. accommodation

   b. convergence

   c. retinal disparity

10. Describe the following two-dimensional, monocular, pictorial depth cues:

    a. linear perspective

    b. relative size

    c. light and shadow

    d. overlap

    e. texture gradients

    f. aerial perspective

    g. relative motion (motion parallax.)

11. Describe the phenomenon of the moon illusion. Include in your explanation the apparent distance hypothesis.

12. Define "perceptual habit" and explain how it allows learning to affect perception.

13.   Explain how the Ames room poses problems for organization and for a person's perceptual habits.

14.   Describe the research which demonstrates the brain's sensitivity to perceptual features in the environment.

15.   Explain how the results of inverted vision experiments support the concept of perceptual habits. Explain why active movement is so important in adapting to inverted vision.

16.   Describe and give an example of the concept of adaptation level. Give an example of context.

17.   Differentiate between an illusion and a hallucination.

18.   Describe the Muller-Lyer illusion and explain how perceptual habits may account for this illusion.

19.   Contrast selective attention from divided attention.

20.　List and describe three characteristics of a stimulus that can make it attention-getting.

　　a.

　　b.

　　c.

21.　Differentiate habituation from sensory adaptation. Include the concept of the orientation response.

22.　Explain and give experimental evidence of how motives may alter attention and perception.

23.　Explain the "boiled frog syndrome" and how it may affect the ultimate survival of humans. (Highlight 6-2)

24.　Explain what bottom-up and top-down processing are.

25.　Explain how perceptual expectancies may influence perception.

26.   Define the terms extrasensory perception and parapsychology.

27.   Describe the following psychic abilities:

    a.   clairvoyance

    b.   telepathy

    c.   precognition

    d.   psychokinesis

28.   Generally describe the Zener cards and why they were developed.

29.   List and explain six reasons why most psychologists remain skeptical about psi abilities.

    a.

    b.

    c.

    d.

    e.

    f.

30.   Describe the best conclusion to make about psi events and the attitude suggested by your author that should be taken toward psychic phenomena.

The following objectives are related to the material in the "Applications" section of your text.

31.   Explain the phrase "We see what we believe."

32.   Explain why most eyewitness testimony is inaccurate. Include the idea of weapon focus. (Also refer to Table 6-2.)

33.   Explain what the term "reality testing" means.

34.   Explain how attention can bring about a dishabituation of perception (i.e., an increase in perceptual awareness).

SELF-QUIZZES

Do You Know the Information?

Multiple Choice

1.   Perception is the
    (a) process of assembling sensations into usable pictures of the world.
    (b) same as the process of sensation.
    (c) transducing of physical stimuli into nerve impulses.
    (d) habituation of attention.

2.   Which of the following constancies holds that an object would appear to remain the same even though the retinal image would actually change?
    (a) size   (b) shape   (c) brightness   (d) all of the above

3.   The perceptual principle that helps us organize sensations so that incomplete figures are completed and have consistent overall forms is called
    (a) continuation.   (c) closure.   (e) contiguity.
    (b) similarity.   (d) figure-ground.

4. Which of the following would be an *incorrect* statement concerning engineering psychology?
    (a) It works to make machines more compatible with our sensory and motor capacities.
    (b) An effective design makes use of perceptual signals that are naturally understood by people.
    (c) An effective design provides clear feedback for each action.
    (d) None of the above statements are true.

5. A _____ is a guess held until the evidence contradicts it.
    (a) perceptual hypothesis   (b) reversible figure   (c) continuity   (d) natural design

6. An ambiguous stimulus is one in which the
    (a) stimulus is not clearly defined.   (c) stimulus is viewed using only depth cues.
    (b) passive nature of perception is revealed.   (d) stimulus allows more than one interpretation.

7. The ability to see three-dimensional space and accurately estimate distances is
    (a) limited to animals (including man) that are capable of learning.
    (b) the definition of the perception of depth.
    (c) facilitated by binocular cues but not by monocular cues.
    (d) all of the above.

8. The visual cliff is
    (a) a device used in investigating depth perception.
    (b) the point on the visible spectrum where our vision begins to decline.
    (c) a mechanism in the eyeball that facilitates depth perception.
    (d) a pictorial representation of how the angles of objects determine our perception of distance.

9. Indicate whether each of the following is a monocular (M) depth cue or a binocular (B) cue.
    (a) _____retinal disparity   (b) _____convergence   (c) _____accommodation   (d) _____stereoscopic vision

10. The process of the lens in the eye bending or bulging to focus nearby objects and then reporting its activities to the brain is called
    (a) stereoscopic vision.   (b) convergence.   (c) accommodation.   (d) retinal disparity.

11. Retinal disparity provides for the perception of depth because
    (a) the eyes turn in slightly to focus on close objects and this muscle activity is sent to the brain.
    (b) each eye receives a slightly different view of the world and the resulting images are fused into one.
    (c) motion parallax works best in combination with this binocular cue.
    (d) accommodation only works well when objects are beyond 50 feet.

12. Which pictorial depth cue refers to the apparent convergence of parallel lines in the environment?
    (a) relative size   (b) linear perspective   (c) aerial perspective   (d) interposition

13. The moon illusion occurs because of
    (a) the image of the moon being magnified and hence appearing larger on the horizon.
    (b) the distance of the moon being greater when it is directly overhead than when it is on the horizon.
    (c) a greater apparent distance when the moon is on the horizon and seen behind houses and trees.
    (d) the moon casting a larger image on the horizon.

14. Established patterns of organization and attention are called
    (a) illusions.   (b) categories.   (c) adaptation levels.   (d) perceptual habits.

15. The Ames room creates perceptual confusion because
    (a) the person is forced either to perceive the room as square or to refuse to perceive the people changing size.
    (b) the brain has no categories to help analyze the situation.
    (c) most people choose size constancy over shape constancy.
    (d) of the illusion of motion parallax.

16. Blakemore and Cooper's experiment with "vertical" and "horizontal" cats demonstrated that the brain's sensitivity to perceptual features in the environment
    (a) is all inherited.   (b) is all learned.   (c) is partly learned.   (d) cannot be explained.

17. Inverted vision experiments with humans have shown that
    (a) with time and active movement, humans can develop new perceptual habits and function normally with completely different visual cues.
    (b) perceptual habits are so ingrained that humans cannot learn to adapt to new visual cues.
    (c) we are like most animals in that we adapt to the differences almost immediately.
    (d) basic physiology can be modified so that when the lens (goggles) are removed, we do not recover.

18. In judging size, weight, etc., you have your own personal "medium" point or frame of reference. This is referred to as
    (a) adaptation level.   (b) perceptual expectancy.   (c) level of habituation.   (d) perceptual sensitivity.

19. The fact that you are tall (6 feet 5 inches) but you appear short when compared to a 7 foot 3 inch person demonstrates
    (a) relative size.   (b) adaptation level.   (c) context.   (d) perceptual prejudice.

20. The difference between an illusion and a hallucination is
    (a) an illusion is present when a person perceives a stimulus that does not exist, such as a mirage in a desert.
    (b) hallucinations are present when a person distorts an existing stimulus.
    (c) a person who is hallucinating believes a stimulus exists when one does not.
    (d) illusions are additive, hallucinations are subtractive.

21. Perceptual habits contribute to the effect of the Muller-Lyer illusion because
    (a) people have more experience with the V-tipped line looking farther away than the arrowhead-tipped line.
    (b) a person who has had little or no experience with perceptual habits dealing with this particular illusion is not fooled by it.
    (c) the illusion is based upon years of experience with the edges and corners of rooms and buildings.
    (d) of all of the above.

22. Allocating your attention to the various parts of a task refers to the process of
    (a) selective attention.   (b) divided attention.   (c) varying attention.   (d) conscious awareness.

23. Which of the following factors does *not directly* affect attention?
    (a) repetition   (b) nativism   (c) motivation   (d) contrast in stimulation

24. If a person is said to have habituated to a stimulus
    (a) there is a decrease in the actual number of sensory messages sent to the brain.
    (b) the person is responding automatically to the orientation stimulus.
    (c) there is a decrease in the orientation response.
    (d) the person begins responding more to the stimulus.

25. The study in which males rated their first impressions of a female college student as more attractive after reading a sexually arousing passage demonstrates that
    (a) intense stimuli are attention-getters.
    (b) motives can affect perception.
    (c) perceptual categories do *not* affect sexual preference.
    (d) an emotional stimulus can shift attention away from relevant information.

26. Ornstein and Ehrlich believe that major threats facing civilization (pollution, deforestation, global warming, population growth) develop very slowly and may escape our attention until too late in a phenomenon known as
    (a) the boiled frog syndrome.   (b) perceptual habituation.   (c) perceptual inattention.   (d) insufficient contrast.

27. If information is analyzed starting with small features and building upward into a complete perception, this is called
    (a) perceptual constancy.   (b) perceptual expectancy.   (c) bottom-up processing.   (d) top-down processing.

28. The fact that motives or context may set you to perceive in a certain way is called
    (a) perceptual habit.   (b) perceptual expectancy.   (c) bottom-up processing.   (d) top-down processing.

29. Parapsychology is defined as the study of
    (a) events which seem to defy accepted scientific laws.
    (b) the changes in the pattern of mental functions.
    (c) hypnosis and meditation.
    (d) Zener cards.

30. Zener cards are used to
    (a) help make the study of ESP more objective.
    (b) test for the presence of psychokinesis.
    (c) differentiate psi from psychic phenomena.
    (d) aid the study of hypnosis.

31. Most psychologists remain skeptical about psi abilities because
    (a) the abilities are so inconsistent.
    (b) some subjects who display the abilities have received credit for a run of luck.
    (c) improvements in research methods have usually yielded fewer positive results.
    (d) of all of the above.

32. The statement "We see what we believe" refers to the idea that
    (a) perception enables us to objectively test reality.
    (b) our perceptions offer us a way to objectively affirm our existence.
    (c) we are what our beliefs tell us we are.
    (d) perception reflects the needs, expectations, and values of the perceiver.

33. One of the main reasons why eyewitness testimony in a court may be inaccurate is because
    (a) the reconstruction of events may contain the attitudes and expectations of the eyewitness.
    (b) the person's level of dishabituation may be higher.
    (c) of sensory adaptation.
    (d) of the the lack of all of the necessary cues for accurate perception.

True-False

_____ 1. A newly sighted person's vision is actually fairly good since most of the necessary concepts can be learned before sight is restored.

_____ 2. Much of perception is empirical, meaning that it is based on prior experience.

_____ 3. In a reversible figure, nearness and similarity can be switched so as to confuse figure-ground organization.

_____ 4. Infants and new-born animals do not show evidence of depth perception; it is an acquired trait.

_____ 5. The most important source of depth perception is retinal disparity.

_____ 6. Pictorial depth cues strive to give the illusion of three dimensions from a two-dimensional cue.

_____ 7. If an artist wishes to depict two objects of the same size at different distances, she should make the more distant object smaller.

_____ 8. People who have lost one eye depend less on motion parallax for depth perception because it is primarily a binocular cue.

_____ 9. The apparent distance hypothesis holds that if two objects form identical images, but one is more distant, the more distant object must be larger.

_____ 10. Learning helps to build perceptual habits that may force us to perceive our world in incorrect or stereotyped ways.

_____ 11. Intense, repetitious, and changing stimuli all draw attention because they are unexpected.

_____ 12. Past experience, motives, context, or suggestions may create a perceptual expectancy that sets a person to perceive in a certain way.

_____ 13. The author of your text says that an open but skeptical mind is probably the best attitude to maintain toward psychic phenomena.

_____ 14. The reason why witnesses to crimes so often disagree is because perceptions formed under stress are prone to distortion.

_____ 15. Reality testing may involve using a different sensory modality to serve as a check on perceptions.

_____ 16. By paying close attention, a person can dishabituate to a stimulus and bring renewed freshness to perception.

Can You Apply the Information?

1. An old joke—
   Two men are in an airplane. First man, "Boy, we sure are high up. Those cars on the ground look like ants." Second man, "You fool! Those *are* ants. We're still on the ground!"
   The problem here is obviously a failure of
   (a) dishabituation.   (c) size constancy.   (e) intelligence.
   (b) shape constancy.   (d) brightness constancy.

2. In a grocery store, if the apples and oranges are all mixed together in a bin but the oranges tend to stand out more than the apples, this demonstrates the principle of
   (a) closure.   (b) continuation.   (c) nearness.   (d) similarity.

3. When a ventriloquist appears to make sound come out of a dummy's mouth, he or she is using which perceptual organizing cue?
   (a) nearness   (b) continuity   (c) similarity   (d) contiguity

4. Soldiers on the ground always wear camouflage uniforms with the pattern of the camouflage similar to the surrounding environment. The purpose is simply to
   (a) break up similarity organization.   (c) break up contiguity organization.
   (b) break up figure-ground organization.   (d) break up nearness organization.

5. A common scenario in detective novels is the point in time when the sleuth puts the available evidence together and comes up with, what he or she believes to be, the identity and motive(s) of the culprit. This does not stop the collection of further evidence even if the initial judgements are overturned. What the sleuth does is develop
   (a) a perceptual hypothesis.   (b) a perceptual habit.   (c) a perceptual expectancy.   (d) a reversible figure.

6. An inkblot from the Rorschach Inkblot personality test is a good example of an ambiguous stimulus.
   (a) True   (b) False

7. If you hold your index fingers approximately four inches in front of your eyes, four inches apart, pointed toward each other, and slowly bring them together, a small finger will "appear" in the middle with a fingernail at each end. This appearance demonstrates which bodily cue for depth perception?
   (a) convergence   (b) accommodation   (c) a monocular one   (d) retinal disparity

8. You have a friend who is a long-distance runner (a 13 mile race is nothing for him) who consents to run with you in a 10,000 meter (6.2 miles) race. He describes the race as "short" or "a breeze," whereas you do well just to finish because you are used to 3 mile races. It is obvious that you and your friend have different
   (a) accommodation levels.   (c) contexts.   (e) numbers of blisters.
   (b) adaptation levels.   (d) averages.

9. You observe a car going 55 mph in a shopping center parking lot. You are instantly alarmed. The same car, driver, and speed on an interstate highway would not even slightly arouse your attention. The difference in the two perceptions is a good example of how _____ affects perceptions.
    (a) nearness   (b) motion parallax   (c) ambiguous stimuli   (d) context

10. You are driving your car down a long flat stretch of highway on a hot summer day and the heat waves coming from the asphalt one-half mile ahead appear to be chickens running across the road. What is this phenomenon?
    (a) an illusion   (b) stroboscopic movement   (c) a hallucination   (d) brightness constancy

11. You are very tired because you stayed up all night studying for exams. When you finally get to bed the following night and turn off the lights, you see what appears to be little green Martians dancing around your bed. What is this phenomenon?
    (a) an example of relative size (b) a hallucination   (c) an illusion   (d) a delusion

12. Having both the radio and the television on at the same time usually causes a problem for most people because of
    (a) selective attention. (b) divided attention.   (c) contrast.   (d) incongruity.

13. Which of the following is an example of habituation?
    (a) A person can see better in the dark after being in a dimly lit room for 30 minutes.
    (b) Your hand is fatigued after carrying a heavy book for six hours.
    (c) Because of a shot of novocaine a person feels less pain in a sore tooth while having it filled.
    (d) While taking a test a person does not think about how the shoes feel on her feet.

14. Bill usually gets mad when his wife Laura comes home even 15 minutes late. On this particular night Laura is one hour late. As Bill waits for his wife, his anger turns into concern. He is genuinely worried about her. When she finally comes in the door Bill says, "Laura, where have you been? I've been worried about you." Accustomed to Bill's usual nasty remarks she snaps back, "What do you mean yelling at me like that? I'm a grown woman!" A fight begins. Laura's unjustified retort is due to
    (a) context.   (b) her adaptation level.   (c) perceptual expectancy. (d) cognitive shift.

15. You are playing poker. Even when your mind is blank, one of the other players is able to become aware of your "hand." Your friend is
    (a) clairvoyant.   (b) telepathic.   (c) psychokinetic.   (d) precognitive.

16. Another friend in the same poker game can perceive the kinds of cards you're holding only when you're concentrating on them. This friend is displaying
    (a) clairvoyance.   (b) telepathy.   (c) precognition.   (d) psychokinesis.

17. Minerva Mrytle, the famous psychic, makes predictions for the coming new year every December. She predicts bumper world food crops and a new breakthrough in nuclear arms control. Which skill is she using?
    (a) clairvoyance   (b) telepathy   (c) precognition   (d) psychokinesis

18. A researcher who is investigating a person's ability to make a desk float in the air is studying
    (a) clairvoyance.   (b) precognition.   (c) psychokinesis.   (d) suggestibility.

19. You are still seeing those little green Martians at night. You reach out to try to grab one. This is an example of
    (a) an illusion.   (b) an ambiguous stimulus. (c) reality testing.   (d) nearness.

20. You're taking a test and the air conditioning blower goes off in the room. You didn't notice how loud the blower was, but now the silence is "deafening." Noticing the silence is an example of
    (a) habituation.   (b) overlap.   (c) illusion.   (d) dishabituation.

Chapter Review

1. The process of assembling sensations into a usable picture of the world is called _____.

2. A newly sighted person does not immediately recognize his environment, but rather must _____ to identify objects, to read clocks, numbers and letters, and to judge size and distances.

3. The fact that the perceived size of an object remains the same even though the size of its retinal image changes is called _____ _____. Even though some of these perceptions may be inborn (_____), most perceptions are believed to be _____, or based on prior experience. _____ _____ refers to the idea that objects are perceived as having the same shape even though the retinal image of the object changes depending on the angle from which the object is viewed. Even though under changing lighting conditions the same object reflects different total amounts of light, we still perceive the brightness of the object as the same. This is known as _____ _____.

4. The simplest organization of sensations is to group them so that an object stands out against some plainer background. This process is called _____ - _____ organization. In normal figure-ground perception, only _____ figure is seen. In _____ _____, however, figure and ground can be switched.

5. There are also other ways to organize perceptions such as when stimuli close together are grouped together. This is called _____. When stimuli are closely related in size, shape, color, or form, they are grouped on the basis of _____.

6. Stimuli may also be perceived together or in a certain way because we tend toward simplicity. This organizational principle is called _____. If an incomplete figure is seen as complete so that it will have a consistent overall form, _____ is influencing perception. When two events appear close together in space and time, then _____ may explain why one event seems to be caused by the other.

7. To adapt machines for human use, the engineering psychologist (or _____ _____ _____) must make them compatible with our sensory and motor capacities. When this is done effectively it is referred to as _____ design. Effective designs make use of perceptual signals that are naturally understood by people and they also provide clear _____.

8. A "guess" about a phenomenon held until evidence contradicts it is called a _____ _____. A stimulus which allows for more than one interpretation is called _____. However, a stimulus which offers such conflicting information that perceptual organization becomes impossible is called _____.

9. The ability to see three-dimensional space and to estimate distances is known as _____ _____. If you believe this ability is learned then you are a(n) _____, but if you believe that it is an innate ability you are a(n) _____. Research indicates that this ability is due to _____. This ability has been investigated by using the _____ _____.

10. Cues that require the use of only one eye for the perception of depth are called _____. Depth cues that require the use of both eyes are called _____ cues.

11. A number of depth cues combine to produce the experience of three-dimensional space. One such cue is _____ which refers to the ability of the lens in each eye to bend more to focus objects close to the eye than at a distance. This cue is a _____ cue.

12. A second bodily cue for depth occurs when the eyes must turn in to focus on an object which is 50 feet or less away. This second bodily source of depth is _____, a _____ cue.

13. _____ _____ is based upon the fact that the eyes are about two and one-half inches apart so each eye receives a slightly different view of an object. When the two images are _____ into one overall visual image, _____ vision occurs. _____ _____ is the most important source of depth perception and is a _____ cue.

14. Pictorial depth cues give the sensation of depth or three-dimensionality from _____ dimensions. All of the pictorial depth cues are _____. One such pictorial depth cue is _____ _____, which refers to the apparent convergence of parallel lines in the environment.

15. If an artist wishes to depict two objects of the same size at different distances, the artist makes the more distant object _____. This is the process of using _____ _____ to produce the sensation of depth.

16. Most objects in the environment are lighted in such a way as to create definite patterns of _____ and _____. The perception of depth is experienced when one object partially _____ the view of another. This monocular cue for depth is also called _____.

17. If you are standing in the middle of a cobblestone street, the street looks coarse near your feet, but the _____ of the stones gets smaller and finer as you look off into the distance. This gradual decrease in fine detail refers to _____ _____.

18. Smog, fog, dust, and haze also add to the apparent distance of an object. Objects seen at a great distance tend to be hazy, light in color, and lacking in detail due to _____ _____.

19. The last monocular pictorial depth cue occurs when looking out of a car window or moving your head. Objects near to you appear to move more than objects in the distance. This cue is known as _____ _____ or _____ _____.

20. The moon illusion refers to the fact that the moon appears _____ when it is low in the sky than when it is over-head. This is because the _____ _____ of the moon is greater when it is on the horizon and seen behind houses, trees and other environmental cues. Since the moon casts the same size image on the horizon, but seems farther away than when it is overhead, you compensate by perceiving it as _____ on the horizon.

21. Learning may affect perception by establishing patterns of organization and attention referred to as _____ _____. These may become so ingrained that they lead us to misperceive a stimulus. A lopsided room that is carefully constructed can be made to appear square. This is the case with the _____ room, named after the man who designed it. In this room the perceiver is faced with maintaining _____ constancy or _____ constancy. Most people choose to maintain _____ constancy, thus objects can be made to appear to shrink or grow merely by placing them at various points in the room.

22. Perceptual habits are just that – habits. This is supported by experiments in which a person's vision is _____. These experiments indicate that humans can learn to _____ to a radically different perception of the world, but the key is _____ _____.

23. An important factor affecting perception is the _____ in which a stimulus is judged. For example, someone who is five feet tall would look tall in a room full of midgets. Standards by which stimuli are judged are called _____ _____ _____. Lifting a ten pound weight would feel easy if you carry around fifty pound sacks of seed all day. This depends on your _____ _____.

24. A stimulus that exists but is distorted by the perceiver is called a(n) _____. This is different from a(n) _____ in which the stimulus actually does not exist.

25. The famous Muller-Lyer illusion illustrates how perceptual habits and past experience combine to produce illusions. In this illusion, a horizontal line with "arrowheads" appears _____ than the horizontal line with "Vs" on each end. People who have not _____ lots of straight lines, sharp edges, and corners are not fooled as much by the Muller-Lyer illusion.

26. The first stage of perception is _____, the selection of incoming messages. When some messages are given priority and some are put on hold, this is known as _____ attention. _____ attention often arises from our limited capacity to process information. Attention, in general, can be affected by stimuli which are _____, _____, or related to _____, _____, or _____.

27. A decrease in the actual number of sensory messages sent to the brain is called _____. After messages are sent to the brain the body makes an _____ _____. When a stimulus is repeated without change, the _____ _____ decreases or _____.

28. Attention can be affected by _____. They may also alter what is _____. For example, subjects rated a picture of a female college student as more attractive after reading an _____ passage.

29. The human perceptual system is impressed most by _____ changes. Ornstein and Ehrlich believe that many of the threats to our civilization are insidious. Like the frog who does not notice the gradual increase in temperature in a pan of water and ultimately dies, man may not notice threats to our civilization like _____.

30. In _____-_____ processing we analyze information starting with small units or features and build into a complete perception. In _____-_____ processing preexisting knowledge is used to rapidly organize features into a meaningful whole.

31. Past experience, motives, context, or suggestion may set you to perceive in a certain way. This set pattern of perceiving is called _____ _____. Frequently this set way of perceiving may be created by _____.

32. _____ is the study of events which lie outside normal experiences and seem to defy accepted scientific laws. Such events are called _____ phenomena.

33. Four areas of psi phenomena are under investigation. One such area deals with the ability to perceive events or gain information in ways that appear unaffected by distance or normal physical barriers. This area is known as _____. Another area of study is _____, the ability to read another person's thoughts.

34. Two other areas are _____ and _____. The first is the ability to predict future events accurately. The second is the ability to exert influence over inanimate objects by will power.

35. Many people doubt the existence of psychic phenomena because of many problems. One of these is _____ which can at least partially be avoided by making the study of ESP more _____. One way of doing this is to use _____ cards.

36. Psychologists are also skeptical about psi abilities because of _____, statistics, and _____. Psi abilities seem to be very _____. Many subjects receive credit for a _____ _____ _____.

37. Another problem is that most of the spectacular findings in parapsychology cannot be _____. Many believers in psychic phenomena _____ negative experimental results in their favor. Your author stresses that the best attitude toward ESP is to maintain an open mind while being carefully _____ of evidence reported in the popular press or by researchers who are "true believers."

38. _____ reflects the needs, expectations, attitudes, values, and beliefs of the perceiver. In this light not only do we "believe what we see," but we "_____ what we _____."

39. Although eyewitness testimony can be a key element in establishing guilt or innocence, such testimony frequently is _____. The perceptions of an emotionally distraught eyewitness may frequently be very _____, but our everyday perceptions may be just as distorted. For instance, many fall prey to _____ _____ where they fix their entire attention on the knife or gun and do not attend to other details. In any situation having an element of doubt or uncertainty, _____ _____ involves obtaining additional information as a check on the accuracy of perceptions.

40. Some people perceive things more _____ than others. Maslow characterized people with especially accurate perceptions of themselves and others as _____, _____, _____, and mentally healthy. He found their perceptual styles were marked by immersion in the _____ and a lack of _____ - _____. Zen masters pay _____ to bring about a _____ of perception.

ANSWER KEYS

Do You Know the Information?

Multiple Choice

1. (a) obj. 1, p. 189
2. (d) obj. 3, p. 190
3. (c) obj. 4, p. 193
4. (d) obj. 5, p. 194
5. (a) obj. 6, p. 193
6. (d) obj. 7, p. 193
7. (b) obj. 8, p. 195
8. (a) obj. 8, p. 196
9. (a) B, (b) B, (c) M, (d) B,
   obj. 9, pp. 196-197
10. (c) obj. 9, p. 197
11. (b) obj. 9, p. 197
12. (b) obj. 10, p. 198
13. (c) obj. 11, pp. 200-201
14. (d) obj. 12, p. 202
15. (a) obj. 13, p. 203
16. (c) obj. 14, p. 203
17. (a) obj. 15, p. 204
18. (a) obj. 16, p. 204
19. (c) obj. 16, p. 204
20. (c) obj. 17, p. 205
21. (d) obj. 18, pp. 205-206
22. (b) obj. 19, p. 207
23. (b) obj. 20, p. 207

24. (c) obj. 21, p. 208
25. (b) obj. 22, p. 209
26. (a) obj. 23, p. 209
27. (c) obj. 24, p. 209
28. (b) obj. 24, p. 210
29. (a) obj. 26, p. 212
30. (a) obj. 28, p. 213
31. (d) obj. 29, p. 213
32. (d) obj. 31, p. 216
33. (a) obj. 32, p. 216

True-False

1. F, obj. 2, p. 189
2. T, obj. 3, p. 190
3. F, obj. 4, p. 191
4. F, obj. 8, p. 196
5. T, obj. 9, p. 197
6. T, obj. 10, p. 198
7. T, obj. 10, p. 199
8. F, obj. 10, p. 199
9. T, obj. 11, p. 201
10. T, obj. 12, p. 202
11. F, obj. 20, p. 208
12. T, obj. 25, p. 210

13. T, obj. 30, p. 215
14. T, obj. 32, p. 216
15. T, obj. 33, p. 216
16. T, obj. 34, p. 218

Can You Apply the Information?

1. (c) obj. 3, p. 190
2. (d) obj. 4, p. 192
3. (d) obj. 4, p. 193
4. (b) obj. 4, p. 193
5. (a) obj. 6, p. 193
6. (a) obj. 7, p. 193
7. (d) obj. 9, p. 197
8. (b) obj. 16, p. 204
9. (d) obj. 16, p. 204
10. (a) obj. 17, p. 205
11. (b) obj. 17, p. 205
12. (b) obj. 19, p. 207
13. (d) obj. 21, p. 208
14. (c) obj. 25, p. 210
15. (a) obj. 27, p. 212
16. (b) obj. 27, p. 212
17. (c) obj. 27, p. 212
18. (c) obj. 27, p. 212
19. (c) obj. 33, p. 216
20. (d) obj. 34, p. 218

Chapter Review

1. perception (p. 189)
2. learn (p. 189)
3. size constancy, native, empirical, Shape constancy (p. 190); brightness constancy (p. 191)
4. figure-ground, one, reversible figures (p. 191)
5. nearness, similarity (p. 192)
6. continuation (continuity), closure, contiguity (p. 193)
7. human factors engineer, natural, feedback (p. 194)
8. perceptual hypothesis, ambiguous, impossible (p. 193)
9. depth perception (p. 195); empiricist, nativist, both, visual cliff (p. 196)
10. monocular, binocular (p. 197)
11. accommodation, monocular (p. 197)
12. convergence, binocular (p. 197)
13. Retinal disparity, fused, stereoscopic, Retinal disparity, binocular (p. 197)
14. two, monocular, linear perspective (p. 198)
15. smaller, relative size (p. 199)
16. light, shadow, overlaps, interposition (p. 199)
17. texture, texture gradient (p. 199)
18. aerial perspective (p. 199)
19. relative motion (motion parallax), motion parallax (relative motion) (p. 199)
20. larger (p. 200); apparent distance, larger (p. 201)

21.	perceptual habits (p. 202); Ames, shape (size), size (shape), shape (p. 203)
22.	distorted (changed, inverted), adapt (adjust) (p. 203); active movement (p. 204)
23.	context, frames of reference, adaptation level (p. 204)
24.	illusion, hallucination (p. 205)
25.	shorter, experienced (p. 205)
26.	attention, selective, Divided, intense (p. 207); repetitious, contrast, change, incongruity (p. 208)
27.	adaptation, orientation response, orientation response, habituates (p. 208)
28.	motives, perceived, arousing (p. 208)
29.	dramatic, pollution (overpopulation, deforestation, etc.) (p. 209)
30.	bottom-up, top-down (p. 209)
31.	perceptual expectancy, suggestion (p. 210)
32.	Parapsychology, psi (p. 212)
33.	clairvoyance, telepathy (p. 212)
34.	precognition, psychokinesis (p. 212)
35.	coincidence (p. 212); objective, Zener (p. 213)
36.	fraud, chance, inconsistent, run of luck (p. 213)
37.	replicated, reinterpret (p. 213); skeptical (p. 214)
38.	Perception (p. 215); see, believe (p. 216)
39.	wrong, distorted, weapon focus, reality testing (p. 216)
40.	accurately, alive, open, aware (p. 217); present, self-consciousness, attention, dishabituation (p. 218)

chapter seven

States of Consciousness

LEARNING OBJECTIVES

To demonstrate mastery of this chapter you should be able to:

1. Explain what hypnogogic images are.

2. Define consciousness according to William James and explain what waking consciousness is.

3.   Define and describe "altered state of consciousness." Include a description of the meaning and uses of altered states of consciousness in other cultures.

4.   Describe two ways in which sleep is a unique state. Describe the limitations of sleep learning.

      a.

      b.

5.   Explain why Webb describes sleep as a gentle tyrant.

6.   Define and describe the term microsleep.

7.   Describe the general effects of 48 hours of sleep deprivation. Name and describe the condition that occurs when a person is deprived of sleep for a longer period of time.

8.   Explain what circadian rhythms are and what is related to them.

9.   State how long the average sleep-waking cycle is and explain how we tie our sleep rhythms to a 24 hour day.

10.   Describe the normal range of sleep needs. Describe how the aging process affects sleep.

11.   State the average ratio of time awake to time asleep.

12.   Explain how and why shift work and jet lag may adversely affect a person. Explain how the direction of travel (or of rotating shifts) affects rhythms and how to minimize the effects of shifting one's rhythms.

13.   Describe how the brain's systems and chemistry promote sleep.

14.   Briefly describe each of the four stages of sleep. Include a description of the brain waves associated with each and those associated with wakefulness.

       a.

       b.

       c.

       d.

15.   Describe the cyclical nature of the sleep stages.

16.   Name and differentiate the two basic states of sleep. State the average amount of time spent in each one and explain how the relative amounts of each can be influenced.

a.

b.

17.   State how many times per night most people dream and how long the dreams usually last.

18.   List the physiological changes that occur during REM sleep including a description of REM behavior disorder.

19.   Characterize the following major sleep disturbances of NREM sleep.

a.   somnambulism

b.   sleeptalking

c.   night terrors (include a differentiation between night terrors and nightmares)

20.   List and briefly describe the eleven sleep disorders that are found in the DSM-IV.

a.	f.
b.	g.
c.	h.
d.	i.
e.	j.
	i.

21.   Explain the concepts of REM rebound and REM myth. Describe the relationship between alcoholism and REM rebound.

22.   Describe the probable functions of REM sleep.

23.   Explain Calvin Hall's view of dreams.

24.   Explain how Freud viewed dreams, and present the evidence against his view.

25.   Describe the activation-synthesis hypothesis concerning dreaming.

26.   Give the general definition of hypnosis and then describe how it is that the general definition is not accepted by all psychologists.

27.   Trace the history of hypnosis from Mesmer through its use today.

28.   State the proportion of people who can be hypnotized.

29.   Explain how a person's hypnotic susceptibility can be determined. Include a brief description of the dimensions of the Stanford Hypnotic Susceptibility Scale.

30. List the four common factors in all hypnotic techniques. Explain why all hypnosis may really be self-hypnosis.

    a.

    b.

    c.

    d.

31. Explain what the basic suggestion effect is.

32. Explain how hypnosis can affect:

    a. strength

    b. memory

    c. pain relief

    d. age regression

    e. sensory changes

33. List three areas in which hypnosis appears to have its greatest value, and then state a general conclusion concerning the effectiveness of hypnosis.

    a.   b.   c.

34. Using the five characteristics of the stage setting outlined in the chapter, explain how a stage hypnotist gets people to perform the way they do in front of an audience.

35.   Name and describe the two major forms of meditation.

    a.

    b.

36.   Describe the relaxation response.

37.   Describe what is known about the effects of meditation.

38.   Explain what sensory deprivation is. Include a discussion of the positive and negative effects of this procedure.

39.   Define the term psychoactive drug.

40.   Differentiate physical dependence from psychological dependence.

41.   Describe the following frequently abused drugs in terms of their effects, possible medical uses, side effects or long term symptoms, organic damage potential, and potential for physical and/or psychological dependence.

    a.   amphetamines

(continued on page 126)

b.   cocaine (include the three signs of abuse)

c.   caffeine

d.   nicotine

e.   barbiturates

f.   alcohol

g.   marijuana

42.   Compare the efficacy of quitting smoking "cold turkey" versus cutting down or smoking low-tar cigarettes.

43.   Explain what a drug interaction is.

44.   List and explain the three steps in the development of a drinking problem.

     a.

     b.

     c.

45.   Generally describe the treatment process for alcoholism. Name the form of therapy that has probably been the most successful.

46.   Explain why drug abuse is such a common problem.

The following objectives are related to the material in the "Applications" section of your text.

47.   Define insomnia. List and describe the characteristics and treatment of the three types of insomnia.

     a.

     b.

     c.

48.   Describe the effects of nonprescription and prescription drugs on insomnia.

49.   List and briefly describe five behavorial remedies which can be used to combat insomnia. (Highlight 7-5)

   a.

   b.

   c.

   d.

   e.

50.   List and describe the four processes identified by Freud which disguise the hidden meaning of dreams.

   a.

   b.

   c.

   d.

51.   Contrast Hall's and Cartwright's views of dream interpretation.

52.   Describe Faraday's approach to dreams and list her eight steps for remembering dreams.

   a.   e.

   b.   f.

   c.   g.

   d.   h.

53. Explain how Perls viewed dreams and how he suggested that people interpret them.

54. Describe how one could use dreams to aid in problem solving. Include a description of lucid dreams and how they have been used in the problem solving process.

SELF-QUIZZES

Do You Know the Information?

Multiple Choice

1. Hypnogogic images are
   (a) like real objects in the environment.
   (b) the same as hallucinations.
   (c) dreamlike and vivid, similar to those experienced just before falling asleep.
   (d) linked to an increase in alpha waves produced by the brain.

2. According to William James, consciousness is
   (a) a state of awareness best characterized by the absence of sleep.
   (b) a stream or an everchanging flow of awareness.
   (c) the state during which rational decisions are made.
   (d) all of the above.

3. Many cultures regard changes in consciousness as
   (a) pathways to enlightenment.
   (b) equivalent to drug intoxication.
   (c) a cleansing of the body and mind.
   (d) life-enhancing breakthroughs.

4. Sleep is considered a unique state because
   (a) the person is completely unconscious.
   (b) it is painless.
   (c) the sleeping individual is unresponsive to the environment.
   (d) the person can learn simple tasks while asleep.

5. Sleep is considered a "gentle tyrant" because (you may choose more than one)
   (a) it is flexible enough to emporarily suspend but it can never be sidestepped.
   (b) it appears to be a learned biological rhythm.
   (c) there appear to be no limits to the extent that you can stay awake.
   (d) a and b above are correct.

6. Microsleep is
   (a) the time required for the onset of sleep in an individual who has been deprived of 24 hours or more of sleep.
   (b) a momentary shift in brain activity to the pattern characteristic of sleep.
   (c) very similar to a nap that lasts 30 minutes or less.
   (d) the shift from NREM to REM sleep.

7. Which of the following statements regarding the effects of losing 48 hours of sleep is *false*?
   (a) Most people display increased pain sensitivity.
   (c) Performance on complex tasks declines.
   (b) The ability to pay attention and remain vigilant declines.
   (d) The ability to follow a simple routine was impaired.

8. The condition caused by long periods without sleep and characterized by body tremors, hallucinations, and staring is called
   (a) hallucinosis.
   (b) sleep-deprivation psychosis.
   (c) dream deficit psychosis.
   (d) Korsakoff's psychosis.

9. Circadian rhythms refer to the
   (a) complex cycle of changes in the body which take place daily.
   (b) body's fluctuating blood sugar level.
   (c) changes in the body as compared to the changes in the moon.
   (d) physical, emotional, and intellectual changes in the body.

10. What is the length of the *average* sleep-waking cycle?
    (a) 23 hours
    (c) 25 hours
    (b) 24 hours
    (d) it depends upon the length of the class

11. Regarding human sleep cycles, it would be most appropriate to say that
    (a) a midmorning nap would take care of the sleepiness that is a natural part of the sleep cycle at that time.
    (b) people should sleep between 7- to 8-hours-per-night.
    (c) age appears to be a significant factor in determining the amount of sleep people get.
    (d) brief naps can leave a person continually drowsy.

12. What is the average ratio of time awake to time asleep?
    (a) 3 to 2
    (b) 4 to 1
    (c) 2 to 1
    (d) 1 to 3

13. The effects of disrupting sleep-waking cycles or circadian rhythms
    (a) are worse for shift work than for jet lag.
    (c) may include upset stomach, nervousness, and depression.
    (b) may take up to a month to resynchronize.
    (d) may be minimized by rotating shifts backwards.

14. Sleep depends on
    (a) the "awake" system in the brain shutting off.
    (b) the "sleep" system in the brain turning on.
    (c) the balance between "sleep" and "awake" systems in the brain.
    (d) the accumulation of a "sleep-promoting" chemical in the brain.

For questions 15-17, match one of the letters of the correct brain waves to each question.

   (a) alpha
   (b) beta
   (c) delta
   (d) theta

_____ 15. the brain wave pattern recorded during deep sleep

_____ 16. the brain wave observed just prior to sleep

_____ 17. the brain wave usually observed during waking hours

18. _____ is the problem that causes about 15 to 20 percent of all cases of insomnia.
    (a) Myoclonus
    (b) Hypnic jerking
    (c) Hypnogogic imaging
    (d) Sleep spindling

19. Dreaming usually appears in
    (a) REM sleep.
    (b) Stage 4 REM.
    (c) Stage 1 NREM.
    (d) NREM sleep.

20. The amount of REM sleep usually is increased by
    (a) an increased amount of daytime stress.
    (c) unusual amounts of exercise or physical exertion.
    (b) daytime fatigue.
    (d) sleep-deprivation psychosis.

21. How many times per night do most people dream?
    (a) 1-2   (b) 4-5   (c) 7-8   (d) 3-4

22. Circle all of the following which occur during REM sleep.
    (a) muscle paralysis   (c) blood pressure fluctuations (e) movement of the eyes (g) change of position
    (b) sexual arousal   (d) irregular heartbeat   (f) acting out of dreams

23. When REM paralysis fails people may physically act out their dreams. This problem is referred to as
    (a) myoclonus.   (c) sleep drunkeness.
    (b) sleepwalking disorder.   (d) REM behavior disorder.

24. Which of the following is *not* a problem occurring during NREM sleep?
    (a) somnambulism   (b) sleeptalking   (c) night terrors   (d) nightmares

25. A person can banish nightmares by
    (a) promoting REM rebound.   (c) drinking a small amount of alcohol prior to falling asleep.
    (b) practicing imagery rehearsal.   (d) simply writing a brief outline of the nightmare.

26. Sleep attacks during the daytime where a person may fall asleep while talking are indicative of
    (a) sleep apnea.   (c) hypersomnia.
    (b) sleep-wake schedule disorder.   (d) narcolepsy.

27. REM rebound refers to
    (a) the increase in total sleep time that occurs when a person is deprived of sleep.
    (b) a person's ability to recover cognitive abilities such as attention and concentration when deprived of REM sleep.
    (c) an increased need to dream because of a deprivation of dream sleep.
    (d) the ability of REM sleep to compensate for a lack of NREM sleep.

28. In adulthood, REM sleep is apparently important for
    (a) processing emotional events.   (c) restoring brain chemicals needed for learning and memory.
    (b) preventing sensory deprivation during sleep.   (d) all of the above.

29. Calvin Hall sees dreams as
    (a) usually more pleasant than unpleasant.   (c) extensions of a person's everyday life.
    (b) predominantly filled with sexual themes.   (d) messages from the unconscious.

30. Freud viewed dreams as
    (a) reflections of our waking personalities.   (c) a message about what is missing in our life.
    (b) an opportunity for wish fulfillment.   (d) an expression of conscious urges.

31. The activation-synthesis hypothesis concerning dreams holds that
    (a) people activate or "create" dreams based on unconsciously repressed urges.
    (b) dreams are created based on psychological processes.
    (c) dreams are brought about by areas of the brain trying to come up with a logical explanation of the activity in lower brain
        areas.
    (d) all of the above are true.

32. Hypnosis is may be
    (a) simple role playing.   (c) a state of increased openness to suggestion.
    (b) characterized by narrowed attention.   (d) all of the above.

33. Interest in hypnosis began in the 1700's with Mesmer. Mesmer believed that
    (a) he could cure diseases by passing magnets over the afflicted person's body.
    (b) hypnosis was a stage of sleep.
    (c) the power of hypnosis releases superhuman strength.
    (d) James Braid, the English surgeon, was a quack and a fraud.

34. In general, the proportion of people who can be hypnotized is
     (a) specifically related to the number of people who are prone to daydreaming.
     (b) 4 out of 10.
     (c) 8 out of 10.
     (d) not a valid question because everyone can be hypnotized.

35. Hypnotic susceptibility can be measured by
     (a) recording the length of time it takes to hypnotize the person.
     (b) investigating whether or not the subject is capable of self-hypnosis.
     (c) assessing the increase in a person's strength.
     (d) recording the number of suggestions to which he or she responds.

36. Which of the following is *not* one of the four common factors in all hypnotic techniques?
     (a) to relax and feel tired   (c) to accept suggestions easily
     (b) to focus attention on what is being said   (d) to feel the sensation of gently falling or floating

37. Which of the following is *not* a feeling that is generally experienced by people who have been hypnotized?
     (a) separation from your body   (c) that suggested actions require effort
     (b) being unaware of what is going on   (d) mild feelings of floating

38. Hypnosis can definitely be used to accomplish which of the following?
     (a) carry out age regression   (c) produce amnesia
     (b) help induce relaxation   (d) significantly improve a person's strength

39. To get people to do what they do in front of audiences most stage hypnotists
     (a) use trickery and deception.
     (b) select responsive subjects.
     (c) take advantage of the fact that the hypnosis label can be disinhibiting.
     (d) do all of the above.

40. Generally speaking, when one sits still and focuses on some external object, one is participating in _____ meditation.
     (a) transcendental   (b) concentrative   (c) receptive   (d) relaxive

41. Which of the following are effects that occur with meditation?
     (a) less oxygen consumption   (d) reduced respiration   (g) greater kidney output
     (b) increased attention span   (e) decreased blood pressure   (h) slowed heartbeat
     (c) increased metabolism   (f) increased alpha brain waves (i) increased muscle tension

42. Sensory deprivation has been found to
     (a) help people quit smoking and break other bad habits.   (c) dull the acuity of senses such as hearing and touch.
     (b) be stressful and aversive, even for brief periods of time. (d) have few benefits.

43. A substance capable of altering attention, memory, judgment, time sense, self-control, emotion, or perception is called a(n) _____ drug.
     (a) addictive   (b) depressant   (c) psychoactive   (d) sedative

44. The difference between physical dependence and psychological dependence is that
     (a) the latter may involve a drug tolerance.
     (b) there may be agonizing withdrawal symptoms when a drug is withheld from a person with a physical dependence.
     (c) there is usually a physiological craving for the drug in cases of psychological dependence.
     (d) only physical depenence strongly affects someone.

For questions 45-54, put the appropriate letter or letters of the drugs which apply to the statements. More than one letter may be used for each of the following questions.

(a) amphetamines   (c) caffeine   (e) barbiturates   (g) marijuana
(b) cocaine   (d) nicotine   (f) alcohol

_____ 45. can lead to psychological dependence

_____ 46. acts as stimulant

_____ 47. most commonly used psychoactive drug in U.S.

_____ 48. encourages breast cysts, may contribute to insomnia, stomach problems, heart problems, and high blood pressure

_____ 49. can cause physical dependence

_____ 50. most commonly combined with alcohol to produce dangerous drug interaction

_____ 51. physiologically depressing

_____ 52. lowers sperm production and may cause abnormal menstrual cycles and problems with ovulation

_____ 53. hallucinogenic

_____ 54. binds with brain cells to produce its effects

55. The real meaning of the phrase "Speed kills" lies in the fact that amphetamines can cause a loss of contact with reality known as
(a) speed delusions.   (b) hallucinations.   (c) euphoric neurosis.   (d) amphetamine psychosis.

56. When one drug enhances the effect of another this is known as a
(a) dosage excess.   (b) drug interaction.   (c) drug intolerance.   (d) drug narcosis.

57. During the crucial phase in the development of a drinking problem
(a) the person begins to lose control over drinking habits.
(b) the person begins to drink more and may begin to worry about drinking.
(c) blackouts usually begin to occur.
(d) the person drinks compulsively and feels a powerful need for alcohol when deprived of it.

58. The usual first step in the treatment of alcoholism is
(a) family therapy.   (b) vitamin therapy.   (c) detoxification.   (d) tranquilization.

59. The approach that has generally had the most success in dealing with alcoholism is
(a) restoration of the alcoholic's physical health.   (c) psychotherapy.
(b) AA.   (d) behavior modification.

60. In general, drug abuse can be viewed as
(a) a result of delinquency.   (c) an escape from feelings of inadequacy.
(b) a logical consequence of stressful life changes. (d) one part of a pattern of problem behavior.

61. Temporary insomnia is caused by
(a) drugs that decrease Stage 4 and REM sleep.   (c) barbiturates.
(b) stress which causes heightened physical arousal. (d) tryptophan.

62. Treatment for chronic insomnia usually begins with
(a) sedatives.   (c) training in relaxation techniques.
(b) urging insomniacs to eat a snack before sleeping. (d) a mild nonprescription sleeping aid such as Sominex.

63.   Prescription sedatives (usually barbiturates)
       (a) can produce a drug-dependency insomnia.
       (b) when taken to combat insomnia, can result in a drug tolerance so that the initial dosage becomes ineffective.
       (c) decrease Stage 4 and REM sleep.
       (d) both a and c.
       (e) can do of the above.

64.   Which of the following is *not* a recommended behavioral remedy for insomnia? (You may choose more than one.)
       (a) Avoid stimulants such as coffee and cigarettes.
       (b) Learn a physical or mental strategy for relaxing in order to reduce muscle tension.
       (c) Watch television or write letters while in bed.
       (d) Avoid drinking alcohol as it impairs sleep quality.

65.   Which of the following is *not* one of the four processes identified by Freud that helps disguise the meaning of dreams?
       (a) symbolization   (b) documentation   (c) displacement   (d) condensation

66.   Thinking of dreams as plays is to _____ as emotional tone of a dream is to _____.
       (a) Hall; Cartwright   (b) Cartwright; Faraday   (c) Hall; Freud   (d) Freud; Faraday

67.   If you consider a dream to be a message from yourself to yourself, then your opinion is most in line with that of
       (a) Freud.   (b) Faraday.   (c) Perls.   (d) Hall.

68.   Dreams are a way of filling in gaps in personal experience. To understand the dream you should play the part of each of the
       principal characters and objects in the dream. This is the point of view of
       (a) Jung.   (b) Faraday.   (c) Hall.   (d) Perls.

69.   Lucid dreams are those that
       (a) you use for solving a problem.
       (b) allow you to "awaken" within the dream and still be capable of normal thought.
       (c) have an easily understood meaning.
       (d) are easily remembered weeks after the dream occurred.

True-False

_____ 1. An altered state of consciousness represents a distinct change in the quantity of mental functioning.

_____ 2. Extended sleep loss results in only physical side-effects.

_____ 3. Circadian rhythms control things such as urine output and liver function.

_____ 4. The average sleep-waking cycle is about 25 hours, but we keep it on a 24 hour schedule by being tied to external time
           markers like light and darkness.

_____ 5. Most individuals average six to seven hours of sleep per night.

_____ 6. Although people find that their sleep habits may change in many ways during old age, the general trend is for older people
           to sleep more than average.

_____ 7. The biological effects of shifting one's circadian rhythms can be minimized by preadapting as much as possible beforehand
           to the new schedule.

_____ 8. Sleep is caused by fatigue which causes the buildup of a sleep-inducing chemical in the blood.

_____ 9. A person moves from Stage 1 sleep through Stage 4 and then begins the cycle again with Stage 1.

_____ 10. The two states of sleep are REM and NREM.

_____ 11. REM sleep averages only about one and one-half hours per night.

_____ 12. The first dream in the night lasts about ten minutes. Each succeeding dream lasts a little longer.

_____ 13. Body movement occurs while in REM sleep and coincides with dream material.

_____ 14. Nightmares and night terrors occur about twice per month for most people.

_____ 15. Hypersomnia is caused exclusively by repeated bouts of narcolepsy.

_____ 16. The belief that a person would go crazy if permanently kept from dreaming is called the "REM myth."

_____ 17. Evidence against Freud's view of dreams includes a study that showed volunteers subjected to the effects of prolonged starvation exhibited no particular decrease in dreams about sex.

_____ 18. The activation-synthesis hypothesis agrees with Freud concerning the hidden meanings of dreams and differs on how the dreams originate.

_____ 19. A hypnotic trance is a form of sleep.

_____ 20. James Braid is most closely associated with "animal magnetism."

_____ 21. Out of every ten people only about four can be hypnotized.

_____ 22. Hypnosis causes such a total loss of self-control that people can routinely be hypnotized to do repulsive and immoral acts.

_____ 23. Since a person must first cooperate in order to become hypnotized, all hypnosis may just be self-hypnosis.

_____ 24. The relaxation response refers to an innate physiological pattern which opposes the stressful activation of the body's fight-or-flight response.

_____ 25. Amphetamines do not supply energy to the body. They speed the expenditure of bodily resources.

_____ 26. The main difference between the effects of amphetamines and cocaine is how long the effects last.

_____ 27. Small amounts of caffiene have been found to produce no side-effects.

_____ 28. Sudden infant death syndrome is a more likely result for children born to mothers who smoke during and after the pregnancy.

_____ 29. Tryptophan can help people sleep, especially those who are slow in getting to sleep.

_____ 30. Dreams can be used to help solve problems because inhibitions are reduced during dreaming.

Matching *(Use the letters on the right only once.)*

_____ 1. altered state of consciousness
_____ 2. hypnosis
_____ 3. key element of hypnosis
_____ 4. to combat insomnia
_____ 5. symbolization
_____ 6. occur in Stage 4
_____ 7. sleep deprivation psychosis
_____ 8. effects last only 15-30 min.
_____ 9. can impair sexual performance
_____ 10. best way to quit smoking
_____ 11. Siamese twins
_____ 12. sleep-wake schedule disorder
_____ 13. REST
_____ 14. sweat lodge
_____ 15. hypnic jerk
_____ 16. receptive meditation
_____ 17. anhedonia
_____ 18. drug-dependency insomnia

A. try to stay awake as long as possible
B. a Sioux Indian approach to alter consciousness
C. cold turkey
D. proved that no sleep chemical accumulates in blood
E. cocaine
F. disorientation, delusions, hallucinations
G. characterized by decreased motivation, loss of energy, lethargy
H. can stimulate creative thinking
I. amphetamines
J. images in dreams are symbolic rather than literal
K. alcohol
L. term coined by James Braid
M. somnambulism & sleeptalking
N. basic suggestion effect
O. part of cocaine withdrawal
P. marijuana
Q. defined as change in quality and pattern of mental functions
R. a mismatch between personal and environmental sleep-wake schedules
S. a reflex muscle contraction
T. widening attention to become aware of everything
U. cut down slowly
V. part of amphetamine withdrawal
W. result of being a "sleeping pill junkie"

Can You Apply the Information?

1. You are a sleepy quality control inspector at a local bottling company. While inspecting a continuously moving line of bottles for 30 minutes you notice that you have not been consciously aware of the bottles for several seconds. You have most likely suffered
    (a) a symptom of sleep-deprivation psychosis.   (c) self-hypnosis.
    (b) waking consciousness.   (d) microsleep.

2. If you know a person who consistently sleeps 6 hours a night, how would you describe this person's sleep patterns?
    (a) below average   (b) average   (c) above average   (d) decidedly abnormal

3. Fred works the graveyard shift (11 p.m. to 7 a.m.). According to circadian rhythms, if Fred has to change shifts, it would be best if
    (a) he rotates forward (7 a.m. to 4 p.m.).
    (b) he could switch shifts every two weeks.
    (c) his shift started three hours earlier.
    (d) he naps during the day rather than sleep for extended periods of time.

4. You are a neurologist and your patient says to you that she feels funny. You notice that the EEG is showing almost pure delta waves. You surmise that
    (a) she has extra sleep chemicals in her blood.   (c) she is in Stage 2.
    (b) she is obviously in REM sleep.   (d) she is sleeptalking in NREM sleep.

5. Bob and Betty both sleep about eight hours per night. One day, Bob came home very late from work after Betty had gone to bed. He noticed that she was in REM sleep. What could he deduce about the length of time she had been asleep?
    (a) She had just fallen asleep and was in her first stage 1 period.
    (b) She had been asleep at least 60 minutes because of the appearance of the REMs but the estimate could be no better than that.
    (c) She was in her second REM period because he observed a period of myoclonus which doesn't happen during the first REM period.
    (d) He could deduce nothing about the length of time she had been asleep.

6. If your doctor tells you that she wants to increase your NREM sleep, which of the following will be most likely to do it?
    (a) Take on added responsibility at work.   (c) Drink a small glass of wine to relax before bedtime.
    (b) Walk briskly around a city block once a day.   (d) Jog in a 10,000 meter race.

7. During a lecture on sleeping and dreaming you hear someone in the audience say, "I'm 65 years old and I've never had a dream in my life." Since you are now knowledgeable on the topic, you think to yourself:
    (a) he is one of those people who never dreams.   (c) he probably just doesn't remember his dreams.
    (b) he probably drinks 8-10 cups of coffee per day.   (d) maybe he is is schizophrenic.

8. Ruth has decided to add a new dimension to her sexual relationship with her husband. What she intends to do is wake him during the night and then "make love." For her plan to succeed, which stage of sleep would be best to wake her husband from?
    (a) any REM period   (c) stage 3   (e) It makes no difference, he won't
    (b) stage 2   (d) stage 4   wake up anyway.

9. A child is plagued by nights when he wakes in a panic, screams and thrashes about, but remembers nothing in the morning. This child is probably suffering from
    (a) sleep terror disorder.   (b) REM behavior disorder.   (c) sleep deprivation psychosis. (d) nightmare disorder.

10. It's Saturday night and you have had too much to drink. In fact, you've had way too much to drink. You fall asleep. It is very likely
    (a) you'll dream about riding in a boat on a rolling ocean.
    (b) you will have an above average number of dreams and many of them will be bizarre.
    (c) the next night you will spend more time in REM sleep.
    (d) that you will get more Stage 4 sleep than any other stage.

11. In which situation would hypnosis probably be most effective?
    (a) childbirth
    (b) World Weightlifting Championships
    (c) a college instructor learning the names of 100 students
    (d) a psychotherapist using hypnosis to take you back to a trauma that you experienced at three years of age

12. If you want to produce relaxation and increased concentration but lessen the body's reaction to stress, which of the following should you use?
    (a) hypnosis   (b) alcohol   (c) barbiturates   (d) meditation

13. A doctor has prescribed a sleeping pill for your insomnia, but after a couple of weeks you have to increase your dosage because one pill a night no longer helps you get to sleep. This occurs because
    (a) the drugs are now stimulating the central nervous system.
    (b) you have developed a physical addiction.
    (c) you have built up a drug tolerance.
    (d) you have a psychological condition rather than a physical one.

14. If you know someone who wakes up in the morning and feels as if he or she has to take Drug X to have a good day, then this person is probably
    (a) psychologically dependent upon the drug.   (c) very tolerant physically to Drug X.
    (b) experiencing severe withdrawal symptoms.   (d) physically addicted to the drug.

15. You are the doctor on duty in the emergency room of a local hospital when an 18 year old female is brought in. She is unconscious with a very slow, irregular heartbeat and shallow respiration. The friend who accompanied the girl says she's not sure what the unconscious patient took. They were both at a party and there were many drugs being taken. If the friend gave you the following list, which would be the most likely candidate?
    (a) marijuana   (b) amphetamines   (c) cocaine   (d) barbiturates

16. Your wife gets up in the morning after a party the previous night at which she had been drinking. At the party she had a loud argument with another woman. She has a Bloody Mary for breakfast. According to your text, in which phase in the development of a drinking problem is she?
    (a) initial   (b) crucial   (c) critical   (d) chronic

17. Probably the *worst* thing a person can do to help cure insomnia is
    (a) to take prescription sedatives.
    (b) avoid beds for everything but sleeping.
    (c) take a nonprescription, heal-yourself drug such as Nytol.
    (d) have a regular time to go to bed.
    (e) once in bed, try to stay awake as long as possible.

Chapter Review

1. Images which occur just before falling asleep and which are dreamlike, very vivid, and often surprising are called _____ images.

2. According to William James, consciousness is a stream or everchanging flow of _____. Waking consciousness is perceived as real, and is marked by a familiar sense of _____ and _____. An altered state of consciousness (ASC) represents a distinct change in the _____ and _____ of mental functioning.

3. Many cultures regard changes in _____ as pathways to _____ even though they may be sought primarily for _____. Special powers, sometimes attributed to shamans, are thought to come from an ability to enter a _____ and _____ with spirits.

4. The state of sleep is unique in many ways. We are not totally unconscious, nor are we _____ to the environment. Some people can even _____ to do simple tasks while asleep, but the tasks can not be _____.

5. Webb describes sleep as a "gentle _____" because it is an _____ _____ rhythm that can never be entirely side-stepped. Animals who are prevented from sleeping fall into a _____ and _____. Animals and humans deprived of sleep will engage in _____, a brief shift in brain activity to patterns normally found in _____.

6. Volunteers who are kept awake for 48 hours show _____ _____ on complex mental tasks. However, most people do show a decline in their ability to pay _____, remain _____, and follow a simple _____. Longer periods of sleep deprivation may bring about _____-_____ _____ which is characterized by confusion, disorientation, _____, and _____.

7. Internal biological clocks which guide the body through many complex cycles of change every 24 hours are called _____ _____. During their high point in these cycles, people are more _____.

8. The sleep-waking cycle is actually _____ hours long, but external time markers like light and dark help us to reset our biological clocks daily. Only 8 percent of the population averages _____ hours sleep or less. Most people sleep _____ to _____ hours per night. Increasing age usually brings a reduction in sleep time, i.e., whereas infants spend up to _____ hours a day sleeping, people over the age of 50 average only _____ hours of sleep per night. Most studies of sleep patterns show a consistent ratio of _____ to _____ between time awake and time asleep.

9. Both shift work and jet lag can cause problems because the rhythms get out of _____ with sun and clocks. This can cause a loss of mental _____ as well as _____. Resynchronization can take from _____ day(s) to _____ week(s) and is aided by getting _____ as much as possible. A _____-hour dose of bright sunlight each day in a new time zone helps to reset the circadium rhythms.

10. If you are traveling, the _____ of travel appears to affect adaptation. Specifically, traveling from _____ to _____ appears to be most disruptive to a person's circadian rhythms. Likewise, work shifts that "rotate" _____ are more disruptive than those that _____. In general, it is best to _____ yourself to a new schedule before it is actually put in place.

11. Early sleep experts thought a _____-related substance accumulated in the _____ causing sleep. A sleep-promoting chemical does, however, collect in the _____ and _____ _____ but this is not the whole explanation. Basically, whether you are awake or asleep depends on the _____ between opposing sleep and waking systems in the brain. Rather than "_____ _____" during sleep, the brain just changes the _____ of its activity rather than the _____.

12. When a person is awake the brain waves are usually small fast ones called _____ waves. Immediately before sleep the EEG patterns shift to larger, slower waves called _____ which continues into Stage 1 with other small, irregular waves. In Stage 2, sleep deepens and the EEG begins to show short bursts of activity called "_____ _____" which seem to mark the boundary of true sleep. In Stage 3 a different brain wave called _____ begins to appear. These waves signal deeper sleep. In Stage 4, the brain wave pattern is almost pure _____, and this stage is called _____ sleep.

13. In Stage 1 sleep, as you lose consciousness and enter _____ sleep, your body muscles relax which sometimes triggers a reflex muscle contraction called a _____ _____. This phenomenon is different from the muscle spasms that occur during sleep itself called _____.

14. Sleeping is a cyclical phenomenon. The sleeper first moves into Stage _____, then through Stages _____ and _____, and finally to Stage _____. After this, the sleeper returns (through Stages _____ and _____) to Stage _____.

15. The two basic states of sleep are _____ and another state during which we usually dream called _____. The first period of stage 1 sleep is usually free of _____ and _____. We generally spend about _____ hours per night in the REM sleep. Exercise and physical exertion generally increase the amount of _____ sleep we get while _____ sleep increases with added _____.

16. Most people dream _____ to _____ times per night. Dreams are usually on a _____ minute cycle. The first dream generally lasts about _____ minutes with each succeeding dream lasting a little longer. The last dream of the night may last _____ minutes. Dreams do not occur in a _____; they occur in _____ time.

17. During REM sleep the heart beats _____ and _____ _____ and _____ waver. Both sexes appear to be _____ aroused. The muscles are still as if the person was _____. However, when REM paralysis fails, a person is said to have _____ _____ _____.

18. Both sleepwalking and sleeptalking occur during _____ sleep. This probably accounts for why most sleeptalking makes little _____ and for why most sleepwalkers wake up rather _____.

19. Another Stage 4 disorder is _____ _____. These are severely frightening experiences that can be distinguished from normal _____ which are simply bad dreams that occur during _____ sleep. The former is most common in _____; the latter occurs for most people _____ times per month.

20. People prevented from dreaming for several nights in a row exhibit what is known as _____ _____ when allowed to dream without interruption. Although people may complain of difficulty in concentrating while being deprived of _____ sleep, it is not true that a person will go _____ if permanently kept from _____. This is now known as the _____ _____.

21. Sleep clinics treat thousands of people each year with sleep disorders with complaints such as: _____ (a difficulty in getting to sleep); myoclonus ("_____ _____" syndrome); _____ (daytime sleep attacks); sleep apnea (where breathing stops for _____ seconds or more during sleep); _____-_____ schedule disorder; REM behavior disorder; nightmare disorder; sleep terror disorder; sleepwalking disorder; _____ _____ (slowed transition to clear consciousness after awakening); and, _____ (excessive daytime sleepiness).

22. Early in life REM sleep may _____ the developing brain thus explaining why newborns spend _____ percent of their sleeptime in REM sleep. REM sleep may serve the purpose of restoring the brain's _____ needed for learning and memory, helping integrate and sort _____ formed during the day, preventing _____ deprivation during sleep, and processing _____ events.

23. Calvin Hall sees dreams as merely extensions of everyday _____. He has collected and analyzed over 10,000 dreams and finds that the favorite dream setting is familiar _____ in a _____.

24. Freud viewed dreams as a vehicle for _____ _____. Some studies do not support Freud. In one study on the effects of starvation, volunteers showed no _____ in dreams about food and eating. One of Freud's insights is that dreams express _____ desires in _____ rather than _____.

25. The _____-_____ hypothesis is a radically different view of dreaming. According to this view, during _____ sleep certain brain cells are activated that normally control eye movements, balance and actions. However, messages from these cells are blocked, so no movement occurs. These cells continue to tell higher _____ _____ of their activities. In order to come up with a reasonable _____ of all of this activity, the _____ manufactures a _____.

26. Some psychologists see _____ as an altered state of consciousness, characterized by narrowed _____ and an increased openness to _____. Others see it as a blend of _____, _____, _____, _____, _____ and role-playing. Either way, hypnosis is not "_____." Interest in this area began in the 1700's with _____. He believed that he could cure disease by passing _____ over a person's body.

27. The term hypnotism was coined by _____. Today we recognize that hypnosis is not _____. Approximately _____ out of ten people can be hypnotized. A typical hypnotic test is the _____ _____ _____ Scale.

28. There are many different hypnotic routines. Common factors in all hypnotic techniques encourage a person to: (1) focus _____ on what is being said; (2) _____ and feel tired; (3) "let go" and accept _____ easily; and (4) use vivid _____. Nevertheless, people will not act out suggestions they consider _____. Because a person must cooperate in order to become hypnotized, all hypnosis may really be just _____-_____. A key element in hypnosis is the _____ _____ effect.

29. Hypnosis does not seem to have a significant effect on _____, however, _____ can be enhanced through hypnosis. Hypnosis can relieve _____ and has been used to _____ subjects to childhood. Hypnotic suggestions concerning _____ seem to be among the most effective.

30. Hypnosis seems to have its greatest value as a tool for inducing _____, as a means of controlling _____ (in dentistry and childbirth, for example), as an aid to maintaining motivation (to diet, quit smoking, etc), and as an adjunct to other forms of psychological _____ and counseling.

31. Little or no _____ is necessary to do a good stage hypnosis act because stage hypnotists make use of several characteristics of the stage setting to perform their act. On stage, people are unusually _____ because they don't want to "ruin the act." Also, the stage hypnotist usually selects volunteers who are quite _____, and the label "hypnotized" acts as a _____. The subjects begin to feel like stars, and all the hypnotist need do is _____ the action. In addition, most stage hypnotists use _____ to put on a good show.

32. There are two major forms of meditation. The first is when attention is given to a single point and is called _____ meditation. The second is open or expansive and is called _____ meditation. It is not necessary to have a customized _____ to do meditation.

33. Medical researcher Herbert Benson believes that the core of meditation is the production of the _____ _____ which is an innate physiological pattern which opposes the stressful activation of the body's fight-or-flight mechanism. Studies have shown that bodily changes during meditation include reduced _____ rate, _____ pressure, and decreases in _____ tension.

34. Any major reduction in external stimulation is referred to as _____ _____. It appears to be one of the surest ways to induce deep _____ and to stimulate _____ thinking.

35. A substance capable of altering attention, memory, judgement, time sense, self-control, emotion, and perception is called a _____ drug.

36. When a person uses a drug to maintain bodily comfort, a _____ dependence exists. This is commonly referred to as _____ and occurs with drugs that cause _____ symptoms. This state is often accompanied by a drug _____ in which the user must use larger and larger doses to achieve the desired effect. When a person feels a need for a drug to maintain emotional well-being, a _____ dependence exists.

37. Amphetamines are synthetic _____ and are used medically to treat _____. Amphetamines are used illicitly to help a person stay _____ or temporarily improve mental or physical _____. Amphetamines rapidly produce a drug _____. They also speed the expenditure of bodily _____. Possible effects include _____, _____, night-mares, confusion, irritability and _____. Amphetamines (speed) may kill because they can cause a loss of contact with reality known as _____ _____ which results from damage to brain cells in the _____.

38. Cocaine is a powerful central nervous system _____ derived from the leaves of the coca plant. It produces sensations of _____, _____, _____-_____, _____, and boundless energy. _____ of all Americans between the ages of 25 and 30 have tried cocaine. Cocaine is very much like _____ in its effect on the central nervous system, but its effects are much more _____-acting. Cocaine's withdrawal pattern starts with a "crash" of _____ and _____ after a _____. Then begins a phase characterized by fatigue, _____, _____, _____, and _____. During withdrawal, cravings for cocaine are _____. Serious signs of cocaine abuse include _____ use, loss of _____, and disregarding _____. It should be noted, however, that _____ to _____ percent of cocaine abusers remaining in treatment programs succeed in breaking their addiction.

39. _____ is the most frequently used psychoactive drug in the U.S. It _____ the brain and increases feelings of _____. It is found in _____, _____, _____ _____, _____, and _____. This drug can lead to an unhealthy dependence called _____. This condition may result in _____, _____, loss of _____, chills, racing _____, and elevated _____. Even in the absence of this condition there are some risks including the development of _____ _____ in women, _____ cancer, _____ problems and high _____ _____. Pregnant women are now urged to avoid this drug entirely because of its suspected link with _____ _____. The equivalent of _____ cups of coffee per day may produce feelings of _____, _____, or fatigue.

40. _____ is a natural _____ found in tobacco. In large doses it causes stomach _____, _____ and _____, cold _____, _____, _____, and _____. There is growing evidence that it is _____. Smoking is responsible for about 97% of all of the _____ cancer deaths in the U.S. Smokers also endanger those nearby through secondary smoke which is thought to cause _____ percent of all lung cancers. Experts believe it is best to quit smoking _____ _____.

41.   Barbiturates are sedative drugs that _____ activity in the brain. They are used medically to calm patients or to induce sleep. In mild doses, barbiturates have an effect similar to _____, but an overdose can cause coma or _____. When combined with alcohol, barbiturates are particularly dangerous. When they are mixed, one drug may enhance the effect of another. This is known as _____ _____. Barbiturates are capable of causing a physical _____ and an emotional depression.

42.   Alcohol is the common name for _____ _____. It is a _____. In small amounts alcohol reduces _____ and produces feelings of _____ and _____. Greater amounts of alcohol cause progressively more dangerous impairment of brain function until the drinker loses _____. Alcohol can cause physical dependence and can definitely cause psychological dependence.

43.   Progression from a "social drinker" to a problem drinker to an alcoholic is often subtle. In the initial phase, the drinker begins to turn more frequently to alcohol to relieve _____. Four danger signals in this period are _____ consumption, drinking in the _____, behavior that is _____, and _____.

44.   After the initial phase comes the _____ phase in which a person begins to lose _____ over his or her drinking. The last phase is called the _____ phase in which the person begins to drink _____ and _____.

45.   Treatment for alcoholism begins by sobering the person up and cutting off the supply of alcohol. The procedure is referred to as _____ and frequently produces all the symptoms of drug withdrawal. The next step is to try to restore the alcoholic's physical _____. After he has dried out and his _____ has been restored, the alcoholic may be treated with _____, _____, or _____. Probably the method which has been the most effective in treating alcoholism is _____ _____.

46.   The active ingredient in marijuana is ___ ___ ___. It is a mild _____, and it also accumulates in the body's _____ tissue – particularly the _____ and the _____ organs. It produces its effects by binding to receptor sites on cells in the _____ _____. The evidence is conflicting as to whether marijuana produces _____ _____, but its danger lies in its _____ _____.

47.   Marijuana generally causes _____, _____, altered _____ sense, and _____ distortions. It is dangerous to _____ under the influence of marijuana or any other intoxicating drug.

48.   Marijuana is quite irritating to the _____. It also lowers _____ production in males or makes what _____ he has _____. THC has also been found to cause abnormal _____ cycles and disrupt _____ in female monkeys. THC has also been found to suppress the body's _____ system. Finally, marijuana causes _____ damage in animals.

49.   People seek drug experiences for a variety of reasons. The predictors for adolescent drug use and abuse are: _____ as well as _____ drug use; _____; _____ maladjustment; poor _____-_____; social _____; and stressful life changes. In other words, drug abuse may just be one part of a general pattern of _____ behavior.

50.   If a person has difficulty going to sleep, wakes up frequently at night, and/or wakes up too early this person has _____.

51.   As remedies for insomnia, nonprescription drugs have almost no effect. Even worse are prescription drugs or sedatives (usually _____) which decrease both Stage _____ and _____ sleep. An additional problem with prescription sedatives is that a drug _____ rapidly builds so that the initial dosage becomes ineffective. A greater number of pills is then required to produce sleep. This can lead to a serious type of insomnia known as _____-_____ insomnia.

52. There are two other types of insomnia. Worry, stress, or excitement can cause _____ insomnia. This sets up a cycle in which the inability to sleep causes more arousal, which causes more insomnia, etc. This cycle suggests that one of the best ways to beat the cycle is to avoid _____ it. Some people with this type of insomnia actually suffer a temporary drop in blood _____ during the night. This can be avoided by eating a small snack before bed, preferably one with the amino acid _____ which can help people sleep.

53. The other type of insomnia is termed _____. Treatment for this type usually begins with _____ training. It is also very helpful to adopt a _____ _____. It may also be helpful to avoid _____, to link only _____ with your bed, to write down _____, to learn a strategy for _____, and to use _____ intention which takes the _____ away from trying to get to sleep.

54. To help discover the meaning of dreams, Freud identified four dream processes. When a single character in a dream represents several people at once, this is known as _____. If the most important emotions of a dream are redirected toward safe images, this is known as _____. Freud believed that the meaning in dreams is _____ rather than literal. The last process is the tendency to reorganize a dream to make it more logical when remembering it. This in known as _____ _____.

55. Hall prefers to think of dreams as _____ and the dreamer as a _____. Hence, one would then consider the _____, cast of characters, _____, and emotions portrayed in a dream. According to Cartwright, the overall _____ _____ of a dream is a major clue to its meaning.

56. Ann Faraday considers dreams a message from _____ to yourself. She suggests the following techniques for catching a dream:
    (a) Before retiring, plan to _____ your dreams.
    (b) If possible, arrange to awaken _____.
    (c) If you rarely remember your dreams, you may want to set your alarm clock to go off _____ hour(s) before you usually awaken.
    (d) Upon awakening, lie still and review the dream images with your _____ _____.
    (e) Make your first dream record with your _____ _____.
    (f) _____ the dream again and record as many additional details as possible.
    (g) Put your dreams into a permanent _____ _____.
    (h) Remember that a number of drugs _____ dreaming.

57. Two such drugs that may have an effect on REM sleep are alcohol and marijuana. Alcohol is known to _____ REM sleep. Marijuana either slightly _____ REM sleep or has no effect at all on it.

58. Fritz Perls, the originator of gestalt therapy, considered dreams a message about what is _____ in our lives. Perls felt that dreams are a way of filling in gaps in _____ _____. He recommended that to understand a dream a person should "take the part of" each of the _____ and _____ in the dream.

59. History is full of cases where dreams have been a pathway to _____ and _____. Dr. Otto Loewi won a Nobel Prize for his research on the chemical transmission of nerve impulses. He was baffled at one point in his research but had a tremendous breakthrough based on a _____.

60. _____ dreams are those during which the dreamer "awakens" while in a dream.

Do You Know the Information?

Multiple Choice

1. (c) obj. 1, p. 221
2. (b) obj. 2, p. 221
3. (a) obj. 3, p. 222
4. (d) obj. 4, p. 222
5. (a) obj. 5, p. 223
6. (b) obj. 6, p. 223
7. (c) obj. 7, p. 223
8. (b) obj. 7, p. 223
9. (a) obj. 8, p. 223
10. (c) obj. 9, p. 224
11. (c) obj. 10, p. 225
12. (c) obj. 11, p. 225
13. (c) obj. 12, p. 226
14. (c) obj. 14, pp. 226-227
15. (c) obj. 14, p. 228
16. (a) obj. 14, p. 228
17. (b) obj. 14, p. 228
18. (a) obj. 14, p. 228
19. (a) obj. 16, p. 229
20. (a) obj. 16, p. 229
21. (b) obj. 17, p. 229
22. (a-e) obj. 18, p. 230
23. (d) objs. 18,20, pp. 230-231
24. (d) obj. 19, p. 230
25. (b) objs. 19-21, p. 231
26. (d) obj. 20, p. 231
27. (c) obj. 21, p. 231
28. (d) obj. 22, p. 232
29. (c) obj. 23, p. 232
30. (b) obj. 24, p. 233
31. (c) obj. 25, p. 233
32. (d) obj. 26, p. 234
33. (a) obj. 27, p. 234
34. (c) obj. 28, p. 234
35. (d) obj. 29, p. 235
36. (d) obj. 30, p. 236
37. (c) obj. 31, p. 236
38. (b) objs. 32-33, p. 236
39. (d) obj. 34, p. 237
40. (b) obj. 35, p. 238
41. (e,h) objs. 36-37, pp. 238-239
42. (a) obj. 38, p. 239
43. (c) obj. 39, p. 240
44. (b) obj. 40, p. 240
45. (a-g) obj. 41, pp. 242-243
46. (a-d) obj. 41, p. 242

47. (c) obj. 41, p. 245
48. (c) obj. 41, p. 246
49. (a,b,d,e,f) obj. 41, pp. 242-243
50. (e) obj. 43, p. 248
51. (e,f) obj. 41, p. 248
52. (g) obj. 41, p. 253
53. (g) obj. 41, p. 251
54. (g) obj. 41, p. 251
55. (d) obj. 41, p. 244
56. (b) obj. 43, p. 248
57. (a) obj. 44, p. 250
58. (c) obj. 45, p. 250
59. (b) obj. 45, p. 250
60. (d) obj. 46, p. 253
61. (b) obj. 47, p. 255
62. (c) obj. 47, p. 255
63. (d) obj. 48, p. 254
64. (c) obj. 49, p. 255
65. (b) obj. 50, p. 256
66. (a) obj. 51, p. 256
67. (b) obj. 52, p. 256
68. (d) obj. 53, p. 257
69. (b) obj. 54, p. 258

True-False

1. F, obj. 3, p. 221
2. F, obj. 7, p. 223
3. T, obj. 8, p. 223
4. T, obj. 9, p. 224
5. F, obj. 10, p. 225
6. F, obj. 10, p. 225
7. T, obj. 12, p. 226
8. F, obj. 13, pp. 226-227
9. F, obj. 15, p. 228
10. T, obj. 16, p. 229
11. T, obj. 16, p. 229
12. T, obj. 17, p. 229
13. F, obj. 18, p. 230
14. F, obj. 19, p. 230
15. F, obj. 20, p. 231
16. T, obj. 21, p. 231
17. F, obj. 24, p. 233
18. F, obj. 25, p. 233
19. F, obj. 27, p. 234
20. F, obj. 27, p. 234
21. F, obj. 28, p. 234
22. F, obj. 30, p. 236

23. T, obj. 30, p. 236
24. T, obj. 36, p. 238
25. T, obj. 41, p. 242
26. T, obj. 41, p. 244
27. F, obj. 41, p. 246
28. T, obj. 41, p. 247
29. F, obj. 47, p. 255
30. T, obj. 54, p. 257

Matching

1. Q, obj. 3, p. 221
2. L, obj. 27, p. 234
3. N, obj. 31, p. 236
4. A, obj. 49, p. 255
5. J, obj. 50, p. 256
6. M, obj. 19, p. 230
7. F, obj. 7, p. 223
8. E, obj. 41, p. 244
9. K, obj. 41, p. 248
10. C, obj. 42, p. 247
11. D, obj. 13, p. 226
12. R, obj. 20, p. 231
13. H, obj. 38, p. 239
14. B, obj. 3, p. 222
15. S, obj. 14, p. 228
16. T, obj. 35, p. 238
17. O, obj. 41, p. 245
18. W, obj. 48, p. 254

Can You Apply the Information?

1. (d) obj. 6, p. 223
2. (a) obj. 10, p. 225
3. (a) obj. 12, p. 226
4. (d) objs. 13,14,16,19, pp. 226-229
5. (b) objs. 14-17, pp. 228-229
6. (d) obj. 16, p. 229
7. (c) obj. 17, p. 229
8. (a) obj. 18, p. 230
9. (a) objs. 19-20, pp. 230-231
10. (c) obj. 21, p. 231
11. (a) objs. 32-33, p. 236
12. (d) obj. 35, p. 238
13. (c) obj. 40, p. 240
14. (a) obj. 40, p. 240
15. (d) obj. 41, pp. 242-243, 248
16. (a) obj. 44, pp. 249-250
17. (a) objs. 48-49, pp. 254-255

Chapter Review

1.   hypnogogic (p. 221)
2.   awareness, time, place, quality, pattern (p. 221)
3.   consciousness, enlightenment, pleasure, trance, communicate (p. 222)
4.   unresponsive, learn, complex (p. 222)
5.   tyrant, innate biological, coma, die, microsleep, sleep (p. 223)
6.   little impairment, attention, vigilant, routine, sleep-deprivation psychosis, delusions, hallucinations (p. 223)
7.   circadian rhythms (p. 223); energetic (alert) (p. 224)
8.   25 (p. 224); five, seven, eight, 20, 6, 2, 1 (p. 225)
9.   phase, agility, fatigue (irritability, nervousness, nausea, depression), several, 2, outside, 5 (p. 226)
10. direction, west, east, backward, advance, preadapt (p. 226)
11. fatigue, bloodstream, brain, spinal cord (p. 226); balance, "shutting down," pattern, amount (p. 227)
12. beta, alpha, sleep spindles, delta, delta, deep (p. 228)
13. light, hypnic jerk, myoclonus (p. 228)
14. one, two, three, four, three, two, one (p. 228 and fig. 7-8 on p. 229)
15. NREM, REM, REMs, dreams, 1 1/2, NREM, REM, stress (p. 229)
16. four, five, 90, 10, 30, flash, real (p. 229)
17. irregularly, blood pressure, breathing, sexually, paralyzed, REM behavior disorder (p. 230)
18. deep, sense, confused (p. 230)
19. night terrors, nightmares, REM, childhood, two (p. 230)
20. REM rebound, REM, crazy, dreaming, REM myth (p. 231)
21. insomnia, restless legs, narcolepsy, 20, sleep-wake, sleep drunkenness, hypersomnia (p. 231)
22. stimulate, 50, chemicals, memories, sensory, emotional (p. 232)
23. experiences, rooms, house (p. 232)
24. wish fulfillment, increase, unconscious, images (pictures), words (p. 233)
25. activation-synthesis, REM , brain areas, interpretation, brain, dream (p. 233)
26. Hypnosis, attention, suggestion, conformity, relaxation, imagination, obedience, suggestion, "magical," Mesmer, magnets (p. 234)
27. Braid, sleep, eight (p. 234); Stanford Hypnotic Susceptibility (p. 235)
28. attention, relax, suggestions, imagination, immoral (repulsive), self-hypnosis, basic suggestion (p. 236)
29. strength , memory, pain, regress, sensations (p. 236)
30. relaxation, pain, therapy (p. 236)
31. hypnosis, suggestible, responsive, disinhibitor, direct, deception (p. 237)
32. concentrative, receptive, mantra (p. 238)
33. relaxation response, heart, blood, muscle (p. 238)
34. sensory deprivation, relaxation, creative (p. 239)
35. psychoactive (p. 240)
36. physical, addiction, withdrawal, tolerance, psychological (p. 240)
37. stimulants, narcolepsy, awake, performance, tolerance (p. 241); resources (p. 242); fatigue, depression, aggression (p. 243); amphetamine psychosis, habenula (p. 244)
38. stimulant, alertness, euphoria, well-being, power, Half, amphetamine, short, mood, energy (p. 244); binge, anxiety, paranoia, boredom, anhedonia, intense, compulsive, control, consequences, 30, 90 (p. 245)
39. Caffeine, stimulates (p. 245); alertness, coffee, tea, soft drinks, chocolate, cocoa, caffeinism, insomnia, irritability, appetite, heart, temperature, breast cysts, bladder, heart, blood pressure, birth defects, 2.5, anxiety, depression (p. 246)
40. Nicotine, stimulant, pain, vomiting, diarrhea, sweats, dizziness, confusion, tremors, addicting (p. 246); lung, 20, cold turkey (p. 247)
41. depress, alcohol, death, drug interaction, dependence (addiction) (p. 248)
42. ethyl alcohol, depressant, inhibitions, relaxation, euphoria, consciousness (p. 248)
43. tension, increasing (p. 249); morning, regretted, blackouts (p. 250)
44. crucial, control, chronic, compulsively, continuously (p. 250)
45. detoxification, health, health, tranquilizers, antidepressants, psychotherapy, Alcoholics Anonymous (p. 250)
46. THC, hallucinogen, fatty, brain, reproductive, cerebral cortex, physical dependence, psychological dependence (p. 251)
47. euphoria, relaxation, time, perceptual, drive (p. 252)
48. lungs, sperm, sperm, abnormal, menstrual, ovulation, immune, genetic (p. 253)
49. peer, parental, delinquency, parental, self-esteem, nonconformity, problem (p. 253)

50. insomnia (p. 254)
51. barbiturates, four, REM, tolerance, drug-dependency (p. 254)
52. temporary, fighting, sugar, tryptophan (p. 255)
53. chronic, relaxation, regular schedule, stimulants, sleep, worries, relaxing, paradoxical, pressure (p. 255)
54. condensation, displacement, symbolic, secondary elaboration (p. 256)
55. plays, playwright, setting, plot, emotional tone (p. 256)
56. yourself, remember, gradually (naturally), one, eyes closed (p. 256); eyes closed, Review, dream diary, suppress (p. 257)
57. decrease, decreases (p. 257)
58. missing, personal experience, characters, objects (p. 257)
59. creativity, discovery, dream (p. 257)
60. Lucid (p. 258)

Conditioning and Learning

learning defined
  reinforcement
antecedents and consequences
classical (respondent) conditioning
  Ivan Pavlov
  elements
    neutral stimulus
    unconditioned stimulus,
    conditioned stimulus,
    unconditioned response,
    conditioned response,
  acquisition
    higher order conditioning
  extinction and spontaneous recovery
  stimulus generalization
  stimulus discrimination
  conditioned emotional response
    desensitization
  vicarious conditioning
operant conditioning
  classical & operant cond. compared

E. L. Thorndike
  law of effect
  reward vs. reinforcer
B. F. Skinner
  response contingent
  shaping (successive approximations)
  oper. extinction/spontaneous recovery
  positive and negative reinforcement
  punishment
reinforcers
  primary and secondary
primary and secondary reinforcement
  delay of reinforcement
    response chaining
    superstitious behavior
schedules of reinforcement
  continuous vs. partial reinforcement
    fixed ratio, variable ratio,
    fixed interval, variable interval
stimulus control

generalization
discriminative stimulus
punishment
  variables affecting punishment
    response cost
    incompatibility
  side effects of punishment
  how to punish
two-factor learning
  informational view
    mental expectancies
feedback (knowledge of results)
  programmed instruction
  computer-assisted instruction
  self-regulated learning
cognitive learning
  cognitive map, latent learning,
    discovery learning
modeling (observational learning)
  effects of television violence
behavioral self-management

To demonstrate mastery of this chapter you should be able to:

1. Define learning.

2. Define reinforcement and explain its role in conditioning. (See also Table 8-1.)

3. Differentiate between antecedents and consequences and explain how they are related to classical and operant conditioning. (See also Table 8-1.)

4. Give a brief history of classical conditioning.

5. Describe the following terms as they apply to classical conditioning:

    a. neutral stimulus (NS)

    b. unconditioned stimulus (US)

    c. unconditioned response (UR)

    d. conditioned stimulus (CS)

    e. conditioned response (CR)

6. Describe and give an example of classical conditioning using the abbreviations US, UR, CS, and CR.

7. Explain how reinforcement occurs during the acquisition of a classically conditioned response. Include an explanation of higher-order conditioning.

8. Describe and give examples of the following concepts as they relate to classical conditioning:

   a. extinction

   b. spontaneous recovery

   c. stimulus generalization

   d. stimulus discrimination

9. Describe the relationship between classical conditioning and reflex responses.

10. Explain what a conditioned emotional response (CER) is and how it is acquired.

11. Explain the concept and the importance of vicarious classical conditioning.

12. State the basic principle of operant conditioning.

13. Contrast operant conditioning with classical conditioning. Include a brief comparison of the differences between what is meant by the terms "reward" and "reinforcement."

14. Explain what response contingent reinforcement is.

15. Describe how Skinner's vision of behavioral engineering has been put into practice.

16. Explain how shaping occurs.

17. Explain how extinction and spontaneous recovery occur in operant conditioning.

18. Describe how negative attention seeking demonstrates reinforcement and extinction in operant conditioning.

19. Compare and contrast positive reinforcement, negative reinforcement, and punishment and give an example of each.

20. Differentiate primary reinforcers from secondary reinforcers and list four of each kind.

primary	*secondary*
a.	a.
b.	b.
c.	c.
d.	d.

21. Discuss three ways in which a secondary reinforcer becomes reinforcing.

a.

b.

c.

22. Discuss the major advantages and disadvantages of primary reinforcers and secondary reinforcers (tokens, for instance), and describe how tokens have been used to help "special" groups of people.

23. Describe how the delay of reinforcement can influence the effectiveness of the reinforcement.

24.   Describe response chaining and explain how it can counteract the effects of delaying reinforcement.

25.   Explain why superstitious behavior develops and why it persists.

26.   Compare and contrast the effects of continuous and partial reinforcement.

27.   Describe, give an example of, and explain the effects of the following schedules of partial reinforcement:

    a.   Fixed Ratio (FR)

    b.   Variable Ratio (VR)

    c.   Fixed Interval (FI)

    d.   Variable Interval (VI)

28.   Explain the concept of stimulus control.

29.   Describe the processes of generalization and discrimination as they relate to operant conditioning.

30. Explain how punishers can be defined by their effects on behavior. Include the concept of response cost in your answer.

31. List and discuss three factors which influence the effectiveness of punishment.

    a.

    b.

    c.

32. Differentiate the effects of severe punishment from mild punishment.

33. List the three basic tools available to control simple learning.

    a.

    b.

    c.

34. Discuss how and why reinforcement should be used with punishment in order to change an undesirable behavior.

35. List and discuss three problems associated with punishment.

    a.

    b.

    c.

36. List seven guidelines which should be followed when using punishment.

    a.

    b.

    c.

    d.

    e.

    f.

    g.

37. Explain how using punishment can be habit forming and describe the behaviors of children who are frequently punished.

38. Name two key elements that underlie learning and explain how they function together in learning situations.

    a.   b.

39. Explain what two factor learning is.

40. Explain classical and operant conditioning in terms of the informational view.

41. Define feedback, indicate three factors which increase its effectiveness, and explain its importance in learning.

    a.   b.   c.

42.   Describe programmed instruction and computer-assisted instruction and discuss their application in learning and teaching.

43.   Briefly describe the six strategies of self-regulated learning.

   a.

   b.

   c.

   d.

   e.

   f.

44.   Define cognitive learning.

45.   Describe the following concepts:

   a.   cognitive map

   b.   latent learning

46.   Explain the difference between discovery learning and rote learning, and describe the students who use each.

47.   Discuss the factors which determine whether or not modeling or observational learning will occur.

48.   Describe the experiment with children and the Bo-Bo doll that demonstrates the powerful effect of modeling on behavior.

49.   Explain why what a parent does is more important than what a parent says.

50.   Briefly describe the general conclusion that can be drawn from studies on the effects of TV violence on children. Explain whether this means that TV violence causes aggression or not and why.

51.   Describe the procedures and results of Williams' natural experiment with TV.

The following objective is related to the material in the "Applications" section of your text.

52. List and briefly describe the seven steps in a behavioral self-management program. Explain how the Premack principle may apply.

   a.

   b.

   c.

   d.

   e.

   f.

   g.

53. Describe how self-recording and behavioral contracting can aid a self-management program.

$$\boxed{\text{SELF-QUIZZES}}$$

Do You Know the Information?

Multiple Choice

1. Learning is a relatively permanent change in behavior due to
   (a) motivation.   (b) fatigue.   (c) experience.   (d) performance.

2. Reinforcement refers to
   (a) any procedure which alters the chances that a response will be made.
   (b) learning which occurs because of practice.
   (c) repeating a response to produce learning.
   (d) any event which increases the probability that a response will occur again.

3. When we discuss antecedents we are talking about
   (a) events that immediately precede consequences.   (c) learning that involves classical conditioning.
   (b) learning that involves operant conditioning.   (d) events that immediately follow consequences.

4.   The person most closely associated with the development and refinement of classical conditioning was
     (a) B. F. Skinner.   (b) Breland.   (c) Pavlov.   (d) Maslow.

5.   In classical conditioning, the US
     (a) usually produces a reflexive response.
     (b) is the stimulus that elicits the CR.
     (c) produces a learned response.
     (d) is the same as the CS.

6.   In classical conditioning the CR produces the
     (a) UR.   (b) CS.   (c) US.   (d) none of these.

7.   In classical conditioning, reinforcement occurs when
     (a) the CS is followed by the CR.
     (b) the CS is paired with or followed by the US.
     (c) the CR is followed by the US.
     (d) the UR is paired with the US.

8.   If the US never follows the CS, what will occur?
     (a) reinforcement   (b) extinction   (c) discrimination   (d) spontaneous recovery

9.   An extinguished response that reappears following a period of separation from the training situation is called
     (a) stimulus generalization.   (b) stimulus control.   (c) spontaneous recovery.   (d) acquisition.

10. When a CS reliably produces a CR, stimuli similar to the CS may also produce the CR by a process known as
     (a) stimulus generalization.   (b) stimulus discrimination.   (c) spontaneous recovery.   (d) disinhibition.

11. Conditioned emotional responses are learned when
     (a) a person is emotionally traumatized in the presence of the stimulus.
     (b) a fearful response is reinforced.
     (c) the response to the stimulus discriminates to related responses.
     (d) associated fearful responses are desensitized.

12. CERs can play an important role in our daily psychological functioning through the development of
     (a) phobias.   (b) reflexes.   (c) instincts.   (d) discriminations.

13. When CERs are learned by observing others this is called
     (a) generalization
     (b) vicarious classical conditioning
     (c) operant conditioning
     (d) nonreward

14. What is the basic principle of operant conditioning?
     (a) Acts followed by reinforcement tend to be repeated.
     (b) The US will not consistently produce the CR unless the CR is rewarding.
     (c) Reward is more effective than reinforcement.
     (d) Punishment is more effective than reinforcement.

15. Unlike classical conditioning, in operant conditioning
     (a) reinforcement is necessary.
     (b) the relevant responses are reflexive.
     (c) combined learning trials are used.
     (d) the response is emitted rather than elicited.

16. If a reinforcement is response contingent then the reinforcement
     (a) depends upon making a response.
     (b) is effective.
     (c) affects the performance of responses already learned.
     (d) does all of the above.

17. Shaping occurs when
     (a) reinforcement is given for any response as long as the organism actively behaves.
     (b) only the first response is reinforced.
     (c) successive approximations to the desired response are reinforced.
     (d) reinforcement is only given for every other response.

18. Two processes that are similar in function for both classical and operant conditioning are
    (a) extinction and successive approximations.
    (b) extinction and spontaneous recovery.
    (c) response contingent reinforcement and shaping.
    (d) none of the above.

19. Negative attention seeking is a good example of the application of _____ and _____ principles.
    (a) reinforcement; extinction (b) reward; reinforcement (c) shaping; punishment (d) discrimination; generalization

20. Negative reinforcement
    (a) is the same as punishment.
    (b) is a pleasant stimulus just like positive reinforcement.
    (c) decreases or suppresses behavior.
    (d) has the same effect on a response as positive reinforcement.

21. Negative reinforcement and punishment are different in that
    (a) negative reinforcement decreases responding.
    (b) one is a pleasant stimulus and the other is unpleasant.
    (c) negative reinforcement increases responding and punishment decreases responding.
    (d) punishment ends discomfort.

22. Praise, affection, and attention are all examples of _____ reinforcers.
    (a) latent   (b) secondary   (c) negative   (d) primary

23. Secondary reinforcers gain their rewarding value by being
    (a) exchanged for primary reinforcers.
    (b) associated with primary reinforcers.
    (c) learned.
    (d) all of these.

24. A major disadvantage of primary reinforcers is that they
    (a) may produce satiation too rapidly.
    (b) may begin producing a reduction in responding like punishment.
    (c) cannot be given immediately.
    (d) function like tokens.

25. If there is a delay between the behavior and the reinforcement
    (a) the two will be paired for a longer period of time and hence, more reinforcement will occur.
    (b) the effectiveness of the reinforcement will be diminished.
    (c) latent learning will occur.
    (d) the reinforcer will be more effective if it is primary.

26. When a series of behaviors or responses is maintained by one reinforcer _____ has occurred.
    (a) feedback   (b) response chaining   (c) cognitive learning   (d) successive approximation

27. Schedules of partial reinforcement, as contrasted with continuous reinforcement, produce
    (a) equally fast learning.
    (b) more rapid shaping.
    (c) more reinforcements per response.
    (d) slower extinction.

28. Which schedule of reinforcement would produce the *highest* rate of responding?
    (a) variable interval   (b) variable ratio   (c) fixed interval   (d) fixed ratio

29. The stimulus control principle of operant conditioning states that
    (a) responses reinforced in a particular situation tend to come under the control of stimuli present in that situation.
    (b) a response following a stimulus will tend to occur again.
    (c) a response not followed by reinforcement may be strengthened.
    (d) stimuli following a response alter the chances of its being repeated.

30. Which factors produce discrimination?
    (a) reinforcement and stimulus control
    (b) generalization and extinction
    (c) shaping and extinction
    (d) stimulus control and partial reinforcement

31. A punisher is
    (a) anything that will reduce the frequency of a desired behavior for all people.
    (b) effective anytime after the occurrence of the undesired response.
    (c) any consequence that reduces the occurrence of a target behavior.
    (d) something that removes response cost.

32. For punishment to be effective it should
    (a) be severe, but humane.
    (b) immediately follow the response.
    (c) be consistent.
    (d) be all of the above.

33. As opposed to mild punishment, more severe punishment
    (a) is not as effective at suppressing behavior.
    (b) abolishes the unwanted behavior.
    (c) more effectively stops behavior.
    (d) actually encourages the behavior to reappear later.

34. Which of the following is *not* one of the basic tools available to control simple learning?
    (a) Negative reinforcement strengthens a response by removing an unpleasant stimulus.
    (b) Nonreinforcement causes a response to extinguish.
    (c) Reinforcement strengthens a response.
    (d) Punishment suppresses a response.

35. Punishment can increase
    (a) avoidance.
    (b) escape.
    (c) aggression.
    (d) all of these.

36. Which of the following is *not* one of the seven guidelines which should be followed when using punishment?
    (a) Use mild punishment in cases where it produces actions incompatible with the response you want to suppress.
    (b) Expect aggression from the punished person.
    (c) Punish with kindness and respect.
    (d) Don't use punishment if you could ignore the behavior and make it go away.

37. Frequent punishment may make a child
    (a) unhappy.
    (b) aggressive.
    (c) fearful of the source of punishment.
    (d) feel all of these.

38. Two underlying elements of learning are
    (a) having responsive machines and information.
    (b) reinforcement and responsive information.
    (c) a responsive environment and information.
    (d) reinforcement and machines that make sounds.

39. Two-factor learning refers to the idea that learning involves both
    (a) primary and secondary reinforcers.
    (b) positive and negative reinforcement.
    (c) classical and operant conditioning.
    (d) reinforcers and punishment.

40. According to the informational view of conditioning,
    (a) CS's and operant reinforcers both predict US's.
    (b) CS's and operant reinforcers both create expectancies.
    (c) CS's predict US's and operant reinforcers predict CS's.
    (d) all of the above are correct.

41. In order to make feedback effective it should be _____, _____, and _____.
    (a) positive, accurate, consistent
    (b) frequent, immediate, detailed
    (c) frequent, immediate, constructive
    (d) timely, consistent, humane

42. Programmed instruction and computer-assisted instruction are examples of new applications of
    (a) KR.
    (b) negative reinforcement.
    (c) latent learning.
    (d) primary reinforcement.

43. Which of the following would *not* add more feedback to your study habits?
    (a) Plan a learning strategy which will help you accomplish your goals.
    (b) Silently ask yourself questions and give guidance as you study.
    (c) Keep records of your progress toward your learning goals.
    (d) Avoid confusion along the way by evaluating your study program only after your goal has been reached.

44. Learning that involves understanding, knowing, and other higher mental processes is termed
    (a) latent learning. (b) cognitive learning. (c) modeling. (d) motor learning.

45. _____ learning occurs with no obvious reinforcement of the correct response.
    (a) Latent (b) Cognitive (c) Verbal (d) Motor

46. As opposed to rote learning, discovery learning involves
    (a) memorization and repetition of facts.
    (b) a useful solution to the problem.
    (c) understanding and insight.
    (d) reinforcement.

47. Which of the following factors affects whether modeling (observational learning) will occur?
    (a) perceived size of the model
    (b) whether the model is live or on TV
    (c) status of the model
    (d) whether or not the learner has imitated before

48. In the experiment on observational learning using the Bo-Bo doll
    (a) most children imitated the attack they had seen an adult perform.
    (b) the live model inspired the most modeling.
    (c) the children seemed to perform only the acts they had previously seen performed.
    (d) the cartoon was actually slightly more effective in encouraging aggression than the live model.

49. Which of the following statements *best* describes the effects of TV on children?
    (a) Identification with aggressive characters does not appear to be a factor.
    (b) Children who watch a great deal of televised violence will be more prone to behave aggressively.
    (c) TV has been shown to cause aggression in children.
    (d) Although found to be a tremendous source of entertainment, TV has not been found to have a definite positive or negative effect on children.

50. Which of the following was *not* one of the findings from Williams' study of the effects of TV on children of a small Canadian town?
    (a) reading development increased
    (b) creativity test scores decreased
    (c) stereotyping of sex roles increased
    (d) verbal and physical aggression increased

51. Indicate (by circling) the steps involved in creating a self-management program to alter one's behavior.
    (a) choose a target behavior
    (b) extinguish non-target behaviors
    (c) record a baseline
    (d) establish goals
    (e) discriminate desired goals
    (f) choose reinforcers
    (g) decide on appropriate CS's
    (h) record your progress
    (i) generalize where necessary
    (j) reward successes
    (k) eliminate secondary reinforcers
    (l) adjust your plan

52. Utilizing _____ is one of the most direct of all approaches to changing personal behavior.
    (a) punishment (b) positive reinforcement (c) feedback (d) negative reinforcement

True-False

_____ 1. Operant conditioning deals with antecedents, whereas classical conditioning deals with consequences.

_____ 2. The US typically produces a UR.

_____ 3. Conditioning is most rapid when there is a delay between the presentation of the CS and the US so that the organism can think about what is being learned.

_____ 4. Classical conditioning depends heavily on voluntary behavior.

_____ 5. Stimulus generalization can create phobias out of CERs.

_____ 6. While deeply relaxed, a person can extinguish a CER through repeated exposure to emotional stimuli.

_____ 7. In contrast to classical conditioning, extinction occurs in operant conditioning when a learned response is reinforced excessively.

_____ 8. Positive reinforcement takes place when a pleasant event follows an action and increases the probability of the recurrence of the action.

_____ 9. A primary reinforcer is unlearned whereas a secondary reinforcer is learned.

_____ 10. A reward reinforces only the last response preceding it. This is the principle that explains superstitious behavior.

_____ 11. The effect of a partial schedule of reinforcement is to make the organism slow down and quit responding faster than continuous reinforcement would.

_____ 12. The slowest response rates are for interval schedules of reinforcement.

_____ 13. Stimulus control refers to the fact that stimuli present when a response is rewarded tend to control that response on future occasions.

_____ 14. Punishment is most effective when everyone has had a chance to cool down and review the situation.

_____ 15. Continued reinforcement of a response will not effect suppression of that response if it is subsequently punished.

_____ 16. If a person chooses to use punishment, an alternate, desirable behavior should be rewarded.

_____ 17. Punishment which attacks a person's self-esteem will be most effective in suppressing unwanted behavior.

_____ 18. The overall emotional adjustment of a child disciplined mainly by reward is usually superior to one disciplined mainly by punishment.

_____ 19. According to the informational view, conditioning creates expectancies which alter behavior.

_____ 20. More frequent feedback in a learning situation generally means faster learning or improved performance.

_____ 21. Rote learning is the first stage of discovery learning.

_____ 22. A cartoon version of aggressive adults attacking a Bo-Bo doll was only slightly less effective in encouraging aggression in children than a live adult model attacking a Bo-Bo doll.

Matching (*Use the letters on the right only once.*)

_____ 1. successive approximations
_____ 2. CS
_____ 3. stimulus generalization
_____ 4. vicarious
_____ 5. operant conditioning
_____ 6. successive approximations
_____ 7. paid by amount of work done
_____ 8. develops a great sense of time
_____ 9. VI
_____ 10. ICS
_____ 11. response cost
_____ 12. non-reinforcement
_____ 13. value of feedback
_____ 14. Premack principle

A. removal of reinforcer
B. secondhand
C. the process behind shaping
D. results in extinction
E. integral to the process of shaping
F. after conditioning, produces a CR
G. FI
H. involves multiple stimuli similar to the CS
I. FR
J. reinforcement after response
K. produces greatest resistance to extinction
L. primary reinforcer
M. KR
N. anything done often can act as a reinforcer

Do you understand concepts of positive reinforcement, negative reinforcement, and punishment? Using the following code, place the correct symbol in each box.

+ pleasant stimulus ↑ increases behavior

– unpleasant stimulus ↓ decreases behavior

	Nature of Stimulus	Effect on Behavior
Positive reinforcement		
Negative reinforcement		
Punishment		

Can You Apply the Information?

For questions 1-6 use the following example:

One day, five-year-old Barbara was running down the street. As she opened the gate to her friend's yard, a big dog jumped out and bit her. She was terribly startled and cried out in pain. She now cries whenever she sees any dog.

1. What was the original US?
   (a) the dog   (b) pain   (c) crying out   (d) the bite

2. Identify the current CS.
   (a) the dog   (b) pain   (c) crying out   (d) being startled

3. What is the CR?
   (a) running down the street   (b) touching the gate   (c) pain   (d) crying

4. If a dog never bites or makes a menacing move toward Barbara again it is possible that _____ may occur.
   (a) reinforcement   (b) conditioning   (c) stimulus generalization   (d) extinction

5. As a result of her experience Barbara becomes afraid and cries when she sees any four-legged furry animal. What has occurred?
   (a) spontaneous recovery   (b) vicarious conditioning   (c) stimulus generalization   (d) extinction

6. In this example, Barbara has developed a(n)
   (a) propensity for vicarious conditioning.   (c) fixed ratio schedule of reinforcement.
   (b) conditioned emotional response.   (d) delayed reinforcement behavior.

7. Mary learns not to play around a hot stove because she saw her brother burned severely while doing so. Mary's avoidance of the stove is a result of
   (a) vicarious conditioning.   (b) stimulus generalization.   (c) partial reinforcement.   (d) US-CR pairing.

8. You have been training your dog Bowzer to howl at the moon. Each time Bowzer has done it right you have given him a doggie treat which he just loves. Now however, as he is getting full, he appears not interested in doing any more howling and he is refusing the treats. What you have just discovered is
   (a) rewards can cease having reinforcing qualities.
   (b) because of the law of effect the response can't be strengthened anymore until Bowzer's appetite comes back.
   (c) response contingent reinforcement did not work in this instance.
   (d) howling has its own inherent reinforcing qualities.

9. You are trying to teach Jose to eat with a spoon. First you praise him for picking it up. Then you reinforce him for lifting it closer to his mouth. Next you reward him for putting food in the spoon. You are teaching Jose using
   (a) generalization. (b) successive discrimination. (c) shaping. (d) all of these.

10. If a child regularly throws temper tantrums in order to get dad's attention
    (a) he or she has had some reinforcement in the past for doing so.
    (b) extinction will probably not work now.
    (c) there has to have been some primary reinforcement for such behavior in the past.
    (d) the child has strong instincts.
    (e) you can bet the parents probably flunked their psych class.

11. You're getting your first kiss. From the sound (a nice, long "Ummm") that your date makes you are encouraged to continue. Your date's sound is a(n)
    (a) negative reinforcer. (b) positive reinforcer. (c) instinct. (d) punishment.

12. Same situation as above except in this case your date belches during the kiss. (Pretty gross, huh?) The next time this person calls to invite you out, you respectfully decline because
    (a) of positive reinforcement. (b) of modeling. (c) of punishment. (d) you can't "stomach" the person.

13. Your father nags you all day to wash the car. Finally, just to "turn his volume down," you wash the jalopy. Learning has been effected through
    (a) negative reinforcement. (b) positive reinforcement. (c) punishment. (d) non-reinforcement.

14. Oxygen is a good
    (a) negative reinforcer. (b) primary reinforcer. (c) secondary reinforcer. (d) generalized reinforcer.

15. "Step on a crack and you'll break your mother's back." If this is an actual superstition and not just a rhyme, you can bet that a long time ago
    (a) stimulus generalization occurred for some child.
    (b) there were successive approximations made which paid off.
    (c) some child came home and found his mother laid out with a broken back.
    (d) a child suffered vicarious classical conditioning.

16. You drive a cab for a living and get paid 40 cents for every passenger mile driven. Sometimes traffic is light and you can drive 50 miles an hour. What schedule of reinforcement are you on?
    (a) VI (b) FI (c) VR (d) FR

17. You work for the federal government and your reinforcement is money. You are salaried and get paid on the 1st and the 16th of each month. You have found that the huge bureaucracy covers up your lazy tendencies. You can get by with almost no work. Which schedule of reinforcement are you on?
    (a) VI (b) FI (c) VR (d) FR

18. Your camera has a built-in flash. A tiny light comes on to signal that the flash is ready. If you push the button before the light comes on, you ruin a picture. If you wait for the light signal, you get a good picture. You very quickly learn when to respond and when not to. A psychologist might say that
    (a) this is a good example of a conditioned response (CR). (c) you have been shaped.
    (b) stimulus generalization has occurred. (d) the tiny light now exerts stimulus control.

19. While walking along a sidewalk you look ahead and see what appears to be a Kennedy half dollar. You reach down and pick it up. It turns out to be a flattened bottle cap. You are embarrassed and hope nobody saw you. What has happened to cause your error?
    (a) shaping (b) spontaneous recovery (c) stimulus discrimination (d) stimulus generalization

20. At first a child calls all men "Dada." When most men do not reinforce her for her efforts but her father does, she limits her use of "Dada" to her father alone. Learning has occurred through
    (a) continuous reinforcement. (b) shaping. (c) discrimination. (d) generalization.

21. Mary hits her little brother frequently. Mary's parents want this behavior to stop. According to the principles in this chapter, which of the following would probably be *best* for all concerned?
    (a) Ignore Mary when she hits him.
    (b) Get mad and spank Mary.
    (c) Pay no attention to Mary when she hits him, but praise and hug her when she plays cooperatively with him.
    (d) Send Mary to her room for a few minutes when she hits her little brother
    (e) Scold Mary when she hits him, but praise her when she plays nicely with her little brother.
    (f) All of the methods would be equally effective.

22. If your child delights in turning off and on your TV set you could merely unplug it. This is an example of using
    (a) non-reinforcement.   (b) punishment.   (c) cognitive learning.   (d) negative reinforcement.

23. If you control your son's behavior by using large amounts of punishment, your son will be likely to
    (a) play very roughly with his friends.
    (b) try to avoid you.
    (c) have a poorer emotional adjustment than the boy next door who is controlled through rewards.
    (d) all of the above.

24. As a young mother, Betty decided never to punish her child by spanking. She felt that hitting her child would be a sign of poor parenting skills. However, one day she impulsively hit her child on the rear end for being particularly rude. The child immediately stopped the bad behavior and apologized. The next time the child is rude Betty is likely to
    (a) hit her again because of the prior negative reinforcement.   (c) wait until the child remembers what happened previously.
    (b) feel bad and ignore the rude behavior.   (d) positively reinforce good behavior when it occurs.

25. Alan's library has a new anti-theft device. If a person walks through it with a book that is not properly checked out, an alarm sounds. Many people (Alan included) have "absentmindedly" walked through after browsing in the library. After a few such experiences, Alan can feel the tension rising as he approaches the device. Circle all of the following statements which are correct.
    (a) The CR is the buzzer.
    (b) Alan would probably like to use a door without the alarm system.
    (c) This is probably an example of two-factor learning.
    (d) As Alan approaches the detection system, a mental expectancy is created. This is in agreement with the informational view.

26. Cynthia has wanted to take flying lessons but she has been afraid of making an error and crashing the plane while she is learning. The flight school at her airport has now installed a CAI flight simulator program to teach many aspects of flying in the classroom. Which of the following are likely results of this move by the flight school? (You may choose more than one.)
    (a) Cynthia's learning will be slower because of the lack of hands-on training.
    (b) The flight simulator program will only work if Cynthia is dedicated.
    (c) Cynthia will learn faster because she can crash many planes while operating the simulator and learn from her mistakes.
    (d) The simulator will provide immediate and detailed feedback about her shills while she is practicing them.

27. The lights go out in your house. It is so dark that you can't see your hand in front of your face. You have to find the flashlight that is in your bedroom. No problem! You can easily walk around your house in the dark. It is likely that
    (a) you know your way around because of discovery learning.
    (b) you have a cognitive map of your house.
    (c) darkness has become a generalized reinforcer.
    (d) you'll be in the local Emergency Room in an hour with swollen toes.

28. Bob and Janet have been lecturing to their 15-year-old son, who weighs 250 pounds, to lose weight by eating low fat foods and exercising regularly. Bob and Janet each weigh about 300 pounds, eat poorly, and get their largest amount of exercise while eating. The likelihood that the son will lose weight is
    (a) *good* because he will see his parents as bad examples.
    (b) *bad* because he is most likely to model their emotions.
    (c) *bad* because he is most likely to model their behaviors.
    (d) *good* because as a 15-year-old he knows he should strictly follow what his parents tell him to do.

29.   Bertha is a heavy smoker and wants to reduce the habit and eventually quit. According to what you learned in the chapter, if she simply records the number of times she smokes in a day, you would expect her
(a)   smoking to decrease.   (c)   smoking to remain the same.
(b)   smoking to increase.   (d)   initially decrease and then return to higher levels.

Chapter Review

1.   _____ is a relatively permanent change in behavior due to _____. In conditioning, some type of _____ must be present. Any event which _____ the chances that a _____ will occur again is called _____.

2.   Events before a response are called _____. Those that follow a response are called _____. Classical conditioning involves learning to associate _____ events with one another. Operant conditioning involves learning affected by _____.

3.   The Russian physiologist _____ first investigated classical conditioning. He taught dogs to salivate to the sound of a bell rung before meat powder was given to the dogs. In this example the meat powder is considered to be the _____ stimulus, and the bell is the _____ stimulus. It is important to recognize that initially the bell was a _____ stimulus because it did not produce salivation.

4.   A dog naturally salivates when food is placed in its mouth. Such "built-in" automatic, unlearned responses are called _____. Pavlov called these unlearned responses _____, whereas salivation to the sound of a bell alone is called a _____ response.

5.   In classical conditioning the connection between a conditioned stimulus and conditioned response is reinforced when the _____ _____ is followed by a(n) _____ _____. Once a response is learned, it can be used to bring about _____-_____ conditioning because a _____-_____ CS may be strong enough to act like a(n) _____ _____.

6.   In classical conditioning if the US does not follow the CS, the CR will be _____. After a rest period, the presentation of the CS may elicit the CR. This is called _____ _____.

7.   Once a subject is conditioned to respond to a particular stimulus, other stimuli similar to the CS may elicit a response. This is called _____ _____. In the opposite process, the subjects learn to respond to one stimulus, but not to others. This is called _____.

8.   Classical conditioning depends upon _____ responses. Fears such as phobias may be learned through classical conditioning and are called _____ _____ _____.

9.   The importance of CERs is extended by the fact that they can be learned _____. Learning to react emotionally to the experiences of others is called _____ classical conditioning.

10.   The basic principle of operant conditioning is that acts followed by _____ tend to be _____. Thorndike called this the _____ of _____. Classical conditioning is _____ and _____. Operant conditioning concentrates on _____ responses.

11.   Psychologists define an _____ _____ as any event that follows a response and increases its probability. To be effective, reinforcement should be _____ _____. In other words, getting a reinforcer depends on making a desired _____.

12.   There have been attempts to put Skinner's vision of _____ _____ into practice. Communities have been established based on his ideas. Reinforcements are given out based on _____ toward rent reduction.

13. When we reward responses that come closer and closer to the final desired behavior, the process is called _____. The basic principle of this process is that gradual or _____ _____ to the desired responses are rewarded.

14. Just as in classical conditioning, if a response learned through operant conditioning is not reinforced, it gradually ceases to be a part of an organism's behavior. This process is called _____. If the organism is removed from the testing apparatus and given a rest period, he is likely to resume making the learned response when returned to the testing situation. This is known as _____ _____.

15. Reinforcement and _____ are often combined to change behavior. For example, when parents pay attention to misbehavior, they are actually reinforcing _____ _____ seeking on the part of their children. To change that pattern of behavior, parents can praise their children for constructive play (i.e., _____) and ignore their disruptive behavior (i.e., _____).

16. When a pleasant event follows an action, the process is called _____ reinforcement. _____ reinforcement occurs when a response causes the _____ of an unpleasant event. Both of these reinforcers _____ behavior. _____ is any event which follows a response and _____ the likelihood of it occurring again. This event can either be the addition of an aversive event or the _____ of a positive event.

17. Reinforcers that are unlearned and biological in nature are called _____ reinforcers. _____ reinforcers are learned.

18. A secondary reinforcer may become reinforcing by being _____ with a primary reinforcer. They may also become rewards when they can be _____ for primary reinforcers. One problem with primary reinforcers is that people and animals receiving them may _____ quickly.

19. Reinforcement usually has its greatest effect on learning when the time lapse between a response and the reward is _____. Experiments show that when reward is _____, learning is retarded or does not occur at all.

20. It is often possible for a single reinforcement to maintain a long _____ of responses such as the sequence of events necessary to prepare a meal.

21. When behaviors develop as a result of _____ but actually have nothing to do with bringing about the _____, the behaviors are called _____. These acts appear to pay off to the person or animal. The existence of such behaviors points to the fact that a reinforcement will reinforce not only the last _____ that precedes it, but also other _____ occurring shortly before the reinforcement is given.

22. When reinforcement follows every response this is known as _____ reinforcement. Reinforcement which does not follow every response is termed _____ reinforcement. This latter type of reward makes a response very resistant to _____.

23. If every 3rd, 4th, 5th, or Nth response is followed by reinforcement, this is a _____ _____ schedule of reinforcement. This type of schedule produces an extremely _____ rate of response. In contrast to this, variable _____ schedules reinforce on an _____ number of responses. Since reward is less predictable, this type of schedule produces slightly greater _____ to extinction than the former type of schedule.

24. If a subject has to wait a set amount of time between one reward and the next, the schedule of reinforcement is called _____ _____. This schedule produces _____ response rates including periods of _____. When subjects are rewarded for the first response made after a variable amount of time has passed, the schedule is called _____ _____. This type of schedule produces _____, _____ responding and tremendous resistance to _____.

25. Responses which are reinforced in a particular situation tend to come under the control of _____ present in that situation. This is the principle of _____ _____.

26. Stimuli similar to those which precede a rewarded response also tend to produce a response because of _____ _____. When an organism responds differently to different stimuli, this is known as _____.

27. Any consequence that reduces the occurrence of a target behavior is, by defiinition, a _____. It can be either the onset of a(n)_____ event or the _____ of a positive state of affairs (i.e., _____ _____.) To be most effective, punishment should occur _____ a response is being made or _____ thereafter. It should also occur_____ _____ a response occurs, and it should be _____, but humane. It other words, the effectiveness of punishment depends upon its _____, _____, and _____.

28. Punishment that is effective in stopping behavior is usually _____. More often, however, punishment only tempo-rarily _____ a response. Responses _____ by _____ punishment usually reappear later.

29. There are three basic tools available to control simple learning: (1) _____ strengthens a response; (2) _____ causes a response to be extinguished; (3) _____ (when mild) suppresses a response but does not remove it. Intense punishment may permanently suppress a response. The three basic tools work best in _____.

30. If you choose to use mild punishment, it is best to also _____ an alternate, desirable response. This is because _____ does not teach new behaviors. In some cases mild punishment may work well when it produces actions _____ with the response you want suppressed.

31. There are three basic problems with punishment. One is that punishment is _____, and as a result situations and people associated with punishment also tend to be perceived as _____. Second, unpleasant stimuli usually encourage _____ learning and _____ learning. Third, punishment can greatly increase _____.

32. Do not use punishment if you can _____ behavior in any other way. Punishment should be applied _____ and one should use the _____ necessary to suppress the target behavior. Be _____, expect _____ from the person being punished, and punish with _____ and _____.

33. The overall emotional adjustment of a child disciplined mainly by reward is usually _____ to one disciplined mainly by punishment. Frequent punishment makes a person _____, _____, _____, _____, and _____ of the source of the punishment. However, punishment can be "_____ _____" because a sudden end to the irritating behavior that caused the punishment to occur acts as a _____ _____. Hence, punishment is more likely to occur in the future if it has been _____.

34. Two key elements that underlie learning are a responsive _____ and _____. Basically, _____ comes from knowing that you succeeded at getting a desired result.

35. Many real world situations involve a combination of classical and operant conditioning and are analyzed using _____-_____ learning.

36. According to the _____ view, learning creates _____ which alter response patterns. In classical conditioning the _____ creates an _____ that the _____ will be presented. Learning in operant conditioning is based on the _____ that a _____ will have a particular _____.

37. Particularly important to human learning is _____, information about what effect a response has had. To be most effective, _____ should be _____, _____, and _____.

38. Recently, new applications of feedback have been developed. One of these is _____ _____ which gives information to students in a format that requires precise answers about information as it is presented. In _____-_____ instruction (abbreviated ___ ___ ___), an individual _____ _____ transmits lessons to a display screen while the student responds by typing answers or by touching the display screen with an electronic pencil. Because CAI removes the fear of being _____ by the teacher, students can freely make _____ and learn from them.

39. A person can add more feedback through _____-_____ learning. Specifically, you should
    (1) set specific, _____ learning _____;
    (2) plan a learning _____;
    (3) be your own _____;
    (4) keep _____ or monitor your progress;
    (5) frequently _____ how well your are progressing in meeting your goals; and,
    (6) take _____ action if you are falling short of your goals.

40. _____ _____ refers to understanding, knowing, anticipating, or otherwise making use of higher mental processes. It extends into the realms of memory, thinking, problem-solving, and the use of concepts and language. A _____ _____ is an internal representation of relationships that acts as a guide in gaining an overall mental picture of some stimulus complex.

41. Cognitive learning is closely related to _____ learning where learning sometimes occurs with no obvious reinforcement at all.

42. In contrast to _____ learning where skills are acquired by repetition and memorization, _____ learning skills are acquired by using insight and understanding.

43. For modeling (observational learning) to occur several things must take place. The learner must pay _____ to the model and _____ what was done. Then the learner must be able to _____ the learned behavior. If a model is _____ or _____ the learner is more likely to imitate the behavior. This is also the case for models who are _____, admired, or high in _____. Once a new response is tried, normal _____ determines if it will be repeated thereafter.

44. The phenomenon of modeling was demonstrated in a classic experiment where children either saw a live model, a filmed model, or a cartoon version of a model displaying _____ toward a blow-up "Bo-Bo" doll. When later frustrated and allowed to play with the Bo-Bo doll, most _____ the _____. The cartoon was only slightly less effective in encouraging _____ than the live model.

45. Hundreds of studies involving over 10,000 children all point to the conclusion that if children watch a great deal of televised violence, they will be more prone to behave _____. It is not fair to say that television violence _____ aggression, just that it makes violence more _____. For example, one factor that influences this relationship between televised violence and aggression is the extent to which the child _____ with aggressive characters.

46. Williams' research with Canadian children and television demonstrated a _____ in reading development, a _____ in creativity scores, more _____ perceptions of sex roles, and an _____ in both verbal and physical aggression two years after the introduction of TV.

47. Reinforcement can be used to change one's behavior. Start by choosing a _____ behavior; that is, identify what you want to change. Then record a _____ so you'll know how much time you already spend performing the behavior. Next, establish _____ and make them realistic.

48. You also need to choose _____ for reaching your daily goals. Be sure to _____ your progress. _____ your successes and _____ your plan as you learn more about your behavior.

49. If you have trouble finding rewards, remember that anything done often can serve as reinforcement. This is known as the _____   _____.

50. You may find that merely _____ how often a certain behavior is performed is enough to modify it to your satisfaction. This is called _____-_____. If you have trouble modifying your behavior, you may find that _____   _____ will help increase your motivation.

ANSWER KEYS

Do You Know the Information?

Multiple Choice

1. (c) obj. 1, p. 261
2. (d) obj. 2, p. 261
3. (c) obj. 3, p. 262
4. (c) obj. 4, p. 263
5. (a) obj. 5, p. 264
6. (d) obj. 5, p. 264
7. (b) obj. 7, p. 264
8. (b) obj. 8, p. 265
9. (c) obj. 8, p. 265
10. (a) obj. 8, p. 266
11. (a) objs. 9-10, p. 267
12. (a) obj. 10, p. 267
13. (b) obj. 11, p. 268
14. (a) obj. 12, p. 268
15. (d) obj. 13, p. 269
16. (d) obj. 14, p. 271
17. (c) obj. 16, p. 272
18. (b) obj. 17, pp. 272-273
19. (a) obj. 18, p. 273
20. (d) obj. 19, p. 273
21. (c) obj. 19, p. 273
22. (b) obj. 20, p. 275
23. (d) obj. 21, p. 275
24. (a) obj. 22, p. 276
25. (b) obj. 23, p. 277
26. (b) obj. 24, p. 277
27. (d) obj. 26, p. 278
28. (d) obj. 27, p. 279
29. (a) obj. 28, p. 281
30. (b) obj. 29, p. 282
31. (c) obj. 30, p. 283
32. (d) obj. 31, p. 284
33. (c) obj. 32, p. 284
34. (a) obj. 33, p. 285
35. (d) obj. 35, p. 286
36. (b) obj. 36, pp. 285-286
37. (d) obj. 37, p. 287

38. (c) obj. 38, p. 287
39. (c) obj. 39, p. 288
40. (b) obj. 40, pp. 288-289
41. (b) obj. 41, p. 289
42. (a) obj. 42, p. 289
43. (d) obj. 43, p. 290
44. (b) obj. 44, p. 291
45. (a) obj. 45, p. 292
46. (c) obj. 46, p. 293
47. (c) obj. 47, p. 294
48. (a) obj. 48, p. 294
49. (b) obj. 50, p. 295
50. (a) obj. 51, p. 296
51. (a,c,d,f,h,j,l) obj. 52, p. 298
52. (c) obj. 53, p. 298

True-False

1. F, obj. 3, pp. 261-262
2. T, obj. 5, p. 264
3. F, obj. 7, p. 265
4. F, obj. 9, p. 267
5. T, obj. 10, p. 267
6. T, obj. 10, p. 267
7. F, obj. 17, p. 272
8. T, obj. 19, p. 273
9. T, obj. 20, pp. 274-275
10. F, obj. 25, p. 277
11. F, obj. 26, p. 278
12. T, obj. 27, pp. 279-281
13. T, obj. 28, p. 281
14. F, obj. 31, p. 284
15. F, obj. 32, p. 284
16. T, obj. 34, p. 285
17. F, obj. 36, p. 286
18. T, obj. 37, p. 287
19. T, obj. 40, p. 288
20. T, obj. 41, p. 289
21. F, obj. 46, p. 293
22. T, obj. 48, p. 295

Matching

1. E, obj. 16, p. 272
2. F, obj. 5, pp. 263-264
3. H, obj. 8, p. 265
4. B, obj. 11, p. 268
5. J, obj. 13, p. 269
6. C, obj. 16, p. 272
7. I, obj. 27, p. 279
8. G, obj. 27, p. 280
9. K, obj. 27, p. 281
10. L, obj. 20, p. 275
11. A, obj. 19, p. 273
12. D, obj. 33, p. 285
13. M, obj. 41, p. 289
14. N, obj. 50, p. 298

	nature	effect
pos. reinf.	+	↑
neg. reinf.	−	↑
punishment	−	↓

Ans.: objs. 3,12,19,31, pp. 262,268,273,284

Can You Apply the Information?

1. (d) objs. 5-6, pp. 263-264
2. (a) objs. 5-6, pp. 263-264
3. (d) objs. 5-6, pp. 263-264
4. (d) obj. 8, p. 265
5. (c) obj. 8, p. 265
6. (b) obj. 10, p. 267
7. (a) obj. 11, p. 268
8. (a) obj. 13, p. 269

Can You Apply the Information? (continued)

9. (c) obj. 16, p. 272
10. (a) obj. 18, p. 273
11. (b) obj. 19, p. 273
12. (c) obj. 19, p. 273
13. (a) obj. 19, p. 273
14. (b) obj. 20, p. 274
15. (c) obj. 25, p. 277

16. (d) obj. 27, pp. 279-281
17. (b) obj. 27, pp. 279-281
18. (d) obj. 28, p. 281
19. (d) obj. 29, p. 281
20. (c) obj. 29, pp. 281-283
21. (c) objs. 32-35,37, pp. 284-287
22. (a) obj. 33, p. 285

23. (d) objs. 35-37, pp. 285-287
24. (a) obj. 37, p. 287
25. (b,c,d) objs. 39-40, pp. 288-289
26. (c,d) objs. 41-42, p. 289
27. (b) obj. 45, p. 291
28. (c) obj. 49, p. 295
29. (a) obj. 53, p. 298

Chapter Review

1. Learning, experience, reinforcement, increases, response, reinforcement (p. 261)
2. antecedents, consequences (p. 261); antecedent, consequences (p. 262)
3. Pavlov, unconditioned, conditioned, neutral (p. 263)
4. reflexes, unconditioned, conditioned (p. 264)
5. conditioned stimulus, unconditioned stimulus, higher-order, well-learned, unconditioned stimulus (p. 265)
6. extinguished, spontaneous recovery (p. 265)
7. stimulus generalization, discrimination (p. 266)
8. reflex (p. 266); conditioned emotional responses (p. 269)
9. indirectly, vicarious (p. 268)
10. reinforcement, repeated, law, effect (p. 268); passive, involuntary, voluntary, (p. 269)
11. operant reinforcer (p. 269); response contingent, response (p. 271)
12. behavioral engineering, credits (p. 271)
13. shaping, successive approximations (p. 272)
14. extinction (p. 272); spontaneous recovery (p. 273)
15. extinction, negative attention, reinforcement, extinction (nonreinforcement) (p. 273)
16. positive, Negative, removal, increase, Punishment, decreases, removal (p. 273)
17. primary (p. 274); Secondary (p. 275)
18. associated, exchanged (p. 275); satiate (p. 276)
19. short, delayed (p. 277)
20. chain (p. 277)
21. reinforcement, reinforcement, superstitious, response, responses (p. 277)
22. continuous, partial, extinction (p. 278)
23. fixed ratio, high, ratio, average, resistance (p. 279)
24. fixed interval, moderate, inactivity (p. 280); variable interval, slow, steady, extinction (p. 281)
25. stimuli, stimulus control (p. 281)
26. generalization, discrimination (p. 281)
27. punisher, unpleasant, removal, response cost (p. 283); while (as), immediately, each time, severe, timing, consistency, intensity (p. 284)
28. severe, suppresses, suppressed, mild (p. 284)
29. reinforcement, nonreinforcement, punishment, combination (p. 285)
30. reinforce, punishment, incompatible (p. 285)
31. aversive, aversive (p. 285); escape, avoidance, aggression (p. 286)
32. discourage, immediately, minimum, consistent, anger, kindness, respect (p. 286)
33. superior, unhappy, confused, anxious, aggressive, fearful, "habit forming," negative reinforcer, reinforced (p. 287)
34. environment, information, reinforcement (p. 287)
35. two-factor (p. 288)
36. informational, expectancies, CS, expectancy, US, expectancy, response, effect (p. 288)
37. feedback (KR), feedback, frequent, immediate, detailed (p. 289)
38. programmed instruction, computer-assisted, CAI, computer terminal, watched (evaluated), mistakes (p. 289)
39. self-regulated, objective, goals, strategy, teacher, records, evaluate, corrective (p. 290)
40. Cognitive learning, cognitive map (p. 291)
41. latent (p. 292)
42. rote, discovery (p. 293)

43. attention, remember, reproduce, successful, rewarded, attractive, status, reinforcement (p. 294)
44. aggression, imitated, attack (p 294); aggression (p. 295)
45. aggressively (p. 295); causes, likely (p. 296); identifies (p. 297)
46. decline, drop (decline), stereotyped, increase (p. 296)
47. target, baseline, goals (p. 298)
48. reinforcers, record, Reward, adjust (p. 298)
49. Premack principle (p. 298)
50. recording, self-recording, behavioral contracting (p. 298)

memory (encoded, stored, retrieved)
sensory memory
  icon
short-term memory (STM)
  selective attention
  magic number 7, + or - 2
  chunking, rehearsal
long-term memory (LTM)
  dual memory, LTM permanence
  hypnosis and memory
  constructive processing
  pseudo-memory
  network model of memory
    redintegration
  procedural, semantic, episodic LTMs
measuring memory

recall, recognition (distractors),
  relearning (savings), implicit memories
priming
tip-of-the-tongue phenomenon
  feeling of knowledge
eidetic imagery
internal images
Herman Ebbinghaus
  curve of forgetting
why forgetting occurs:
  encoding failure, memory trace,
  decay, disuse, cue-dependent forgetting,
  state-dependent forgetting,
  interference,
    retroactive & proactive inhibition
repression versus suppression,

flashbulb memories
retrograde amnesia
  consolidation
  electroconvulsive shock
hippocampus
engram
  brain mechanisms of memory
how to improve memory
  knowledge of results (feedback),
  recitation, rehearsal, selection,
  organization, whole versus part learning,
  progressive part method,
  serial position effect, cues, overlearning,
  spaced practice versus massed practice,
  sleep, review, strategies
mnemonics

| LEARNING OBJECTIVES |

To demonstrate mastery of this chapter you should be able to:

1. Explain how memory functions like a computer.

2. Describe sensory memory. Explain how icons function in this memory system.

3. Describe short-term memory in terms of capacity, permanence, susceptibility to interference, and how information is stored. Explain the function of selective attention in this memory system.

4. Describe long-term memory in terms of permanence, capacity, and how information is stored.

5. Explain what dual memory is.

6. Explain what is meant by "the magic number seven (plus or minus two)."

7. Describe chunking and rehearsal and explain how they help memory.

8. Discuss the permanence of memory including the work of Penfield and the Loftuses.

9. Discuss the effects of hypnosis on memory. (Box 9-1)

10. Explain how memories are constructed. Include the concepts of constructive processing and pseudo-memories.

11. Briefly describe how long-term memories are organized including the network model and redintegration.

12. Differentiate procedural (skill) memory from fact memory. Differentiate the two kinds of fact memory — semantic memory and episodic memory.

13. Explain the tip-of-the-tongue phenomenon and the related feeling of knowledge.

14. Describe and give an example of each of the following ways of measuring memory:

    a. recall

    b. recognition (compare to recall and include the idea of distractors)

    c. relearning (include the concept of savings)

15. Distinguish between explicit and implicit memory. Describe how the concept of priming can demonstrate the existence of memories outside the realm of awareness.

16. Describe eidetic imagery and its effects on long-term memory.

17. Describe the concept of internal imagery and explain how it differs from eidetic imagery.

18. Characterize memory loss as demonstrated by Ebbinghaus' curve of forgetting. Discuss his findings as they relate to cramming versus spaced review.

19. Discuss the following explanations of forgetting:

    a. encoding failure

    b. decay of memory traces

    c. disuse (Give three reasons to question this explanation.)

        (1)

        (2)

        (3)

d. cue-dependent forgetting

e. state-dependent learning

f. interference (List and explain the two types of interference [inhibition] and how they are investigated in the laboratory.)

    (1)

    (2)

g. repression (and differentiate it from suppression)

20. Describe flashbulb memories and explain how they may be formed.

21. Describe the role of consolidation in memory, and explain how retrograde amnesia and electroconvulsive shock (ECS) can affect it.

22. Name the structure in the brain which is responsible for switching information from STM to LTM.

23. Discuss how memories are recorded in the brain by describing how learning is related to engrams, transmitter chemicals, or brain circuits.

24.   Describe each of the following in terms of how it can improve memory:

a.   knowledge of results

b.   recitation

c.   rehearsal

d.   selection

e.   organization

f.   whole versus part learning

g.   serial position effect

h.   cues

i.   overlearning

j.   spaced practice

k.   sleep

l.   review

m.   using a strategy for recall

25.   List and describe the four strategies of a cognitive interview.

a.

b.

c.

d.

The following objectives are related to the material in the "Applications" section of your text.

26.   Define mnemonics and explain the four basic principles of using mnemonics.

    a.

    b.

    c.

    d.

27.   List and describe three procedures for using mnemonics to remember things in order.

    a.

    b.

    c.

SELF QUIZZES

Do You Know the Information?

Multiple Choice

1.   Memory functions like a computer because
    (a) information is encoded.
    (b) information is stored.
    (c) memories must be retrieved.
    (d) of all of the above.

2.   Memory that holds an exact copy for about a second of what is seen or heard is called
    (a) eidetic imagery.   (b) LTM.   (c) sensory memory.   (d) short-term memory.

3.   Which of the following statements about short-term memory is *incorrect*?
    (a) It is severely affected by interference.
    (b) Its capacity is limited only by time.
    (c) Information removed from STM is lost.
    (d) Selective attention determines what information moves from sensory memory to STM.

4.   Which of the following statements about long-term memory is *incorrect*?
    (a) It has a limited (although large) capacity to store information.
    (b) Information which is meaningful is transferred from STM to this system.
    (c) It acts as a permanent storehouse for information.
    (d) It contains everything you know about the world.

5.   Short-term memories are to _____ as long-term memories are to _____.
    (a) images; sound   (b) sound; images   (c) meaning; meaning   (d) sound; meaning

6. Which of the following statements concerning STM and LTM is *correct*?
    (a) LTM is more subject to the effects of interference than is STM.
    (b) Selective attention screens the memories going directly into LTM.
    (c) The permanent loss of information once it is removed from STM keeps some useless trivia from cluttering up our brains.
    (d) Even if rehearsal is prevented, STM can still hold information for long periods of time.

7. Humans can normally retain about how many bits of information in STM?
    (a) 2   (b) 4   (c) 7   (d) 10

8. Which of the following statements concerning LTM is (are) *true*?
    (a) Brain stimulation produces memory like experiences in most people
    (b) Most long-term memories are only relatively permanent
    (c) Hypnosis can significantly improve memory
    (d) Memories are frequently updated in a process called constructive processing

9. The information in long-term memory is organized in terms of
    (a) networks of linked ideas.   (c) rules, images, categories, symbols, similarity.
    (b) formal or personal meaning.   (d) all of the above.

10. Which of the following statements regarding memory is *true*?
    (a) Procedural memory is involved in recalling who was the first president of the United States.
    (b) Episodic memories are more easily forgotten than semantic memories.
    (c) Our basic factual knowledge of the world is stored in episodic memory.
    (d) Semantic memories record life events.

11. The tip-of-the-tongue phenomenon occurs when
    (a) a memory is in STM but is not consolidated to LTM.   (d) an answer or memory is just out of reach.
    (b) the amount of memory saved exceeds the amount relearned. (e) a feeling-of-knowing reaction occurs.
    (c) a person depends upon internal images more than language.

12. Remembering or reproducing important facts and information without explicit cues or stimuli is called
    (a) redintegration.   (b) recall.   (c) relearning.   (d) recognition.

13. A test involving matching and multiple choice items measures memory using
    (a) redintegration.   (b) recall.   (c) relearning.   (d) recognition.

14. The importance of savings lies in its
    (a) ability to make relearning at a later date easier.   (c) beneficial effect on short-term memory.
    (b) ability to make recall easier.   (d) organizational and coding effects.

15. _____ memories are to awareness as _____ memories are to experience without awareness.
    (a) Explicit; long-term   (b) Explicit; implicit   (c) Implicit; short-term   (d) Redintegrative; recall

16. Which of the following statements regarding eidetic imagery and internal images is *incorrect*?
    (a) Most eidetic imagery disappears during adolescence and is quite rare in adulthood.
    (b) Eidetic images are projected out in front of a person.
    (c) Most eidetic memorizers have a better than average long-term memory.
    (d) Internal images occur when a person can "visualize" a memory in his or her head.

17. Ebbinghaus' curve of forgetting demonstrates that
    (a) forgetting is slow at first but increases dramatically as time increases.
    (b) meaningful words are forgotten more rapidly than shorter nonsense syllables.
    (c) intense review (cramming) before a test is an ineffective study technique.
    (d) forgetting is rapid at first and then levels off to a slow decline.

18. One of the most probable explanations of STM forgetting centers around
    (a) the decay of memory traces.
    (b) too much overlearning which may cause confusion.
    (c) cue-dependent forgetting.
    (d) disuse.

19. If a memory is not used, it may be forgotten through disuse. One problem with this explanation is
    (a) that some memories that are used are unable to be retrieved.
    (b) disuse fails to explain why some unused memories fade and others do not.
    (c) sometimes an elderly person has fantastic memory for recent events but can't remember the long-forgotten, trivial incidents.
    (d) all of the above.

20. You're trying to remember something. The memory is available but not accessible because the stimuli present at the time of learning are now absent. This is called
    (a) repression.   (b) interference.   (c) decay.   (d) cue-dependent forgetting.

21. The tendency for new memories to interfere with old memories is called
    (a) retroactive inhibition.   (b) repression.   (c) retrograde forgetting.   (d) proactive inhibition.

22. To investigate proactive inhibition the experimental group learns A, learns B, and then is tested on B. What happens with the control group?
    (a) They rest, then learn B and are tested on B.
    (b) They are the same as the experimental group except they rest during B.
    (c) They do nothing but test A to measure the effects of relaxation.
    (d) They learn A, learn B, and then are tested on B.

23. When you cannot recall a memory that is unpleasant or disturbing, you may be experiencing which of the following?
    (a) repression   (b) depression   (c) suppression   (d) regression

24. The difference between suppression and repression is
    (a) suppression is an active attempt not to think of something.
    (b) true repression is an unconscious event.
    (c) when we use repression we are unaware that forgetting has even occurred.
    (d) all of the above.

25. Most flashbulb memories are
    (a) negative.
    (b) positive.
    (c) probably of important, surprising, or emotional events.
    (d) the result of increased levels of growth hormone secreted during emotion or stress.

26. The process of consolidation refers to how information
    (a) gets into STM.
    (b) is retrieved from LTM.
    (c) is recalled from STM.
    (d) is formed into a long-term memory.

27. Which of the following can *prevent* a memory from being consolidated?
    (a) lack of rehearsal   (b) electroconvulsive shock   (c) a head injury   (d) all of these

28. Recent studies have shown that learning may occur because
    (a) the electrical activity, structure, and chemistry of the brain may be altered.
    (b) nerve cells in a circuit may alter the amount of transmitter chemicals they release.
    (c) certain circuits may be strengthened or weakened.
    (d) of all of the above.

29. Circle any of the following which will tend to *increase* your ability to retain information in memory.
    (a) boil the information in paragraphs down to several key ideas
    (b) using massed instead of spaced practice
    (c) rehearsing the items or concepts
    (d) learning in a novel environment to heighten your attention
    (e) using sleep learning devices
    (f) learning the information in a place where there is little distraction or interference

30. The serial position effect indicates the last material to be learned in a sequence and the most difficult to recall is
    (a) the last part.   (b) the first part.   (c) the middle part.   (d) all are learned equally well.

31. Which of the following is *not* a search strategy for finding a "lost" memory?
    (a) Mentally re-create the learning environment.
    (b) Recall from a single viewpoint to avoid the inherent confusion factor.
    (c) Recall events in different orders.
    (d) Write down everything you can remember.

True-False

_____ 1. The three memory systems are sensory memory, short-term memory, and long-term memory.

_____ 2. One might accurately say that long-term memories are relatively permanent.

_____ 3. Memories for things which never happened but which nevertheless are firmly believed by people are called pseudo-memories.

_____ 4. Redintegration is the process that connects short-term memories for recoding.

_____ 5. Redintegration is the amount of material that is left before a person must remaster information.

_____ 6. Recognition as a measure of memory is usually superior to recall.

_____ 7. The incidence of eidetic imagery is much greater among adults than among children.

_____ 8. According to Ebbinghaus' curve of forgetting, most forgetting occurs at first.

_____ 9. The less time there is between reviewing for a test and the taking of the test, the more forgetting that will occur.

_____ 10. An obvious reason for forgetting is that a memory was never formed in the first place.

_____ 11. Information learned in one particular emotional or physiological state is best remembered in that same state. This is state-dependent learning.

_____ 12. The hypothalamus plays an important role in the formation of long-term memories.

_____ 13. In the progressive part method of memorizing, the learner learns part A, then part B, then part C, and then puts them all together.

_____ 14. Learning something beyond bare mastery is called overlearning. It improves learning.

_____ 15. A mnemonic is a kind of memory system or aid.

Matching *(Use the letter on the right only once.)*

_____ 1. image
_____ 2. most memory chores handled by
_____ 3. chunking
_____ 4. STM prolonged by
_____ 5. updating memories
_____ 6. semantic memory
_____ 7. proactive inhibition
_____ 8. a head injury may cause it
_____ 9. hippocampus
_____ 10. Karl Lashley looked for this
_____ 11. middle of list harder to learn
_____ 12. relies heavily on mental pictures

A. serial position effect
B. hypothalamus
C. prior learning interferes with later learning
D. rehearsal
E. mnemonics
F. dual memory
G. STM
H. LTM
I. putting smaller units together into larger ones
J. retrograde amnesia
K. retroactive inhibition
L. constructive processing
M. icon
N. particularly important brain structure for memory
O. basic factual knowledge about the world
P. procedural memory
Q. engram

Can You Apply the Information?

1. Which of the following would require the use of only sensory memory and STM?
   (a) remembering the measured height of a cabinet as you write the number down
   (b) remembering your name as you write it on a job application
   (c) remembering the letters of the alphabet
   (d) remembering your mother's name

2. If you smell a perfume that reminds you of what happened on a date 20 years ago at a drive-in movie, you are experiencing
   (a) recognition.   (b) recall.   (c) relearning.   (d) redintegration.

3. Remembering that the funny-lookings at the end of your feet are called toes is an example of
   (a) sensory memory.   (b) semantic memory.   (c) procedural memory.   (d) episodic memory.

4. Gloria is a vice-president at IBM and must travel to France on business. She decides to take a refresher course in French. She finds that the language is easier to master the second time around. She has experienced the phenomenon of
   (a) internal images.   (b) recall.   (c) savings.   (d) recognition.

5. One of your classmates always does well on psychology exams. One day after class you get the opportunity to corner her to find out her secret. She reports that during a test she can actually see her notes on the desk in front of her. You surmise that she probably has
   (a) eidetic imagery.
   (b) fantastic relearning skills.
   (c) efficient organizing skills for LTM.
   (d) internal images.
   (e) pulled a little whoopee in class.

6. According to Ebbinghaus' curve of forgetting, if a person is studying for a test he or she should
   (a) use spaced practice for review and not get anxious and cram shortly before a test.
   (b) study for a week to 10 days before the test but put the books away a day before the test.
   (c) avoid interference by studying only a couple of hours before the test with an hour or so of cramming.
   (d) use spaced practice with short, daily study sessions and cram right before the test.

7. You're out shopping and someone gives you a phone number to remember. You say it over and over many times but can't find a pencil to write it down for 20 minutes. You forget the number. In this case the forgetting is probably due to
   (a) repression.   (b) disuse.   (c) decay.   (d) lack of relevant cues.

8. You have a psychology test scheduled for 11 a.m. You studied for it last night and again this morning. It is now 10 a.m. and you decide to take a break and study anthropology. It is likely that as you are taking the psychology test
   (a) you will suffer retroactive inhibition for the psychology material.
   (b) consolidation of the psychology will not occur.
   (c) proactive inhibition will occur for the psychology material.
   (d) your hippocampus will not be allowed to function properly.

9. Last year while ice skating you fell in front of a group of people and made a fool of yourself. When reminded of the incident this year you cannot remember it at all. This forgetting is probably a result of
   (a) interference.   (b) suppression.   (c) repression.   (d) electroconvulsive shock.

10. You are embarrassed when you think of how you acted at the party, so you try not to remember it. This is an example of
   (a) repression.   (b) suppression.   (c) lack of consolidation.   (d) a disorder of the hippocampus.

11. John is 42 years old and can vividly remember his first day in school when he was only 6 . He remembers being excited and scared at the same time. This memory is most likely a(n)
   (a) eidetic image.   (b) pseudo-memory.   (c) short-term memory.   (d) flashbulb memory.

12. You are plotting to overthrow a government. You want to develop a technique to keep people from remembering what you are planning to do, but you don't want to permanently affect their memories or their ability to remember. Which of the following should you do?
   (a) destroy the hippocampus   (c) interrupt the consolidation process
   (b) wipe out their LTM systems   (d) all of the above

13. Herman can easily learn his multiplication tables but can't remember what he was doing on the ladder before he fell and hit his head. Herman is suffering from
   (a) retrograde amnesia.   (b) suppression.   (c) a lack of icons.   (d) decay of engrams.

14. Remembering the 12 cranial nerves by learning a rhyme to go with them is an example of
   (a) chaining.   (b) using a mnemonic system.   (c) memory transfer.   (d) chunking.

Chapter Review

1. In some ways memory acts like a _____ because information is first _____. Then the information is _____, and finally it is _____.

2. There are several steps in placing information in permanent memory. First, incoming information enters _____ memory. If the information is seen, an _____ (image) persists.

3. _____ _____ determines what information goes from _____ memory to _____ - _____ memory where it is most often stored by _____. This memory system is not _____ and is severely affected by _____ or _____.

4. The third stage of memory is called _____ - _____ memory and is relatively _____ with almost limitless _____. These memories are stored on the basis of _____. Most of our daily memory chores are handled by _____ memory, a combination of __ __ __ and __ __ __ .

5. S T M can only hold about ____ (___ or ___ two) bits of information. If separate bits of information can be combined or _____, more information can be handled. S T M can be prolonged if it is _____.

6. It is probably most accurate to say that long-term memories are _____ permanent. As new memories are formed, older memories are often _____. This process is called _____ processing. Gaps in memory may be filled in by _____ , _____ , or _____. Such memories are then called _____ - _____.

7. Research shows that a _____ person is more likely than normal to use _____ to fill in gaps in memory. It can be concluded that _____ does not greatly improve memory.

8. The information in LTM is usually organized around _____, _____, _____, _____, _____, _____ meaning, or _____ meaning. Some researchers believe that LTM is organized as a _____ of linked _____, hence the term _____ model. _____ memories demonstrate the "branches" of memory networks.

9. LTM tends to fall into two categories. _____ memory includes actions like typing or playing tennis. Specific information which is learned is placed in _____ memory. This kind of memory is further divided into two other types. Most of our factual knowledge about the world is almost totally immune to forgetting and is called _____ memory. _____ memory records life events day after day and is more easily forgotten than _____ memories.

10. The experience of having an answer or a memory just out of reach is known as the _____ - _____ - _____ - _____ phenomenon. On the other hand, knowing that you are likely to remember something is called the _____ of _____.

11. There are some common techniques for retrieving information. To _____ means to remember or reproduce important facts and information without explicit cues. A multiple-choice examination is based on the retrieval mechanism known as _____. This is a more sensitive testing procedure than _____, but this depends greatly on the kinds of _____ used.

12. Testing memory by _____ shows that it takes less time and effort to master previously learned material. This difference in time is known as _____.

13. When dealing with _____ memories, one deals with past experiences of which one is aware. _____ memories on the other hand lie outside awareness. Hidden memories can be _____.

14. _____ _____ occurs when a person has visual images clear enough to be scanned or retained for at least 30 seconds after viewing a picture. Such memory is usually only observed in _____. The majority of _____ memorizers have no better _____-_____ memory than the average person.

15. Although most adults do not exhibit _____ memory, some adults have extremely vivid _____ _____ which can result in very accurate memories.

16. In Ebbinghaus' famous experiment involving memory and the _____ of _____, he found that _____ was _____ at first and then _____ declined. Students who _____ periodically and then intensely right before an exam have been found to remember much more than students who do not.

17. Probably the most obvious reason for forgetting is that a _____ was never formed in the first place. Another view of forgetting is that _____ _____ (changes in nerve cells or brain activity) fade or _____ over a period of time. Such fading applies to _____ memory and __ __ __.

18. The decay of memory traces also has appeal as an explanation for long-term forgetting. Perhaps long-term memory traces fade from _____. There are reasons to question this idea. One is the recovery of seemingly forgotten memories through _____. Another is that _____ fails to explain why some unused memories _____ and others are carried for life. A third contradiction deals with the apparent fading of _____ memories in elderly people while they can remember trivial events from 30 years ago.

19. There are other explanations of LTM forgetting. One of them emphasizes that many memories appear to be _____ but not _____ because _____ present at the time of learning are no longer present when the memory needs to be retrieved. This is called _____-_____ forgetting. This is similar to _____-_____ learning in which information learned under one internal state is best recalled when in a similar _____.

20. Another possibility is that much forgetting can be attributed to _____ of memories with one another. When recent learning interferes with memory of prior learning, _____ inhibition has occurred. The opposite is when old learning interferes with new learning. This is called _____ inhibition.

21. When memories which are painful or threatening are held out of consciousness by forces within one's personality, this is called _____. This can be distinguished from _____, an active attempt to put something out of mind.

22. _____ memories describe lasting images that are frozen in memory when an event is _____, important, or _____.

23. The forming of a long-term memory is called _____. One part of the brain (the _____) is especially important for this purpose. Memory is especially susceptible to _____ during the time that it takes for it to be transferred from temporary storage to long-term storage.

24. If a person suffers a head injury as a memory is being formed, some of the memory may be lost. This is called _____ amnesia. Another way to wipe out a memory that is being formed is to apply a mild electrical shock to the brain. This is called _____ _____. In any event, _____ memories are more easily disrupted than are _____ memories.

25. Initially, researchers sought to find evidence of an _____ or memory trace. Researchers have found that learning may be related to the amount of _____ chemicals released by certain nerve cells in a circuit. Such changes essentially determine which circuits get _____ and which become _____.

26. Several suggestions have been made for improving memory. One of these emphasizes the importance of _____ or knowledge of results. This method can help you identify material that needs extra practice. A very good way to provide knowledge of results is through _____, repeating to yourself what you have learned.

27. Rehearsal refers to _____ repeating, paraphrasing, and _____ information. This process is similar to _____ but an be done privately. Another suggestion is to boil down paragraphs to one or two important terms or ideas. This is the process of _____.

28. Students may find it helpful to _____ class notes and the important ideas or concepts in a class. Also, it is generally better to study _____ units of information rather than small parts. Try to study the largest _____ amount of information possible at one time.

29. For very long or complex material, try the _____ _____ method. In this approach, you study part "A" until it is mastered. Next you study parts "___" and "___"; then "___", "___", and "___", and so forth.

30. Whenever you must learn something in order, be aware of the _____ _____ effect. This is the tendency to make the most errors in remembering the _____ of the list, so you should give those items the most attention.

31. It helps to _____ information as you learn it because knitting _____ cues into your memory code helps in retrieving information when you need it.

32. Numerous studies have shown that memory is greatly improved by _____, that is, study continued beyond bare mastery. _____ practice is generally superior to _____ practice. By scheduling your time into brief study sessions, you maximize your study skills.

33. Remember that _____ after study produces the least interference. It is wise to _____ shortly before an exam to cut down the time during which you must remember details.

34. In addition, successful recall is usually the result of a planned _____ of memory using a variety of cues to help open more _____ to a memory.

35. Memory systems or aids are called _____ techniques. By using these techniques _____ learning (learning by simple repetition) can be avoided. The superiority of _____ learning over rote learning has been demonstrated many times.

36. The basic principles of mnemonics are to use mental _____, make things _____, make information _____, and form _____ mental associations.

ANSWER KEYS

Do You Know the Information?

Multiple Choice

1. (d) obj. 1, p. 302
2. (c) obj. 2, p. 302
3. (b) obj. 3, p. 303
4. (a) obj. 4, p. 304
5. (d) objs. 3-4, pp. 303-304
6. (c) objs. 3-4, p. 303
7. (c) obj. 6, p. 305
8. (b,d) objs. 8-10, p. 307
9. (d) obj. 11, p. 308
10. (b) obj. 12, p. 310
11. (d) obj. 13, p. 311
12. (b) obj. 14, p. 311
13. (d) obj. 14, p. 312
14. (a) obj. 14, p. 313
15. (b) obj. 15, p. 314
16. (c) objs. 16-17, p. 315
17. (d) obj. 18, p. 317
18. (a) obj. 19, p. 319
19. (b) obj. 19, p. 319
20. (d) obj. 19, p. 319
21. (a) obj. 19, p. 321
22. (a) obj. 19, p. 321
23. (a) obj. 19, p. 322
24. (d) obj. 19, p. 323
25. (c) obj. 20, p. 323
26. (d) obj. 21, p. 324

27. (d) objs. 7, 21, pp. 306, 324
28. (d) obj. 23, p. 325
29. (a,c,f) obj. 24, pp. 327-328
30. (c) obj. 24, p. 327
31. (b) obj. 25, p. 328

True-False

1. T, objs. 2-4, pp. 302-304
2. T, obj. 8, p. 307
3. T, obj. 10, p. 307
4. F, obj. 11, p. 308
5. F, obj. 11, p. 308
6. T, obj. 14, p. 310
7. F, obj. 16, p. 314
8. T, obj. 18, p. 317
9. F, obj. 18, p. 318
10. T, obj. 19, p. 318
11. T, obj. 19, p. 320
12. F, obj. 22, p. 325
13. F, obj. 24, p. 327
14. T, obj. 24, p. 328
15. T, obj. 26, p. 330

Matching

1. M, obj. 2, p. 303
2. F, obj. 5, p. 304
3. I, obj. 7, p. 305
4. D, obj. 7, p. 306
5. L, obj. 10, p. 307
6. O, obj. 12, p. 310
7. C, obj. 19, p. 321
8. J, obj. 21, p. 323
9. N, obj. 22, p. 325
10. Q, obj. 23, p. 325
11. A, obj. 24, p. 327
12. E, obj. 26, p. 330

Can You Apply the Information?

1. (a) obj. 3, pp. 302-303
2. (d) obj. 11, p. 308
3. (b) obj. 12, p. 310
4. (c) obj. 14, p. 313
5. (a) objs. 16-17, pp. 314-315
6. (d) obj. 18, p. 318
7. (c) obj. 19, p. 318
8. (a) obj. 19, p. 321
9. (c) obj. 19, p. 322
10. (b) obj. 19, p. 323
11. (d) obj. 20, p. 323
12. (c) obj. 21, p. 324
13. (a) obj. 21, p. 323
14. (b) obj. 26, p. 330

Chapter Review

1. computer, encoded, stored, retrieved (p. 302)
2. sensory, icon (p. 302)
3. Selective attention, sensory, short-term, sound, permanent, interruption, interference (p. 303)
4. long-term, permanent, capacity, meaning (importance), dual, STM, LTM (p. 304)
5. seven, plus, minus, chunked, rehearsed (p. 305)

6. relatively, updated (changed, revised, lost), constructive, logic, guesses, new information, pseudo-memories (p. 307)
7. hypnotized, imagination, hypnosis (p. 308)
8. rules, images, categories, symbols, similarity, formal, personal, network, ideas, network, Redintegrative (p. 308)
9. Procedural (skill), fact (p. 309); semantic, Episodic, semantic (p. 310)
10. tip-of-the-tongue, feeling, knowing (p. 311)
11. recall (p. 311); recognition, recall (p. 312)
12. relearning, savings (p. 313)
13. explicit, Implicit, primed (p. 314)
14. Eidetic imagery, children (p. 314); eidetic, long-term (p. 315)
15. eidetic, internal images (p. 315)
16. curve, forgetting, forgetting, rapid, slowly, review (p. 317)
17. memory, memory traces, decay, sensory, STM (p. 318)
18. disuse, redintegration, disuse, fade, recent (p. 319)
19. available, accessible, cues, cue-dependent, state-dependent, state (p. 319)
20. interference, retroactive, proactive (p. 321)
21. repression, suppression (p. 322)
22. Flashbulb, surprising, emotional (p. 323)
23. consolidation (p. 324); hippocampus, interference (p. 325)
24. retrograde, electroconvulsive shock, reent, older (p. 324)
25. engram (p. 325); transmitter, stronger, weaker (p. 326)
26. feedback, recitation (p. 326)
27. mentally, summarizing, reitation, selection (p. 327)
28. organize, whole (large), meaningful (p. 327)
29. progressive part, A, B, A, B, C (p. 327)
30. serial position, middle (p. 327)
31. elaborate, meaningful (p. 327)
32. overlearning, Spaced, massed (p. 328)
33. sleep, review (p. 328)
34. search, paths (p. 329)
35. mnemonic, rote, mnemonic (p. 330)
36. pictures, meaningful, familiar, bizarre (unusual, exaggerated) (p. 330)

chapter ten

Cognition, Intelligence, and Creativity

---| **KEY TERMS, CONCEPTS, AND INDIVIDUALS** |---

thinking
  cognition
  internal representation
basic units of thought
  images, muscular responses,
  concepts, language (symbols)
stored versus created images
  size of images
muscular imagery
concepts and their formation
  conjunctive, relational, disjunctive
  prototypes
denotative versus connotative meanings
semantic differential
semantics
symbols
  phonemes, morphemes
grammar
syntax
transformation rules
language must be productive
  talking chimps
conditional relationship

mechanical problem solving
  trial and error, rote
solutions by understanding
  general properties, functional solutions
heuristics vs. random search strategies
abilities for insight
  selective encoding
  selective combination
  selective comparison
fixation
artificial intelligence
  computer simulations
  expert systems
Alfred Binet
intelligence defined
  operational definition
Stanford-Binet Intelligence Scale
  mental and chronological age
  intelligence quotient (IQ)
Wechsler scales
  verbal and performance scales
group vs. individual tests
  normal curve

Terman's study of the gifted
Gardner's real world success criteria
mental retardation
  levels of retardation
  causes of retardation
   organic vs. familial
heredity/environment in intelligence
  twin studies, enriching environments
culture-fair tests
fluency, flexibility, originality of thought
divergent versus convergent thought
ways to measure divergent thinking
stages of creative thought
characteristics of creative people
thinking errors
  representativeness,
  ignoring the base rate,
  framing.
problems in problem solving
  rigid mental set, problems with logic,
  oversimplification
brainstorming

---| **LEARNING OBJECTIVES** |---

To demonstrate mastery of this chapter you should be able to:

1. Define the term "thinking."

2. List the four basic units of thought.

  a.

  b.

  c.

  d.

3. Describe mental imagery (including the concept of mental rotation). Explain how both stored and created images may be used to solve problems.

4. Explain how the size of a mental image is important.

5. Explain how muscular imagery aids thinking.

6. Define the terms "concept" and "concept formation," explain how they aid thought processes, and describe how they are learned.

7. Define the terms conjunctive concept, disjunctive concept, and relational concept.

8. Explain the importance of prototypes.

9. Explain the difference between the denotative and the connotative meaning of a word or concept, and describe how the connotative meaning of a word is measured.

10. Define semantics and explain how semantic problems may arise.

11. Briefly describe the following three requirements of a language and their related concepts:

    a. symbols

        1. phonemes

        2. morphemes

    b. grammar

        1. syntax

        2. transformation rules

    c. productivity

12. Describe the research involving attempts to teach primates (especially Washoe and Sarah) to use language. Describe the criticisms and practical value of such attempts.

13.   Compare and contrast mechanical problem solving with problem solving through understanding.

14.   Define the term heuristic and contrast it with random search strategies.

15.   Describe the process of insight as a problem solving technique.

16.   List and describe the three abilities which comprise insight.

   a.

   b.

   c.

17.   Explain how fixation and functional fixedness block problem solving, and give an example of each.

18.   List and explain four common barriers to creative thinking.

   a.

   b.

   c.

   d.

19.   Define the term artificial intelligence and state what it is based upon.

20.   Explain how computer simulations and expert systems are used.

21.   Explain the differences between experts and novices.

22.   Describe Binet's role in intelligence testing.

23.   State Wechsler's description of intelligence.

24.   Explain what an operational definition of intelligence is.

25.   Generally describe the construction of the Stanford-Binet Intelligence Scale.

26.   Define intelligence quotient, and use an example to show how it was computed. Explain the purpose of deviation IQ scores.

27. Distinguish the Wechsler tests from the Stanford-Binet tests, and distinguish between group and individual intelligence tests.

28. Describe the pattern of distribution of IQ scores observed in the general population.

29. Discuss the relationship between IQ and intellectual potential.

30. Briefly describe Terman's study of gifted children. State how successful subjects differed from the less successful ones.

31. List seven early signs of giftedness.

    a.   e.

    b.   f.

    c.   g.

    d.

32. Describe Gardner's broader view of intelligence and list the seven different kinds he discusses.

    a.   e.

    b.   f.

    c.   g.

    d.

33. State the dividing line between normal intelligence and retardation (or developmental disability), list the degrees of retardation, and describe the similarities between people of normal intelligence and those regarded as retarded.

34. Differentiate between organic and familial retardation.

35. Explain how the twin (identical and fraternal) studies can be used to support either side of the heredity/environment controversy.

36. Describe the evidence that strongly supports the environmental view of intelligence.

37.   Describe the studies which indicate how much the environment can alter intelligence.

38.   Define the term culture-fair test, and explain how IQ tests may be unfair to certain groups.

39.   Discuss how the heredity/environment debate is resolved.

40.   Describe the following four kinds of thought:
    a.   inductive

    b.   deductive

    c.   logical

    d.   illogical

41.   Describe the following characteristics of creative thinking:
    a.   fluency

b.   flexibility

c.   originality

42.   Explain the relationship of creativity to divergent and convergent thinking. Describe how the ability to think divergently can be measured.

43.   List and describe the five stages of creative thinking, and relate them to a problem that you have solved.

a.

b.

c.

d.

e.

44.   List MacKinnon's five conclusions about creative people.

a.

b.

c.

d.

e.

45.   List the ten qualities which characterize creative individuals.

a.   f.

b.   g.

c.   h.

d.   i.

e.   j.

46.   Explain the following errors made when using intuition:

   a.   representativeness

   b.   base rate

   c.   framing

The following objectives are related to the material in the "Applications" section of your text.

47.   List and explain three common problems which cause difficulties in thinking and problem solving.

   a.

   b.

   c.

48.   Describe six practical steps for encouraging creativity.

   a.

   b.

   c.

   d.

   e.

   f.

49.   Describe the process of brainstorming, and explain how it can be used to solve problems.

Do You Know the Information?

Multiple Choice

1. Thinking is
   (a) mentally processing images, concepts, words, rules, and symbols.
   (b) a uniquely human activity.
   (c) dependent upon tiny, sometimes unobservable muscular responses.
   (d) all of the above.

2. Which of the following is *not* one of the basic units of thought?
   (a) language   (b) muscular responses   (c) conditional relationships   (d) images

3. Stored images can be used to solve problems by
   (a) using ideas already stored in memory to generate more original solutions.
   (b) translating kinesthetic sensations into phonemes.
   (c) bringing prior experience to bear on the problem.
   (d) allowing language to help solve the problem.

4. The larger the size of the mental image, the
   (a) more confusing the image will be to existing precepts.
   (b) easier it is to see details.
   (c) fewer muscular responses that will be needed to solve the problem.
   (d) smaller the created image necessary to solve the problem.

5. People who "talk" with their hands thereby using gestures to help themselves think are demonstrating
   (a) implicit actions.   (b) micromovements.   (c) kinesthetic sensations.   (d) none of the above.

6. Concepts aid the thought process by
   (a) allowing us to function on an abstract level.
   (b) helping us understand ideas so we can better apply transformation rules.
   (c) preventing us from overlooking the minute details of a particular situation.
   (d) allowing us to break down experiences into integral component parts.

7. Disjunctive concepts
   (a) classify objects on the basis of their relationship to something else.
   (b) include classes of objects that have one or more features in common.
   (c) include things such as "large," "above," and "left."
   (d) refer to objects that have at least one of several possible features.

8. The explicit definition of a word or concept is its
   (a) semantic definition.   (b) denotative meaning.   (c) functional meaning.   (d) connotative meaning.

9. The semantic differential measures the _____ meaning of a word or concept.
   (a) inductive   (b) connotative   (c) functional   (d) denotative

10. Semantic problems usually occur when
    (a) the world is encoded into symbols.   (c) a word has an unclear meaning.
    (b) we study the meaning of words.   (d) the link between language and thought become evident.

11. Which of the following is *not* one of the requirements of a language?
    (a) must carry meaning   (b) must have a set of rules   (c) must be regenerative   (d) must be productive

12. Phonemes are
    (a) the basic speech sounds.
    (b) the set of rules used to form sounds into words.
    (c) speech sounds which have been collected into meaningful units.
    (d) rules pertaining to word order in sentences.

13. Which of the following statements about teaching language to primates is *incorrect?*
    (a) Such research has proven helpful for teaching language to aphasic children.
    (b) One chimp even learned to state conditional relationships, that is, if...then statements.
    (c) Washoe the chimp was probably the most successful, learning over 240 signs.
    (d) One chimp learned to vocalize about 150 words.

14. Mechanical problem solving involves
    (a) a high level of thinking based on understanding.
    (b) trial and error or rote solutions.
    (c) the sudden appearance of the answer after a period of unsuccessful thought.
    (d) the use of transformation rules.
    (e) for example, a mechanic trying to figure out how to get his zipper down in an emergency.

15. Which of the following is *not* a heuristic strategy?
    (a) Identify how the current state of affairs differs from the desired goal.
    (b) Work in a step-by-step fashion from the starting point toward the desired goal.
    (c) If you can't reach the goal directly, try to identify an intermediate goal.
    (d) Try representing the problem in other ways.
    (e) Generate a possible solution and then test it.

16. Bringing together seemingly unrelated bits of useful information to solve a problem is called
    (a) selective encoding.   (c) selective comparison.   (e) doing your taxes.
    (b) selective combination.   (d) selective representation.

17. The inability to see new uses for familiar objects or objects that have been used in a particular way is called
    (a) illogical problem solving. (b) perceptual rigidity.   (c) functional fixedness.   (d) simplicity.

18. If you have values which block creative thinking because you believe that fantasy is a waste of time, then you are suffering from _____ barriers.
    (a) learned   (b) perceptual   (c) emotional   (d) cultural

19. Artificial intelligence is based upon
    (a) the fact that many tasks can be reduced to a set of rules applied to a body of knowledge.
    (b) organized knowledge and acquired strategies.
    (c) programs used to simulate human behavior.
    (d) the speed of computers when it comes to doing things like mathematical computations.

20. Computer programs which have advanced knowledge of a specific topic by virtue of having converted complex skills into rules which a computer can follow are called
    (a) computer simulations.   (b) cognitive programs.   (c) automatic processors.   (d) expert systems.

21. Experts differ from novices in any given field by virtue of their
    (a) stronger minds.
    (b) willingness to explore and reject unproductive alternatives.
    (c) ability to define problems in terms of their specific rather than general principles.
    (d) ability to see the true nature of problems.

22. In constructing his test of intelligence, Binet
    (a) chose items at each age level which could be passed by an average child of that chronological age.
    (b) selected the children in the French school system with average grades at each grade level and determined what intellectual skills they possessed.
    (c) chose items at each level that all French-speaking children of that age could correctly answer.
    (d) consulted with Stanford University.

23. According to Wechsler, intelligence is
    (a) that which an intelligence test measures.
    (b) the ability to succeed in school.
    (c) the capacity to act purposefully, think rationally and deal effectively with the environment.
    (d) regarded as a person's capacity to learn.

24. The IQ test which uses a set of increasingly more difficult items to categorize age groups is the
    (a) Wechsler Adult Intelligence Scale.   (c) Wechsler Intelligence Scale for Children.
    (b) Stanford-Binet Intelligence Scale.   (d) MGM Scale.

25. Of the following, which are associated with the Stanford-Binet Intelligence Scale?
    (a) chronological age   (c) mental age   (e) overall IQ score
    (b) morphological age   (d) separate subscales   (f) intelligence quotient

26. The formula for figuring IQ is
    (a) $\dfrac{M}{A} \times (100) = IQ.$ (b) $\dfrac{CA}{MA} \times (100) = IQ.$ (c) $\dfrac{MA}{CA} \times (100) = IQ.$ (d) $\dfrac{MA}{CA(100)} = IQ.$

27. First, it is determined how far above or below average a person's score is relative to others taking the test. Then, tables are used to convert the person's relative standing in the group to an IQ score. This process is used to calculate
    (a) an IQ score.   (c) a deviation IQ score.   (e) the person's age + weight.
    (b) a mental age score.   (d) a performance score.

28. Which of the following statements is *incorrect*?
    (a) The WAIS-R is a group intelligence test.
    (b) The WAIS-R is specifically designed to measure adult intelligence.
    (c) The WISC-R and the WAIS-R rate performance and verbal intelligence.
    (d) The Stanford-Binet gives one overall IQ score.

29. Concerning the relationship between IQ and intellectual potential,
    (a) measured intelligence is the only factor affecting grades in school.
    (b) one can learn a lot from even IQ differences of just a few points.
    (c) off-campus educational opportunities have little influence on school grades.
    (d) IQ is not a good predictor of performance in creative writing.

30. Which of the following was *not* a conclusion reached from Terman's study of the mentally gifted?
    (a) More of them than average held professional positions.
    (b) The likelihood of outstanding achievement seemed to be higher.
    (c) The highly intelligent person is more susceptible to mental illness.
    (d) Highly successful subjects were more persistent and more motivated than less successful subjects.

31. Gardner's broader view of intelligence
    (a) is supportive of studies which suggest that IQ test scores mainly reflect a general intelligence factor.
    (b) has been the basis of much of the search for culture-fair tests.
    (c) encompasses abilities including art, music, and athletics.
    (d) hopes to be able to make the most accurate prediction of school success.

32. What IQ score has traditionally been used as the dividing line between retardation and normal intelligence?
    (a) 60   (b) 70   (c) 80   (d) 100

33. Which of the following is *not* a cause of organic retardation?
    (a) genetic abnormalities   (b) fetal damage   (c) nutrition   (d) metabolic disorders

34. The correlation of intelligence test scores of identical twins
    (a) is only slightly lower when they are raised apart than when they are raised together.
    (b) is only slightly lower than that of parents and children.
    (c) is higher than for any other blood relatives except siblings.
    (d) is lower when they are raised together than that of siblings reared together.

35. In the studies of families having one biological child and one adopted child,
    (a) the adopted child's IQ is more like the biological mother's than the adoptive mother's.
    (b) children reared by the same mother resemble her in IQ to the same degree.
    (c) the adoptive child's IQ is more like the biological mother's if her educational level is higher than the adoptive mother's.
    (d) the children were more alike in IQ than ordinary siblings were.

36. In the Skeels study, children who were considered retarded were moved from an orphanage to a more stimulating environment where
    (a) their IQ test scores improved slightly.
    (b) their IQ test scores rose an average of 29 points.
    (c) they became better adjusted and happier but not intellectually superior.
    (d) their IQs rose sufficiently to allow reclassification from mildly to moderately retarded.

37. Tests developed so that they will not place certain groups at a disadvantage
    (a) include the Dove test.   (c) are best exemplified by the Wechsler scales.
    (b) are called culturally balanced.   (d) are culture-fair.

38. Thinking which goes from general principles to specific situations is termed
    (a) deductive   (b) logical   (c) inductive   (d) illogical

39. Which of the following is *not* an aspect of creative thinking?
    (a) flexibility   (b) fluency   (c) originality   (d) convergency

40. What is the one factor that the Unusual Uses, Consequences, and Anagrams tests have in common?
    (a) They are all tests of divergent thinking.   (c) They are all tests of logical thinking.
    (b) They are all tests of convergent thinking.   (d) They are all tests of illogical thinking.

41. Indicate which of the following are characteristics of creative individuals.
    (a) highly intelligent   (d) introverted   (g) a high level of energy and activity
    (b) an openness to experience   (e) neurotic
    (c) a preference for complexity   (f) a willingness to take risks

42. When people give different answers to the same problem when it is posed in a slightly different way, this is known as
    (a) ignoring the base rate.   (c) representativeness.   (e) fibbing.
    (b) rigid mental set.   (d) framing.

43. Indicate which of the following are difficulties in thinking and problem solving.
    (a) overcomprehension   (c) disjunctive conceptual thinking   (e) divergent thinking
    (b) problems with logic   (d) rigid mental set   (f) oversimplification

44. Which of the following are suggestions for enhancing creativity?
    (a) Be a convergent thinker.
    (b) Allow time for incubation.
    (c) Develop a narrow but consistent chain of thought.
    (d) Create the right atmosphere by spending time with creative individuals.
    (e) Look for analogies.

45.   The idea of brainstorming is to
      (a) produce as many ideas as possible.
      (b) encourage ideas that seem to be workable.
      (c) critically evaluate each proposed idea before moving on to the next idea.
      (d) allow for selective encoding.

Matching (*Use the letters on the right only once.*)

_____ 1. mental imagery
_____ 2. concept
_____ 3. semantics
_____ 4. morphemes
_____ 5. syntax
_____ 6. mechanical solutions
_____ 7. heuristic
_____ 8. expert system
_____ 9. operational definition
_____ 10. deviation IQ
_____ 11. SAT
_____ 12. giftedness
_____ 13. familial retardation
_____ 14. inductive
_____ 15. illumination

A. rules pertaining to word order
B. going from specific facts to general principles
C. person's score compared to the average score; tables then used to figure an IQ
    score
D. example of a group intelligence test
E. problem defined
F. intuitive
G. study of meaning of words
H. mental sensory representation
I. ends with insight
J. intellectual and educational level of home is low
K. achieved by rote or trial and error
L. solving on unconscious level
M. sounds collected into meaningful units
N. represents class of objects or events
O. problem-solving strategy
P. clearly stated rules that a computer can follow
Q. procedures used to measure it have been specified
R. synesthesia
S. answer suddenly appears
T. going from general principles to specific situations
U. early fascination with explanations and problem solving

True-False

_____ 1. Thinking could be considered tiring because it is accompanied by an undercurrent of muscular tension and implicit muscular
         activity.

_____ 2. Concept formation is the process whereby we classify information into meaningful categories.

_____ 3. Adults are likely to acquire concepts by learning or formulating rules.

_____ 4. Conjunctive concepts refer to objects that have at least one of a number of features.

_____ 5. Identifying concepts is difficult even when we come up with a prototype relevant to what we see.

_____ 6. We create sentences by using transformation rules.

_____ 7. A language that is productive can generate new ideas.

_____ 8. Solutions based on understanding use habitual modes of thought.

_____ 9. Insight is said to have occurred when an answer appears after a period of logical divergent thought.

_____ 10. The point at which a useful idea or insight becomes set in one's mind is known as fixation.

_____ 11. In the general population fewer people score above average than score below average on IQ tests.

_____ 12. A child who shows cooperation toward others is less likely to be gifted than one with a good memory.

_____ 13. Environmentalists argue that separated identical twins are almost always placed in homes socially and educationally similar to their biological parents. This artificially inflates the similarity in the separated twins' IQ scores.

_____ 14. Strong evidence of the environmental view of intelligence comes from studies of children who were separated at birth.

_____ 15. There is probably no limit to how far down intelligence can go in an impoverished environment, but heredity may impose some limits on how far up IQ can go, even under ideal conditions.

_____ 16. A person who thinks creatively thinks divergently.

_____ 17. Creative individuals tend to be flexible in social situations.

Can You Apply the Information?

1. Mark is trapped in a burning room. There are three objects in the room. He can use one of the objects to help him get out of the room, but he's never seen any of them before. Mark had better rely on
   (a) Superman.   (b) muscular imagery.   (c) created images.   (d) stored images.

2. In order to be a bird, an organism must have feathers and wings. This is an example of a
   (a) disjunctive concept.   (b) relational concept.   (c) conjunctive concept.   (d) mental imagery.

3. Amy says the word "vomit" at the dinner table. Her mother doesn't like the word at all. They both know what the word means. The word doesn't bother Amy, but her mother is disgusted. It is likely that her mother is reacting to the word's _____ meaning.
   (a) connotative   (b) relational   (c) denotative   (d) encoded

4. A three-month-old baby makes all sorts of sounds and noises. Most of these sounds are probably
   (a) grammar.   (b) morphemes.   (c) phonemes.   (d) following transformation rules.

5. Tom doesn't really know much about cars, but he loves to work on them. To fix a car he takes out parts and replaces them until the car runs better. He is solving a problem using
   (a) insight.   (b) understanding.   (c) a mechanical solution.   (d) heuristics.

6. You are a mathematician and have been trying to solve a perplexing problem for two weeks. One evening while walking in the garden you suddenly realize you've been trying to solve the problem in the wrong way. How stupid! You merely have to move two variables and the equation makes sense. This is an example of
   (a) rote problem solving.   (b) insight.   (c) trial and error learning.   (d) a random search strategy.

7. Tom is still working on his car. He figures that since the oil filter is on the lower part of the engine, he should crawl under the car to change it. He does so but finds all sorts of stuff between him and the filter. He works for 45 minutes trying to get to the filter to unscrew it. All he really needs to do is unscrew the filter while standing up looking down at the engine. Tom is experiencing
   (a) functional fixedness.   (b) internal misrepresentations. (c) fixation.   (d) consummate stupidity.

8. Benjamin is studying and a gnat keeps buzzing around his ears bugging him. He uses his psychology book as a weapon to smash the little bugger between the pages. It is obvious that Benjamin is **not** suffering from
   (a) functional fixedness.   (c) negative oversimplification.   (e) unnatural fears.
   (b) problems with general properties.   (d) images.

9. Your professor asks a really "off the wall" question in class. You can't come up with a creative solution because you're worried about making a fool of yourself. Your barrier to creative thinking is called a(n) _____ barrier.
   (a) perceptual   (b) learned   (c) cultural   (d) emotional

10. "The temperature at sea level at 6:58 a.m. was 20 degrees Celsius." This is an example of an operational definition.
    (a) True   (b) False

11. You're looking at a patient's chart trying to figure out her age on the date of her intelligence testing. You can't read the number written down for her age. You know her IQ was 83 and her MA was 10. What was her CA on the date of testing?
    (a) 8   (b) 9   (c) 12   (d) 10

12. The average twelve-year-old child has a mental age of
    (a) 10.   (b) 120.   (c) 12.   (d) 100.

13. If a college professor's grade distribution"fit" her classes the way the normal curve fits randomly selected people, most students would make a(n) _____ in her class
    (a) A   (c) C   (e) F
    (b) B   (d) D   (f) insufficient data to choose an answer

14. You are asked to think of as many uses for a paper clip as you can. It is likely that you are taking a test for
    (a) solutions through understanding.   (c) inductive reasoning.
    (b) divergent thinking.   (d) convergent thinking.

Chapter Review

1. Thinking refers to the _____ _____ and combination of images, concepts, words, rules, symbols, and precepts. At its most basic, it is the _____ _____ of a problem or situation.

2. There are many basic units of thought. Four basic units that serve as internal representations include _____, _____ responses, _____, and _____. All four ways may be combined in complex _____.

3. If you use mental pictures to help you solve problems, this is called _____. Problem solving can be aided by using _____ _____ to bring prior experience to bear on the problem. To generate more original solutions _____ _____ may be used. The larger the _____, the _____ it is to see the _____ in it. Regardless of size, most people report that they can mentally _____ an image to see all sides of it.

4. Jerome Bruner believes that we often represent things in a kind of _____ imagery created by actions or implicit actions. The underlying premise is that there is a great deal of information contained in _____ _____ (feelings from the muscles and joints). Research supports this contention by showing that most thinking is accompanied by muscular tension and _____ throughout the body.

5. A _____ is a word or idea that represents a class of objects or events. _____ allow us to function on an _____ level. _____ _____ is the process whereby we classify information into meaningful _____. At its most basic, concept formation is based on experience with _____ and _____ instances of the concept. However, as adults we often acquire concepts by learning _____.

6. Several general types of concepts have been identified. A _____ concept embraces a class of objects that have one or more features in common. _____ concepts classify objects on the basis of their relationship to something else or by the relationship between features of an object. _____ concepts refer to objects that have at least one of a number of features.

7. Regardless of the type of concept, most people also use _____, or ideal models to identify concepts. Identifying concepts is _____ when we cannot come up with a relevant prototype.

8. Concepts have two types of meaning. The _____ meaning of a word or concept is its explicit definition. The _____ meaning of a word is its emotional or personal meaning. The latter type of meaning has been measured using Osgood's _____ _____.

9. The study of word meaning and language is called _____.

10. A language must provide _____ that can be used to stand for objects and ideas. The symbols we call words are built out of _____ (basic speech sounds) and _____ (speech sounds collected into meaningful units).

11. Language must also have a _____ or set of rules for the combination of sounds into words and words into sentences. _____ refers to the rules pertaining to word order in sentences. The rules used to change core ideas into sentences are called _____ rules.

12. Language must be able to be used to produce new possibilities or to generate new ideas. In other words, it must be _____.

13. Some of the most revealing research on thinking and problem solving capacities has centered on attempts to teach _____ to chimpanzees and other primates. The first major breakthrough occurred with a female chimp named Washoe. She was taught to use _____ _____ _____, a set of hand gestures used by the deaf in which each gesture stands for a word.

14. Washoe now has a vocabulary of about 240 signs and can construct six-word sentences. Some critics are skeptical of Washoe's haphazard _____ of words. An answer to this criticism has come from the work of Premack who taught a female chimp named Sarah to use 130 words consisting of _____ _____ arranged on a magnetic board.

15. Sarah has been required to use proper _____ _____. She has learned to answer _____, to label things as the same or different, to classify objects, and to construct _____ sentences. One of her most outstanding achievements is the use of sentences involving _____ _____. A pygmy chimpanzee has been taught to construct _____ several words long. He can also understand about 650 spoken _____. The results of such linguistic research are inconclusive, but the research has already proven helpful for teaching language to _____ children.

16. A number of different approaches to thinking and problem solving can be identified. _____ solutions may be achieved by trial and error or by rote.

17. Many problems are unsolvable by mechanical means. In this case a higher level of thinking based on _____ is necessary. Usually this process involves a discovery of the general _____ of a solution followed by the proposing of a number of _____ solutions.

18. A problem solving strategy can also be called a _____. When solving problems, a trial-and-error strategy in which all possibilities are tried is called a _____ _____ strategy.

19. Insight apparently involves three abilities. The ability to select information which is relevant to a problem is called selective _____. Selective _____ brings together seemingly unrelated bits of information. The ability to compare new problems to old information or to problems already solved is termed selective _____.

20. A barrier to problem solving occurs when a person gets "hung up" on wrong solutions or becomes blind to other alternatives. This is called _____. _____ _____ occurs when a person cannot see a new use for a familiar object or for objects that have previously been used in a particular way. This is an example of _____.

21. There are four common barriers to creative thinking. Fear of making a fool of oneself leads to _____ barriers. _____ barriers are a result of values which portray fantasy as a waste of time. Conventions about uses may lead to _____ barriers, and _____ barriers result from habits which lead to a failure to identify important elements of a problem.

22. Artificial intelligence refers to computer programs capable of doing things that require _____ when done by people. It is based on the fact that many tasks can be reduced to a set of _____ applied to a body of _____.

23. In computer simulations, programs are used to simulate human _____. Programs that display advanced knowledge of a specific topic or skill are called _____ _____.

24. Working with artificial intelligence has helped to clarify differences between _____ and _____. Experts are better able to see the true nature of _____ and to define them in terms of general _____. Their skills are based on _____ knowledge and _____ strategies.

25. In 1904, Binet created a test made up of "_____" questions and problems. He then learned which questions an average _____ could answer at each age. Children _____ in intellectual ability were identified by below-par scores on the test.

26. A general description of intelligence by David Wechsler defines it as the global capacity of the individual to act _____, to think _____, and to deal effectively with the _____.

27. A(n) _____ definition of intelligence is one that specifies the procedures used to _____ it.

28. One example of intelligence tests is the Stanford-Binet Intelligence Scale which uses a set of increasingly more difficult items to categorize _____ _____. These types of questions allow a person's _____ age to be determined.

29. To know the meaning of _____ age one must also consider _____ age. Using these two age values, an _____ or _____ _____ can be determined. This is defined as _____ age divided by _____ age multiplied by 100.

30. On tests currently in use, there is no longer any need to calculate IQ scores. Instead, a _____ _____ score is used. To compute this score, we determine how far above or below _____ a person's score is compared to others taking the test. Tables are then used to convert the person's _____ _____ in the group to an IQ score.

31. A widely used alternative to the Stanford-Binet is the _____ _____ Intelligence Scale—Revised. This test has a form adapted for use with children called the _____ Intelligence Scale for _____ —III.

32. The Stanford-Binet only gives an overall IQ, whereas both the WISC-III and WAIS-R rate _____ intelligence in addition to _____ intelligence. Both the Stanford-Binet and the Wechsler tests are _____ intelligence tests. _____ intelligence tests are designed for use with large groups of people.

33. The distribution of IQs in the population approximates a _____ curve in which the majority of scores fall close to the _____, and relatively few at the _____.

34. The correlation between IQ and school grades is _____ which might be higher if measured _____ was the only thing affecting grades. However, _____, special _____, off-campus _____ opportunities, and many other factors influence school grades and _____.

35. Terman's study of the mentally _____ found them to be generally _____. It appears that even though IQ scores are not generally good predictors of _____-_____ success, when they are in the gifted range, the likelihood of outstanding _____ seems to be higher. The highly successful subjects differed mainly in their greater _____ and _____ to succeed.

36. Early signs of giftedness include seeking out _____ children and adults; a fascination with _____ and _____ _____; talking in complete sentences at age ____; good _____; precocious "artistic" talent; early interest in _____; and show-ing _____ towards others.

37. An IQ of _____ or below has traditionally been the dividing line between normal intelligence and _____. However, performance of adaptive _____ also figures into evaluating retardation. The degrees of retardation are _____, _____, _____, and _____.

38. About 50 percent of all cases of mental retardation are _____, or related to known physical disorders. These can be traced to one or more of the following conditions: (1) _____ injuries (such as lack of oxygen); (2) _____ damage caused by maternal drug abuse, disease, or infection; (3) _____ disorders; and (4) _____ abnormalities.

39. _____ retardation, where no known biological problem can be identified, occurs most often in very low income or impoverished households. Many cases of retardation might be prevented by better _____, _____, and early _____ _____ programs.

40. Gardner feels that the definition of intelligence needs to be _____ so that it can predict "_____ _____" success and not just success in _____. He feels that intelligence should include such things as language, logic and _____, visual and _____ thinking, music, _____ skills, _____ skills (self-knowledge), and _____ skills (social skills).

41. In assessing the relative importance of heredity and environment on the development of intelligence, studies have looked at the similarity in IQ between various relatives. It is typically found that as the genetic similarity increases, the similarity in IQ _____.

42. For example, _____ twins when reared together have virtually identical IQs. When reared apart, the correlation _____ but only slightly. This tends to support the _____ side of the controversy. However, the _____ argue that the separated twins are nearly always put into _____ homes.

43. The strongest evidence for the environmentalist view comes from families in which there is one _____ child and one _____ child. Studies show that children reared by the same mother resemble her in IQ to the same degree.

44. The environment can have considerable impact on a person's intelligence. One study showed that then 25 children who were considered mentally retarded were transferred to a more _____ environment, the result was an average gain of _____ IQ points. In that same study, a second group of initially less retarded children who remained in the orphanage lost an average of _____ IQ points.

45. Most psychologists agree that _____ and _____ are inseparable, interacting factors in determining intelligence. There is probably no _____ to how far _____ intelligence can go in an impoverished environment. Heredity may impose some _____ on how far _____ IQ can go, even under ideal conditions.

46. Intelligence test scores tell nothing about heredity if they result from unequal educational opportunity. In recognition of this problem, some psychologists are trying to develop _____-_____ tests that will not disadvantage certain groups.

47. Going from specific facts or observations to general principles is _____ thinking. Going from general principles to specific situations is _____ thinking. Thinking which is _____ proceeds from given information to new conclusions on the basis of _____. Thinking which is intuitive, associative, or personal is _____.

48. Creative thinking is characterized by _____ (the total number of ideas), _____ (the number of times thought shifts from one class of possibilities to another), and _____ (the degree of novelty of ideas).

49. Creative thinking requires _____ thought, not _____ thought, which occurs when the lines of thought converge on a correct thought. The former type of thought is generally measured by tests requiring that _____ possibilities be generated from one starting point.

50. The best summary of the sequence of events in thinking proposes five stages. The first step is _____, where the problem must be defined and important dimensions identified. _____ is next, where the persons saturate themselves with as much information as possible pertaining to the problem.

51. The third stage, _____, involves a period during which all attempted solutions have proven futile, and the person leaves the problem "cooking" in the background. This stage is often ended by a rapid insight or series of insights which mark the fourth stage referred to as _____. The final step, _____, involves testing and critically evaluating the solution obtained during the stage of illumination If the solution proves faulty, the thinker reverts to the stage of _____.

52. Researcher David MacKinnon has discovered several important factors about creative people. First, there is little correlation between creativity and _____.

53. Creative people usually have a greater than average range of _____ and _____. They also have an _____ to experience.

54. Creative people enjoy _____ thought, ideas, concepts, and possibilities. They value _____ and have a preference for _____.

55. There are many errors that we can make when using intuition. A choice that seems to be _____ of what we already know may be erroneously given greater weight. One might also ignore the _____ _____ or underlying probability of an event. Also the way a problem is stated or _____ can make a difference.

56. There are several factors which can contribute to difficulties in thinking and problem solving. One of these difficulties is a rigid _____ _____. Another major thinking difficulty centers on the process of _____ _____. It is entirely possible to draw true conclusions using faulty _____ or to draw false conclusions using valid _____. Another basic source of thinking errors is the process of _____.

57. Several suggestions have been offered as to how to begin increasing creativity. One of these is to define the problem _____. A broad range of knowledge can mean more creative possibilities. A variety of experiments show that people make more original, spontaneous, and imaginative responses when exposed to others (models) doing the same thing, so you should create the right _____.

58. Trying to hurry or force a problem's solution may simply encourage fixation on a dead end, so always allow time for _____. Creativity requires divergent thinking, so remember to seek varied _____. Representing a problem in a variety of ways is often the key to solution. One way to do this is to look for _____. Also, delaying _____ tends to increase rather than inhibit creativity.

59. _____ is an alternative approach to enhancing creativity. It involves encouraging participants to produce as many ideas as possible while absolutely prohibiting _____ of the ideas. This technique helps people solve problems by allowing them to consider many possible solutions before negatively rejecting them.

ANSWER KEYS

Do You Know the Information?

Multiple Choice

1. (a) obj. 1, p. 335
2. (c) obj. 2, p. 336
3. (c) obj. 3, p. 336
4. (b) obj. 4, p. 337
5. (c) obj. 5, p. 337
6. (a) obj. 6, p. 338
7. (d) obj. 7, p. 338
8. (b) obj. 9, p. 339
9. (b) obj. 9, p. 339
10. (c) obj. 10, p. 340
11. (c) obj. 11, p. 341
12. (a) obj. 11, p. 340
13. (d) obj. 12, p. 342
14. (b) obj. 13, p. 345
15. (b) obj. 14, p. 346
16. (b) obj. 16, p. 347
17. (c) obj. 17, p. 348
18. (d) obj. 18, p. 349
19. (a) obj. 19, p. 349
20. (d) obj. 20, p. 349
21. (d) obj. 21, p. 350
22. (a) obj. 22, p. 351
23. (c) obj. 23, p. 351
24. (b) objs. 25, 27, p. 352
25. (a,c,e,f) objs. 25, 27, pp. 352-353
26. (c) obj. 26, p. 353
27. (c) obj. 26, p. 353
28. (a) obj. 27, p. 354
29. (d) obj. 29, p. 355
30. (c) obj. 30, p. 356
31. (c) obj. 32, p. 356

32. (b) obj. 33, p. 357
33. (c) obj. 34, pp. 357-358
34. (a) obj. 35, p. 359
35. (b) obj. 36, p. 359
36. (b) obj. 37, p. 359
37. (d) obj. 38, p. 360
38. (a) obj. 40, p. 361
39. (d) obj. 41, p. 361
40. (a) obj. 42, p. 361
41. (b,c,f,g) objs. 44-45, pp. 364-365
42. (d) obj. 46, p. 366
43. (b,d,f) obj. 47, pp. 367-369
44. (b,d,e) obj. 48, p. 369
45. (a) obj. 49, p. 369

Matching

1. H, obj. 3, p. 336
2. N, obj. 6, p. 338
3. G, obj. 10, p. 340
4. M, obj. 11, p. 340
5. A, obj. 11, p. 341
6. K, obj. 13, p. 345
7. O, obj. 14, p. 346
8. P, obj. 20, p. 349
9. Q, obj. 24, p. 352
10. C, obj. 26, p. 353
11. D, obj. 27, p. 354
12. U, obj. 31, p. 356
13. J, obj. 34, p. 358
14. B, obj. 40, p. 361
15. I, obj. 43, p. 363

True-False

1. T, obj. 5, p. 337
2. T, obj. 6, p. 338
3. T, obj. 6, pp. 338-339
4. F, obj. 7, p. 338
5. F, obj. 8, p. 338
6. T, obj. 11, p. 341
7. T, obj. 11, p. 341
8. F, obj. 13, p. 345
9. F, obj. 15, p. 346
10. F, obj. 17, p. 348
11. F, obj. 28, pp. 354-355
12. F, obj. 31, p. 356
13. T, obj. 36, p. 359
14. F, obj. 36, pp. 359-360
15. T, obj. 39, p. 360
16. T, obj. 42, p. 361
17. T, obj. 45, p. 364

Can You Apply the Information?

1. (c) obj. 3, p. 336
2. (c) obj. 7, p. 338
3. (a) obj. 9, p. 339
4. (c) obj. 11, p. 340
5. (c) obj. 13, p. 345
6. (b) obj. 15, p. 346
7. (c) obj. 17, p. 348
8. (a) obj. 17, p. 348
9. (d) obj. 18, p. 349
10. (a) obj. 24, p. 352
11. (c) obj. 26, p. 353
12. (c) obj. 26, p. 353
13. (c) obj. 28, p. 355
14. (b) obj. 42, p. 361

Chapter Review

1. mentally processing, internal representation (p. 335)
2. images, muscular, concepts, language (symbols), thinking (p. 336)
3. imagery, stored images, created images, image, easier, detail, rotate (p. 336)

4. muscular, kinesthetic sensations, micromovements (p. 337)
5. concept, Concepts, abstract, Concept formation, categories, positive, negative, rules (p. 338)
6. conjunctive, Relational, Disjunctive (p. 338)
7. prototype, difficult (p. 338)
8. denotative, connotative, semantic differential (p. 339)
9. semantics (p. 340)
10. symbols, phonemes, morphemes (p. 340)
11. grammar, Syntax, transformation (p. 340)
12. productive (p. 341)
13. language, American Sign Language (p. 342)
14. arrangement, plastic chips (p. 343)
15. word order, questions, compound, conditional relationships, sentences, sentences, aphasic (p. 343)
16. Mechanical (p. 345)
17. understanding, properties, functional (workable) (p. 345)
18. heuristic, random search (p. 346)
19. encoding,, combination, comparison (p. 347)
20. fixation, Functional fixedness, fixation (p. 348)
21. emotional, Cultural, learned, perceptual (p. 349)
22. intelligence, rules, information (p. 349)
23. behavior, expert systems (p. 349)
24. experts (novices), novices (experts), problems, principles, organized, acquired (p. 349)
25. Binet, child, low (p. 350)
26. purposefully, rationally, environment (p. 351)
27. operational, measure (p. 352)
28. age groups, mental (p. 352)
29. mental, chronological, IQ, intelligence quotient, mental, chronological (p. 352)
30. deviation IQ, average, relative standing (p. 353)
31. Wechsler Adult, Wechsler, Children (p. 353)
32. performance (verbal), verbal (performance), individual, Group (p. 353)
33. normal, average, extremes (p. 354)
34. .50, intelligence, motivation, talents, educational, success (p. 355)
35. gifted, successful, real-world, achievement, persistence, motivation (p. 356)
36. older, explorations, problem solving, 2 (3), memory, books (reading), kindness (understanding, cooperation) (p. 356)
37. 70, retardation, behaviors (p. 357); mild, moderate, severe, profound (p. 358)
38. organic, birth, fetal, metabolic, genetic (p. 358)
39. Familial, nutrition, education, childhood enrichment (p. 358)
40. broader, real world, school, math, spatial, bodily, intrapersonal, interpersonal (p. 356)
41. increases (p. 359)
42. identical, decreases, heredity, environmentalists, similar (p. 359)
43. biological (adopted), adopted (biological) (p. 359)
44. stimulating, 29, 26 (p. 359)
45. heredity, environment, limit, down, limits, up (p. 360)
46. culture-fair (p. 360)
47. inductive, deductive, logical, rules, illogical (p. 361)
48. fluency, flexibility, originality (p. 361)
49. divergent, convergent, many (p. 361)
50. orientation, Preparation (p. 362)
51. incubation, illumination, verification, incubation (p. 363)
52. intelligence (p. 364)
53. knowledge, interests, openness (p. 364)
54. symbolic, independence, complexity (p. 364)
55. representative, base rate, framed (p. 366)
56. mental set (p. 367); logical reasoning, logic, logic (p. 368); oversimplification (p. 369)
57. broadly, atmosphere (p. 369)
58. incubation, input, analogies, evaluation (p. 369)
59. Brainstorming, criticism (p. 370)

chapter eleven

Motivation and Emotion

LEARNING OBJECTIVES

To demonstrate mastery of this chapter you should be able to:

1. Define motivation.

2. Describe or analyze a motivational sequence using the "need reduction" model.

3.   Explain how the incentive value of a goal can affect motivation, and describe how incentive value is related to internal need.

4.   List and describe the three types of motives and give an example of each.

a.

b.

c.

5.   Define homeostasis.

6.   Discuss why hunger cannot be fully explained by the contractions of an empty stomach.

7.   Describe the relationship of each of the following to hunger:

a.   blood sugar

b.   liver

c.   hypothalamus

feeding system (lateral hypothalamus)

satiety system (ventromedial hypothalamus)

blood sugar regulator (paraventricular nucleus)

(continued on page 214)

    d.   cultural factors

    e.   taste

8.   Explain how a persons's set point is related to obesity in childhood and adulthood.

9.   Explain the paradox of "yo-yo" dieting.

10.   Explain the relationship between how much a person overeats and the person's obesity.

11.   Describe the relationship between emotionality and overeating.

12.   Explain how a taste aversion is acquired, give a practical example of the process, and briefly explain why psychologists believe these aversions exist.

13. Describe the essential features of the eating disorders anorexia nervosa and bulimia. Explain what causes them and what treatment is available for them.

14. Name the brain structure that appears to control thirst (as well as hunger). Differentiate extracellular and intracellular thirst.

15. Explain how the drive to avoid pain and the sex drive differ from other primary drives.

16. Describe the evidence for the existence of drives for exploration, manipulation, curiosity, and stimulation.

17. Explain the arousal theory of motivation including the inverted U function. Relate arousal to the Yerkes-Dodson law and give an example of it.

18. Describe the two major components of test anxiety and describe four ways to reduce it.

    Components   *Ways to reduce test anxiety*

    a.   a.

                                          b.

    b.   c.

                                          d.

19. Define need for achievement (nAch) and differentiate it from the need for power.

20. Describe people who are achievers, and relate nAch to risk taking.

21. Explain the influences of drive and determination in the development of success for high achievers.

22. List (in order) the needs found in Maslow's hierarchy of motives.

23. Explain why Maslow's lower (physiological) needs are considered prepotent.

24. Define meta-need and give an example of one.

25. Distinguish between intrinsic and extrinsic motivation, and explain how each type of motivation may affect a person's interest in work and leisure activities.

26. Explain what is meant by the phrase, "emotions aid survival."

27. List and describe the three major elements of emotions.

    a.

    b.

    c.

28. List the eight primary emotions proposed by Plutchik and explain his concept of mixing them.

    a.   c.   e.   g.
    b.   d.   f.   h.

29. Describe, in general, the effects of the sympathetic and the parasympathetic branches of the ANS during and after emotion.

    Sympathetic   *Parasympathetic*

30. Describe the relationship between pupil dilation and emotion.

31. Define "parasympathetic rebound" and discuss its possible involvement in cases of sudden death.

32. Explain how the polygraph detects "lies."

33. Discuss the limitations and/or accuracy of lie detector devices.

34. Discuss Darwin's view of human emotion.

35. Describe the evidence that supports the conclusion that most emotional expressions are universal.

36. Define kinesics. List and describe the emotional messages conveyed by facial expressions and body language. Explain how overall posture can indicate one's emotional state.

37. Describe the characteristics or behaviors that are related to lying.

38. Describe the commonsense theory of emotion.

39.   Briefly describe the James-Lange theory of emotion.

40.   Briefly describe the Cannon-Bard theory of emotion.

41.   Briefly describe Schachter's cognitive theory of emotion and give experimental evidence to support his theory.

42.   Describe and give an example of the effects of attribution on emotion.

43.   Briefly describe the facial feedback hypothesis.

44.   Discuss the role of appraisal in the contemporary model of emotion.

The following objective is related to the material in the "Applications" section of your text.

45.   Explain what is meant by behavioral dieting, and describe the techniques which can enable you to control your weight.

Do You Know the Information?

Multiple Choice

1. Needs cause a psychological state or feeling to develop called a
    (a) response.   (b) motive.   (c) drive.   (d) incentive.

2. The pull exerted by a goal is called its
    (a) incentive value.   (b) intrinsic motivation.   (c) drive reduction effect.   (d) stimulus factor.

3. Motives which appear to be innate but which are *not* necessary for the survival of the organism are called
    (a) learned.   (b) secondary.   (c) primary.   (d) stimulus.

4. Circle the secondary motives.
    (a) need for air   (d) exploration   (g) need to explore   (i) need for security
    (b) need for affiliation   (e) need for status   (h) need to manipulate   (j) regulation of body temperature
    (c) need for sleep   (f) need to avoid pain

5. Within the body there are ideal levels for temperatures, concentration of blood chemicals, etc. When the body deviates from these ideal levels, automatic reactions restore equilibrium. This process is known as
    (a) the Yerkes-Dodson law.   (b) homeostasis.   (c) biothermoregulation.   (d) primary motivation.

6. The stomach can't be the main regulator of hunger because
    (a) there is no correlation between hunger pangs and stomach contractions.
    (b) when the stomach can no longer send sensory messages about its fullness, hunger is still present.
    (c) if blood from a starving dog is transferred into another dog, the second dog will no longer eat.
    (d) of all of the above.

7. Hunger and thirst appear to be primarily controlled by
    (a) blood content.   (b) stomach contractions.   (c) cultural factors.   (d) the hypothalamus.

8. The hypothalamus receives information about hunger from the
    (a) level of sugar in the blood.   (b) stomach.   (c) liver.   (d) all of these.

9. If the feeding center in an animal is destroyed the animal will
    (a) overeat and die.
    (b) begin eating only if its stomach is empty.
    (c) eat until it is full and the hunger motive is gone, then it will cease eating and die.
    (d) refuse to eat and will die.

10. Which of the following statements regarding hunger is *false*?
    (a) Cultural values greatly affect the incentive value of various foods.
    (b) Overeating occurs mainly while a person is gaining weight.
    (c) The satiety center in the hypothalamus tells a person when to stop eating.
    (d) Obese people are thought to be externally cued eaters.

11. Which of the following statements regarding set-point is *incorrect*?
    (a) Your personal set point is the weight you maintain when you are making no effort to gain or lose weight.
    (b) The set-point appears to be partially inherited and partially determined by early feeding patterns.
    (c) It would be better (in terms of fat cells) to be overweight as a child instead of overweight as an adult.
    (d) When an overweight person loses weight, the body goes below the set point, and the person feels hungry most of the time.

12. "Yo-yo" dieting is a name given to the process of frequent weight cycling and its effect on metabolic rate whereby a person finds it _____ to lose weight with each new diet and _____ to regain weight when the diet ends.
    (a) harder, harder
    (b) harder, easier
    (c) easier, harder
    (d) easier, easier

13. Which of the following statements about emotionality and obesity is *incorrect*?
    (a) Overweight people are generally slightly less emotionally reactive than normal-weight people.
    (b) Obesity is frequently accompanied by unhappiness.
    (c) People with weight problems are just as likely to eat when they are anxious or angry as when hungry.
    (d) The overweight person may develop a pattern of overeating which produces distress, and, in turn, leads to more overeating.

14. If a food causes sickness or if it precedes sickness caused by something else a(n) _____ _____ may be acquired.
    (a) taste aversion
    (b) specfic hunger
    (c) physiological hypoglycemia
    (d) episodic drive

15. Anorexia is best described as
    (a) a relentless pursuit of excessive thinness.
    (b) a loss of the desire for food.
    (c) a disorder than may ultimately result in hair loss, sore throat, kidney damage.
    (d) all of the above.

16. Which of the following statements regarding eating disorders is *false*?
    (a) Anorexics have a distorted body image.
    (b) Many people with eating disorders actually resist help.
    (c) Treatment of eating disorders involves therapy to explore the personal conflicts and family issues which are involved in the disorder.
    (d) Anorexia, but not bulimia, is far more prevalent in females than males.

17. People generally become bulimic because
    (a) of a desire for perfection.
    (b) of a very distorted body image.
    (c) they have a need to maintain control over things around them.
    (d) they are generally overweight in the first place.

18. When fluid is drawn out of cells and the cells shrink, this thirst is called
    (a) extracellular.
    (b) intracellular.
    (c) hypothalamic.
    (d) Miller Time.

19. The sex drive is different from most other primary drives in that it
    (a) increases as deprivation increases.
    (b) is necessary for individual survival.
    (c) is nonhomeostatic.
    (d) is all of the above.

20. The Yerkes-Dodson law relates _____ to _____.
    (a) fear of success, need for achievement
    (b) task difficulty, need for achievement
    (c) drive level, homeostasis
    (d) arousal level, task difficulty

21. According to the Yerkes-Dodson law, if a task is relatively simple, the optimal level of arousal will be
    (a) high.
    (b) moderate.
    (c) low.
    (d) it really doesn't matter.

22. The two major components of test anxiety are
    (a) worry plus physiological arousal.
    (b) sweating and self-doubt.
    (c) upsetting thoughts and feelings.
    (d) underpreparation plus fear.
    (e) stupidity plus not knowing where your classroom is.

23. Which of the following is *not* a good way to reduce test anxiety?
    (a) overprepare for tests
    (b) get physiologically "up" for the test
    (c) diminish your self-defeating thoughts
    (d) rehearse how you will cope with upsetting events

24. Which of the following statements regarding the need for achievement is ***incorrect***?
    (a) People high in nAch are moderate risk-takers.
    (b) College students high in nAch tend to blame their failure on someone else.
    (c) The need for achievement can be defined as a desire to meet some internalized standard of excellence.
    (d) The need for achievement differs from the need for power in that the latter is more concerned with the desire to have impact or control over others.

25. According to Bloom, which of the following conditions is necessary for the achievement of extraordinary success by high achievers? (You may choose more than one.)
    (a) natural talent
    (b) whole hearted parental support
    (c) intensive practice
    (d) innate ability

26. The needs in Maslow's hierarchy are ranked in which of the following ways?
    (a) physiological, safety and security, love and belonging, esteem, self-esteem, self-actualization
    (b) safety and security, physiological, love and belonging, esteem, self-actualization
    (c) physiological, love and belonging, safety and security, esteem, self-actualization
    (d) self-actualization, esteem, love and belonging, physiological, safety and security

27. Maslow's physiological needs are considered to be prepotent over the higher needs because
    (a) the higher needs can be more easily met.
    (b) the physiological needs are necessary for survival.
    (c) self-actualization is not a universal drive.
    (d) a person must always satisfy the physiological needs before dealing with the higher needs.

28. Motivation that makes an activity an end in itself is called
    (a) internal.   (b) extrinsic.   (c) ulterior.   (d) intrinsic.

29. Emotions appear to aid which of the following?
    (a) the meaning of life
    (b) depth of caring in our social relationships
    (c) motivation
    (d) survival
    (e) all of the above

30. Which of the following is a correct match?
    (a) emotional expressions – "butterflies" in the stomach
    (b) physiological changes – trembling hands
    (c) emotional feelings – your private experience
    (d) none of the above is a correct match

31. Circle the following emotions that Plutchik considers primary.
    (a) love   (e) disappointment   (i) awe   (l) surprise
    (b) hate   (f) joy   (j) aggression   (m) sadness
    (c) disgust   (g) anticipation   (k) terror   (n) anger
    (d) fear   (h) acceptance

32. The sympathetic branch of the ANS
    (a) calms a person after emotional arousal.
    (b) arouses some bodily systems and inhibits others.
    (c) helps build up and conserve bodily energy.
    (d) does none of the above.

33. Parasympathetic rebound refers to
    (a) overreaction of the parasympathetic system to any intense emotion.
    (b) overreaction of the parasympathetic system to fear.
    (c) the cause of all unexplained cases of sudden death.
    (d) the trauma caused by disruption of a close relationship.

34. Lie detection devices
    (a) measure the difference between the physiological and the psychological responses to a question.
    (b) are accurate indicators of when a person is not telling the truth.
    (c) measure the difference between the baseline and the increased levels of physiological arousal in response to questions.
    (d) are regulated by federal law.

35. Which of the following statements about lie detectors is *incorrect*?
    (a) Studies of the accuracy of lie detector devices show them only at or slightly above the chance level.
    (b) Bodily changes caused by the ANS are good indicators of emotion.
    (c) Lie detector devices only record general emotional arousal.
    (d) The machines' most common error is to label a guilty person innocent, rather than vice versa.

36. According to Charles Darwin, humans have emotions because
    (a) they are learned.
    (b) in the evolutionary chain animals did not use them.
    (c) of genetic mutations.
    (d) they are an aid to survival.

37. Emotional expressions appear to be the same for all people because
    (a) the grimace is the most recognizable facial expression of emotion.
    (b) children who are blind and deaf at birth use the same facial expression as more "normal" children.
    (c) everybody expresses emotions.
    (d) the physiological arousal for different emotions is the same for all people.

38. Which of the following is *not* a dimension of emotion conveyed by facial expression?
    (a) arousal   (b) attention-rejection   (c) hope-disappointment   (d) pleasantness-unpleasantness

39. Which of the following are communicated by the body (as opposed to strictly the face)?
    (a) liking or disliking   (b) deception or fibbing   (c) relaxation or tension   (d) all of these

40. Which of the following statements is *false*?
    (a) Arousal, interest, or attention can dilate the pupils.
    (b) Making faces may bring about changes in the autonomic nervous system.
    (c) The physiological reactions parents feel when hearing a baby cry encourage the parents to tend to his/her needs, thus increasing its chances for survival.
    (d) The commonsense theory of emotion holds that we encounter a scary situation, run, and feel fear.

41. Which theory first stressed that emotion follows bodily arousal?
    (a) Cannon-Bard   (b) commonsense   (c) James-Lange   (d) Schachter

42. The theory of emotion that says emotion and bodily changes occur simultaneously is the _____ theory.
    (a) cognitive   (b) commonsense   (c) Cannon-Bard   (d) James-Lange

43. Schachter's theory of emotion puts emphasis on
    (a) bodily arousal.
    (b) the reversal of parasympathetic and sympathetic cues.
    (c) the simultaneous perception of emotional feelings and their bodily expressions.
    (d) the labels or interpretations of bodily arousal.

44. The observation that arousal can be attributed to various sources, thereby altering the perception of emotions, works best with which overall theory of emotion?
    (a) Commonsense   (b) James-Lange   (c) Cannon-Bard   (d) Schachter

45. The facial feedback hypothesis appears to demonstrate that
    (a) facial expressions may affect emotions.
    (b) emotions may determine facial expressions.
    (c) physiological changes are reflected in facial expression.
    (d) the face is a "physiological billboard."

46. Appraisal of a situation or stimulus would mean different things to different people because
    (a) feedback from arousal adds to emotional experience.
    (b) of the facial feedback hypothesis as it applies to each individual.
    (c) the personal meaning for each individual would be different.
    (d) each person would use different adaptive behaviors.

47. Indicate by circling which of the following are behavioral dieting techniques.
    (a) Avoid exercise – it increases appetite.
    (b) Weaken personal eating cues.
    (c) Focus on the amount of food not the calories.
    (d) Keep a diet diary.
    (e) Involve other people in your diet program.
    (f) Eat small snacks in between light meals to keep your appetite down.
    (g) Set a threshold for maintaining control over your weight.

True-False

_____ 1. Motivation is defined as the process of balancing needs against goals.

_____ 2. Obese people generally eat normal amounts of food after they have gained their weight.

_____ 3. Studies of people with anorexia nervosa demonstrate that a considerable weight loss results in a loss of appetite.

_____ 4. Avoiding pain is an unlearned motive basic to the survival of humans and animals.

_____ 5. As evidence for the existence of drives such as curiosity and exploration, it has been noted that monkeys will learn to perform a simple task to open a window that allowed them to view the outside world.

_____ 6. According to the arousal theory of motivation, there is an ideal level of arousal for activities, and individuals behave in ways that keep arousal near this ideal level.

_____ 7. Test anxiety is at its greatest when heightened physiological arousal is coupled with overpreparation.

_____ 8. People low in nAch will seek out goals that require more luck than skill to achieve.

_____ 9. The meta-needs are self-actualization motives.

_____ 10. The complexity and challenge of a task are barriers to reaching a goal when intrinsic motivation is stressed.

_____ 11. According to Plutchik, adjacent primary emotions can be mixed to yield a third, simpler emotion.

_____ 12. The actions of the parasympathetic branch generally calm and relax the body.

_____ 13. Most people tend to interpret large pupil size as a sign of pleasant feelings and small pupil size as a sign of negative feelings.

_____ 14. Because children who are born deaf and blind have little opportunity to learn emotional expression from others, they have very different facial gestures for joy and sadness than other hearing and sighted children.

_____ 15. The study of kinesics reveals that body language usually just communicates a person's overall emotional tone.

_____ 16. Shifty eyes and squirming are examples of illustrators which increase in number when a person is telling a lie.

_____ 17. James (of the James-Lange theory of emotion) pointed out that we often do not experience an emotion until after we react.

_____ 18. According to the attribution theory, the perception of emotion in any situation depends on the intensity of the bodily arousal.

_____ 19. According to Schacter, emotional arousal, behavior, and experience are controlled by the thalamus and are nearly simultaneous.

Can You Apply the Information?

1. If you're in an airplane crash and left without food for many days or weeks, you may find yourself eating roots, insects, leaves, or even human bodies. In this case it can be said that
   (a) the internal need was low but the incentive value high.
   (b) the internal need and the incentive value were both low.
   (c) the pull of the goal was high but its push was low.
   (d) the pull of the goal was low but the internal need was strong.

2. Coming into a warm room and taking off your sweater is an example of
   (a) the motivation of homeostasis.
   (b) a learned motive.
   (c) intrinsic motivation.
   (d) none of these.

3. Unfortunately you find out that you have a cancerous tumor in your stomach and your stomach must be removed. What will likely happen to you?
   (a) You will have trouble deciding when you are hungry.
   (b) You will probably overeat because you won't know when you're full.
   (c) You will probably feel hunger and eat regularly.
   (d) You will lose weight due to the absence of hunger pangs.

4. You are going to redecorate your Italian restaurant with soft lights, background music, pleasant colors, candles, etc. In short, you want to make the atmosphere conducive to eating. You will probably make
   (a) some obese people eat more.
   (b) some normal-weight people eat more.
   (c) some thin people eat more.
   (d) all of the above.

5. A weight problem that begins in adulthood is more serious than a weight problem beginning in childhood because fat cells are more easily added to adults.
   (a) True   (b) False

6. Bob has tried to lose weight by going on six different diets in the last six months. By now, he has discovered that
   (a) he loses weight quickly and has no trouble keeping it off.
   (b) he loses about one pound per week during the diet and regains one pound per day when the diet is over.
   (c) he loses about one pound per week during the diet and can now keep it off for months.
   (d) pounds drop off him quickly but he regains the weight just as fast when the diet is over.

7. You go out for a good time on Saturday night and eat too much pizza and drink too much cheap wine. Your stomach can't take anymore and after your 8th piece of pizza you get very sick. It is likely that
   (a) you have acquired a taste aversion through classical conditioning, and you won't want to eat pizza for a while.
   (b) you will develop specific hungers for the nutrients in pizza.
   (c) your appetite for pizza will now become episodic.
   (d) the incentive value of pizza will increase.

8. Felice is a 14 year old female who has conflict in her family. There is discord between the parents. Her brother who is two years older is constantly in trouble at home and at school. Because of her brother, Felice feels that she must try to be the "perfect" daughter—helpful, considerate, obedient. She is 5'6" tall and weighs 90 pounds, but she decides to go on a diet. Which of the following statements is *least* appropriate in her situation?
   (a) She is more likely to become anorexic than bulimic.
   (b) The probability is considerable that unless her problem is avoided or brought under control quickly that she will die.
   (c) She may eventually need to be hospitalized and started on a strictly controlled diet.
   (d) She has some major problems with the idea of control.

9. Gladys is a neurosurgeon and has decided not to operate on her mother's hypothalamus. According to the Yerkes-Dodson law Gladys
   (a) made a wise choice because her arousal would probably have been too low for a complex task.
   (b) should have operated anyway.
   (c) would have had too much arousal for a complex task, and her performance (and her mother) would have suffered.
   (d) would have done fine since her arousal would have been high for a simple task.

10. Bill is taking the final examination in his psychology class. All of a sudden he finds that he is drawing a blank on five of the last six essay questions. Twenty minutes later he looks at the clock and realizes that he has only ten minutes remaining. He begins to panic. Which of the methods to reduce test anxiety should Bill have concentrated on before he took the test? (use two.)

(a) be prepared
(b) learn to relax
(c) rehearse how to cope
(d) change self-defeating thinking

11. A person who has a high need for achievement is gambling. The casino has a $100 limit on bets. Our high nAch person will be most likely to

(a) bet all he has on one roll.
(b) avoid all risk.
(c) make many bets of very small amounts.
(d) take a moderate amount of risk if there seems to be a chance of winning.

12. Roberta started a high-paying but tedious assembly line job four months ago. She can now pay all her bills and meet all her basic needs easily. The only drawback is the lack of time for anything else in her life but the job. We should expect Roberta to

(a) be happy over improving her credit rating.
(b) be looking for a new apartment.
(c) experience a mixture of happiness and anticipation over the changes in her life.
(d) feel alienated from her family and co-workers.

13. Rick cooks because he loves it (and he can cook one heck of a TV dinner). Tom cooks because his family has to eat. What can be said of this situation?

(a) Rick's cooking motives are extrinsic.
(b) Rick's primary reason for cooking is to strive for self-actualization.
(c) The incentive value of cooking is primarily external.
(d) The motive to cook by Rick is intrinsic.

14. Ed and Terri enjoyed doing ceramics as a hobby. To make some money they decided to open up a ceramics shop. Their love of ceramics has decreased dramatically because

(a) their motivation went from intrinsic to extrinsic.
(b) there was no longer any incentive value to the ceramics.
(c) intrinsic value overtook extrinsic value.
(d) their motivation was prepotent.

15. Over the last two weeks, most of your co-workers have been laid off. You're worried that you might be next but you don't want to upset your spouse. When you got home from work today all of the following indicators of emotional distress were present. Which one told your spouse you were upset?

(a) increased heart rate
(b) shifty eyes
(c) perspiration
(d) trembling hands

16. You are confronted by a person on a dark street. Which physiological mechanism will probably take over?

(a) parasympathetic branch of the ANS
(b) central nervous system
(c) sympathetic branch of the ANS
(d) peripheral nervous system

17. You're a private detective investigating embezzlement at a large department store. Which of the following would probably give you the best results?

(a) Interview each employee where you can get a videotape of their lower body without them knowing it.
(b) Test each employee with a polygraph.
(c) Watch for facial expressions indicating tension.
(d) Use a polygraph with an experienced tester.

18. You're an insurance investigator examining the theft of some valuable artworks. You believe it is an "inside job" after talking with the four family members who claimed to have been home during the robbery but heard nothing. Which one was probably lying?

(a) Bob, the retired accountant, who squirmed in his chair during the questioning.
(b) Rita, the sign language teacher, who sat with her arms folded during the questioning.
(c) Billy, the graduate student, who played with his beard during most of the questions.
(d) Mary, the little rich girl, who bit her lips during the interrogation.

19. You're in your car driving on an icy road when all of a sudden you lose control and your car begins spinning around and around. You remain calm and manage to regain control after skidding about 75 yards. You pull over to the side of the road and begin to shake almost uncontrollably. You realize you're scared to death. This situation best supports which theory of emotion?
   (a) commonsense   (b) James-Lange   (c) Cannon-Bard   (d) Schachter's cognitive

20. According to the attribution theory which of the following statements is *correct*?
   (a) Bill and Jane will love each other more if their feelings are accurately attributed to their physiological arousal.
   (b) Jane is more likely to respond to Bill's kiss after riding a gigantic roller coaster than after riding on the merry-go-round.
   (c) The intensification of feelings between two people is most often due to frustration.
   (d) None of these is correct.

21. You are preparing for your final exam in psychology and it is not going well. Which of the following steps would best keep you from feeling depressed?
   (a) a brief period of intense exercise   (c) make a "happy face" for ten minutes
   (b) reviewing the key points of the covered material   (d) going ahead and letting yourself feel bad for ten minutes

Chapter Review

1. _____ refers to the dynamics of behavior, the process of initiating, sustaining, and directing activities of the organism. Many motivated behaviors begin with a _____.

2. In the need reduction model of motivation, a need causes a psychological state called a _____ to develop. This in turn activates a _____ (or a series of actions) designed to attain a _____. Relieving the need temporarily ends the motivational chain of events. After achieving the _____ a person experiences _____ _____.

3. Motivated behavior can be energized by _____ stimuli as well as by the "push" of _____ needs. The "pull" exerted by a goal or _____ stimulus is called its _____ _____.

4. Motives can be divided into three major categories. The first, referred to as _____ motives, are based on _____ needs which are _____ and must be met for _____. _____ motives also appear to be _____, but they are not necessary for the _____ of the organism. The last category, called _____ motives, are _____ and they account for the great diversity of human activity.

5. While it is certainly true that eating is limited when the stomach is _____, it can be shown that the stomach is not essential for experiencing _____. For one thing, cutting the _____ from the stomach does not abolish _____. Also people who have had their stomachs _____ continue to feel _____ and eat regularly.

6. One important factor involved in hunger appears to be the level of _____ in the blood. Another important factor is the _____ which responds to a lack of bodily fuel by sending nerve impulses to the _____ in the brain.

7. If the _____ system of the hypothalamus is stimulated, even a well-fed animal will begin eating. If it is destroyed the animal will die of _____. The hypothalamus also has an area that seems to operate as a _____ system (or "stop center") for eating. If this area is destroyed, dramatic _____ results. A third area of importance is the _____ nucleus of the hypothalamus. This area keeps _____ _____ levels steady.

8. Recent evidence suggests that fat stored in the body also influences hunger. The body acts as if there is a _____-_____ for the proportion of body fat that is maintained. This point appears to be partially _____ and partially determined by early _____ patterns.

9. The _____-_____ may be lastingly altered when a child is overfed. If a weight problem begins in childhood, the person as an adult will have _____ fat cells and _____ fat cells in the body. If the person does not have a weight problem until adulthood, his or her fat cells will be _____, but there will not be an _____ in the number.

10. It is now known that people of all weights can be found who are especially sensitive to _____ cues. Obese people generally eat _____ amounts of food. Once excess weight is gained, it can be maintained with a _____ diet.

11. People with weight problems are just as likely to eat when _____ _____ as when _____. Another problem is that their additional weight causes them _____ distress.

12. Dieting causes the body to become highly effecient at _____ calories and storing them as _____. Frequent weight _____ appears to _____ the body's metabolic rate. Hence it becomes _____ to lose weight with each diet and _____ to regain weight when the diet ends.

13. In some countries people eat what Americans would find disgusting and vice versa. This demonstrates that eating is partially controlled by _____ factors. It has also been shown that _____ may affect hunger because the hungrier a person is, the more pleasant a sweet food tastes.

14. If a food causes sickness or if it simply precedes sickness caused by something else, we may develop a _____ _____ which is a special case of _____ conditioning. Using this method coyotes have been trained to develop_____ _____ to lamb.

15. The problem which is characterized as a relentless pursuit of excessive thinness is called _____ _____. The binge-purge syndrome is known as _____. Both disorders seem to occur more in _____.

16. Both disorders are related to an exaggerated fear of becoming _____. Anorexics have a distorted _____ _____ and are described as _____ daughters. Both seem to be concerned with _____. Besides treatment to restore a person's _____, anorexics usually need _____ to explore _____ conflicts and _____ issues. Bulimics must work on extinguishing the urge to _____ after eating.

17. Like hunger, thirst appears to be controlled by the _____, where separate thirst and thirst satiety centers are found. Thirst caused by a loss of water from the fluids surrounding your body's cells is termed _____. When fluid is drawn out of cells because of an increase in salt this is called _____ thirst.

18. Two primary drives, _____ and the avoidance of _____, are unlike the rest. The avoidance of _____ is different because it is _____ in nature, because we _____ the other primary motives, and because the drive is partially _____.

19. Compared to the other primary drives, the _____ drive is unusual because it is not necessary for the _____ of an individual, it is _____, and its _____ is sought as actively as its _____.

20. The drives for exploration, manipulation, and curiosity are examples of _____ needs. These drives were demonstrated in experiments showing that monkeys would learn tasks for no _____ except exploration and manipulation.

21. The _____ theory of motivation assumes that there is an ideal level of _____ for various activities and that individuals behave in ways to keep themselves near this ideal level. The relationship of a person's _____ to the _____ of the task is referred to as the _____-_____ law. If a task is _____, the optimal level of _____ will be _____.

22. Test anxiety involves the combination of heightened _____ and excessive _____. To reduce this anxiety it is best to be fully _____ for the test and one must be able to _____. It also helps to _____ how to cope with upsetting events. Changing _____ - _____ thinking can be the best solution of all.

23. The desire to meet some internalized standard of excellence is called need for _____. It is different from a need for _____ which is a desire to have _____ or _____ over others.

24. People who are high in nAch tend to be _____ risk-takers. College students high in nAch tend to attribute success to their own _____ and failure to insufficient _____.

25. Bloom found that _____ and _____, not great natural talent, led to success in the high achievers he studied. Basically, _____ is nurtured by dedication and hard _____. This would be most likely to happen when parents give their wholehearted _____ to a child's _____ interest.

26. Maslow has proposed a _____ (or ordering) of human needs. The first of the needs are the _____ ones. They are considered _____ because generally the higher needs are not expressed until the lower needs are met and the lower needs are necessary for _____.

27. After the physiological needs come the needs for _____ and _____, then _____ and _____, _____ and _____-_____, and last, _____-_____. More generally the needs are ordered _____, _____, and _____.

28. _____ motivation occurs when there is no external reward for your actions while _____ motivation stems from obvious external factors. For some behaviors external incentives may be required to get a person's skills to the level where _____ motivation can take over. However, increasing external incentives does not always strengthen motivation. In most cases motivation is best when it is _____.

29. Emotions have a powerful influence on _____. First, the body is _____ aroused during emotion. Second, emotions are linked to _____ behaviors. Emotions can be _____ but more often they aid _____.

30. Emotional expressions, or _____ _____ of what a person is feeling, are a major element of emotions along with _____ changes and _____ feelings.

31. Plutchik believes that there are eight _____ _____ and that adjacent ones can be mixed to yield a third more complex _____.

32. The consistency of the physical reactions to emotion is due to the acitivity of the _____ nervous system. The _____ branch is primarily responsible for _____ the body to prepare for action. In contrast, the _____ branch _____ the body.

33. Arousal, interest, or attention can activate the _____ nervous system and cause the pupils to _____. This can occur during _____ or _____ emotions.

34. The parasympathetic system may overreact during intense _____, a process called _____ _____, sometimes resulting in death. However, in the case of older people or those with _____ problems, direct effects of _____ _____ may be enough to cause a heart attack. For example, Engel found the traumatic disruption of a _____ _____ related to almost _____ of all sudden deaths.

35. Devices called "lie detectors" record general _____ _____. Such devices appear to be rather _____ because there is no unique _____ _____ that everyone gives when not telling the truth. The most common error of "lie detectors" is to label a(n) _____ person _____.

36.   According to _____, emotional expressions were retained during the course of human evolution because communicating feelings to others was an aid to _____.

37.   There is evidence to support the contention that there is a universality of emotional expressions. Children born _____ and _____ use the same facial expressions as other children to display many emotions. It is nice to note that the most universal and easily recognizable facial expression of emotion is the _____.

38.   The study of communication through body movement, posture, gestures, and facial expressions is called _____. It is generally agreed that body language does not communicate specific emotional messages but just the overall _____ _____.

39.   Facial expressions are capable of accurately portraying three feelings: _____- _____, _____-_____, and _____. The most general emotional feelings communicated by the body are _____ or _____ and _____ or _____. Overall _____ can also indicate a person's emotional state. In addition, it has been shown that _____ is best revealed by the _____ body.

40.   The _____ theory of emotion says that when we see a bear, we feel fear, become aroused and run.

41.   The James-Lange theory of emotion says that emotional _____ follow _____ _____. James pointed out that often we do not experience an emotion until _____ reacting.

42.   The Cannon-Bard theory of emotion states that emotional feelings and bodily arousal occur at the _____ _____ and that the emotions are organized in the _____.

43.   Schachter's cognitive theory of emotion emphasizes the importance of _____ applied to feelings of bodily arousal. Support for this theory comes from studies that show subjects who experience _____ rated a slapstick movie as much funnier than subjects who received a tranquilizer before the movie.

44.   Closely related to the cognitive theory of emotion is the process of _____ which refers to the emotional effects of associating bodily _____ with a particular person, object, or situation. This theory predicts that adding fear, anger, frustration, etc., to a relationship tends to _____ a couple's love for each other.

45.   Researchers have found that making faces brings about changes in the _____ nervous system. Apparently emotional activity causes changes in _____ _____ which in turn provides _____ to the brain to help us determine what emotion we are feeling. This is the core of the _____ _____ hypothesis.

46.   Current thought holds that each theory is partly true: James and Lange were right about feedback from _____ and _____ adding to emotional experience; Cannon and Bard were right about _____ of events; and, _____ showed the importance of cognition. In addition, the _____ of a situation affects the course of emotion.

47.   What is really needed to control weight is a complete overhaul of _____ _____ and control of the _____ for eating. This approach has been called _____ _____ and has repeatedly proved superior to simple dieting for weight control.

48.   Behavioral dieting involves several steps. Keeping a diet _____ can be useful as a means of learning your eating habits. Along with this, count _____. Also, develop techniques to control the act of eating like taking _____ portions and _____ your mouthfuls.

49. You should also learn to _____ your personal eating cues by avoiding situations that stimulate your eating behavior. You should also avoid _____ and be sure to get regular _____. It helps to make a list of _____ you will receive if you change your eating habits and _____ that will occur if you don't. _____ your progress daily.

ANSWER KEYS

Do You Know the Information?

Multiple Choice

1. (c) obj. 2, p. 374
2. (a) obj. 3, p. 375
3. (d) obj. 4, p. 376
4. (b,e,i) obj. 4, p. 376
5. (b) obj. 5, p. 376
6. (b) obj. 6, p. 377
7. (d) objs. 7,14, pp. 378, 384
8. (d) obj. 7, p. 378
9. (d) obj. 7, p. 378
10. (d) objs. 7,10, pp. 378,380-381
11. (c) obj. 8, p. 379
12. (b) obj. 9, p. 381
13. (a) obj. 11, p. 380
14. (a) obj. 12, p. 381
15. (a) obj. 13, p. 382
16. (d) obj. 13, p. 382
17. (c) obj. 13, p. 383
18. (b) obj. 14, p. 384
19. (c) obj. 15, p. 385
20. (d) obj. 17, p. 389
21. (a) obj. 17, p. 389
22. (a) obj. 18, p. 390
23. (b) obj. 18, p. 390
24. (b) objs. 19-20, p. 391
25. (b,c) obj. 21, pp. 391-392
26. (a) obj. 22, p. 393
27. (b) obj. 23, p. 392
28. (d) obj. 25, p. 394
29. (e) obj. 26, pp. 395-396
30. (c) obj. 27, p. 396

31. (c,d,f,g,h,l,m,n) obj. 28, p. 396
32. (b) obj. 29, p. 398
33. (b) obj. 31, p. 399
34. (c) obj. 32, p. 400
35. (d) objs. 32-33, p. 401
36. (d) obj. 34, p. 402
37. (b) obj. 35, p. 402
38. (c) obj. 36, p. 403
39. (d) obj. 36, p. 403
40. (d) objs. 30,34,38,43, p. 404
41. (c) obj. 39, p. 404
42. (c) obj. 40, p. 404
43. (d) obj. 41, p. 405
44. (d) obj. 42, p. 406
45. (a) obj. 43, p. 406
46. (c) obj. 44, p. 409
47. (b, d, e) obj. 45, pp. 410-411

True-False

1. F, obj. 1, p. 374
2. T, obj. 10, p. 380
3. F, obj. 13, p. 382
4. F, obj. 15, p. 385
5. T, obj. 16, p. 386
6. T, obj. 17, p. 387
7. F, obj. 18, p. 390
8. T, obj. 20, p. 391
9. T, obj. 24, p. 394
10. F, obj. 25, p. 394
11. F, obj. 28, p. 397

12. T, obj. 29, p. 398
13. T, obj. 30, p. 399
14. F, obj. 35, p. 402
15. T, obj. 36, p. 403
16. F, obj. 37, p. 404
17. T, obj. 39, p. 404
18. F, obj. 42, p. 406
19. F, obj. 44, p. 408

Can You Apply the Information?

1. (d) obj. 3, p. 375
2. (a) obj. 5, p. 376
3. (c) obj. 6, p. 377
4. (d) objs. 7, 10, p. 380
5. (b) obj. 8, p. 379
6. (b) obj. 9, p. 381
7. (a) obj. 12, p. 381
8. (b) obj. 13, pp. 382-383
9. (c) obj. 17, p. 389
10. (a,c) obj. 18, p. 390
11. (d) obj. 20, p. 391
12. (d) obj. 24, p. 394
13. (d) obj. 25, p. 394
14. (a) obj. 25, p. 394
15. (d) obj. 27, p. 396
16. (c) obj. 29, p. 398
17. (a) objs. 32,33,36,37, p. 403
18. (b) obj. 37, p. 403
19. (b) obj. 39, p. 404
20. (b) obj. 42, p. 406
21. (c) obj. 43, p. 407

Chapter Review

1. Motivation, need (p. 374)
2. drive, response, goal, goal, need reduction (p. 374)
3. external, internal, external, incentive value (p. 375)
4. primary, biological, innate, survival, Stimulus, innate, survival, secondary, learned (p. 376)
5. full (distended), hunger, nerves, hunger, removed, hunger (p. 377)
6. sugar, liver, hypothalamus (p. 378)
7. feeding, starvation, satiety, overeating, paraventricular, blood sugar (p. 378)
8. set-point, inherited, feeding (p. 379)
9. set-point, more, larger, larger, increase (p. 379)

10. external (p. 379); normal, normal (p. 380)
11. emotionally upset, hungry, emotional (p. 380)
12. conserving, fat, cycling, slow, harder, easier (p. 381)
13. cultural, taste (p. 381)
14. taste aversion, classical, bait shyness (p. 381)
15. anorexia nervosa, bulimia, females (p. 382)
16. fat, body image, perfect, control, health (weight), counseling, personal, family, vomit (p. 382)
17. hypothalamus, extracellular, intracellular (p. 384)
18. sex, pain, pain, episodic, seek, learned (p. 385)
19. sex, survival, nonhomeostatic, arousal, reduction (p. 383)
20. stimulus, reward (p. 386)
21. arousal, arousal (p. 387); arousal, complexity, Yerkes-Dodson, simple (complex), arousal, high (low) (p. 389)
22. arousal, worry, prepared, relax, rehearse, self-defeating (p. 390)
23. achievement, power, impact, control (p. 391)
24. moderate, ability, effort (p. 391)
25. drive, determination, talent, work, support, special (p. 391)
26. hierarchy, physiological, prepotent, survival (p. 392)
27. safety, security, love, belonging, esteem, self-esteem, self-actualization, basic, growth, meta (p. 393)
28. Intrinsic, extrinsic, intrinsic, intrinsic (p. 394)
29. motivation, physically, adaptive, disruptive, survival (p. 396)
30. outward signs, physiological, emotional (p. 396)
31. primary emotions, emotion (p. 396)
32. autonomic, sympathetic, arousing, parasympathetic, calms (relaxes) (p. 398)
33. sympathetic, dilate, pleasant, unpleasant (p. 398)
34. fear, parasympathetic rebound, heart, sympathetic activation, close relationship, half (p. 399)
35. emotional arousal, inaccurate, lie response, innocent, guilty (p. 400)
36. Darwin, survival (p. 402)
37. deaf, blind, smile (p. 402)
38. kinesics, emotional tone (p. 403)
39. pleasantness-unpleasantness, attention-rejection, activation, relaxation, tension, liking, disliking, posture, deception, lower (p. 403)
40. commonsense (p. 404)
41. feelings, bodily arousal, after, physical (p. 404)
42. same time, brain (p. 404)
43. labels, arousal (p. 405)
44. attribution, arousal, increase (intensify) (p. 406)
45. autonomic, facial expression, cues, facial feedback (p. 406)
46. arousal, behavior, timing, Schacter, appraisal (p. 407)
47. eating habits, cues, behavioral dieting (p. 410)
48. diary, calories, smaller, counting (p. 410)
49. weaken, snacks, exercise, rewards, punishments, Chart (p. 411)

chapter twelve
Health, Stress, and Coping

stress
   factors affecting it
burnout
appraising stressors
   primary vs. secondary
threats
   problem vs. emotion-focused coping
frustration
   external, personal
factors affecting frustration
reactions to frustration
   aggression, persistence,
   circumvention, displacement,
   escape/withdrawal

scapegoating
conflict
   approach-approach
   avoidance-avoidance
   approach-avoidance
   double approach-avoidance
psychological defense mechanisms
   denial, repression, reaction formation,
   regression, projection, rationalization,
   compensation, sublimation
learned hopelessness
   attribution
   depression
   hope

Social Readjustment Rating Scale
hassles
acculturative stress
psychosomatic vs. hypochondriac
Type A vs. Type B personality
biofeedback
strategies for reducing hostility
   hardy personality
General Adaptation Syndrome
   alarm reaction, resistance, exhaustion
health psychology
   behavioral risk factors
stress management
stereotyped response

LEARNING OBJECTIVES

To demonstrate mastery of this chapter you should be able to:

1. Explain the similarity between your body's stress reaction and emotion.

stress reaction-(physical response to stress-i.e - bodily change Re to autonomic nervous system arousal

2. List five aspects of stress that make it more intense and damaging.

  a. — *heart beat- rapid surge*

  b. *blood pressure increases*

  c. *muscle tension*

  d. *respirational problem*

  e. *fatigue*

emotional shock intense, repeated or unpredictable, (linked to pressure — stress then magnified & damage likely to result

3. Describe burnout. List and describe the three aspects of the problem. Describe three things that can be done to help reduce it.

Job related condition - mental/physical/emotional exhaustion ("used up

Aspects: ② depersonalization (detachment)   To help reduce burnout:

a. mental exhaustion

— a. redesigning jobs → improve balance between demands & satisfaction

③ reduced personal accomplishment feeling

b. physical exhaustion — b. build stronger social support system at work

① c. emotional exhaustion (fatigued, tenseness, apathy) Focus us to

c. — demonstrate greater understanding of stress felt by those whose work requires caring about the needs of other

4. Give an example of how primary and secondary appraisal are used in coping with a threatening situation.

P. A = deciding if situation is relevant or irrelevant - positive or threatening - "Am I ok or in trouble?

2nday A = assess resources, select way to meet threat or challenge - "What can I do?

5. Explain how the perception of control of a stressor influences the amount of threat felt.

sense of Control results from a feeling (belief) that one can reach desired goals — the greater the sense of control, the lesser the amt of threat felt [in one's mind]

6. Differentiate problem-focused coping from emotion-focused coping and explain how they may help or hinder each other.

Problem Focused coping – aimed at managing or altering the distressing situation) In attempts

Emotion Focused coping – an attempt at controlling his/her emotional reaction (at coping

2 types aiding one another) hypo. situation - anxiety before a speech - deep breathing reduces anxiety [emotion focus] coping

this leads to a glance at notes & a speech delivery improvement [problem focus coping]

2 types hindering one another) hypo. situation) time to arrive at difficult decision → seemingly unbearable emotional distress - temptation – a quick, ill-advised choice – this brings about coping with emotions – but it short changes problem Focused coping

7. List and describe the two different kinds of frustration.

a. External - based on conditions' outside the the individual - Conditions that impede goal achievement (stuck with a flat tire)

b. Personal — based on personal characteristics } ex. 4' tall aspiring to NBA   D student " " " law school }

8. List four factors which increase frustration.

a. increase in strength, urgency or importance of a blocked motive

b. being stopped just shy of the goal

c. repetition of frustration

d. improper I.D. of source of frustration

9. List and describe five common reactions to frustration (see Figure 12-2).

a. aggression) any response made intended to bring harm to person or object you lost e'th - no results

b. persistence) characterize by more vigorous efforts - & more varied responses (lost e'h in vend. machine - press harder - faster)

c. redirecting or displacing aggression) ale the bullegee incident - "taking out" frustrations - a delayed reaction -

d. scapegoating) - targeting of displaced aggression - ale USBlacks) Germ. Jews

e. escape or withdrawal) leaving a source of frustration

10. Explain how scapegoating is a special form of displaced aggression.

it is particularly damaging - it may cause expensive harm to individuals) or groups.

11. Describe and give an example of each of the following four types of conflict:
occurs) whenever one must choose between contradictory needs) desires) motives.

a. approach-approach — that which results from being forced to choose between 2 positive or desirable alternatives - (selecting one of two tempting desserts)

b. avoidance-avoidance — that which results from a forced choice between two negative, or undesirable alternatives - when one is caught between "the devil & the deep blue sea"; between "the frying pan & the fire" to study or to fail) pregnancy vs abortion) sustained pain vs medication) employment vs poverty

c. approach-avoidance (Include the terms ambivalence and partial approach in your response.)
<that resulting from a simultaneous attraction to & repulsion from the same goal - or activity 1st date & an obnoxious parent - does one seek 2nd date? Result - ambivalence in feelings. ∴ ambivalence in feelings becomes a c'trl characteristic of approach-avoidance conflicts - it results in a partial approach - No 2nd Date - but socializing outside framework of a date!

d. double approach-avoidance (Include the term vacillate in your response.)
that resulting from the presence of both positive & negative qualities in each alternative choice (w 2 job offers - Job A good salary, lousy hrs, monotonous routine - Job B - interesting work, great hrs - lousy pay

12. Define the term defense mechanism and discuss the positive and negative aspects of using them. {See also p. 426 for [+] and [-] points.} any /device or technique used to avoid, deny, or distort sources of threat or anxiety — they're used to cultivate idealized self image - makes us feel more comfortable about ourselves - (set f'th by Dr. Freud - his contention - they're unconsciously operative!
+ aspect) they're of assistance in preventing one from becoming overwhelmed
+ aspect) they "buy time" aiding us in learning to cope with adversity

- aspect) over excessive usage → lessening of adaptability potential

- aspect) unconscious defensiveness could cause a "blind spot" in awareness - ale stinginess causing the trytued image could go un noticed by its displayer

13. Describe the following defense mechanisms and give an example of each:

a. denial protecting oneself from unpleasantness via refusing to acknowledge its existence
   e.g.) these X rays must be wrong - I'm in good shape!

b. repression – unconsciously preventing painful or dangerous thoughts from entering our awareness of them
   (loss of memory of any past unpleasantness in life)

c. reaction formation
   – preventing dangerous impulses from being expressed in behavior by exaggerating opposite behavior
   "covering" child resentment – via display of inordinate affection for child

d. regression reacting to an earlier level of development or to earlier, less demanding habits or situations
   ∟ older child resorting to habits earlier acceptable – in order to detract from 2th given to newborn (bed wetting -) childish speech – "baby talk"

e. projection – attributing one's own feelings, shortcomings – or unacceptable impulses to others
   – cheating on others – thinking everyone's out to get me – I'll get them first.

f. rationalization – justifying behavior via giving reasonable – "rational" but false reasons for something
   ∟ I'll not study now. – why? I've got to be in the mood! – The mood will arrive later – then I'll study!

g. compensation – counteracting a real/imagined weakness by emphasizing desirable traits or seeking to excel in the area of weakness or in other areas.
   – FDR – political success – following his partial conquest of polio!

h. sublimation – "working off" unfulfilled desires – or unacceptable impulses – in other constructive activities
   aggressiveness – substitute defensive NFL lineman!

   Seek student reaction:
   lying may be sublimated into
   creative writing (or) – political!

14. Describe the development of learned helplessness and relate this concept to depression and attribution. Explain how helplessness may be unlearned.

is a a Learned inability to overcome obstacles or to avoid punishment 2 this occurs when events appear to be uncontrollable. Learned passivity to aversive stimuli

there are similarities between learned helplessness & depression. Common symptoms – feelings of powerlessness hopelessness decreased activity, lowered aggression, loss of sex drive & appetite

the unlearning of 2 via Kindling of hope & control Providing experience & training in mastering "impossible" challenges Survival Training

persons who are made to feel helpless in one situation are more likely to act helpless in other situations – if they attribute their failure to lasting gen'l factors!

15. Describe the four problems which typically contribute to depression among college students.

a. stress from difficulty of college work - career choice pressure -

b. isolation feeling (home sickness)

c. study problems - unsatisfactory grades - ex validictorian - is now little fish in big pond - necessary skills conspicuously absent

d. termination of an intimate relationship (student "cracked" at local tavern - pouring out ♡ to any listener)

16. List the five conditions of depression and describe how it can be combatted.

a. Constant negative self evaluation

b. Frequency of self criticism

c. - negative attachments to normally insignificantly perceived events

d. - pessimistic future outlook

e. - perception of overwhelment by personal responsibilities

Possible depression reduction devices
- improved time management via schedule
- provide a "jam packed" day
- initiate easy activities — graduate to difficulties
- use soft system for activities
- list personal accomplishments
- seek help in "overcoming" deficiencies
  └ upon arrival of improvement signs, embrace concept
    ' There's light at end of tunnel "

17. Discuss the relationship between life changes and long-term health, immediate health and how acculturative stress can cause problems.

stresses caused by adaptation - changes requisite in a move to a culture outside one's homebase

this can lead to health problems, (psychosomatic illnesses) —

Describe the SRRS.
Social Readjustment Rating Scale - rates the impact of various life events on the likelihood of illness

Explain how hassles are related to
The greater the importance attached to the hassle — the more adverse its impact upon immediate health!

18. Distinguish between psychosomatic disorders and hypochondria.

actual damage inflicted upon bodily tissues

imagined damages to one's health

19. List the causes of psychosomatic disorders and name several of the most common types of psychosomatic problems.

repeated stress
hereditary differences
specific organ weaknesses
learned reactions to stress
personality factors

gastronomical (ulcers) respiratory (asthma)
eczema (skin rash) hives, migraines rheumatoid arthritis,
hypertension (blood pressure) colitis (colon ulcer) heart disease

20.   Differentiate between Type A and Type B personalities. "A"- runs high risk of ♡ attack (hard driving, ambitious, highly competitive, achievement oriented, striving (cik John Skewski) - he/she in a hurry - slave to time —

"B"- unlikely unlikely candidate for ♡ attack! — stress resistant

21.   Discuss biofeedback in terms of the process involved, its possible applications, and the contradictory evidence as to its value. (Students should note the twelve strategies for reducing hostility and appluy them where applicable

a technique that provides auditory or visual signal based on some bodily activity - it allows one to monitor & control his/her own bodily function

— It might be useable in treating psychosomatic problems (ck) prevention of migraines via sensory redirection of bloodflow from head to extremities — its benefits result from g'nl. relxation.

— there's no "magic" in bio feed back
— it doesn't do anything by itself

NOTE TO STUDENTS: Be aware of the twelve strategies for reducing hostility and be able to apply them where applicable.

22.   Describe what a hardy personality is and list the three ways such people view the world. — One who is highly stress resistant & who

    a.   nourishes a personal commitment to self/work/family/& "other stabilizing values"- seek student definition

    b.   feels he/she has control over his/her life & work

    c.   views life as a series of challenges (which can be met) — Not AS A SERIES of THREATS OR PROBLEMS

23.   Explain the concept of the General Adaptation Syndrome. List and describe its three stages. — General Adaptation Syndrome is a consistent series of bodily reactions to prolonged stress occurring in three stages

    a.   alarm reaction - body mobilizes its resources to cope with added stress)

stage b.   resistance - body is better able to cope with the original source of stress - its resistence to other stresses is lowered

stage c.   exhaustion body's resources are exhausted - stress hormones are depleted

24.   Explain how stress affects the immune system and how control may be related.

weakens the immune system — makin one disease prone

controlling stress may prevent this weakening of the immune system.

25. Describe health psychology including its focus or core.) an approach to health whose core is using psychological principles to promote health & to prevent illness.

26. List eight behavioral risk factors which can be controlled and explain their relationship to life expectancy. ✳
    a. stress
    b. accident
    c. disease
    d. untreated high blood pressure
    e. cigarette smoking
    f. alcohol abuse
    g. overactivity   — high speed driving
    h. underexercising

their absence = longer life!

27. Briefly describe the research demonstrating the relationship of health-promoting behaviors and longevity.
    Alameda Co. (Calif) – study – 7000 people given detailed health questionnaire – focusing on 7 basic health practices – In ensuing yrs. health/death records of these people closely watched. (7 plus sleep, ideal weight, smoking/non smoking, use or refraining fr alcohol – regular exercise – daily breakfast fast between meals (men engaged in 7 health practices – death rate 4x men who didn't

28. Describe the impact of (refusal-skills training) and (community health programs) on illness prevention.
    training that teaches how to resist influences to try smoking – Also applicable to other drugs.
    — Community wide prgm. (educates) provider information re factors that affect health & how to handle them
    } — these reduce likelihood of contraction of these illnesses.

The following objectives are related to the material in the "Applications" section of your text.

29. List the three responses that are triggered by stress and discuss the stress management techniques that can be used to diminish or break the cycle.
    a. bodily effects } each worsens the
    b. upsetting thoughts } other in a
    c. ineffective behavior } vicious cycle
    — Learning a reliable, drug free way of relaxing
    — Full body exercise (swimming, dancing, sports, walking – good outlets) ✳ most effective on a daily basis!
    — meditation – quiets the body, promoting relaxation. Forms of meditation (Listening to & playing music, taking nature walks.
    — progressive relaxation – (tighten certain muscles, then voluntarily relax them – this is tension reducing)
    — guided imagery (visualizing peaceful scenes)
    — slow down (goal is distance, not speed)
    — organize (keep it simple)

30.   Define stereotyped response and give an example of it.

31.   Discuss three effective ways to avoid frustration.

   a.

   b.

   c.

SELF-QUIZZES

Do You Know the Information?

Multiple Choice

1.   Circle the four aspects of stress which make it more intense.
   (a) related to family   (c) personal   (e) unpredictable   (g) repetition
   (b) linked to pressure   (d) uncontrollable   (f) it's physical demands   (h) intense or repeated

2.   The aspect of burnout called depersonalization refers to
   (a) workers doing poor work and feeling helpless, hopeless, or angry.
   (b) a detached feeling toward other people.
   (c) workers feeling fatigued, tense, and apathetic.
   (d) a chronic feeling of not caring about anything.

3.   Which of the following characteristics would go hand-in-hand with a feeling of incompetence about a particular situation?
   (a) dressing powerfully to overcome the feeling   (c) feeling a lack of control over the situation
   (b) building a stronger social support system   (d) a low stress reaction in the body

4.   Jethro has aspirations of being a brain surgeon but has the IQ of a chicken. It is likely that he will encounter
   (a) external frustration.   (b) personal frustration.   (c) internal frustration.   (d) Type B behavior.

5.   Frustration usually increases as the _____ of a blocked motive increases.
   (a) urgency   (b) loss   (c) delay   (d) rejection

6.   Circle the five common reactions to frustration listed by your author.
   (a) crying   (d) displaced aggression   (g) depression   (i) anger
   (b) withdrawal, escape   (e) cursing   (h) direct aggression   (j) persistence
   (c) disgust   (f) variability

7.   When aggression is habitually redirected toward a person or group, _____ has occurred.
   (a) scapegoating   (b) prejudice   (c) stereotyping   (d) escape

8.   When a person is being simultaneously attracted to and repelled by the same goal or activity, the conflict is called
   (a) approach-avoidance.   (b) avoidance-avoidance.   (c) approach-approach.   (d) double approach-avoidance.

9. Because avoidance conflicts are extremely stressful and rarely solved, people sometimes leave the situation entirely — a reaction known as _____.
   (a) ambivalent avoidance
   (b) complete avoidance
   (c) leaving the field
   (d) playing against the house

10. Psychological defense mechanisms
    (a) are conscious acts designed to display a more favorable external personality to the world.
    (b) have no adaptive value because they use great amounts of emotional energy to control anxiety.
    (c) distort sources of anxiety to maintain an idealized self-image.
    (d) are rarely self-deceptive.

11. When you protect yourself from something unpleasant by refusing to perceive it, _____ has occurred.
    (a) suppression
    (b) denial
    (c) regression
    (d) compensation

12. When painful thoughts are prevented from entering consciousness, _____ has occurred.
    (a) repression
    (b) compensation
    (c) sublimation
    (d) suppression

13. When dangerous impulses are avoided by exaggerating opposite behavior, _____ has occurred.
    (a) sublimation
    (b) compensation
    (c) repression
    (d) reaction formation

14. _____ is justifying one's own behavior by making an unobtainable goal seem less appealing.
    (a) Sublimation
    (b) Rationalization
    (c) Denial
    (d) Compensation

15. The defense mechanism which is used to rechannel frustrated energy and desires into productive and socially acceptable behaviors is called _____.
    (a) projection
    (b) substitution
    (c) sublimation
    (d) compensation

16. The condition in which people give up because they perceive a situation to be hopeless is called
    (a) learned helplessness.
    (b) lowered internal aggression.
    (c) anxiety.
    (d) the avoidance reaction.

17. Which of the following is *not* one of the common problems which causes depression among college students?
    (a) problems with studying and grades
    (b) money and sex worries
    (c) isolation and loneliness
    (d) the breakup of an intimate relationship

18. One technique to combat depression is to write down negative thoughts as they occur and then
    (a) write a rational answer to each one.
    (b) read and review them over the course of the day.
    (c) burn them in a symbolic display of rejection of the thoughts.
    (d) keep them in a diary so that you can keep them and review them over time.

19. The SRRS scale seems to be *most* appropriate for
    (a) military personnel.
    (b) young adults whose lives are constantly changing.
    (c) single, college-age students.
    (d) older, more established adults.

20. Hypochondriacal disorders are those in which
    (a) the symptoms are imaginary.
    (b) physiological damage is caused by psychological stress.
    (c) the symptoms are vague and diffuse.
    (d) individuals have physiological symptoms but no underlying physiological cause.

21. Causes of psychosomatic diseases include
    (a) personality traits.
    (b) specific organ weaknesses.
    (c) hereditary differences.
    (d) all of these.

22. As opposed to Type B personalities, Type A personalities have
    (a) a higher rate of heart disease.
    (b) a chronic sense of time urgency.
    (c) chronic anger or hostility.
    (d) all of the above.

23. Which of the following have been changed using biofeedback?
    (a) brain waves   (d) epileptic seizures   (g) blood flow
    (b) blood pressure   (e) visual accuracy   (h) hand temperature
    (c) memory   (f) muscle tension   (i) heart rhythms

24. The hardy personality is one who
    (a) is able to suffer frustration without getting upset.
    (b) seems to be unusually resistant to stress.
    (c) suffers as much stress as the average person but tends to have a low endocrine response to it.
    (d) has control over his/her life and work.

25. The _____ is a consistent series of stages of physical reaction to stress.
    (a) stress management response   (c) autonomic response system
    (b) resistance pattern   (d) general adaptation syndrome

26. In which stage of the general adaptation syndrome is the body better able to cope with the original source of stress but less resistant to other stresses?
    (a) alarm reaction   (b) stage of exhaustion   (c) stage of resistance   (d) stage of preparation

27. The immune system
    (a) appears to be less affected by stress when a person feels less responsibility for or control over a situation.
    (b) is adversely affected by stress and illness may be the result.
    (c) is regulated by the endocrine system.
    (d) none of these statements are true.

28. Which of the following statements is *incorrect*?
    (a) Today people die primarily from infectious diseases and accidents.
    (b) The core of health psychology is to use psychological principles to promote health and prevent illness.
    (c) Most causes of poor health are under our control.
    (d) Engaging in health-promoting practices can double the remaining life expectancy of a middle-aged man.

29. Which of the following statements is *incorrect*?
    (a) Challenging "good stress" and relaxation are one and the same thing.
    (b) Anything that reliably interrupts upsetting thoughts and promotes relaxation can be helpful.
    (c) People who have difficulty learning progressive relaxation may find biofeedback helpful.
    (d) People can learn to fight fear and anxiety with an internal monologue of positive coping statements.

Can You Apply the Information?

1. You are confronted by a person on a dark street, your first step in coping will be
   (a) primary appraisal in which you decide if the situation is threatening or not.
   (b) to instinctively shout or scream.
   (c) to choose a means to meet the threat.
   (d) secondary appraisal.

2. It's 11:30 p.m. and Brenda has a test tomorrow. She has procrastinated up until now and hasn't studied more than 15 minutes. She's really getting into a panic. She's wringing her hands, she's nervous, she's shaking. The wise thing to do at this point would be to
   (a) engage in primary appraisal.   (d) try some emotion-focused coping.
   (b) try to beat the effects of learned helplessness.   (e) call out for that fourth pizza.
   (c) attribute the situation to surplus of arousal.

3. Beulah really wants to put on a size 6 dress but she weights 185 pounds. Her frustration is probably
   (a) internal.   (c) personal.   (e) due to a Twinkie overdose.
   (b) external.   (d) situational.

4. If you are in a hurry to get to a meeting and someone stops you to talk about the weather, you will probably experience _____ frustration.
   (a) internal   (b) external   (c) personal conflict   (d) conflict

5. When you get an "F" on a test and then go home and yell at your children, you are displaying
   (a) compensation.   (c) aggression.   (e) an American tradition.
   (b) scapegoating.   (d) displaced aggression.

6. You love to swim. Should you buy a house on a lake or on the ocean? This is an example of a(n) _____ conflict.
   (a) approach-avoidance   (b) avoidance-avoidance   (c) approach-approach   (d) double approach-avoidance

7. Take a flu shot or get the flu. This is an _____ conflict.
   (a) avoidance-avoidance   (b) approach-avoidance   (c) approach-approach   (d) double approach-avoidance

8. You are trying to lose weight and are hungry. When you look into the refrigerator you see a bunch of celery and a piece of pie. This is an example of a(n) _____ conflict.
   (a) avoidance-avoidance   (b) approach-approach   (c) double approach-avoidance   (d) approach-avoidance

9. In your class your professor says, "Tell me about the defense mechanisms that you use." Which of the following statements about this situation is *true*?
   (a) Most of the students will report using denial.
   (b) Students will enjoy discussing repressed events since it is the most primitive defense mechanism.
   (c) According to Freud, since the defense mechanisms are unconscious, we can't really meaningfully talk about the mechanisms which may be of most value to us.
   (d) All of the above are true.

10. A man who is upset because he thinks other men are "making eyes" at him may unconsciously be transferring his own sexual interests to them. This would be a case of the defense mechanism
    (a) reaction formation.   (b) projection.   (c) sublimation.   (d) denial.

11. Teaching yourself chess because you are missing a leg and cannot play football is an example of
    (a) reaction formation.   (b) rationalization.   (c) compensation.   (d) sublimation.

12. Gladys and Bill are secretaries at a large law firm. They both intensely dislike each other, but they are so sugary, syrupy sweet to each other that it makes everyone in the office want to barf. They are probably both exhibiting the defense mechanism known as
    (a) reaction formation.   (b) compensation.   (c) sublimation.   (d) regression.

13. Bill was abused as a young child. Now as a teenager his parents act as if they do not love him and they call him stupid. He would like to move away from home, but he has no money, no job, no skills to get a job, and he flunked out of school. It is very likely that Bill
    (a) will not use primary appraisal again.   (c) will avoid love relationships for fear of attribution.
    (b) is experiencing learned helplessness.   (d) will always fail at problem-focused solutions.

14. Linda has been feeling blue the last couple of days. She should probably go see a therapist about her depression.
    (a) True   (b) False

15. Overall, Bob realizes that a lot has changed in his life in the past year. To demonstrate that, he scored over 300 LCUs on Holmes' Social Readjustment Rating Scale. Yet, he feels that he has met the challenges and is making constructive changes in his life. From this one could assume
    (a) that Bob has an 80% chance of illness in the next 6 months.
    (b) that Bob's level of daily hassles must also be high.
    (c) that Bob's perceptions may reduce the effects of the high LCUs.
    (d) nothing because there is not enough information.

16. Lucy is in a high stress position but seems to thrive. When she and her colleagues are confronted with new demands, others see the demands as threats but Lucy sees them as a challenge. Lucy usually perceives herself as in control of her life. It can be said with some assurance about Lucy that
    (a) she is a Type A personality.   (c) she is usually in the G.A.S. resistance stage.
    (b) she is a Type B personality.   (d) she has a hardy personality.

17. Willard is a 45-year-old manager at a local retail store. He gets 7 to 8 hours of sleep each night, has never smoked cigarettes, and eats breakfast almost every day. All things being equal, we should expect him to live to the ripe old age of
    (a) 55.   (b) 67.   (c) 76.   (d) 88.

18. Ralph puts a quarter in a machine and the coin immediately comes out the coin return slot. He tries again and the same thing happens. Instead of trying another coin, Ralph keeps putting the same one in. This is an example of
    (a) persistence.   (b) denial.   (c) aggression.   (d) stereotyped response.

19. Your friend Kathy has come to you for some help. She has been offered a new job with a substantial pay increase, but she will have to move to Europe, leaving her fiance (who can't go with her) and family behind. The job has tremendous potential for the future, but she has to commit to three years overseas before she can return home. Your advice is to
    (a) take a two week vacation to the place in Europe where she will have her job in order to "try it out."
    (b) reject the offer because it is obviously so demanding that a compromise would be unlikely.
    (c) take the job and stick it out for the three years even if after 2 months it turns out that that was obviously wrong.
    (d) avoid making a comparison of the pros and cons and go with her intuition.

Chapter Review

1. Your body's stress reaction begins with the same _____ nervous system arousal that occurs during _____. _____-_____ stresses can be uncomfortable, but they rarely do any damage.

2. When stressors are _____ or _____, _____, _____, or linked to _____, the stress will be magnified and damage is likely to occur.

3. The condition in which an employee is physically, mentally, and emotionally drained is called _____. It involves emotional _____, _____ (a detachment from others), and a feeling of reduced personal _____. This problem is especially prevalent for those in the _____ professions. It may help to _____ jobs and build a stronger social _____ system at work.

4. The appraisal of a situation as a threat or not greatly affects the stress reaction to it. _____ appraisal is when a person makes a decision about the nature of a situation. When the person makes a decision about how to meet a threatening or challenging situation, this is called _____ appraisal. Therefore, the way a situation is "_____" becomes very important to coping with it.

5. Threat has a lot to do with the idea of _____. A perceived _____ of control is as important as an _____ lack of control in causing us to feel threatened. Your personal sense of control in any situation also comes from believing that you can reach desired _____, or that you are _____ to cope with a particular demand.

6. _____-_____ coping is aimed at managing or altering the distressing situation itself and is most useful when you are facing a controllable _____. In _____-_____ coping the person tries instead to control his/her emotional reaction.

7. There are two different types of frustration. If an individual cannot get his or her money or merchandise out of a candy machine, this person will probably experience _____ frustration. Wanting to be a jockey but weighing 300 pounds would lead to _____ frustration.

8. Frustration usually increases as the _____, _____ or _____ of a blocked motive increases. Also, frustrations which are _____ are more frustrating.

9. Although _____ is one of the most persistent and frequent responses to frustration, there are several other responses. Frustration is often met with _____, characterized by more vigorous efforts and more variable responses. When a person uses a new or variable response to try to get around the frustration, this is called variability or _____.

10. Since aggression in response to frustration is disruptive and generally discouraged, the aggression is frequently _____ or redirected. Another major reaction to frustration is _____ or withdrawal, either physically or psychologically leaving the frustrating situation.

11. _____ is a form of displaced aggression. The aggression is not aimed directly at the frustrating event or person but is _____ directed at another person or group of people.

12. There are four types of conflict. The simplest conflict comes from having to choose between two desirable alternatives and is called an _____-_____ conflict.

13. When forced to choose between two undesirable alternatives an _____-_____ conflict develops. This conflict often leads to _____, _____, and _____. In an _____-_____ conflict a person is simultaneously attracted to and repelled by the same activity or goal. This conflict almost certainly leads to feelings of _____.

14. The last type of conflict is the most typical of the choices we must usually make. In _____ _____-_____ conflicts a person is forced to choose between two alternatives, each of which has positive and negative qualities. This causes them to _____ or waver.

15. A defense mechanism is any technique used to distort sources of _____ or to maintain an idealized _____-_____. Defense mechanisms operate _____.

16. When defense mechanisms are overused, a person becomes less _____ because great amounts of emotional energy are used to control _____. The value of defense mechanisms lies in their ability to help prevent a person from being overwhelmed by a temporary threat. Defense mechanisms may also provide time to learn to _____.

17. One of the most primitive defense mechanisms is _____, or protecting oneself from an unpleasant reality by refusing to accept it. Another defense mechanism occurs when a person can't recall a very unpleasant memory. This is called _____.

18. _____ _____ is a defense mechanism in which impulses are not only repressed, but they are also held in check by exaggerated, opposite behavior. A person who escapes into the past is using the defense mechanism _____. Another defense mechanism known as _____ is the unconscious transference of a person's own shortcomings or unacceptable impulses to others.

19. The defense mechanism which unconsciously provides us with convincing reasons for behavior which we ourselves find somewhat questionable is called _____.

20. _____ is a form of behavior whereby a person tries to make up for some personal defect or fault. The defense mechanism which is defined as working off frustrated desires in constructive substitute activities is called _____.

21. _____ _____ may develop when an organism has little or no control over his or her destiny. In humans, _____ _____ is usually accompanied by feelings of hopelessness, powerlessness, and decreased activity. These are the same symptoms that generally accompany _____. In addition, people may act helpless in situations if they _____ their failure to lasting, general factors. These conditions may be eliminated if the person experiences _____ which promotes the development of the emotion of _____.

22. Four problems which typically cause depression in college students are _____, _____ and loneliness, problems with _____ and _____, and the _____ of an intimate relationship.

23. To combat depression, Beck and Greenberg suggest making a _____ _____ of activities for yourself. In addition, write down _____-_____ or _____ thoughts and write a rational answer for each one.

24. Dr. Thomas Holmes has found that stressful events reduce the body's natural defenses against disease and increase the likelihood of _____. More surprising is the finding that almost any major life _____, whether positive or negative, requires adjustment and increases susceptibility to _____ and _____. Lazarus believes that daily _____ are related to immediate _____. In any event, stress is always related to _____, _____, _____, and personal _____. Cultural shock marked by confusion, alienation, depression, etc., is called _____ stress.

25. A _____ disorder is one in which _____ factors are associated with actual _____ to tissues of the body. _____ suffer from _____ diseases. The most common examples of the former disorders are _____ and _____.

26. _____ is not the only cause of psychosomatic troubles. Usually several factors are combined to produce damage. The factors may include _____ differences, _____ traits, specific _____ weaknesses, and _____ tendencies to focus stress on a particular part of the body.

27. Researchers have studied the personality characteristics of people who are especially prone to suffer heart attacks. People who run a high risk of heart attack are classified _____ _____. This type of person is _____, highly _____, _____ oriented and has a chronic sense of _____ _____ and _____. This person runs a high risk of _____ _____.

28. The process whereby bodily activities are monitored and converted into a signal that provides the person with information about what the body is doing is called _____. This process has been useful for helping people control things such as _____ _____. Many questions remain about the value of this process. Many of the reported benefits may simply reflect _____ _____. The procedure may simply act as a "_____" to help a person accomplish tasks involving _____-_____.

29. People who seem to be unusually resistant to stress are said to possess a _____ personality. These people possess a sense of personal _____, the perceive _____ over their life and work, and they have a tendency to see life as a series of _____.

30. The answer to how stress causes physical damage seems to lie in the body's defenses against stress, a pattern of reactions known as the _____ _____ _____, or the _____. _____. _____.

31. The first stage of G.A.S. is the _____ reaction. During this stage the body mobilizes its defenses against stress. If stress continues, the second stage, called the stage of _____, begins. At this point the body's defenses are stabilized. If the stress does not cease, the stage of _____ may be reached. In this stage the body's resources are _____ and the stress hormones are _____.

32. The immune system is regulated at least in part by the _____. Stress, upsetting thoughts, and emotions may affect the immune system in ways that increase susceptibility to _____. If a person perceives himself/herself to be in _____ of a situation, this susceptibility is diminished.

33. The approach of _____ psychology is to use psychological principles to promote _____ and prevent _____. Eight major behavioral risk factors have been identified which can be controlled and which increase the chances of accident, disease and early death: high _____ _____, _____, abuse of _____, over _____, under _____, Type _____ behavior, and driving too _____.

34. Health psychologists are interested in increasing behaviors that actively promote _____. These include regular _____, maintaining a balanced _____, and managing _____. Adding these and other health-promoting behaviors may increase _____ _____.

35. Role playing ways to resist pressures from peers, adults, and advertisements to smoke (a process called _____ _____ training) has helped teenagers be less likely to begin smoking.

36. Stress triggers _____ effects, _____ behavior, and upsetting _____. To combat each of these problems, _____ _____ may be of some help.

37. To lessen the effects on the body, _____, _____, and progressive _____ may help. To make your ineffective behavior more effective, it may be helpful to _____ _____, get _____, strike a _____ among all of your interests and demands, recognize and accept your _____, and seek _____ support.

38. To diminish upsetting thoughts, it may be helpful to make _____ statements instead of _____ self-statements. _____ statements are used to block out or _____ self-talk in stressful situations.

39. A person who continues to engage in inflexible behavior has adopted a _____ response. This is not the same as _____ because the former is not _____.

40. There are several suggestions to help avoid needless frustration:
    (a) Try to identify the _____ of your frustration.
    (b) If possible try to _____ the source of frustration.
    (c) Ask yourself whether or not the efforts are worth changing the source of your frustration.
    (d) Try to distinguish between barriers which are _____ or _____.

ANSWER KEYS

Do You Know the Information?

Multiple Choice

1. (b,d,e,h) obj. 2, p. 416
2. (b) obj. 3, p. 417
3. (c) obj. 5, p. 417
4. (b) obj. 7, p. 419
5. (a) obj. 8, p. 419
6. (b,d,f,h,j) obj. 9, pp. 419-421
7. (a) obj. 10, p. 420
8. (a) obj. 11, p. 422
9. (c) obj. 11, p. 422
10. (c) obj. 12, p. 424
11. (b) obj. 13, p. 424
12. (a) obj. 13, p. 425

13. (d) obj. 13, p. 425
14. (b) obj. 13, p. 425
15. (c) obj. 13, p. 426
16. (a) obj. 14, p. 427
17. (b) obj. 15, p. 429
18. (a) obj. 16, p. 429
19. (d) obj. 17, p. 431
20. (a) obj. 18, p. 432
21. (d) obj. 19, p. 433
22. (d) obj. 20, p. 433
23. (b,d,f,g,h,i) obj. 21, p. 434
24. (b) obj. 22, p. 436
25. (d) obj. 23, p. 437
26. (c) obj. 23, p. 437

27. (b) obj. 24, p. 438
28. (a) objs. 25-26, pp. 438-439
29. (a) obj. 29, p. 444

Can You Apply the Information?

1. (a) obj. 4, p. 417
2. (d) obj. 6, p. 418
3. (c) obj. 7, p. 419
4. (b) obj. 7, p. 419
5. (d) obj. 9, p. 420
6. (c) obj. 11, p. 420
7. (a) obj. 11, p. 421
8. (c) obj. 11, p. 423

Can You Apply the Information? (cont.)

9. (c) obj. 12, p. 424
10. (b) obj. 13, p. 425
11. (c) obj. 13, p. 426
12. (a) obj. 13, p. 425

13. (b) obj. 14, p. 427
14. (b) objs. 15-16, pp. 428-429
15. (c) obj. 17, p. 432

16. (d) obj. 22, p. 436
17. (b) obj. 27, p. 440
18. (d) obj. 30, p. 445
19. (a) obj. 31, p. 446

Chapter Review

1. autonomic, emotion, Short-term (p. 415)
2. intense, repeated, unpredictable, uncontrollable, pressure (p. 416)
3. burnout, exhaustion, depersonalization, accomplishment, helping, redesign, support, (p. 417)
4. Primary, secondary, sized up (p. 417)
5. control, lack, actual, goals, competent (p. 417)
6. Problem-focused, stressor, emotion-focused (p. 418)
7. external, personal (p. 419)
8. strength, urgency, importance, repeated (p. 419)
9. aggression, persistence (p. 419); circumvention (p. 421)
10. displaced (p. 420); escape (p. 421)
11. Scapegoating, habitually (p. 420)
12. approach-approach (p. 420)
13. avoidance-avoidance (p. 421); indecision, inaction, freezing, approach-avoidance, ambivalence (p. 422)
14. double approach-avoidance, vacillate (p. 423)
15. anxiety, self-image, unconsciously (p. 424)
16. adaptable, anxiety, cope (p. 426)
17. denial (p. 424); repression (p. 425)
18. Reaction formation, regression, projection (p. 425)
19. rationalization (p. 425)
20. Compensation, sublimation (p. 426)
21. Learned helplessness, learned helplessness (p. 427); depression, attribute, success, hope (p. 428)
22. stress, isolation, studying, grades, breakup (p. 429)
23. daily schedule, self-critical, negative (p. 429)
24. illness, change, accident, illness (p. 430); hassles, health, personality, values, perceptions, resources, acculturative (p. 432)
25. psychosomatic, psychological, damage, Hypochondriacs, imaginary, gastrointestinal (ulcers), respiratory (asthma) (p. 432)
26. Stress, hereditary, personality, organ, learned (p. 433)
27. Type A, ambitious, competitive, achievement, time urgency, anger (hostility), heart attack (p. 433)
28. biofeedback, migrane headaches (brain waves, blood pressure, heart rhythms), general relaxation, mirror, self-regulation (p. 434)
29. hardy, commitment, control, challenges (p. 436)
30. General Adaptation Syndrome, G.A.S. (p. 437)
31. alarm, resistance, exhaustion, exhausted, depleted (p. 437)
32. brain, disease, control (p. 438)
33. health, health, illness (p. 438); blood pressure, smoking, alcohol (drugs), eating, exercise, A, fast (p. 439)
34. health, diet, stress, life expectancy (p. 440)
35. refusal skills (p. 441)
36. bodily, ineffective, thoughts, stress management (p. 442)
37. exercise, meditation (p. 442); relaxation (p. 443); slow down, organized, balance, limits, social (p. 444)
38. coping, negative, Coping, counteract, (p. 444)
39. stereotyped, persistence, flexible (p. 445)
40. source, change, real (imagined), imagined (real) (p. 445)

KEY TERMS, CONCEPTS, AND INDIVIDUALS

---

personality defined
character, temperament
  stability of personality
trait vs. type approach
self-concept
personality theory:
  trait theories
    common vs. individual
    cardinal, central, secondary (Allport)
    surface vs. source (Cattell)
    five factor model
    factor analysis
    16 PF, trait profile
    trait-situation interaction
    twin studies
    influence of heredity
  psychodynamic theories
    Sigmund Freud
    id, ego, superego
    pleasure principle
    libido
    life (Eros) vs. death (Thanatos)
      instincts
    reality principle
    neurotic and moral anxiety

levels of awareness
    unconscious, preconscious,
    conscious
  psychosexual stages
    oral, anal, phallic,
    latent, genital
  erogenous zone
  fixation
  critical evaluation of Freud
behavioristic theories
  learning theory
  situational determinants
  habits – drive, cue, response, reward
  social learning theory
  psychological situation
  expectancy
  reinforcement value
  self-reinforcement
  behaviorist view of development
  critical situations
    feeding, toilet training
    sex training, anger expression
  identification, imitation
humanistic theory
  human nature

subjective experience
Maslow, Rogers
self-actualization
steps for self-actualization
fully functioning person
incongruent
self, ideal self, possible self
conditions of worth
organismic valuing
personality assessment
  interview – structured vs. unstructured
  halo effect
  direct observation
  rating scale
  behavioral assessment
  situational testing
  personality questionnaire (MMPI-2)
  projective tests
    ambiguous stimulus
    Rorschach Inkblot
    Thematic Apperception
  honesty tests
limits of assessment techniques
sudden murderers
shyness (elements, causes, and the shy
    personality)

| LEARNING OBJECTIVES |

To demonstrate mastery of this chapter you should be able to:

1. Define the term personality and explain how personality differs from character and temperament. Discuss the stability of personality (Highlight 13-1).

2. Define the term trait. Describe the trait approach and the type approach to personality, and explain the shortcoming of the type approach.

3. Explain what the self-concept is and how it affects behavior and personal adjustment.

4. Define the term personality theory. List and describe the four broad perspectives covered by this author.

    a.

    b.

    c.

    d.

5. Characterize the general approach to the study of personality taken by a trait theorist.

6. Distinguish common traits from individual traits.

7. Define, differentiate, and give examples of Allport's cardinal traits, central traits, and secondary traits.

8. Distinguish between surface traits and source traits, and state how Cattell measures source traits.

9. Explain how Cattell's approach to personality traits differed from Allport's approach.

10. Discuss the five-factor model of personality.

11. Explain what a trait-situation interaction is.

12. Explain how twin studies are used to assess the effect of heredity on personality. Contrast the relative influence of heredity on physical attributes as compared to personality.

13. Explain why Freud became interested in personality.

14. List and describe the three parts of the personality according to Freud.

    a.

    b.

    c.

15. Describe the dynamic conflict between the three parts of the personality and relate neurotic and moral anxiety to the conflict.

16. Describe the relationships among the three parts of the personality (according to Freud) and the three levels of awareness.

17. List and describe Freud's four psychosexual stages. In your answer include an explanation of fixation and the corresponding age range for each stage.

    a.

    b.

    c.

    d.

18. Discuss the positive and the negative aspects of Freud's developmental theory.

19.   Explain how behaviorists view personality.

20.   Explain how learning theorists view the structure of personality. Include in your discussion the terms habit, drive, cue, response, and reward.

21.   Explain how learning theory and social learning theory differ. Include in your discussion a description of the terms psychological situation, expectancy, reinforcement value, and self-reinforcement. Explain how self-reinforcement is related to self-esteem and depression (see Highlight 13-4).

22.   Using the behavioristic view of development, explain why feeding, toilet training, sex training, and learning to express anger or aggression may be particularly important to personality formation.

23. Describe the role of social reinforcement, imitation, and identification in personality development.

24. Briefly explain how the humanists set themselves apart from the Freudian and behaviorist viewpoints of personality.

25. Describe the development of Maslow's interest in self-actualization.

26. Using at least five of the characteristics of self-actualizers listed in your text, describe a self-actualizing person. From the original list of ten, evaluate yourself and explain what may be helping or hindering your self-actualization.

27. List and briefly explain or describe (where applicable) eight steps to promote self-actualization.

    a.

    b.

    c.

    d.

    e.

    f.

    g.

    h.

28. Differentiate Freud's and Rogers' views of the normal or fully functioning individual.

29. Describe Rogers' view of an incongruent person.

30. Explain how "possible selves" help translate our hopes, dreams, and fears and ultimately direct our future behavior.

31. Explain how "conditions of worth" and "organismic valuing" may affect personality formation.

32. Discuss the following assessment techniques in terms of purpose, method, advantages, and limitations:

    a.   structured and unstructured interviews

    b.   direct observation (combined with rating scales, behavioral assessment and situational testing)

    c.   personality questionnaires (MMPI)

(continued on page 256)

    d.   projective tests (Rorschach, TAT)

    e.   honesty tests

33.   Describe the personality characteristics of sudden murderers, and explain how their characteristics are related to the nature of their homicidal actions.

The following objectives are related to the material in the "Applications" section of your text.

34.   List and describe the three elements of shyness. State what usually causes shyness.

    a.

    b.

    c.

35.   Compare the personality of the shy and the nonshy. Include the concepts labeling and self-esteem.

36.   List and discuss the four major areas that can help reduce shyness.

    a.

    b.

    c.

    d.

SELF-QUIZZES

Do You Know the Information?

Multiple Choice

1. Personality is
   (a) a person's unique and enduring behavior patterns.
   (b) best typified by the type approach.
   (c) made up of surface and cardinal traits.
   (d) the same as temperament.

2. Of the following, which implies an evaluation of the person?
   (a) temperament   (b) character   (c) hypothetical construct   (d) personality

3. Most studies indicate that personality becomes quite stable by age
   (a) 10.   (b) 15.   (c) 20.   (d) 30.

4. Which of the following statements about types and traits is *incorrect*?
   (a) The trait approach attempts to specify those traits which best describe a particular individual.
   (b) The trait approach tends to oversimplify personality.
   (c) Personality traits are relatively permanent and enduring qualities that a person shows in most situations.
   (d) A personality type represents a category of individuals who have a number of traits in common.

5. A person's self-concept
   (a) determines what he/she pays attention to, remembers, and how events are interpreted.
   (b) represents a person's perception of how others view him or her.
   (c) has a minor influence on our behavior.
   (d) is built out of how we imagine other people view us.

6. Which of the following is a *correct* match?
   (a) trait theories — inner workings of personality as they relate to behavior
   (b) psychodynamic theories — importance of the external environment
   (c) behavioristic theories — personal growth as an extension of conditioning and learning
   (d) humanistic theories — private, subjective experience

7. Traits which are shared by most members of a culture are classified by Allport as _____ traits.
   (a) cardinal   (b) central   (c) secondary   (d) common

8. According to Allport some traits are so basic that all of a person's activities can be traced to existence of these traits. Allport calls such traits
   (a) central traits.   (b) cardinal traits.   (c) source traits.   (d) secondary traits.

9. Cattell attributes _____ traits to more basic underlying characteristics called _____ traits.
   (a) individual, common   (b) surface, source   (c) common, cardinal   (d) central, cardinal

10. Cattell's Sixteen Personality Factor Questionnaire is designed to measure
    (a) cardinal traits.   (b) central traits.   (c) source traits.   (d) surface traits.

11. Cattell's approach to personality differs from Allport's approach in that Cattell
    (a) asked random subjects to rank order what they considered to be the most important personality traits.
    (b) classified traits subjectively.
    (c) used a more circular research procedure than Allport did.
    (d) tried to be more objective by using factor analysis to reduce surface traits to source traits.

12. The five-factor theory of personality is an attempt to
    (a) relate the MMPI-2 to a trait profile.
    (b) uncover the most basic dimensions of personality.
    (c) use the 16PF as a diagnostic tool.
    (d) identify the most salient cardinal traits.

13. Trait-situation interactions would predict that
    (a) although your behavior might be different in different situations, your underlying personality traits would still be apparent.
    (b) your behavior would probably be about the same in most situations because of your personality traits.
    (c) the situation is more important than the relevant personality trait.
    (d) your behavior would be different in different situations because traits cannot predict a person's behavior.

14. Which of the following statements regarding the influence of heredity on personality is *false*?
    (a) Identical twins who are reared apart are used to compare the similarity of their personality traits.
    (b) Identical twins usually are similar in traits such as dominance and extroversion.
    (c) Separated twins tend to share similar talents such as art, music, or dance.
    (d) There is a genetic factor in personality, but it is relatively small when compared to the effect that genetics has on physical attributes.

15. In the Freudian view of personality, the _____ is totally unconscious and dominated by the pleasure principle.
    (a) ego   (b) id   (c) superego   (d) libido

16. According to Freud any behavior that is aggressive or destructive in nature
    (a) originated in the superego.
    (b) reflects the influence of Eros.
    (c) is learned.
    (d) is derived from Thanatos.

17. In Freud's theory the aspect of the personality that acquires the values and ideals of the parents and the society is the
    (a) id.   (b) superego.   (c) ego.   (d) life instinct.

18. According to Freudian theory, the basic conflict within an individual's psyche is between
    (a) psychic and physical energy.
    (b) the id and superego.
    (c) the ego and the id.
    (d) the ego and superego.

19. According to Freud, which part or parts of the personality operate at all three levels of consciousness?
    (a) id   (b) ego   (c) superego   (d) id, ego, and superego

20. According to Freud, the Oedipus and Electra conflicts occur during the
    (a) phallic stage.   (b) anal stage.   (c) oral stage.   (d) genital stage.

21. According to Freud, a person whose personality is characterized as obstinate, stingy, orderly, and compulsively clean would be classified as
    (a) oral-aggressive.   (b) anal-expulsive.   (c) anal-compulsive.   (d) anal-retentive.

22. The behaviorist position is that personality is
    (a) a collection of learned behavior patterns.
    (b) dominated by the self-concept.
    (c) an expression of the life instincts and the death instinct.
    (d) best understood in terms of subjective experiences.

23. Learning theorists
    (a) consider personality to be made up of traits.
    (b) believe personality is made up of responses to specific situations.
    (c) see man's personality as basically good.
    (d) closely reflect sociological thought regarding personality.

24. According to the social learning theorists, in order to understand a person's personality and his or her responses in a situation
    (a) the different values attached to activities must be understood.
    (b) it must be known if the person expects reinforcement.
    (c) it is important to know how the person interprets the situation.
    (d) all of the above will occur.

25. Feeding is a developmental situation, from a behaviorist viewpoint, where a child learns
    (a) attitudes toward cleanliness.
    (b) to get pleasure from asserting him/herself.
    (c) associations that will affect later social relationships.
    (d) none of the above.

26. Learning sex-appropriate behavior is greatly influenced by
    (a) toilet-training and early feeding contacts.
    (b) self-reinforcement and resolution of unconscious conflicts.
    (c) identification and imitation.
    (d) organismic valuing and self-regard.

27. The humanistic viewpoint emphasizes
    (a) the effects of reinforcement and prior learning.
    (b) biological instincts and unconscious forces.
    (c) subjective experience and self-actualization.
    (d) identification and imitation.

28. Maslow believed that all humans strive for this. These people are spontaneous, autonomous, task-centering, etc. The term is
    (a) self-actualization.   (b) growth fulfillment.   (c) conditions of worth.   (d) congruence.

29. Which of the following is *poor* advice for a person who wishes to promote self-actualization?
    (a) Seek peak experiences.
    (b) Take responsibility for your life.
    (c) Try to live up to the positive expectations others may hold for you.
    (d) Be willing to change.

30. Whereas Freud thought the normal personality was adjusted to internal conflict, Rogers thought the fully functioning person
    (a) was able to symbolize the phenomenal field.
    (b) would find the self-image incongruent.
    (c) achieved an openness to feelings and experiences.
    (d) learned to trust other's expectations for him or her.

31. In Carl Roger's view, information or feelings inconsistent with the self-image are said to be
    (a) separated from "not me" experiences.
    (b) incongruent.
    (c) symbolized.
    (d) a source of meta-needs.

32. Rogers believes that congruence and self-actualization are encouraged by substituting organismic valuing for
    (a) positive self-regard.   (b) imitation.   (c) conditions of worth.   (d) self-image.

33. Which is *not* considered a limitation of interviewing?
    (a) The interviewer may overlook certain qualities in his own personality.
    (b) The interviewer may affect what is said.
    (c) The interviewer can be swayed by preconceptions.
    (d) The interview may uncover relevant body language cues.

34. A valuable technique for improving the accuracy of direct observation is the use of
    (a) personality questionnaires.
    (b) introspection.
    (c) projective devices.
    (d) rating scales.

35. "Shoot—Don't Shoot" training is a good example of
    (a) a behavioral assessment.   (b) situational testing.   (c) the halo effect.   (d) rating scales.

36. Probably the best known and the most widely used objective test of personality is the
    (a) 16 PF.   (b) MMPI.   (c) Rorschach.   (d) TAT.

37. Which of the following statements about the MMPI is *incorrect*?
    (a) The answer to a single item may reveal something important about a person's personality.
    (b) By comparing a person's profile with scores produced by normal adults, various disorders can be identified.
    (c) There is a lie scale to detect if a person is trying to look better or worse than they really are.
    (d) One of the problems with the MMPI is that people other than psychologists may use it.

38. Of the following, which is designed to uncover deep-seated or unconscious wishes, thoughts, and needs?
    (a) personality questionnaires (b) projective tests   (c) behavioral assessments   (d) direct observation

39. Ambiguous stimuli are part of which type of assessment technique?
    (a) direct observation   (b) personality inventories   (c) projective tests   (d) situational testing

40. Projective tests of personality
    (a) are considered almost worthless by most clinicians.   (c) are extremely reliable.
    (b) are computer scored.   (d) are low in validity.

41. Concerning honesty tests,
    (a) studies have failed to demonstrate that they can accurately predict if a person will be a poor risk on the job.
    (b) most job applicants rate their honesty as above average.
    (c) they are accepted as valid in most states.
    (d) all of the above are true.

42. Sudden murderers have been found to
    (a) be masculine and undercontrolled.
    (b) be shy, restrained, and inexpressive.
    (c) be aggressive and impulsive and become violent because of their unrestrained impulses.
    (d) not show any significant pathology on personality tests.

43. Which of the following is *not* one of the three elements of shyness?
    (a) self-defeating mental bias   (c) lack of eye contact
    (b) social anxiety   (d) underdevelopment of social skills

44. Which of the following statements about shyness is *incorrect*?
    (a) Shy people tend to consider their social anxiety to be caused by external events.
    (b) People who are shy are high in public self-consciousness.
    (c) Nonshy persons tend to have higher self-esteem than shy persons.
    (d) Nonshy persons give themselves credit for successes.

True-False

_____ 1. Temperament implies that a person has been evaluated, not just described.

_____ 2. Psychologists are hesitant to speak of personality "types" because this approach tends to oversimplify personality.

_____ 3. In general, trait theorists identify traits that best describe a particular individual.

_____ 4. Freud became interested in personality because there were no complete theories that explained healthy personality development to his satisfaction.

_____ 5. Threats of punishment from the superego cause neurotic anxiety.

_____ 6. Fixation early in the oral stage tends to produce people who are passive, gullible, and need lots of attention.

_____ 7. Freud's theory of the development of personality has been influential partly because it was the first theory to propose the idea that the first years of life help shape adult personality.

_____ 8. Freud's portrayal of the latency stage as free from sexuality and unimportant for personality development has been shown to be true.

_____ 9. With the concept of situational determinants, learning theorists have entirely removed the "person" from personality.

_____ 10. A basic active or passive orientation toward the world may be established by early feeding experiences.

_____ 11. Freud viewed a normal person as one who has learned to be open to the defense mechanisms resulting from internal conflict.

_____ 12. The interview is called structured if the interviewee is allowed to determine what subjects are discussed.

_____ 13. Personality questionnaires are more subjective than interviews or observation.

_____ 14. "Sudden murderers" are likely to be habitually violent and impulsive individuals who feel cheated or betrayed.

_____ 15. Shyness is most often triggered by novel or unfamiliar social situations.

_____ 16. "I don't need to pretend to be someone I'm not; it just makes me more anxious" is an example of an innocuous opening line.

Can You Apply the Information?

1. A proud father is talking about his new son. "That kid was born with lots of personality." Technically, his statement is
   (a) True.   (b) False.

2. David views himself as a person who can't cope with the world. He believes that almost everyone thinks that he is stupid. If he was warmly welcomed into a room by nine people and the tenth person was rather cool toward him, he would interpret the situation as having been totally rejecting and that nobody liked him. It is probable that David
   (a) would score poorly on the MMPI.   (c) has a very poor self-concept.
   (b) would be evaluated as not having much character.   (d) has fewer positive personality traits than the average person.

3. The Scottish are thrifty. This is a _____ trait.
   (a) central   (b) source   (c) cardinal   (d) common

4. Bill is considered timid. This is a _____ trait.
   (a) central   (b) secondary   (c) common   (d) cardinal

5. At the end of football practice today, Edgar "high-fived" all of his teammates as they left the locker room. Tonight as he leaves his church choir practice, Edgar will probably also "high-five" the other choir members.
   (a) True   (b) False

6. Fred really wants to have a package of Twinkies but he knows they will add to his weight problem. Impulses such as these probably come from the
   (a) collective unconscious.   (b) superego.   (c) ego.   (d) id.

7. If a person unconsciously wants to kill someone but feels anxiety because of the impulse, which part of the personality decides on a socially acceptable response?
   (a) superego   (b) ego   (c) id   (d) ego-ideal

8. Louise went home to see her parents for the weekend. Driving back to college on Sunday night she had a vague feeling of guilt. She figured she must have done something wrong. Her feelings probably came from
   (a) conventional moral thinking.   (c) the superego.
   (b) the preconscious.   (d) organismic valuing.

9. Fred is still struggling with the Twinkie problem. He's visiting the Twinkie factory with his college marketing class. He doesn't want to look ridiculous, but he has an almost irrestible urge to jump into a bowl of Twinkie batter. Fred is probably experiencing
   (a) pangs of extroversion.   (c) images from the anima.   (e) Weight Watchers' condemnation.
   (b) moral anxiety.   (d) neurotic anxiety.

10. Brenda is 15 years old. She loves to be the center of attention and is always looking in mirrors because she says she's concerned about her appearance. Freud would likely say that Brenda is fixated at the _____ stage.
    (a) anal   (b) genital   (c) phallic   (d) oral

11. Mary has barely passed each of her last three psychology tests and she doesn't have much hope of getting a higher score on her final exam even though she has studied. She is most likely to
    (a) resign herself to do better, put her nose to the grindstone, and get a good final score.
    (b) spend a lot of time praising herself for at least doing as well as she has.
    (c) take the course over next term with the confidence that she could do better.
    (d) do only as well as she expects to do.

12. Which of the following would *not* be conducive to self-actualization?
    (a) Try to allow enough time for contemplation and self-exploration.
    (b) Engage in wishful thinking to stimulate creative ideas or problem solving.
    (c) Act as if you are personally responsible for every aspect of your life.
    (d) Be prepared to be unpopular or different when your views don't agree with others.

13. Dick considers himself warm, sensitive, loving and intelligent. His close associates perceive him to be cold, insensitive, manipulative, and not so bright. Dick refuses to believe such feedback. Dick is
    (a) incongruent.   (c) a fully functioning person.
    (b) reducing his phenomenal field.   (d) symbolizing his experiences.

14. Steve is a struggling downhill skier who practices diligently because he pictures himself as someday receiving an Olympic gold medal. He is utilizing
    (a) congruent personality self-images.   (c) the key to self-actualization.
    (b) a very positive possible self.   (d) superego functioning.

15. Sigmund is a college professor but also operates a business on the side. He hires Susan, one of his best students, because he figures if she is such a good student she'll make a great oyster shucker. Sigmund is
    (a) confusing central traits and source traits.   (c) assuming that Susan is androgynous.
    (b) suffering from the halo effect.   (d) in need of a personality questionnaire.

16. Regina is obsessive-compulsive and washes her hands up to 300 times per day. In order to show her how often she engages in this behavior and to accurately inform her therapist of the exact magnitude of the problem, the nurses on the ward decide to
    (a) do a rating scale.   (c) do a behavioral assessment on Regina.
    (b) give her a projective test.   (d) administer a personality questionnaire to Regina.

17. In order to see how a secretary performs under the pressure of the job, the corporation executives decide to give each job applicant a
    (a) situational test.   (b) computer simulation.   (c) trait factor test.   (d) rating scale.

18. You suspect that your patient has repressed a traumatic event from childhood. Which personality assessment technique seems most appropriate for this situation?
    (a) direct observation   (c) a projective test
    (b) a personality questionnaire   (d) situational testing

19. John is 30 years old. He is very quiet and shy and keeps his emotions and actions under tight control. What might you expect when he gets angry and releases his rigid self-control?
    (a) an overreaction to the situation and perhaps violence
    (b) no more reaction than he ever shows because research indicates that these individuals do not lose control
    (c) an underreaction to the situation since this is his predominant mode of responding
    (d) guilt, embarrassment, and neurotic anxiety

Chapter Review

1. Most psychologists regard personality as one's _____ and _____ _____ patterns. Personality is different from character, which implies that a person has been _____. The raw material from which personality is formed is called _____. Most personality traits are quite stable by age _____.

2. Psychologists think of _____ as lasting qualities within a person that are inferred from behavior. The study of personality _____ is a natural extension of interest in personality. We often speak of the executive type, the motherly type, the strong, silent type, etc. However, too frequently they represent an _____ of personality.

3. A person's perception of his or her own personality traits is called the _____-_____. It greatly affects personal adjustment by determining what we _____ to, _____, and _____ about.

4. A system of assumptions, ideas, and principles proposed to explain personality is called a _____ _____. The four broad theories are: _____, _____, _____, and _____.

5. Regarding trait theories, any quality of an individual is considered to be a trait if it is _____ of their behavior. In general, the trait approach attempts to identify traits that best describe a particular _____.

6. Allport makes a distinction between _____ and _____ traits. _____ traits are those shared by most members of a culture and help reveal the similarities among people. _____ traits characterize unique personal characteristics.

7. Allport has also distinguished three other types of traits. _____ traits are so basic that all of a person's activities can be traced to the existence of the trait. _____ traits are the basic building blocks that make up the core of personality. _____ traits are less consistent and less important aspects of a person.

8. Cattell distinguishes between the visible portions of personality called _____ traits and the underly- ing personality characteristics called _____ traits. Allport classifies traits_____, whereas Cattell used _____ _____. The attempt to reduce Cattell's list down to five traits has resulted in the _____-_____ model of personality. The factors are _____, _____, _____, _____, and _____ to experience.

9. Cattell's list of _____ traits forms the basis of a personality test called the ____ ____ ____.

10. Personality traits show a degree of _____ over time, but also _____ can exert a powerful influence on behavior. This is called the _____-_____ interaction.

11. Psychologists study the effect of heredity on personality by studying identical twins who have been _____ at birth. Studies have shown that they are amazingly similar _____ and less so in terms of their _____. It seems reasonable to conclude that there is a _____ factor in _____.

12. The first truly comprehensive approach to understanding personality was developed by _____. He became interested in the treatment of mental disorders when he determined that many of his patients' problems were without _____ cause. Starting about 1890 and continuing to his death in 1939 Freud evolved a theory of _____.

13. Freud conceived personality as a dynamic system of energies directed by three structures: the _____, _____, and _____. The _____ is made up of innate _____ _____ and urges present at birth. It operates on the _____ principle. The energy for the personality is called_____ and derives from _____.

14. The _____ is the executive and draws its energy from the _____. The _____ operates on the _____ principle. The _____ acts as a judge or censor.

15. The _____ demands immediate gratification but the _____ may place moral restrictions on the impulses. The _____ is left to make the decision. Impulses from the _____ which threaten a loss of control cause _____ anxiety. Threats of punishment from the _____ cause _____ anxiety.

16. The id works totally on the _____ level. The ego and the superego may also work on this level and also on the _____ and _____ levels.

17. Freud theorized that the core of personality is formed before age six in a series of _____ stages. These stages in order from earliest to latest are the _____, _____, _____, and _____.

18. At each stage a different part of the body becomes an _____ zone (an area capable of producing pleasure). It serves as the principle source of pleasure, frustration, and self-expression. Freud believes that many adult personality traits can be traced to _____ (an unresolved conflict or emotional "hang-up") in one or more of the stages.

19. Fixation early in the oral stage produces an oral-_____ personality who is gullible, passive and needs lots of attention. Fixation later in the oral stage causes an oral-_____ adult who is argumentative, cynical, and exploitive of others.

20. Fixation during the anal stage can lead to anal-_____ personality, who is obstinate, stingy, orderly, and compulsively clean. It may also lead to the anal-_____ personality who is disorderly, destructive, cruel or messy.

21. During the phallic stage, increased sexual interest causes the child to become physically attracted to the parent of the opposite sex. In males this generates the _____ conflict in which the boy feels rivalry with his father for the affection of the mother. The counterpart to this is the _____ conflict. Fixation during this stage produces the _____ personality who exhibits vanity, exhibitionism, sensitive pride, and narcissism.

22. During the genital stage, personality is marked by a growing capacity for mature and responsible social-sexual relationships. This last stage comes after a long period of _____ during which psychosexual development is temporarily interrupted.

23. Freud's theory has been influential for a number of reasons. First, it pioneered the idea that the first years of life help shape adult _____. Secondly, it identified _____, _____ training, and early _____ experiences as critical events in personality formation. Third, Freud was among the first to propose that development proceeds through a series of _____.

24. Some of Freud's ideas are not universally accepted. In some cases he was clearly _____. Most psychologists feel that much more is going on during _____ than Freud recognized. Freud also overemphasized _____ in personality development.

25. Behaviorists believe that personality is a collection of _____ _____ patterns. Personality is acquired through _____ and _____ conditioning, observational learning, reinforcement, extinction, generalization, and discrimination. Learning theorists have kept the "person" in personality by drawing our attention to the _____ determinants of behavior.

26. A behavioral view of personality proposed by Dollard and Miller holds that _____ form the structure of personality. These theorists believe that _____ are governed by four elements of the learning process: _____, _____, _____, and _____.

27. Social learning theorists have expanded the original learning theory view to give added emphasis to _____ relationships and _____. Such theorists include _____, _____, and other _____ events in their view of personality. Such elements are exemplified by Rotter's concepts of the _____ situation, _____, and _____ value. The social learning theorists have also added _____-_____ to the behavioristic view. This might be considered the equivalent to the Freudian _____. People who have high rates of _____-_____ have been found to have high _____-_____.

28. Many of Freud's major points can be restated in terms of modern learning theory. Miller and Dollard consider four situations of critical importance. These are: _____, _____ or cleanliness training, _____ training, and learning to express _____ or _____. Behaviorists tend to stress two processes that contribute greatly to personality development in general, and particularly to sex training. They are _____ and _____.

29. Identification refers to the child's _____ _____ to admired adults especially to those the child depends upon for love and care. Many sex traits come from identification with the behavior patterns of the _____-_____ parent. Identification typically encourages _____.

30. _____ is a reaction to the _____ of psychoanalytic theory and the _____ of learning theory. The _____ view human nature as inherently _____ and that we are creative beings capable of free _____. This viewpoint leads to a greater emphasis being placed on immediate _____ experience than on prior learning. According to Maslow, people strive for_____-_____.

31. According to Maslow, housewives and clerks could live _____ and make full use of their _____ just like people of high _____. He termed this tendency _____-_____ and considered it an ongoing process, not a simple _____ _____ to be attained only once.

32. Self-actualizers have efficient perceptions of _____, and they have a comfortable _____ of self, others and nature. They are _____, task-_____, and _____. They have a continued freshness of _____ of life, a fellowship with _____, and profound interpersonal _____. They have an _____ sense of humor and _____ experiences.

33. While self-actualization offers the promise of personal growth, creativity, and fullness of life, it requires hard work, patience, and commitment. It is primarily a _____, not a goal or an endpoint.

34. Several suggestions can be gleaned from the writings of Abraham Maslow on how to promote self-actualization. One is to be willing to _____. You must learn to take _____. You can become an architect of self by acting as if you are personally responsible for every aspect of your life.

35. Another point is to examine your _____. Use self-discovery to try to make each life decision a choice for growth, not a response to fear or anxiety. Try to see things as they are, not as you would like them to be. In other words, experience things _____ and _____.

36. Make use of positive experiences to promote growth. You might actively repeat activities that cause "_____ _____" (temporary moments of self-actualization). Actualizing potentials may place you at odds with cultural expectations. This may produce fear which keeps many people from becoming what they might. You must be prepared to be _____.

37.   Maslow found that self-actualizers tend to have a _____ or "_____" in life. Therefore, get involved and committed to problems outside yourself. Self-awareness takes time to develop.

38.   As a final note, _____ your progress. It is important to gauge your progress and to renew your efforts. _____ is a good sign that you are in need of further growth and change.

39.   One influential humanist, Rogers, saw the _____ _____ person as one who has achieved an openness to feelings and experiences, and who has learned to trust inner urges and intuitions. This is different from Freud's view of the "normal" personality as adjusted to internal _____. Rogers' theory of personality centers on the concept of the _____.

40.   According to Rogers, much of human behavior is an attempt to maintain consistency between one's _____-_____ and one's _____. Information or feelings inconsistent with the self-image are said to be _____.

41.   When we translate our hopes, fears, fantasies, and goals into personal images of who we could be, we are utilizing _____ _____. They may either be positive or negative and tend to direct future _____.

42.   Rogers holds that positive and negative evaluations by others cause a child to develop internal standard of evaluation called _____ of _____. By this he means that we learn that some actions win our parents' love and approval while others are rejected. This is directly related to a later capacity for positive _____-_____.

43.   He believes congruence and self-actualization are encouraged by substituting _____ _____ for conditions of worth. This process is a direct, gut-level response to life experiences that avoids the filtering and distortion of _____.

44.   Psychologists use various tools to assess personality. A very direct way to learn about a person's personality is to engage in conversation. An _____ is described as _____ if the conversation is informal and the_____ is allowed to determine what subjects are discussed. In a _____ _____, information is obtained by asking a series of preplanned questions.

45.   Interviews are used to identify personality _____, to select persons for _____, _____, or special programs, and for research on the dynamics of _____.

46.   In addition to providing _____, interviews give rapid insight into _____. They also allow observation of a person's tone of voice, posture, and other body cues. They also have certain limitations. Interviewers can be swayed by _____.

47.   The interviewer's own _____ may cause him to accentuate, overlook, or distort qualities of the interviewee. Another problem in interviewing is the _____ effect, the tendency to generalize a favorable or unfavorable impression to unrelated details of personality.

48.   When used as an assessment procedure, _____ _____ is a simple extension of the natural interest in "people watching." It is a useful technique but, like interviewing, has limitations. For this reason, _____ _____ are used which limit the chance of overlooking some traits while exaggerating others.

49.   An alternative to rating scales is to do a _____ _____ which records how often various _____ occur. A specialized form of direct observation is _____ _____ which is based on the premise that the best way to learn how a person reacts to a certain situation is to _____ that situation.

50. Most personality _____ are paper-and-pencil tests requiring a person to answer questions about himself. As measures of personality, they are more _____ than interviews or observation. However, that is not enough to insure the test's _____. It must also be _____ and _____. The best known and most widely used objective test of personality is the ___ ___ ___ __ - 2.

51. The ___ ___ ___ ___ - 2 is composed of _____ (how many?) items to which a subject must respond _____, _____, or _____ _____. It is through the _____ of responses that personality dimensions are revealed. The MMPI - 2 assumes that people are willing to tell the _____ about themselves.

52. In contrast to personality assessments that provide information on observable traits, _____ tests are designed to uncover deep-seated or _____ wishes, thoughts, and needs.

53. A projective test provides an _____ stimulus which the subjects must describe or about which they must make up a story. People tend to structure their descriptions according to their own life experiences. One of the oldest and most widely used projective tests is the _____ _____ Test. It consists of a set of ten standardized inkblots. Scoring is complex. _____ is less important than what _____ of the inkblot are used and how the image is _____.

54. Another popular projective test is the _____ _____ Test. This test consists of twenty sketches depicting various scenes. Subjects are asked to make up a _____ about the people in each sketch. Scoring is restricted to analysis of the _____ of the stories. Tests measuring a person's attitude toward dishonest acts are called _____ tests.

55. The _____ of projective tests is considered lowest among tests of personality. The _____ of judgments is low. Despite the drawbacks of projective tests, many psychologists attest to their value, especially as part of a _____ of tests and interviews.

56. Researchers like Lee, Zimbardo, and Bertholf have investigated the personalities of "_____ _____"—those who explode and commit violent crimes without warning. These people attack _____ of their personality, not in spite of it. They found that these people were _____, _____, and _____ individuals.

57. Fifty percent of American college students consider themselves to be shy. Shyness combines social _____ with a tendency to avoid others. There are three elements of shyness. The first involves an underdevelopment of _____ skills. The second is social _____, and the third is a confidence-lowering _____ - _____ _____ in their thinking.

58. Shyness is most often triggered by _____ or _____ social situations. Shyness is linked to public _____-_____. Shy people consider their social anxiety a lasting _____ _____, whereas nonshy people believe that _____ _____ cause their occasional feelings of shyness. Shy people have lower _____-_____ than nonshy people.

ANSWER KEYS

Do You Know the Information?

Multiple Choice

1. (a) obj. 1, p. 449
2. (b) obj. 1, p. 449
3. (d) obj. 1, p. 451
4. (b) obj. 2, pp. 451-452

5. (a) obj. 3, p. 452
6. (d) obj. 4, p. 452
7. (d) obj. 6, p. 453
8. (b) obj. 7, p. 454
9. (b) obj. 8, p. 455
10. (c) obj. 8, p. 455

11. (d) obj. 9, p. 455
12. (b) obj. 10, pp. 455-456
13. (a) obj. 11, p. 457
14. (b) obj. 12, p. 457
15. (b) obj. 14, p. 459
16. (d) obj. 14, p. 459

Multiple Choice *(continued)*

17. (b) obj. 14, p. 460
18. (b) obj. 15, p. 460
19. (b,c) obj. 16, p. 461
20. (a) obj. 17, p. 462
21. (d) obj. 18, p. 462
22. (a) obj. 19, p. 464
23. (b) obj. 20, p. 464
24. (d) obj. 21, p. 464
25. (c) obj. 22, p. 467
26. (c) obj. 23, p. 468
27. (c) obj. 24, p. 469
28. (a) objs. 25-26, pp. 470-471
29. (c) obj. 27, pp. 470-471
30. (c) obj. 28, p. 471
31. (b) obj. 29, p. 471
32. (c) obj. 32, p. 473
33. (d) obj. 32, p. 475
34. (d) obj. 32, p. 476
35. (b) obj. 32, p. 477
36. (b) obj. 32, p. 479
37. (a) obj. 32, p. 479
38. (b) obj. 32, p. 480

39. (c) obj. 32, p. 480
40. (d) obj. 32, p. 482
41. (a) obj. 32, p. 481
42. (b) obj. 33, p. 483
43. (c) obj. 34, p. 484
44. (a) obj. 35, p. 484

True-False

1. F, obj. 1, p. 449
2. T, obj. 2, p. 452
3. T, obj. 5, p. 453
4. F, obj. 13, p. 458
5. F, obj. 15, p. 460
6. T, obj. 17, p. 461
7. T, obj. 18, p. 463
8. F, obj. 18, p. 463
9. F, obj. 19, p. 464
10. T, obj. 22, p. 467
11. F, obj. 28, p. 471
12. F, obj. 32, p. 475
13. F, obj. 32, p. 478
14. F, obj. 33, p. 483
15. T, obj. 34, p. 484
16. F, obj. 36, p. 486

Can You Apply the Information?

1. (b) obj. 1, p. 449
2. (c) obj. 3, p. 452
3. (d) obj. 6, p. 453
4. (a) obj. 7, p. 454
5. (b) obj. 11, p. 457
6. (d) obj. 14, p. 459
7. (b) objs. 14-16, pp. 459-460
8. (c) objs. 14-15, p. 460
9. (d) obj. 15, p. 460
10. (c) obj. 17, p. 462
11. (d) obj. 21, p. 464
12. (b) obj. 27, p. 471
13. (a) obj. 29, pp. 471-472
14. (b) obj. 30, p. 473
15. (b) obj. 32, p. 475
16. (c) obj. 32, p. 476
17. (a) obj. 32, p. 476
18. (c) obj. 32, p. 480
19. (a) obj. 33, p. 483

Chapter Review

1. unique, enduring behavior, evaluated, temperament, 30 (p. 449)
2. traits (p. 450); types (p. 451); oversimplification (p. 452)
3. self-concept, attend, remember, think (p. 452)
4. personality theory, trait, psychodynamic, behavioristic, humanistic (p. 452)
5. typical (p. 452); individual (p. 453)
6. common, individual, Common, Individual (p. 454)
7. Cardinal, Central, Secondary (p. 454)
8. surface, source, subjectively, factor analysis, five-factor, extroversion, agreeableness, conscientious, neuroticism, openness (p. 455)
9. source, 16 PF (p. 455)
10. consistency, situations, trait-situation (p. 457)
11. separated, physically, personality, genetic, personality (p. 457)
12. Freud, physical, personality, (p. 458)
13. id, ego, superego, id, biological instincts, pleasure, libido, Eros (p. 459)
14. ego, id, ego, reality, superego (p. 459)
15. id, superego, ego, id, neurotic, superego, moral (p. 460)
16. unconscious, conscious, preconscious (p. 460)
17. psychosexual, oral, anal, phallic, genital (p. 461)
18. erogenous, fixation (p. 461)
19. dependent, aggressive (p. 461)
20. retentive, expulsive (p. 462)
21. Oedipus, Electra, phallic (p. 462)
22. latency (p. 463)
23. personality, feeding, toilet, sexual, stages (p. 463)
24. wrong, latency, sexuality (p. 463)
25. learned behavior, classical, operant, situational (p. 464)
26. habits, habits, drive, cue, response, reward (p. 465)

27. social, modeling, perception, thinking, mental, psychological, expectancy, reinforcement, self-reinforcement, superego (p. 466); self-reinforcement, self-esteem (p. 467)
28. feeding, toilet, sex, anger, aggression (p. 467); identification, imitation (p. 468)
29. emotional attachment, same-sex, imitation (p. 468)
30. Humanism, pessimism, mechanism, humanists, good, choice, subjective, self-actualization (p. 469)
31. creatively, potentials, achievement, self-actualization, end point (p. 470)
32. reality, acceptance, spontaneous, centering, autonomous, appreciation, humanity, relationships, unhostile, peak (p. 470)
33. process (p. 470)
34. change, responsibility (p. 471)
35. motives, honestly, directly (p. 471)
36. peak experiences, different (p. 471)
37. mission, calling (p. 471)
38. assess, Boredom (p. 471)
39. fully functioning, conflict, self (p. 471)
40. self-image, actions, incongruent (p. 471)
41. possible selves, behavior (p. 473)
42. conditions, worth, self-regard (p. 473)
43. organismic valuing, incongruence (p. 473)
44. interview, unstructured, interviewee, structured interview (p. 475)
45. disturbances, employment, college, personality (p. 475)
46. information, personality, preconceptions (p. 475)
47. personality, halo (p. 475)
48. direct observation, rating scales (p. 476)
49. behavioral assessment, actions, situational testing, simulate (p. 476)
50. questionnaires, objective, accuracy, reliable, valid (p. 478); MMPI-2 (p. 479)
51. MMPI-2, 567, true, false, cannot say, patterns, truth (p. 479)
52. projective, unconscious (p. 482)
53. ambiguous, Rorschach Inkblot, Content, parts, organized (p. 480)
54. Thematic Apperception, story, content, honesty (p. 481)
55. validity, objectivity, battery (p. 482)
56. sudden murderers, because, passive, shy, overcontrolled (p. 483)
57. inhibition, social, anxiety, self-defeating bias (p. 484)
58. novel, unfamiliar (p. 484); self-consciousness, personality trait, external events, self-esteem (p. 485)

chapter fourteen

Abnormal Psychology

KEY TERMS, CONCEPTS, AND INDIVIDUALS

psychopathology
views of normality
   subjective discomfort
   statistical
   social noncomformity
   context
   cultural relativity
   male bias in DSM-IV
   notes on labeling
DSM-IV
psychological disorders
   psychotic, organic mental,
   psychoactive substance related
   mood, anxiety
   somatoform, dissociative
   personality, sexual
insanity
personality disorders (10 types)
antisocial personality (sociopath)
   characteristics and causes
sexual deviances
   types, causes
   exhibitionism, pedophilia
rape
anxiety (definition and characteristics)
adjustment disorder
nervous breakdown
anxiety disorders
   generalized anxiety, panic

phobic (social vs. specific)
   agoraphobia
obsessive-compulsive
acute
post-traumatic stress
dissociative disorders
   amnesia, fugue
   dissociative identity
     (multiple personality)
somatoform disorders
   hypochondriasis
   somatization pain disorder
   conversion reactions
understanding psychopathology
   psychodynamic, humanistic,
   behavioristic
psychosis:
   delusions
     depressive, somatic,
     grandeur, influence,
     persecution, reference
   hallucination, flat affect
   word salad, personality disintegration
organic psychosis:
   general paresis, senile dementia
Alzheimer's disease
Delusional disorders
   paranoia psychosis
schizophrenia

   disorganized, catatonic,
   paranoid, undifferentiated
schizotypal personality
causes of schizophrenia
   environment – trauma, family
     environment, communication
   heredity
   body chemistry – biochemistry,
     dopamine
CT scan, MRI, PET scan
mood disorders
   depressive
     dysthymia, cyclothymia
     reactive depression
   bipolar, depressive, unipolar
   affective psychosis
     endogenous
causes of depression
treatment
   psychotherapy
   somatictherapy
     chemotherapy, ECT,
     psychosurgery
   hospitalization
   revolving-door policy
   community mental health center
   prevention, paraprofessional
   suicide – who, why, how to prevent

| LEARNING OBJECTIVES |

To demonstrate mastery of this chapter you should be able to:

1. Present information to indicate the magnitude of mental health problems in this country.

2. Define psychopathology.

3. Describe the following ways of viewing normality including the shortcoming(s) of each:

   a. subjective discomfort

   b. statistical definitions

   c. social nonconformity (include the concept of context)

   d. cultural relativity

4. State the conditions under which a person is usually judged to need help.

5. Explain the caution which is necessary to keep in mind when using psychiatric labels.

6. Explain why more women than men are treated for psychological problems.

7. Generally describe each of the following categories of mental disorders found in the DSM-III-R:

    a. psychotic disorders

    b. organic mental disorders

    c. substance related disorders

    d. mood disorders

    e. anxiety disorders

    f. somatoform disorders

    g. dissociative disorders

    h. personality disorders

    i. sexual and gender identity disorders

8. List the four general categories of risk factors for mental disorders (Table 14-3)..

    a.

    b.

    c.

    d.

9. Differentiate psychosis from insanity.

10. List and briefly describe the ten different types of personality disorders (see Table 14-4).

    a.

    b.

c.

d.

e.

f.

g.

h.

i.

j.

k.

11.   Describe the distinctive characteristics, causes, and treatment of the antisocial personality.

12.   Explain the difference between public and private standards of sexual behavior, what sets true sexual deviations apart from other sexual activity (p. 499), and what generally causes sexual deviations (p. 500).

13.   List and define eight behavior patterns that fit the definition of sexual deviation.

a.

b.

c.

d.

e.

f.

g.

h.

14.   Describe exhibitionism including who the offenders are, why they do it, and how one's reactions may encourage them.

15.   Describe pedophilia (child molestation) including who does it, what the offenders are like, and the factors that affect the seriousness of the molestation.

16.   Explain why rape is *not* viewed by experts as primarily a sexual act.

17.   Differentiate anxiety from fear.

18.   Outline the general features and characteristics of anxiety-related problems.

19.   State what is usually meant when the term "nervous breakdown" is used. Differentiate this category from an anxiety disorder.

20.　Define the key element of most anxiety disorders. Differentiate generalized anxiety disorders from panic disorders.

21.　Describe the following conditions:

a.　specific phobia

differentiate a social phobia from a simple phobia.

b.　agoraphobia

c.　obsessive-compulsive disorder

d.　post-traumatic stress disorder

e.　acute stress disorder

f.　dissociative reactions:
amnesia

fugue

multiple personality (dissociative identity disorder)

g.　somatoform disorders

hypochondriasis

somatization pain disorder

(continued on page 276)

h.   conversion reactions

22.   Discuss how each of the three major perspectives in psychology views neurosis. (Include the terms self-defeating, paradox, avoidance learning and anxiety reduction hypothesis.)

a.   psychodynamic

b.   humanistic

c.   behavioral

23.   Define what is meant by the term psychosis.

24.   List the five characteristics of a psychosis.

a.   d.

b.   e.

c.

25.   Define delusion. List and describe the six different types of delusions.

a.

b.

c.

d.

e.

f.

26.   Define hallucination and name the most common type.

27. Describe the emotion, communication, and personality changes that may occur in someone with a psychosis. Include an explanation of the frequency of occurrence for these changes.

28. Differentiate an organic from a functional psychosis.

29. Describe general paresis and senile dementia.

30. Briefly describe Alzheimer's disease including its incidence, symptoms, and neurological concomitants.

31. List the four categories of functional psychoses.

    a.   c.

    b.   d.

32. Describe the characteristics of delusional disorders including each of the five delusional types.

    a.

    b.

    c.

    d.

    e.

33.   Describe a paranoid psychosis. Explain why treatment of this condition is difficult.

34.   Generally describe schizophrenia.

35.   Describe the symptoms of a person with a schizotypal personality.

36.   List and describe the four major types of schizophrenia.

   a.

   b.

   c.

   d.

37.   Explain how paranoid delusional disorder and paranoid schizophrenia differ.

38.   Describe the roles of the following three areas as causes of schizophrenia:

   a.   Environment   T521

      1. psychological trauma – *early psychological trauma may contribute to the later development of schizophrenia – revelations viz case studies – its victims were exposed to violence, sexual abuse, death, divorce or separation in childhood & gnlly. it appears those experiencing schizophrenia – have been exposed to significant degree of stress (Minsley & Duncan 1986)*

TS21-522

2. disturbed family environment — *theoretically- Its an added risk Factor in schizophrenia* — *ak) this viewpoint originates with a 15 yr study of disturbed adolescents — study results —* *chance of developing schizophrenia — relates to patterns* of (deviant communication in families)

Family — reaction(s) Filled with confusion, conflict, guilt, prying, criticism, negativity & emotional attacks

b. (Heredity) X (Asarnow, Golastein & Ben-Meir (1988)

(evidence of this as a Factor in schizophrenia has become recently stronger current indications are that some individuals inherit a potential for developing schizophrenia (Fowler 1992) — ak

c.. Body Chemistry (include a description of the CT, MRI, and PET scans) — *some psychosis may be based on biochemical abnormalities → CT = Computed Tomography scan a computer enhanced X-ray image of the brain Magnetic Resonance Imaging) - a computer enhanced image based on the body's response to a magnetic Field Positron Emission Tomography - a computer generated color image of brain activity -illus via concentration of*

1. dopamine *substance produced by the brain — resembles a PSYCHEDELIC (brain altering) drug [radioactive sugar]* *one of these substances is called — dopamine a a chemical messenger in the brain — Currently popular belief among researchers — schizophrenia relates to overactivity in brain dopamine systems (Heinrichs 1993) —Schizophrenics might be on a kind of drug trip — caused by their own bodies —.˙. schizo— is a brain disease*

39. X Summarize the relationship among inheritance, stress, and body chemistry as causes of schizophrenia (p. 518).

anyone exposed to sufficient stress contribute derives → a psychotic break *Some people's hereditary brain structure renders them more susceptible* *.˙. Combo. of hereditary vulnerability & environmental stress = mind altering changes in brain chemistry*

40. X Describe the characteristics of depressive disorders. Include a description of dysthymia, cyclothymia, and reactive depression.

exaggeration of Sadness, despondency — on a prolonged basis — (symptoms: dejection, hopelessness) inability to Feel pleasure, fatigue —negative self image, recurrent thoughts of suicide

√ moderate depression — more days than not —for 2 yrs

↓ depression alternates with pds. of elevation, expansion or irritation

continuous intense depression person un- prepared to cope with loss — due to prior

41. √ List and describe the four major mood disorders. As a group, explain how they differ from affective psychoses (include the concept of endogenous).

a. bipolar I — (person manic hyperactive + 1 or) plus. of depression

b. bipolar II - person depressed despondent -

c. major depressive — person suffers of 1 or) intense depression

d. (episodes) intense depression

those markedly casting extremely mood or emotion — accompanied by psychotic symptoms

—Combo. of mood disorders & break with reality = affective psychosis — these major mood disorders usually involve more severe emotional changes. — personal emotional excesses can be accompanied by psychotic delusions & hallucinations — these mood disorders appear to be produced from within — as opposed to reactions to external events/Forces — *.˙. these disorders are said to be endogenous (within the person)*

T523

T525

X 42. Generally describe the likely causes of mood disorders (include the condition known as SAD). ↓

— psychoanalytic theory - maintains - depression traceable to repressed anger (displaced & turned inward in Form of self-blame, self hate cite Isenberg & Schatzberg 1976) -

— cite stresses also might trigger some forms of mood disorder; women 2x vulnerable as men - why? (parenting vs work conflict; reproductive stress - providing emotional support For others - sexual abuse

— genetic factors - heredity   (when a persons' symptoms of depression are lasting &

— seasonal conditions —   disabling the problem is called Seasonal Affective Disorder -

X 43. List and describe the two basic kinds of treatment for psychosis.

a. psychotherapy (2 people talking about one person's problem

b. somatic (bodily) therapy - chemotherapy, electroconvulsive therapy, psychosurgery

X 44. Define chemotherapy. List and describe the three classes of drugs used to treat psychopathology.
Use of drugs or chemical substances to relieve symptoms of emotional disturbance

a. minor tranquilizers [calm agitated persons]

b. major tranquilizers (anti-psychotics) - control hallucinations & other symptoms of psychosis

c. energizers (anti-depressants) - improve the mood of depressed

X45. Discuss the advantages and disadvantages of the use of chemotherapy in the treatment of psychosis. (Include the term tardive dyskinesia in your discussion.) ↳ their use has improved recovery chances (Re psychiatric disorders)
their use has abbreviated duration of hospitalization; their use has Facilitated "out patient" procedures

— disadvantages) (lengthy use of tranquilizers (by as many as 10%) of patients leads → TARDIVE DYSKINESIA,
to
a condition in which patients make rhythmic Facial & mouth movements & unusual arm movements

X (Rosenthal -1983)

It offers only temporary improvement - can cause permanent memory loss - should be a last resort measure —
it valid only in select cases of depression

X46. Describe what is known about the uses and effectiveness of the following techniques in the treatment of psychosis:

a. electroconvulsive therapy — drastic medical treatment For depression — in usual treatment session
=== a 150 volt current passed through brain < 1 second — convulsion triggered - patient loses
consciousness - during short pd. — to soften its impact - pre session muscle relaxants & sedatives administered
PRO) shock-induced seizure → alters bio-chemical brain balance - ending depression & suicidal behavior (FRANKL 1977) X
some argue confusion results - patients can't recall source of depression (Kohn 1988) X

b. psychosurgery
↳ an extreme biological treatment — gnl. term applied to any surgical alteration of the brain —
most known type Lobotomy (brain lobes disconnected From other area of brain - objective - calm persons' unresponsive to
other treatments - 1st introduced 1940s — initially success highly acclaimed (later discovery - such treatment produced
undesirable side effects -ie seizures, stupors - creation of human 'vegetables' (cite the Kennedy Family) —
its impact - irreversible (its still experimental (Penkoff 1980) X

47.X Describe the role of hospitalization in the treatment of psychological disorders. — removes a troubled individual from problem sustaining situations — provides sanctuary (controlled environment — where diagnosis, support, refuge & psychotherapy are all available (Bachrach 1984)✗

48.X Describe the impact that community mental health centers have had on the treatment of mental health. — describes as a bright spot in mental health area —; their objective — provide direct aid to [mentally] troubled citizens. 2nd goal prevention — via consultation education, crisis intervention — those processes end problems — or prevent problems from becoming serious — some of these mental health ctrs. try to raise g'nl. mental health level in "target areas" — via combatting unemployment, delinquency & drug abuse.) — On the achievement score of community mental health ctrs. — they've succeeded in making mental health service more accessible than ever before — their pgms. made available by paraprofessionals who have "been there" — mental health ctrs have also been staffed by volunteers.

The following objectives are related to the material in the "Applications" section of your text.

49. Present a composite picture of the person most likely to commit suicide. ✗ male (3x as many M as W do it) — an adolescent — young adult — or anyone 24-84 45 yrs yge n older, a college student; one who's experienced family troubles; one who's become victim of alcoholism) one who previously attempted suicide; — one who's family history includes attempted & completed suicides;

50. Discuss why people try to kill themselves. ✗
    - interpersonal — family difficulties } those conditions ——→ conclusion that death is the answer to suffering
    - alcoholism
    - sexual adjustment problems
    - job difficulties
    - feeling of isolation

51. List four common characteristics of suicidal thoughts and feelings. y
    a. escape — one feels like permanently running away from distress
    b. Emotional pain
    c. frustrated need
    d. helplessness (I can't do anything else but suicide)

52.   Explain how you can help prevent suicide.

─────────────────────────────┤ SELF-QUIZZES ├─────────────────────────────

Do You Know the Information?

Multiple Choice

1.   Each year, some _____ percent of the population experience an anxiety related disorder.
      (a) 10   (b) 7   (c) 18   (d) 12

2.   A problem with the statistical definition of normality is
      (a) the line between normality and abnormality is not specified.
      (b) subjective discomfort is overemphasized.
      (c) the method is not objective.
      (d) all of the above are problems with the statistical definition of normality.

3.   Which of the following statements is *incorrect*?
      (a) A lack of subjective discomfort indicates that there are no psychological problems present.
      (b) Before any behavior can be defined as abnormal we must consider the context in which it occurs.
      (c) Before the judgment that a person needs help is made, a person in a position of power must notice the behavior and then do
           something about it.
      (d) There may be a damaging male bias to traditional conceptions of normality.

4.   Because everyone has felt "crazy" during brief periods, persons whose adjustment problems extend over long periods differ from
      you in the
      (a) way the problem is labeled.   (c) amount of stress experienced.
      (b) severity of the difficulty.   (d) amount of emotion felt.

5.   _____ disorders are problems caused by known and verifiable brain pathology.
      (a) Substance use   (b) Organic mental   (c) Dissociative   (d) Anxiety

6.   The presence of physical symptoms suggesting disease or injury for which there are no identifiable causes is an indication of
      _____ disorders.
      (a) organic   (b) dissociative   (c) anxiety   (d) somatoform

7.   Which of the following is *not* one of the four general categories of risk factors for mental disorders?
      (a) psychological   (b) biological   (c) mental   (d) social

8.   A lack of interest in close relationships with other people is a characteristic of a(n) _____ personality disorder.
      (a) narcissistic   (b) schizotypal   (c) schizoid   (d) avoidant

9.   The sociopath
      (a) usually gives a bad first impression.   (c) is relatively easy to treat by psychotherapy.
      (b) tends to be selfish and impulsive.   (d) avoids other people as much as possible.

10. The early history of sociopaths is usually marked by
    (a) deviant family communication.
    (b) tension and stress.
    (c) emotional deprivation and disregard.
    (d) sexual perversion and obscenity.

11. From a psychological point of view, the mark of true sexual maladjustments is that they are
    (a) against the law.
    (b) compulsive and a source of guilt or discomfort for one or both partners.
    (c) in violation of public standards regarding appropriate sexual behavior.
    (d) listed in the DSM-IV.

12. Which of the following statements about exhibitionism and pedophilia is (are) *incorrect*?
    (a) Exhibitionists are typically single men from repressed backgrounds.
    (b) More than half of the child molesters are known to the child.
    (c) Molestations by strangers can be most devastating because of the lack of trust involved.
    (d) Most exhibitionists have a deep sense of inadequacy and a need to prove their manhood.

13. Forcible rape is now considered by experts to be
    (a) primarily a sexual act.
    (b) an act designed to humiliate and degrade the victim.
    (c) an act that reveals the sexual immaturity of the rapist.
    (d) all of the above.

14. Anxiety
    (a) is a response to a nonspecific threat or an anticipation of harm.
    (b) is usually associated with psychosis.
    (c) is another term for fear.
    (d) is both a and b.

15. Which of the following is *not* a characteristic of disruptive anxiety?
    (a) self-defeating behaviors
    (b) elaborate defense mechanisms to maintain minimal functioning
    (c) dissatisfaction with life
    (d) amount of anxiety is proportional to the situation

16. A nervous breakdown is *not* the same as an anxiety disorder because
    (a) a nervous breakdown is really an adjustment disorder whose symptoms disappear when life circumstances improve.
    (b) an anxiety disorder has lower levels of anxiety than do adjustment disorders.
    (c) a nervous breakdown is self-defeating.
    (d) a person having a nervous breakdown shows a greater loss of contact with reality.

17. A relatively simple behavioral pattern characterized by continuous tension and occasional attacks in which the person thinks he or she is going insane or is about to die is called
    (a) phobic disorder.
    (b) generalized anxiety disorder.
    (c) panic disorder.
    (d) conversion reaction.

18. Irrational and very specific fears that persist even when there is no real danger to a person are called
    (a) phobias. (b) anxieties. (c) delusions. (d) obsessions.

19. Avoiding speaking in public for fear of being evaluated could be a symptom of a(n)
    (a) agoraphobia. (b) simple phobia. (c) social phobia. (d) panic disorder.

20. Thoughts or images that intrude into consciousness against a person's will and which cause anxiety or extreme discomfort are called
    (a) phobias. (b) obsessions. (c) compulsions. (d) hallucinations.

21. Compulsions
    (a) give rise to obsessions.
    (b) make a person feel more secure by keeping activities highly structured.
    (c) tend to increase immediate anxiety but reduce it in the long run.
    (d) are all of the above.

22. The story of Sybil, a woman who had sixteen separate personalities, illustrates multiple personality or dissociative identity disorder which is a rare form of
    (a) fugue.   (b) dissociative disorder.   (c) schizophrenia.   (d) psychosis.

23. _____ _____ are said to occur when anxiety or severe emotional conflicts are converted into physical symptoms resembling disease or disability.
    (a) Dissociative reactions   (b) Hypochondria disorders   (c) Somatosensory disorders   (d) Conversion reactions

24. Which of the following *best* characterizes Carl Rogers' interpretation of the cause of dissociative, anxiety, and somatoform disorders?
    (a) a learned response   (c) an attempt to handle guilt generated by the superego
    (b) a form of avoidance learning   (d) the end product of a faulty self-image

25. In the behavioristic explanation of self-defeating behavior, the paradox is an example of
    (a) avoidance learning.   (b) observational learning.   (c) classical conditioning.   (d) latent learning.

26. The psychodynamic, humanistic, and behavioristic explanations of disordered behavior agree that
    (a) such behavior is made up of reinforced habits.   (c) self-image is a central issue.
    (b) guilt underlies most of it.   (d) it is paradoxical and self-defeating.

27. Psychosis is a break in contact with shared views of reality typically characterized by
    (a) self-pity and other schizophrenic symptoms.
    (b) delusions, hallucinations, personality disturbances, disturbed emotions, and disturbed communications.
    (c) increased anxiety, mounting tensions, loneliness, and despair.
    (d) mania and depression.

28. A delusion is
    (a) a false belief that is held even though the facts contradict it.   (c) seeing insects that are not really there crawling on your arm.
    (b) sensory experience that occurs in the absence of a stimulus.   (d) all of the above.

29. Among psychotics, the most common hallucination is
    (a) hearing voices.   (c) seeing places or people related to the source of the psychosis.
    (b) seeing objects fly around the room.   (d) feeling insects crawling under the skin.

30. Extremely psychotic behavior typically occurs
    (a) without flat affect.   (c) when word salad is present.
    (b) without involving personality disintegration.   (d) in brief episodes.

31. A psychosis based on unknown or psychological factors is termed a(n)
    (a) organic psychosis.   (b) affective disorder.   (c) senile psychosis.   (d) functional psychosis.

32. A psychosis resulting from an advanced stage of syphilis in which the disease attacks brain cells is called
    (a) general paresis.   (b) affective psychosis.   (c) functional psychosis.   (d) senile dementia.

33. Which of the following statements about Alzheimer's disease is *false*?
    (a) It effects from 5 to 10% of all people over age 65.
    (b) It is the major cause of senility.
    (c) It is thought to be caused by a subtle buildup of toxins in certain areas of the brain.
    (d) It eventually involves serious physical as well as psychological problems.

34. Delusional disorders marked by a belief that one's body is infested with insects would be of the _____ type.
    (a) grandiose   (b) somatic   (c) erotomanic   (d) persecutory

35. The major symptom of a paranoid psychosis is
    (a) hallucinations.   (b) flat affect.   (c) delusions of persecution.   (d) depression.

36. Schizophrenia involves
    (a) the delusions, hallucinations, and thought abnormalities found in other types of psychosis.
    (b) a withdrawal from contact with others; an inability to deal with daily events.
    (c) a split between thought and emotion.
    (d) all of the above.

37. Which personality disorder develops gradually and is characterized by isolation and withdrawal?
    (a) schizotypal   (b) dependent   (c) catatonic   (d) paranoid

38. The most common form of schizophrenic disorder is
    (a) undifferentiated.   (b) disorganized.   (c) catatonic.   (d) paranoid.

39. In paranoid schizophrenia there is _____ that is not evident in paranoid delusional disorder.
    (a) depression   (b) personality disintegration   (c) delusional thought   (d) persecution

40. Which of the following is *not* a potential environmental cause for schizophrenia?
    (a) the number of dopamine receptors in the brain   (c) deviant communication in families
    (b) early psychological trauma   (d) exposure to death in childhood

41. Studies with identical twins show that
    (a) knowing the mental health of one has no predictive value for knowing the mental health of the other.
    (b) if one twin is schizophrenic the other will be no more likely to be schizophrenic than another sibling.
    (c) if one twin is diagnosed schizophrenic, the other twin has about a 50-50 chance of becoming schizophrenic.
    (d) none of the above are true.

42. In view of current research, choose the best summary statement concerning the causes(s) of schizophrenia.
    (a) Extremely traumatic experiences early in childhood cause the first split in personality to form.
    (b) The right combination of inherited potential and environmental stress brings about important changes in brain chemicals.
    (c) A by-product of adrenaline called dopamine accumulates in the schizophrenic's body.
    (d) Schizophrenics are really adapting to an impossible environment created by deviant family communications.

43. Depression can be termed to be _____ if a person is intensely depressed following a major failure.
    (a) dysthymic   (b) cyclothymic   (c) reactive   (d) delusional

44. Major mood disorders are characterized by
    (a) feelings that someone is out to get you.   (c) lasting extremes of emotion.
    (b) a state of total panic which results in a stuporous condition.   (d) a heightened state of anxiety.

45. A person with a major mood disorder who is continuously loud, inappropriately elated, hyperactive, and energetic would be classified as which of the following types?
    (a) manic-depressive   (b) unipolar disorder   (c) bipolar I disorder   (d) bipolar II disorder

46. Depression may be caused by
    (a) problems with the chemicals in the brain.   (c) repressed anger.
    (b) not being prepared to cope with a major loss.   (d) all of the above.

47. Therapy which emphasizes two people talking about a person's problems is called
    (a) somatic therapy.   (b) hospitalization.   (c) bodily therapy.   (d) psychotherapy.

48. The minor tranquilizers
    (a) improve the mood of those who are depressed.
    (b) are used to treat flat affect.
    (c) lessen anxiety and calm patients.
    (d) help control hallucinations.

49. Which of the following is a neurological side effect of extended major tranquilizer usage?
    (a) tardive dyskinesia
    (b) loss of memory
    (c) senility
    (d) dry mouth and constipation

50. Which one of the following statements about chemotherapy is *incorrect*?
    (a) Chemotherapy is often overused and keeps patients docile and easy to manage.
    (b) Drugs generally cure mental illness.
    (c) Drugs provide symptomatic relief and may allow patients to benefit more fully from psychotherapy.
    (d) Drugs have greatly improved the chances for recovery from a psychiatric disorder.

51. Most experts seem to agree that ECT
    (a) produces permanent improvement.
    (b) only causes temporary memory loss.
    (c) should be used primarily for depression.
    (d) can now be used in lieu of drug therapy.

52. Psychosurgery is rarely used for the treatment of mental illness because
    (a) it is irreversible and unpredictable.
    (b) chemotherapy has made the procedure worthless.
    (c) regrowth of brain cells occurs very slowly.
    (d) it has been shown to have little or no effect on personality.

53. Which of the following statements about hospitalization is (are) *true*?
    (a) Long-term hospitalization has better results than short-term.
    (b) It works best when it is the treatment of choice.
    (c) It does nothing to improve a troubled individual by itself.
    (d) None of the above statements are true.

54. Which set of factors would be *most* likely to increase the odds that suicide will occur?
    (a) being a poor woman at Christmas time.
    (b) being a student with a need for recognition during final exams.
    (c) being a divorced male psychiatrist over the age of 45.
    (d) being a mentally retarded woman with strong religious convictions.

55. Which of the following is *not* one of the common characteristics of suicidal thoughts and feelings?
    (a) Frustrated psychological needs.
    (b) Reduced behavioral output.
    (c) Constriction of options.
    (d) Unbearable psychological pain.

True-False

_____ 1. Psychopathology may be defined as the inability to behave in ways that conform to other's expectations.

_____ 2. Psychotic disorders are problems where people retreat from the shared views of reality.

_____ 3. People who are psychotic are also insane.

_____ 4. Sexual offenders are usually sexually immature and inhibited and choose a relatively infantile method of sexual expression because it is less threatening.

_____ 5. Exhibitionism is displaying the genitals to voyeurs.

_____ 6. Anxiety is a response to a specific threat or an anticipation of harm.

_____ 7. The presence of anxiety attacks characterizes panic disorders whereas a generalized anxiety disorder is characterized by chronic anxiety.

_____ 8. According to Freud, neurosis represents a raging conflict between conscious and unconscious thought patterns.

_____ 9. Paranoid psychotics are rarely treated.

_____ 10. The term undifferentiated is used to describe many schizophrenic disorders because patients may shift from one pattern of behavior to another.

_____ 11. The diagnosing of schizophrenia is fairly objective and straightforward.

_____ 12. There is a greater than average degree of stress in the childhood of those who develop schizophrenia.

_____ 13. Mood disorders include manic behavior, but depression is by far the most common problem.

_____ 14. Manic behavior can be viewed as a reaction of individuals trying to escape feelings of worthlessness and depression.

_____ 15. A person who gets severely depressed only in the winter is probably suffering from unipolar depression.

_____ 16. Psychiatric patients recover better the longer they stay in the hospital (up to 3-4 months.)

_____ 17. Hospitalization may be considered a form of therapy since it removes a disturbed person from a stressful environment.

_____ 18. Community mental health centers emphasize curing mental illness.

_____ 19. More women than men attempt suicide, but more men complete the act due to the techniques selected.

_____ 20. Generally, suicide is more common among lower socioeconomic status individuals than those higher in material wealth.

_____ 21. People who try to kill themselves are considered mentally ill.

_____ 22. In order to help a suicidal person it is important to accept his or her feelings as well as the idea of the act of suicide itself.

Matching _(use the letters on the right only once)_

_____ 1. psychotic disorder	A.	brought about by stress beyond the range of normal experience
_____ 2. somatoform disorder	B.	measures how much sugar is used in each area of the brain
_____ 3. personality disorder	C.	fear of leaving home
_____ 4. legal term	D.	chemotherapy, ECS, and psychosurgery
_____ 5. agoraphobia	E.	unrelated events given personal significance
_____ 6. post-traumatic stress disorder	F.	hypochondriasis
_____ 7. dissociative reaction	G.	physical flight to escape extreme conflict or threat
_____ 8. fugue	H.	sensory experience but no stimulus
_____ 9. delusion of reference	I.	deeply ingrained maladaptive personality problems
_____ 10. hallucination	J.	most severe form of psychopathology
_____ 11. senile dementia	K.	silliness, laughter, bizarre behavior
_____ 12. schizotypal personality	L.	amnesia
_____ 13. catatonic schizophrenic	M.	insanity
_____ 14. disorganized schizophrenic	N.	most common of organic problems
_____ 15. undifferentiated schizophrenia	O.	waxy flexibility
_____ 16. dopamine	P.	nearly double the normal number of these receptors in the brains of schizophrenics
_____ 17. PET scan	Q.	may live on fringe of society as vagrant, eccentric, or derelict
_____ 18. dysthymia	R.	label for overlap among the types
_____ 19. endogenous	S.	produced from within
_____ 20. somatic therapy	T.	improves mood of depressed person
_____ 21. energizers	U.	depressed for at least two years
_____ 22. escape	V.	characteristic of suicidal thought
	W.	CT scan
	X.	general paresis

Can You Apply the Information?

1.   You are sitting in a room full of convicted murderers. You are not a murderer. According to which definition of normality could you be considered abnormal in this situaion?
     (a) social nonconformity   (b) statistical   (c) subjective discomfort   (d) all of these

2.   You are a psychiatrist talking to a patient who thinks he has a sexual problem. Your patient only likes the missionary position but feels guilty because his wife wants a little variety. Can this situation be considered abnormal or a sexual deviation?
     (a) Yes   (b) No

3.   Tom has trouble controlling his thoughts and has hallucinations. He probably has a(n) _____ disorder.
     (a) mood   (b) anxiety   (c) psychotic   (d) somatoform

4.   Ralph is a con-artist. He is a pro at pulling scams. He feels no guilt after bilking little old widows out of their savings. Ralph is probably suffering from
     (a) an anxiety disorder.   (b) a psychotic problem.   (c) sociopathy.   (d) an adjustment disorder.

5.   Thinking about going to college makes you nervous. In this case you would be feeling
     (a) anxiety.   (b) fear.

6.   Susan has lost the job she held for eighteen years. She really loved going to work. Now she has insomnia, she can't eat, she cries for no reason at all, and she feels worthless. It is likely that Susan is experiencing
     (a) a depressive reaction.   (b) obsessions.   (c) an adjustment disorder.   (d) both a and c.

7.   You are deathly afraid of giving an oral report in front of class. Shortly before you are due to give your report you feel your heart pounding, you feel like you're dizzy, and you feel like you might fall over dead. You're having the classic symptoms of a(n)
     (a) generalized anxiety disorder.   (c) panic disorder.
     (b) phobic attack.   (d) adjustment disorder.

8.   Herman is afraid to leave the familiar surroundings of his home. He would be diagnosed as having
     (a) hydrophobia.   (b) claustrophobia.   (c) acrophobia.   (d) agoraphobia.

9.   A househusband, whose dedication to household cleanliness is so great that he runs the vacuum cleaner five times a day whether or not the house needs it, probably has a(n) _____ disorder.
     (a) mood   (c) conversion reaction
     (b) phobic dosorder   (d) obsessive-compulsive disorder

10. Barbara witnesses her father committing a homosexual act. She immediately becomes blind and does not remember the event. Doctors can find nothing organically wrong with her eyes. The doctors diagnose her blindness as
     (a) a conversion reaction.   (b) fugue.   (c) amnesia.   (d) a phobic disorder.

11. Tim says he hears a radio inside his head. The CIA is speaking to him through the radio and telling him what to do. Tim is having delusions of
     (a) reference.   (b) persecution.   (c) grandeur.   (d) influence.

12. Flat affect would be *least* likely in which of the following disorders?
     (a) affective psychosis   (b) senile psychosis   (c) catatonic schizophrenia   (d) paranoid schizophrenia

13. Mary and Frank have an apartment in a very old building. They also have a two year old child. From an organic psychosis point of view regarding their child, Mary and Frank should be most concerned about
     (a) whether the elevator works or not in their building.   (c) the possibility that the child might develop senile dementia.
     (b) whether one of them might be carrying syphilis.   (d) whether the paint on the walls might contain lead or not.

14. The medical record of Patient X reveals that she was admitted to the hospital complaining of being chased by the Mafia because of her secret knowledge of how to win money on game shows. Her parents noted that she seemed to be a completely different person than she was a year ago. Patient X probably has
(a) paranoid psychosis.
(b) disorganized schizophrenia.
(c) paranoid schizophrenia.
(d) schizotypal personality.

15. On your first visit to a psychiatric ward you notice a patient sitting motionless and in an odd position on a couch. He holds the position for the full 30 minutes you are there. The patient probably is
(a) manic-depressive.
(b) catatonic.
(c) disorganized.
(d) schizotypal.

16. Steve breaks into uncontrollable laughter when told of his mother's death. Steve is probably suffering from
(a) undifferentiated schizophrenia.
(b) paranoid schizophrenia.
(c) catatonic schizophrenia.
(d) disorganized schizophrenia.

17. The father who says "I love you. Come give me a hug," to his daughter but then stiffens and nonverbally rejects her when she gets into his lap is probably
(a) experiencing a schizophrenic break.
(b) paranoid.
(c) hallucinating.
(d) deviant in his communication.

18. Sara's mother and father were both schizophrenic. If you're playing the odds, do you think Sara will also become schizophrenic?
(a) Yes
(b) No

19. Betsy has unlimited energy but cannot keep her mind on one thing for more than a few seconds. She talks constantly and is easily distracted. Eventually she becomes incoherent and disorganized. She probably is
(a) in the manic phase of an affective psychosis.
(b) paranoid.
(c) a disorganized schizophrenic.
(d) suffering from an organic psychosis.

20. David feels worthless. He has lost 25 pounds in the last three months and he can't sleep at night. His boss is on the verge of firing him because he has missed so much work, and when he is there, his performance is far below average. David had a manic episode one year ago. Now he appears to be suffering from
(a) cyclothymia
(b) bipolar II disorder
(c) bipolar I disorder
(d) unipolar disorder, major depression

21. Drugs haven't diminished Frank's severe depression. He is now talking about suicide. As a psychiatrist, the next form of therapy you might consider would be
(a) psychosurgery.
(b) psychotherapy.
(c) ECT.
(d) none of these.

Chapter Review

1. _____ may be defined as the inability to behave in ways that foster the well-being of the individual and ultimately of society. Some _____ to _____ percent of the population experience major depression in their lifetime.

2. Defining normality is difficult. We can begin by saying that _____ _____ is characteristic of psychopathology and accounts for most instances in which a person makes a decision to voluntarily seek professional help. However, a problem with this definition of abnormality is that in some cases a person's behavior may be quite _____ without producing any discomfort. Additionally, in some cases a _____ of discomfort may indicate a problem.

3. Some psychologists have tried to define normality more objectively by using _____ definitions. Unfortunately this kind of definition of abnormality tells us nothing about the meaning of _____ from the _____. Another major problem with a statistical definition is the question of where to draw the line between _____ and _____.

4. _____ _____ may also serve as a basis for judgments of normality. Abnormal behavior can sometimes be viewed as a failure in _____. Before any behavior can be defined as normal or abnormal we must consider the _____ in which it occurs. One of the most influential _____ in which any behavior is judged is that of _____. There is always a high degree of _____ _____ in perceptions of normality and abnormality.

5. It should be clear that all definitions of abnormality are _____. In practice, the judgment that a person is abnormal or needs help usually occurs when the person does something that annoys or gains the _____ of a person in a position of _____ who then does something about it. If doing something about it includes giving a label, some psychologists believe that the DSM-IV has a distinct male _____. In any case, it is better to label _____ than it is to label _____ in order to aid communication about human problems.

6. The most widely accepted system of classification of disorders is the _____-IV. Some of the disorders which are included in it follow. _____ mental disorders are problems caused by brain pathology. Psychological dependence on mood- or behavior-altering drugs results in a _____ _____ disorder.

7. _____ disorders are the most severe type of psychopathology, often requiring hospitalization. Here there is a loss of contact with shared views of _____ and a major loss of ability to control thoughts and actions. _____ disorders involve significant disturbances in mood or emotion.

8. _____ disorders may take the form of _____ (irrational fear of objects, activities, or situations), panic (in which the person suffers unexplainable feelings of total panic), _____ _____ (chronic and persistent anxiety). or _____-_____ stress (following extremely distressing events). Also associated with anxiety disorders is a pattern known as _____-_____ behavior.

9. _____ disorders are indicated when a person has physical symptoms suggesting physical disease or injury (paralysis, blindness, chronic pain, etc.) for which there is no identifiable cause. _____ disorders include cases of sudden, temporary amnesia, fugue, and instances of _____ personality.

10. _____ disorders are deeply ingrained, maladaptive personality patterns, usually recognizable by adolescence which continue throughout most of the individual's adult life.

11. _____ disorders include gender identity disorders, transsexualism, and paraphilias.

12. There are four general categories of risk factors for mental disorders. These include _____ conditions, _____ factors, _____ factors, and _____ factors.

13. Insanity is a _____ term. Psychosis is a _____ term.

14. Personality disorders are generally classified into three groups by degree of impairment. The first group (_____ impairment) includes dependent, _____, _____, and antisocial disorders. The second group (_____ impairment) includes _____-_____, _____ aggressive, schizoid, and _____ disorders. The last group (_____ impairment) includes _____, _____, and schizotypal disorders.

15. The individual possessing an antisocial personality, known as a _____ or _____, is irresponsible, impulsive, selfish, lacking in judgment, unable to feel guilt, emotionally shallow, unable to learn from _____, and lacking in moral values. The sociopath's childhood is usually a history of _____ deprivation and neglect which prevents the development of concern for the feelings of others.

16. Sociopathy is _____ treated with any success since the sociopaths _____ therapy as they might any other situation. There is, however, some evidence that antisocial behavior declines somewhat after age _____.

17. Public standards of proper sexual behavior are often at odds with _____ found privately acceptable. The mark of true sexual deviations is that they are _____ and _____, or that they cause guilt, anxiety, or discomfort for one or both participants. In characterizing sexual offenders, the picture of sexual deviance that usually emerges is one of sexual _____ and _____. The outlet for sexual expression is selected because it is less _____ than normal sexuality.

18. Sexual behaviors that fit the definition of sexual deviation include: _____ (sex with children), incest, fetishism, exhibitionism, _____ (viewing the genitals of others), transvestic fetishism, sexual _____ (deriving sexual pleasure from inflicting pain), sexual _____ (desiring pain as a part of the sex act), and frotteurism.

19. The category of sexual offenses that has the highest rate of repeaters is _____. Most of these offenders have a deep sense of _____. A woman should try not to become visibly _____ when confronted by one of these men.

20. In one-half to two-thirds of all cases of _____, the offender is known to the child. A single incident of _____ is unlikely to psychologically harm a child, but _____ incidents especially by someone the child knows, can cause problems.

21. Many psychologists no longer think of _____ as a sexual act; rather it is an act of _____. The goal of the act is not sexual intercourse, but to attack, subordinate, humiliate, and degrade the victim. The impact is so great that most women who successfully ward off a rape attempt are just as _____ as rape survivors.

22. Anxiety is similar to fear except anxiety is a response to an _____ threat. What were formally called the neuroses are now classified separately as _____ disorders, _____ disorders, and _____ disorders. In general these disorders involve high levels of _____ and/or restrictive, self-defeating _____ patterns, a tendency to use elaborate _____ _____ or _____ responses, and pervasive feelings of _____ and dissatisfaction with life.

23. The term nervous breakdown has no formal meaning. It is best described as an _____ disorder. This disorder is the result of obvious environmental _____ that pushes people beyond their ability to cope effectively. In a generalized _____ disorder there is at least 6 months of excessive _____. In a _____ disorder the affected person feels heart _____, _____ sensations, or feels that he or she is about to die because of the tremendous _____.

24. _____ are irrational fears that persist even when there is no real danger to a person. Phobias can be broken down into either _____ or _____ phobias depending on whether the person is fearful of social situations or objects, respectively. The most common and disruptive phobic disorder is _____, a fear of leaving _____.

25. _____ are thoughts or images that intrude into consciousness against a person's will. These usually give rise to _____, irrational acts a person feels driven to repeat which may help to lessen the associated _____. Such phenomena are characteristic of _____-_____ disorders.

26. Most anxiety disorders are relatively lasting patterns. An exception to this is _____ _____ disorder and _____ _____ _____ disorder. These problems occur when _____ (like disasters or war) outside the range of normal human experience cause a disturbance. If reactions last less than a month, the disorder is the _____.

27. A _____ reaction is marked by striking episodes of _____ (the inability to recall one's name, address, or past), _____ (physical flight to escape threat or conflict), or _____ _____ disorder (a rare condition in which two or more separate personalities exist in an individual).

28. The person who has multiple physical complaints for which medical attention is sought but for which no clear physical cause can be found suffers from what is called _____ (one of the _____ disorders). Another form of this, _____ disorder, is said to occur when anxiety or severe emotional conflicts are converted into physical symptoms resembling disease or disability.

29. At least three perspectives on causes of dissociative, anxiety, and somatoform disorders can be identified. The first explanation was proposed by _____ and is called the _____ approach. According to this view, these disorders represent a raging conflict between the three subparts of the personality: the _____, _____, and _____.

30. Psychologist _____ _____, exemplifying the humanisticapproach, interprets these disorders as the end-product of a faulty _____-_____. _____ have generally rejected previous explanations. They stress that such behavior is _____ just like any other behavior.

31. All theorists agree that this behavior is ultimately _____-_____ and _____. This means the behavior makes the person more miserable in the long run, but its immediate effect is to make him feel temporarily less _____.

32. The behavioristic explanation is that self-defeating behavior begins with _____ learning. Anxiety has been conditioned to various situations, and the immediate reinforcement of relief keeps the behavior pattern alive. This is called the _____ _____ hypothesis.

33. Psychosis—a major loss of contact with shared views of _____—is the most serious of all mental problems. It is characterized by the presence of _____ and _____, disturbed _____, and personality _____.

34. _____ are false beliefs that are held even when facts contradict them.

35. One common form of delusion is a _____ delusion in which people feel they have committed some horrible crime or sinful deed.

36. Also common in psychosis are _____ delusions, such as belief that one's body is "rotting" away or emitting foul odors. Delusions of _____ may occur as well. Here the individuals think they are extremely important persons. Delusions of _____ occur when individuals feel that they are being controlled by other persons or unseen forces.

37. Delusions of _____ in which the people feel others are "out to get them" are also common. Finally, there may be delusions of _____, in which unrelated events are given personal significance.

38. _____ are sensory experiences that occur in the _____ of a stimulus. The most common psychotic hallucination is _____ _____.

39. In the person with a psychosis, emotions may swing violently between the extremes of _____ and _____, or there may be instances of _____ _____ where there are almost no signs of emotion.

40. Some psychotic symptoms can be thought of as a primitive form of _____. Psychotic speech tends to be _____ and _____, and sometimes sounds like a "_____ _____."

41. The occurence of psychotic symptoms or disturbances bring about personality _____ and a break with _____. When the disturbances and disintegration are present for weeks or months, the person has suffered a _____.

42. A psychosis based on known brain pathology caused by disease, gunshot wound, accident, etc., is termed an _____ psychosis. A psychosis based on unknown or psychological factors is called a _____ psychosis.

43. One example of organic psychosis is _____ _____, which occurs in a small number of cases of untreated syphilis. Probably the most common of organic problems is _____ _____, premature deterioration of the brain caused by circulatory problems, repeated strokes, or general shrinkage and atrophy of the brain. It is typically marked by disturbances in _____, abstract reasoning, _____, _____ control, and personality, leaving the individual confused, suspicious, apathetic, or withdrawn.

44. The major cause of senility is _____ disease. Initially victims have trouble remembering _____ events. Slowly, they become more _____. Eventually they are mute, bedridden, and unable to walk, sit up, or smile. Two brain areas seem to be implicated. They are the _____ and the _____ _____.

45. The three major types of functional psychoses are _____ disorders, _____, and _____ _____ disorders. There is also a general category for psychotic disorders that are not elsewhere classified.

46. People with _____ _____ usually do not suffer from hallucinations, emotional excesses, or personality disintegration. Their main feature is the presence of _____.

47. _____ _____ is the most common type of delusional disorder centering on delusions of _____. Persons suffering paranoid delusions are rarely treated thereby leading isolated lives dominated by constant _____ and _____.

48. Other types of delusional disorders include the _____ (believing one is loved by someone famous), _____ (believing one's body is diseased or rotting), _____ (an all-consuming belief that one's spouse or lover is unfaithful), _____ (believing one has some great, unrecognized talent), and _____ (believing that one is being conspired against).

49. Another major type of functional psychosis is _____, which accounts for approximately half of all admissions to mental hospitals. The word _____ refers to a split between _____ and _____.

50. _____ personality disorder develops gradually, usually starting in adolescence. The individual becomes _____ and _____, and they are often considered _____, _____, or _____. Problems of this type resemble _____ but do not involve a break with _____.

51. In _____ schizophrenia the individual's personality disintegrates almost completely, resulting in silliness, laughter, bizarre and often obscene behavior. Chances of improvement are limited and social impairment is usually extreme.

52. In _____ schizophrenia the person seems to be in a state of total panic. This brings about a stuporous condition in which odd positions may be held for hours or days. In this condition _____ _____ occurs in which the person can be arranged into any position like a mannequin.

53. _____ schizophrenia is the most common form of schizophrenic disorder. This type of schizophrenia, like paranoia, centers around delusions of _____ and _____, but in the schizophrenic disorder there is major personality _____ not evident in paranoia.

54. There is considerable overlap among the types of schizophrenia, with patients often shifting from one pattern of behavior to another at different times during the course of the psychosis. Many are simply classified as suffering from _____ schizophrenia.

55.   Some psychologists suspect that early _____ _____ may contribute to the later development of schizophrenia. There seems to be a greater than average degree of _____ in the childhood of those who develop schizophrenia. Many psychologists theorize that a disturbed _____ environment is a causal factor in schizophrenia. The chance of developing schizophrenia appears related to patterns of _____ _____ in families.

56.   Although attractive, environmental explanations of schizophrenia are incomplete. When the children of schizophrenic parents are raised away from their home environment, they are just as likely to become psychotic. Thus children may at least inherit a _____ for schizophrenia. This is shown in studies with twins. If one identical twin becomes schizophrenic, there is a _____ percent chance the other will also.

57.   Many scientists believe that psychosis may be based on _____ abnormalities which cause the body to produce some substance similar to a psychedelic drug. The most likely candidate is _____.

58.   Medical researchers are now able to directly observe the schizophrenic by looking at an x-ray picture of the brain called a _____ scan. Researchers can also measure how much sugar is used in each area of the brain. This is called a _____ scan.

59.   Although no single cause fully accounts for psychosis, it appears that anyone subjected to enough _____ may be pushed to a psychotic break. Some people _____ a difference in brain _____ or _____ and this makes them more susceptible.

60.   _____ disorders are among the most serious of all, with between _____ and _____ percent of the _____ population having had a major depressive episode at some time. In depressive disorders, sadness and despondency are _____. A person suffers from _____ if they have been depressed more days than not for at least 2 years or from _____ if depression alternates with periods when the person's mood is elevated.

61.   Depression is to be expected when it is an _____ _____ to a death or major loss and is completed within a reasonable time. However, when someone is continually or intensely depressed after a triggering incident, it is termed a _____ _____.

62.   Another major type of functional disorder is major_____ disorder which accounts for about 14 percent of the patients admitted to mental hospitals. In addition to the usual psychological disturbances, this disorder includes lasting extremes of _____ or _____.

63.   In these disorders one of the following patterns predominates: In _____ disorders, persons go up or down emotionally. Individuals may be continually loud, inappropriately elated, hyperactive and energetic (_____ ____ disorder), but has had one or more periods of depression. When a person is sad and guilt-ridden, the problem is considered _____ ____ disorder if the person has ever been _____ in the past. The person who only goes down emotionally suffers from a major _____ disorder.

64.   The affective psychoses differ from the other affective disorders in that the former usually involves more severe _____ changes. Also, psychotic _____ and _____ are present. In addition, this disorder appears to be _____ (produced from _____) rather than a reaction to external events.

65.   _____ _____ disorder (SAD) is a depressive disorder which appears to be related to an increased release of _____ during the winter. The most efficacious treatment appears to be _____.

66.   Depression and other _____ disorders have resisted adequate explanation and treatment. Some researchers are focusing on the biology of mood changes with some success. For example, the chemical named _____ _____ can be effective in treating some cases of depression, particularly those also showing _____ behavior.

67. Others have sought psychological explanations for depression. Psychoanalytic theory, for instance, holds that depression is caused by repressed _____ that is displaced and turned inward as self-blame and self-hate. Behavioral theories of depression emphasize learned _____.

68. In addition, the fact that major mood disorders appear to be endogenous implies that _____ may be involved, especially in _____ disorders.

69. Two basic forms of treatment for psychosis can be distinguished. The first, called _____, can be described as two people talking about one person's problems. A second major approach to treatment is _____ (or bodily) therapy.

70. One of the principal somatic treatments is _____, the use of drugs to control or alleviate the symptoms of emotional disturbance. This therapy is most often used to combat _____ but may also be used to relieve the anxiety attacks and other discomforts of nonpsychotic disorders.

71. _____ tranquilizers calm anxious or agitated persons, _____ improve the mood of those who are depressed, and _____ control hallucinations and other symptoms of psychosis.

72. While drugs have improved the chances of recovery from a psychiatric disorder, there are some _____. For example, as many as 10 percent of patients taking major tranquilizers for extended periods develop _____ _____, a neurological condition where patients develop rhythmical facial and mouth movements, as well as unusual movements of the limbs and other parts of the body. Concern over _____ _____ and _____ of drugs may temper the popularity of chemotherapy.

73. Another somatic treatment is _____ therapy in which convulsions are produced by electric current. This is a rather drastic medical treatment used mainly for _____. Generally, ECT produces _____ improvement, causes permanent _____ _____ in many patients, and should only be used when drug therapy has failed

74. The most extreme type of somatic therapy is _____, a general term applied to any surgical alteration of the brain. The best known of these treatments is the _____ _____, where the frontal lobes are surgically disconnected from other areas of the brain.

75. The original goal of this procedure was to _____ a person who had not responded to any other type of treatment. Unfortunately, studies indicate it has very unpredictable results, and at the very least is _____, since damage to the brain is permanent.

76. Most neurosurgeons now use a technique called _____ _____ in which small areas in the brain's interior are destroyed electrically.

77. In the last 20 years, the resident population in large mental hospitals has been reduced by two-thirds. Hospital stays are now held to a minimum through use of _____ - _____ policies in which patients are released as soon as possible and readmitted only if necessary. Recent research indicates that patients do as well with _____- _____ hospitalization as they do with _____ periods.

78. A bright spot in the area of mental health care has been the creation of _____ _____ _____ centers. A distinctive feature of these centers is an emphasis on _____. These centers have made mental services more accessible than ever before. Much of their work is made possible by _____, individuals who work under the supervision of more highly trained staff.

79. Several factors appear related to suicide; other popular beliefs appear untrue. For example, there is little connection between major holidays and the suicide rate. The peak actually occurs in _____. More _____ actually complete suicide, but _____ make more attempts. More than half of all suicides are committed by individuals over _____ years old, although there has been a recent increase in rates for adolescents and young adults. Studies also show that the person who is likely to commit suicide is in a _____ line of work and in terms of marital situation is probably _____.

80.   There are many factors which cause suicide. There is usually a history of _____ troubles, a _____ problem, a _____ problem, or _____ difficulties. There is usually a break in _____ and the _____-_____ becomes very negative. There also may be unrealistic _____.

81.   There are several common characteristics of suicidal thoughts or feelings. Most people who want to kill themselves believe that this is the ultimate _____ from unbearable psychological _____. These people also usually have frustrated psychological _____ and they feel that this is the only _____ to their problems.

82.   To help a suicidal person you should _____ their feelings and the idea of _____, try to get day-by-day _____ from them, don't end your efforts too soon, put the person in touch with a suicide _____ center, and if the suicidal person has a concrete _____, ask him or her to accompany you to a local emergency ward.

ANSWER KEYS

Do You Know the Information?

Multiple Choice

1. (b) obj. 1, p. 489
2. (a) obj. 3, p. 491
3. (a) objs. 3-6, pp. 490-493
4. (b) obj. 5, p. 492
5. (b) obj. 7, p. 494
6. (d) obj. 7, p. 496
7. (c) obj. 8, p. 496
8. (c) obj. 10, p. 498
9. (b) obj. 11, p. 498
10. (c) obj. 11, p. 498
11. (b) obj. 12, p. 499
12. (a,c) objs. 14-15, pp. 499-501
13. (b) obj. 16, p. 500
14. (a) obj. 17, p. 501
15. (d) obj. 18, pp. 501-502
16. (a) obj. 19, p. 501
17. (c) obj. 20, p. 502
18. (a) obj. 21, p. 503
19. (c) obj. 21, p. 504
20. (b) obj. 21, p. 504
21. (b) obj. 21, p. 504
22. (b) obj. 21, p. 506
23. (d) obj. 21, p. 507
24. (d) obj. 22, p. 508
25. (a) obj. 22, p. 508
26. (d) obj. 22, p. 508
27. (b) objs. 23-24, pp. 509-510
28. (a) obj. 25, p. 510
29. (a) obj. 26, p. 510
30. (d) obj. 27, p. 510
31. (d) obj. 28, p. 511
32. (a) obj. 29, p. 511
33. (c) obj. 29-30, p. 511
34. (b) obj. 32, p. 512

35. (c) obj. 33, p. 512
36. (d) obj. 34, p. 513
37. (a) obj. 35, pp. 513, 515
38. (d) obj. 36, p. 515
39. (b) obj. 37, p. 515
40. (a) obj. 38, p. 516
41. (c) obj. 38, p. 517
42. (b) obj. 39, p. 518
43. (c) obj. 40, p. 521
44. (c) obj. 41, p. 521
45. (c) obj. 41, p. 521
46. (d) objs. 40, 42, pp. 521-523
47. (d) obj. 43, p. 525
48. (c) obj. 44, p. 525
49. (a) obj. 45, p. 525
50. (b) objs. 44, 45, p. 525
51. (c) obj. 46, p. 526
52. (a) obj. 46, p. 527
53. (d) obj. 47, p. 527
54. (c) obj. 49, pp. 529-530
55. (b) obj. 51, pp. 531-532

True-False

1. F, obj. 2, p. 490
2. T, obj. 7, p. 494
3. F, obj. 9, p. 497
4. T, obj. 12, p. 500
5. F, obj. 13-14, p. 499
6. F, obj. 17, p. 501
7. T, obj. 20, p. 502
8. F, obj. 22, p. 508
9. T, obj. 33, p. 512
10. T, obj. 36, p. 515
11. F, obj. 36, p. 515

12. T, obj. 38, p. 516
13. T, obj. 40, p. 521
14. T, obj. 41, p. 522
15. F, obj. 42, p. 524
16. F, obj. 47, p. 528
17. T, obj. 47, p. 527
18. F, obj. 48, p. 528
19. T, obj. 49, p. 529
20. F, obj. 49, p. 530
21. F, obj. 50, p. 530
22. T, obj. 51, p. 532

Matching

1. J, obj. 7, p. 494
2. F, objs. 7, 21, pp. 496, 506
3. I, obj. 7, p. 497
4. M, obj. 9, p. 497
5. C, obj. 21, p. 503
6. A, obj. 21, p. 505
7. L, obj. 21, p. 506
8. G, obj. 21, p. 506
9. E, obj. 25, p. 510
10. H, obj. 26, p. 510
11. N, obj. 29, p. 511
13. O, obj. 36, p. 514
14. K, obj. 36, p. 513
15. R, obj. 36, p. 515
12. Q, obj. 35, p. 515
16. P, obj. 38, p. 518
17. B, obj. 38, p. 518
18. U, obj. 40, p. 521
19. S, obj. 41, p. 522
20. D, obj. 43, p. 525
21. T, obj. 44, p. 525
22. V, obj. 51, p. 531

Can You Apply the Information?

1. (b) obj. 3, pp. 490-491
2. (a) objs. 3, 12, pp. 490, 499
3. (c) obj. 7, p. 494
4. (c) obj. 11, p. 498
5. (a) obj. 17, p. 501
6. (d) objs. 19, 40, pp. 501, 521
7. (c) obj. 20, p. 502

8. (d) obj. 21, p. 503
9. (d) obj. 21, p. 504
10. (a) obj. 21, p. 507
11. (d) obj. 25, p. 510
12. (a) objs. 27, 41, pp. 510, 521
13. (d) obj. 29, p. 511
14. (c) objs. 33, 35-37, p. 515

15. (b) obj. 36, p. 514
16. (d) obj. 36, p. 513
17. (d) obj. 38, p. 516
18. (b) obj. 38, p. 517
19. (a) obj. 41, p. 522
20. (b) obj. 41, p. 521
21. (c) obj. 46, p. 526

Chapter Review

1. Psychopathology, 10, 20 (p. 489)
2. subjective discomfort, maladaptive (abnormal), lack (p. 490)
3. statistical, deviations, norm, normality, abnormality (p. 490)
4. Social nonconformity, socialization, context, contexts, culture, cultural relativity (p. 491)
5. relative, attention, power, bias, problems, people (p. 492)
6. DSM, Organic, substance related (p. 494)
7. Psychotic, reality, Mood (p. 494)
8. Anxiety, phobias, generalized anxiety, post-traumatic, obsessive-compulsive (p. 494)
9. Somatoform, Dissociative, multiple (p. 496)
10. Personality (p. 496)
11. Sexual (p. 496)
12. social, family, psychological, biological (p. 496)
13. legal, psychiatric (p. 497)
14. moderate, histrionic, narcissistic, high obsessive-compulsive, passive, avoidant, severe, borderline, paranoid (p. 498)
15. sociopath, psychopath, experience, emotional (p. 498)
16. rarely, manipulate, 30 (p. 498)
17. behavior, compulsive, destructive (p. 499); inhibition, immaturity, threatening (p. 500)
18. pedophilia, voyeurism, sadism, masochism (p. 501)
19. exhibitionism, inadequacy, upset (p. 499)
20. molestation, molestation, repeated (p. 500)
21. rape, aggression (brutality), depressed (p. 500)
22. nonspecific, anxiety, behavior, defense mechanisms, avoidance, stress (insecurity, inferiority, unhappiness) (p. 501)
23. adjustment, stress, anxiety, anxiety (worry), panic, palpitations, choking (smothering), anxiety (p. 501)
24. Phobias, social, specific, agoraphobia, home (p. 503)
25. Obsessions, compulsions, anxiety, obsessive-compulsive (p. 504)
26. acute stress, post-traumatic stress, stresses, former (p. 505)
27. dissociative, amnesia, fugue, dissociative identity (p. 506)
28. hypochondriasis, somatization, conversion (p. 506)
29. Freud, psychodynamic, id, ego, superego (p. 508)
30. Carl Rogers, self-image, Behaviorists, learned (p. 508)
31. self-defeating, paradoxical, anxious (p. 508)
32. avoidance, anxiety reduction (p. 509)
33. reality, delusions, hallucinations, emotions, disorganization (disintegration) (p. 509)
34. Delusions (p. 510)
35. depressive (p. 510)
36. somatic, grandeur, influence (p. 510)
37. persecution, reference (p. 510)
38. Hallucinations, absence, hearing voices (p. 510)
39. elation, depression, flat affect (p. 510)
40. communication, garbled, chaotic, word salad (p. 510)
41. disintegration, reality, psychosis (p. 510)
42. organic, functional (p. 510)
43. general paresis, senile dementia, memory, judgment, impulse (p. 511)

44. Alzheimer's, recent, disoriented (suspicious, confused), hippocampus, nucleus basalis (p. 511)
45. delusional, schizophrenia, psychotic mood (p. 511)
46. delusional disorders, delusions (p. 512)
47. Paranoid psychosis, persecution, suspicion, hostility (p. 512)
48. erotomanic, somatic, jealous, grandiose, persecutory (p. 512)
49. schizophrenia, schizophrenia, thought, emotion (p. 513)
50. Schizotypal, isolated, withdrawn, odd, shiftless, eccentric, schizophrenic, reality (p. 515)
51. disorganized (p. 513)
52. catatonic, waxy flexibility (p. 514)
53. Paranoid, grandeur, persecution, disintegration (p. 515)
54. undifferentiated (p. 515)
55. psychological trauma, stress, family, deviant communication (p. 516)
56. potential, 46 (p. 517)
57. biochemical, dopamine (p. 518)
58. CT, PET (p. 518)
59. stress, inherit, chemistry, structure (p. 518)
60. Mood, 10, 20 adult, exaggerated (prolonged, unreasonable), dysthymia, cyclothymia (p. 519)
61. emotional adjustment, reactive depression (p. 521)
62. mood, mood, emotion (p. 521)
63. bipolar, bipolar I, bipolar II, manic, depressive (p. 521)
64. mood, delusions, hallucinations, endogenous, within (p. 522)
65. Seasonal affective, melatonin, phototherapy (p. 524)
66. mood lithium carbonate, manic (p. 522)
67. anger, helplessness (p. 523)
68. genetics, bipolar (p. 523)
69. psychotherapy, somatic (p. 525)
70. chemotherapy, psychosis (p. 525)
71. Minor, energizers, antipsychotics (p. 525)
72. drawbacks, tardive dyskinesia, side effects, overuse (p. 525)
73. electroconvulsive, depression, temporary, memory loss (p. 526)
74. psychosurgery, prefrontal lobotomy (p. 526)
75. calm, irreversible (p. 527)
76. deep lesioning (p. 527)
77. revolving-door, short-term, longer (p. 528)
78. community mental health, prevention, paraprofessionals (p. 528)
79. May, men, women, 45, professional, divorced (p. 529)
80. interpersonal, drinking, sexual, job, communication, self-image, expectations (p. 530)
81. escape, pain, needs, solution (p. 531)
82. accept, suicide, commitments, prevention, plan (p. 532)

chapter fifteen

Therapies

LEARNING OBJECTIVES

To demonstrate mastery of this chapter you should be able to:

1. Define psychotherapy.

2. Describe each of the following approaches to therapy:

    a. individual therapy

    b. group therapy

    c. insight therapy

    d. action therapy

    e. directive therapy

    f. non-directive therapy

    g. time-limited therapy

3. Evaluate what a person can expect as possible outcomes from psychotherapy.

4. Briefly describe the history of the treatment of psychological problems, including in your description trepanning, demonology, exorcism, ergotism, and Pinel.

5. Explain why the first psychotherapy was developed.

6. List the four basic techniques used in psychoanalysis and explain their purpose.

    a.

    b.

    c.

    d.

7. Name and describe the therapy that is frequently used today instead of psychoanalysis. Describe the criticism that helped prompt the switch.

8. Contrast client-centered (humanistic) therapy and psychoanalysis.

9. Describe client-centered therapy including the four conditions that should be maintained for successful therapy.

    a.

    b.

    c.

    d.

10. Explain the approach of existential therapy and compare and contrast it with client-centered therapy. Name and generally describe one example of existential therapy.

11. Briefly describe gestalt therapy.

12. Describe the advantages of group therapy.

13. Briefly describe each of the following group therapies:
    a. psychodrama

    b. family therapy

    c. group awareness training (including sensitivity groups, encounter groups, and large group awareness training)

14. Discuss the limitations of phone-in psychologists and describe what the APA recommends should be the extent of their activities.

15. Evaluate the effectiveness of encounter groups and sensitivity groups and include the concept of the therapy placebo effect.

16. Contrast the goal of behavior therapy with the goal of insight therapies.

17. Define behavior modification and state its basic assumption.

18. Describe aversion therapy and explain how it can be used to stop smoking and drinking.

19. Explain the relationship of aversion therapy to classical conditioning. State two problems associated with aversion therapy.

    a.

    b.

20. Explain how relaxation, reciprocal inhibition, and use of a hierarchy are combined to produce desensitization. State what desensitization is used for and give an example of desensitization therapy or vicarious desensitization therapy. Very briefly describe eye-movement desensitization.

21.   List and briefly describe the seven operant principles most frequently used by behavior therapists.

   a.

   b.

   c.

   d.

   e.

   f.

   g.

22.   Explain how nonreward and time out can be used to bring about extinction of a maladaptive behavior.

23.   Describe a token economy including its advantages and possible disadvantages. Include the terms token and target behavior in your description.

24.   Describe what sets a cognitive behavior therapist apart from other behavior therapists. List and describe four thinking errors which underlie depression and explain what can be done to correct such thinking.

   a.

   b.

   c.

   d.

25. Describe rational-emotive therapy. List the three core ideas which serve as the basis of most irrational beliefs.

    a.

    b.

    c.

26. Discuss the effectiveness of psychotherapy. Describe the rate at which typical doses of therapy help people improve.

27. List the six goals of psychotherapy, and state the four means used to accomplish the goals.

    Goals:

    a.

    b.

    c.

    d.

    e.

    f.

    Means:

    a.

    b.

    c.

    d.

28. List and briefly describe the nine points or tips which can help a person when counseling a friend.

a.

b.

c.

d.

e.

f.

g.

h.

i.

29. List and explain the six characteristics of culturally skilled counselors.

a.

b.

c.

d.

e.

f.

The following objectives are related to the material in the "Applications" section of your text.

30. Describe how covert sensitization, thought-stopping, and covert reinforcement can be used to reduce unwanted behavior.

31.   Give an example of how you can overcome a common fear or break a bad habit using the steps given for desensitization.

32.   List and describe four indicators that may signal the need for professional psychological help.

   a.

   b.

   c.

   d.

33.   List six methods a person can use for finding a therapist.

   a.

   b.

   c.

   d.

   e.

   f.

34.   Describe how one can choose a psychotherapist.

35.   Summarize what is known about the importance of the personal qualities of the therapist and the client for successful therapy.

SELF-QUIZZES

Do You Know the Information?

Multiple Choice

1.   Psychotherapy is defined as
     (a)   a technique used to cure mental illness.
     (b)   a technique that facilitates positive changes in a person's adjustment, behavior, or personality.
     (c)   two people facilitating each other's personal growth.
     (d)   any technique which provides an understanding of one's problems.

For questions 2-5 use a letter from the following list:

(a)   insight therapy   (d)   nondirective therapy   (f)   group therapy
(b)   action therapy   (e)   individual therapy   (g)   time-limited therapy
(c)   directive therapy

_____ 2.   places responsibility for the course of therapy on the client

_____ 3.   focuses on directly changing troublesome habits and behavior

_____ 4.   one-to-one basis between client and therapist

_____ 5.   fosters a deeper understanding of the assumptions, beliefs, emotions, and conflicts underlying a problem

6.   Which of the following statements about psychotherapy is *incorrect?*
     (a)   Chances of improvement are fairly good for circumscribed problems such as phobias, sexual problems, marital conflicts, etc.
     (b)   Therapy's major benefit is that it provides comfort, support, and a way to make positive changes.
     (c)   Therapy usually helps bring about a dramatic end to a person's suffering.
     (d)   Therapy is not just done to solve problems but also to encourage personal growth and enrichment.

7.   Trepanning was the technique in which
     (a)   a hole was bored into a person's skull to release evil spirits.   (c)   a person was chained to a wall to prevent injury.
     (b)   a person was tortured as a part of a religious ritual.   (d)   a person's system was purged of the ergot fungus.

8.   During the Middle Ages, treatment for the mentally ill in Europe focused on
     (a)   demonology.   (b)   poisoning.   (c)   unconscious motives.   (d)   physiological abnormalities.

9.   A compassionate view of the mentally ill slowly emerged after 1793, primarily as a result of the efforts of
     (a)   Freud.   (b)   Pinel.   (c)   Rogers.   (d)   Frankl.

10. The first psychotherapy was developed because Freud
    (a) could not understand his dreams.
    (b) believed that deeply hidden unconscious conflicts caused hysteria.
    (c) became convinced that the driving forces of personality were conscious ideas that needed controlling.
    (d) found the symptoms of hysteria were caused by dreams.

11. A patient in psychoanalysis does not wish to talk about her ideas and thoughts during free association or dream analysis. This problem is known as
    (a) transference.　　　(b) empathy.　　　(c) resistance.　　　(d) identification.

12. Which of the following statements about psychotherapy is *incorrect*?
    (a) Most therapists who use psychoanalytic theory have switched to short-term dynamic therapy.
    (b) The success of psychoanalysis may be attributable to spontaneous remission.
    (c) Some people in psychoanalysis improve with the mere passage of time.
    (d) The number of therapists practicing psychoanalysis has increased.

13. The goal of psychoanalysis is
    (a) adjustment.　　　(b) self-knowledge.　　　(c) self-actualization.　　　(d) to rebuild connected wholes.

14. Which of the following statements concerning client-centered therapy and psychoanalysis is *incorrect*?
    (a) The client-centered therapist tends to take a position of authority from which he or she offers interpretations.
    (b) Psychoanalysts delve into childhood, dreams, and the unconscious.
    (c) Client-centered therapy and the other humanistic therapies view therapy as a means of giving a person's natural tendencies toward mental health a chance to emerge.
    (d) In client-centered therapy the client determines what will be said in each session.

15. The terms unconditional positive regard and empathy are most closely associated with _____ therapy.
    (a) psychoanalytic　　　(b) client-centered　　　(c) existential　　　(d) rational-emotive

16. The idea of existential therapy is to
    (a) probe hidden desires that relate to the nature of one's being.
    (b) confront a person's unrealistic expectations.
    (c) eliminate undesirable behavior by manipulating reinforcers.
    (d) promote self-knowledge and self-actualization and emphasize free will.

17. Which of the following therapies stresses confrontation between client and therapist?
    (a) psychoanalysis　　　(b) logotherapy　　　(c) short-term dynamic therapy　　　(d) client-centered therapy

18. A therapist who tries to help an individual rebuild thinking, feeling, and acting into connected wholes would most likely be a
    (a) Gestalt therapist.　　　(b) psychoanalyst.　　　(c) encounter group therapist.　　　(d) sensitivity group therapist.

19. According to Perls, the founder of Gestalt therapy, emotional health comes from getting in touch with what you
    (a) should do.　　　(b) ought to do.　　　(c) want to do.　　　(d) should want to do.

20. An advantage of group therapy is that it
    (a) provides an important link between the real world and therapy.
    (b) enables patients to have more individual time with the therapist to talk over personal problems.
    (c) provides a more protected atmosphere than individual therapy.
    (d) all of the above are advantages of group therapy.

21. In which of the following therapies would a person role play incidents resembling those which cause problems in real life?
    (a) psychoanalysis　　　(b) encounter groups　　　(c) psychodrama　　　(d) sensitivity groups

22. The therapy in which a person is encouraged to get rid of his or her psychological defenses and to be totally honest and confronting is
    (a) psychoanalysis.　　　(b) encounter groups.　　　(c) psychodrama.　　　(d) sensitivity groups.

23. Which of the following statements is *incorrect*?
    (a) The APA recommends that radio psychologists discuss only problems of a general nature and not discuss the particular problem of an individual caller.
    (b) Many radio psychologists stress that their work is educational, not therapeutic.
    (c) Many of the claimed benefits of sensitivity and encounter groups are the result of a therapy placebo effect.
    (d) The therapy placebo effect is related to things such as the therapist's theoretical orientation, the number of years of schooling, etc.

24. The goal of insight therapies is _____, whereas the goal of behavior therapy is to _____.
    (a) insight; allow the person to achieve his or her full potential   (c) understanding; discover the cause of the behavior
    (b) understanding; alter troublesome thoughts and behavior   (d) self-actualization; improve the negative behavior

25. Behavior modification is based upon which of the following principal assumptions?
    (a) Conflicts between the conscious and unconscious produce maladaptive behaviors.
    (b) Habits that cause problems are learned and therefore can be unlearned.
    (c) The thwarting of self-actualization processes produces abnormal ego-states.
    (d) Insight is the key to normal adjustment.

26. The basic idea of aversion therapy is
    (a) a person learns to associate a strong aversion with an undesirable habit.
    (b) behavior is extinguished by punishment.
    (c) maladaptive behavior is eliminated or decreased by rewarding desirable behavior.
    (d) in none of the above answers.

27. Of the following, which is a problem in the use of aversion therapy?
    (a) ineffectiveness with some personality types
    (b) lack of a sound theoretical base
    (c) poorly defined connections between applications and basic research
    (d) difficulties of generalization of results from the therapy setting to the real world

28. Desensitization is based on the principle of
    (a) retroactive inhibition.   (b) proactive inhibition.   (c) reactive inhibition.   (d) reciprocal inhibition.

29. Desensitization is used primarily for
    (a) diminishing hallucinations and delusions.   (c) hysteria.
    (b) treating depression.   (d) alleviating phobias and anxieties.

30. When constructing a hierarchy for desensitization, care should be taken to insure that the situations
    (a) do not provide any reinforcement.
    (b) are ordered from the least disturbing to the most disturbing.
    (c) do not provoke undue anxiety.
    (d) are balanced between situations that are perceived as disturbing and those that are not.

31. _____ prevents reward from following an undesirable response.
    (a) Punishment   (b) Extinction   (c) Time out   (d) Nonreinforcement

32. When a child misbehaves in order to gain attention, an effective way of decreasing this misbehavior is to
    (a) ignore the child's misbehavior.
    (b) be reinforcing and kind to the child when he or she misbehaves.
    (c) direct negative statements at the child when he or she misbehaves.
    (d) give the child what he or she desires so he or she will no longer misbehave.

33. One advantage of a token economy is
    (a) it often works on seemingly hopeless cases.
    (b) it overcomes the problem of generalization by using tokens.
    (c) target behaviors can be more easily identified than in aversion therapy.
    (d) in none of the above answers.

4. As compared to a behavior therapist, a cognitive behavior therapist
   (a) uses less relaxation training.
   (b) has been generally more concerned with why certain thoughts or behavior occur.
   (c) is interested in thoughts instead of just visible behavior.
   (d) uses more tokens in therapy.

5. Which of the following statements about cognitive behavior therapy is *incorrect*?
   (a) Cognitive therapy has been especially effective in the treatment of depression.
   (b) To combat depression clients are asked to collect information to test the beliefs that cause the depression.
   (c) Cognitive therapists may look for the presence of effective coping skills and thought patterns, not for the absence of self-defeating thinking.
   (d) According to Beck depressed people engage in selective perception, over-generalization, all-or-nothing thinking, and magnification of the importance of undesirable events.

6. The basic idea of rational-emotive therapy is that
   (a) people who exhibit psychotic behavior should just try to live more rationally.
   (b) emotions cause people to hold irrational thoughts about themselves.
   (c) therapists who use desensitization will not get good generalization to the outside world.
   (d) people develop self-defeating habits because of unrealistic or faulty beliefs.

7. Which of the following statements about psychotherapy is *incorrect*?
   (a) In a study of the rate of improvement, half of the patients reported feeling better after one month.
   (b) In the above study, the majority of patients had improved after 6 months.
   (c) The typical "dose" of therapy is one hour per week.
   (d) In hundreds of studies of the effectiveness of therapy, a modest but consistent positive effect was found.

8. Which of the following is *not* a goal of psychotherapy?
   (a) better interpersonal relations   (c) a more pleasant personality
   (b) resolution of conflicts   (d) insight

9. To accomplish part or all of the goals of psychotherapy, the different therapies offer
   (a) an explanation or a rationale for the suffering the client has experienced.
   (b) a protected setting in which emotional catharsis can take place.
   (c) a caring relationship between client and therapist.
   (d) a new perspective about self and their situation.
   (e) all of the above.

0. Which of the following is *not* good to keep in mind when comforting someone in distress?
   (a) Focus on feelings to avoid making the person defensive.
   (b) Resist the temptation to contradict the person with your point of view.
   (c) Show your understanding and support by giving your advice freely.
   (d) Encourage free expression through open questions.

1. Culturally skilled counselors need to
   (a) set aside their own cultural values and biases.   (c) avoid thinking of clients in terms of stereotypes.
   (b) realize that cultural barriers are rarely transcended.   (d) mentally take the role of the ethnic or racial group.

2. Which of the following is *not* a typical step in using desensitization to overcome a common fear?
   (a) Learn how to relax.   (c) Identify the fear you would like to control.
   (b) Reward yourself for each stage of the hierarchy completed.   (d) As you progress through the hierarchy, relax between steps.

3. Which of the following would *not* be considered an important indicator that a person needs professional psychological help?
   (a) significant change in observable behavior   (c) persistent suicidal thoughts or impulses
   (b) inability to meet the expectations of others   (d) high level of psychological discomfort

44. In choosing a psychotherapist, it is best to
(a) choose a psychologist instead of a psychiatrist.
(b) start with a short consultation first for evaluation purposes.
(c) avoid paraprofessionals at all costs.
(d) be sure you have enough money to cover the costs of a long therapeutic interaction.

45. Which of the following statements is *incorrect*?
(a) All therapists are not equally effective.
(b) The therapist's personal qualities are far more important than the techniques used in therapy.
(c) If a client likes the therapist, that will get in the way of making progress in the relationship.
(d) The relationship between a client and therapist is the therapist's most basic tool.

True-False

_____ 1. Time-limited therapy is used when each therapy session is to last no more than one hour.

_____ 2. Therapy is about equally effective for all problems.

_____ 3. Ergotism, which occurred in the Middle Ages, was poisoning from a fungus that produced psychotic-like symptoms.

_____ 4. Psychoanalysis as originally conducted by Freud is still in widespread use today.

_____ 5. Although not extremely effective, psychoanalysis is usually better than no treatment at all.

_____ 6. Client-centered therapy emphasizes the idea of free will whereas existential therapy seeks to uncover a "true self" hidden behind an artificial screen of defenses.

_____ 7. In psychodrama an individual role-plays dramatic incidents resembling those that cause problems in real life.

_____ 8. Family therapists believe that problems are rarely limited to a single family member, but that it is the person who should receive therapy.

_____ 9. Encounter groups are usually more confrontive and emotionally intense than sensitivity groups.

_____ 10. Because there is a danger of psychological damage, encounter group participation is safest when members are carefully screened and when groups are professionally led.

_____ 11. The idea of aversion therapy is to associate something like alcohol (the CS) with something aversive (the CR) like vomiting.

_____ 12. Constructing a hierarchy is not essential to the desensitization process.

_____ 13. A variation of nonreinforcement is the time-out procedure whereby an individual is removed from a situation in which reinforcement occurs.

_____ 14. In the A-B-C of rational-emotive therapy the "B" stands for behavior.

_____ 15. One of the core ideas which forms the basis of irrational beliefs is that a person must perform well and be approved of by significant others.

_____ 16. When counseling a friend, contradict his or her opinion of a situation if you feel it is wrong.

_____ 17. Covert sensitization involves associating very unpleasant thoughts or images with a habit you wish to diminish.

_____ 18. The simplest thought-stopping technique makes use of mild punishment to suppress upsetting mental images and internal "talk."

_____ 19. The main purpose of public mental health services is to make referrals to private therapists.

_____ 20. Psychotherapy techniques tend to be about equally successful in helping clients with emotional/behavioral problems.

_____ 21. Whether a client likes their therapist or not seems to have no relationship to the success of the therapy.

Can You Apply the Information?

1. Alex is going to a therapist in hopes of breaking his smoking habit. The therapy which would most likely be best for him would be _____ therapy.
   (a) nondirective   (b) action   (c) insight   (d) group

2. In the above question, if Alex were going to a therapist to find out why he smokes, he would probably be participating in _____ therapy.
   (a) action   (b) insight   (c) nondirective   (d) none of these

3. In a psychoanalytic session the patient is talking about her relationship with her father. She begins to get angry with the psycho-analyst when he makes comments. It is likely that the therapist would begin to concentrate on
   (a) analysis of resistance.   (b) dream interpretation.   (c) analysis of transference.   (d) free association.

4. Which of the following therapists would be *least* likely to give you suggestions on how to solve an emotional problem?
   (a) Perls (Gestalt therapy)   (c) Davanloo (short-term dynamic therapy)
   (b) Frankl (logotherapy)   (d) Rogers (client-centered therapy)

5. You are a humanistic therapist doing client-centered therapy. What is probably your *first* step with most of your clients?
   (a) Convince your client that you are a competent therapist capable of guiding them to good adjustment.
   (b) Reflect upon the client's mistakes and tell them what you would do to improve behavior.
   (c) Offer the client unconditional positive regard and strive to be authentic in your relationship.
   (d) None of these answers should be done first.

6. David's therapist is emphasizing the idea that David is totally free to make his own choice concerning his future. David is probably in
   (a) existential therapy.   (c) client-centered therapy.
   (b) short-term dynamic therapy.   (d) Gestalt therapy.

7. With the help of her therapist, Rebecca is now able to decide what she wants to do for herself rather than dwelling on what others may want her to do or on what she feels she ought to be doing. Rebecca has probably been in
   (a) existential therapy.   (b) logotherapy.   (c) client-centered therapy.   (d) Gestalt therapy.

8. Frank is in group therapy. During one session he and the rest of the group act out his latest confrontation with his alcoholic wife. Frank is probably engaged in
   (a) logotherapy.   (b) sensitivity training.   (c) Gestalt therapy.   (d) psychodrama.

9. Betty is depressed and suicidal. Her best friend Linda has asked her to go to an encounter group as her guest and consider this type of therapy. Betty should
   (a) go with Linda because the group will probably help her understand her problem in a nonthreatening manner.
   (b) stay away because she is probably not psychologically suited for the brutal honesty.
   (c) go with Linda and bring other family members along.
   (d) not do anything now and expect to improve with time.

10.   Mary is having trouble sleeping at night, and she believes that she can get help by calling her local radio psychologist. It takes 30 minutes of constant dialing to finally get through. Even though the psychologist only talks about insomnia in a general manner and not about her specific problem, Mary's insomnia is alleviated and she can now sleep normally. What would account for this apparent "relief?"
(a) the therapy placebo effect
(b) the indepth discussion of Mary's personal life
(c) the psychologist's unconditional positive regard for Mary and her situation
(d) the use of awareness training during the call

11.   For which of the following would behavior modification be *inappropriate*?
(a) making an autistic child more socially responsive   (c) understanding why you smoke
(b) losing weight   (d) overcoming procrastination

12.   A pedophile (a person who achieves sexual gratification through contact with children) desperately wants to overcome his problem. To help you show him slides of naked children and every time he begins to get an erection you give him a severe shock. This therapy is an example of
(a) desensitization.   (b) implosive therapy.   (c) covert sensitization.   (d) aversion therapy.

13.   Donald has been offered a job as a janitor in the reptile house at the local zoo but he is deathly afraid of snakes. Which of the following therapies would probably be *most* appropriate for him?
(a) desensitization   (b) nonreinforcement   (c) insight therapy   (d) cognitive behavior therapy

14.   Your husband has started telling you jokes that you really don't like. The best "therapy" for him would be
(a) desensitization.   (b) nonreinforcement.   (c) insight therapy.   (d) covert sensitization.

15.   Benjamin is argumentative and belligerent with his parents. To correct the behavior his parents make him sit on the stairs by himself for ten minutes. Benjamin's parents are using
(a) desensitization.   (b) cognitive behavior therapy. (c) time out.   (d) a token economy.

16.   Bob is very depressed. He was accepted at the college of his choice, he has a good summer job, and has a great date for the prom, but all he can think about is the one college which rejected his application. He seems to be suffering from
(a) all-or-nothing thinking.   (c) thought stopping.   (e) a good case of the geeks.
(b) selective perception.   (d) target behaviors.

17.   "I can't take it anymore. I've tried to be the perfect mother, the perfect lawyer, and the perfect wife, and I'm blowing all three. I want to be the best in everything I do." This person is probably a good candidate for
(a) covert sensitization.   (b) time out.   (c) behavior modification.   (d) rational-emotive therapy.

18.   Pat wants to reduce the amount of red meat she eats. When she thinks about eating a hamburger she envisions cholesterol clogging her arteries. This is an example of
(a) covert sensitization.   (b) thought stopping.   (c) desensitization.   (d) covert reinforcement.

19.   Bill suffers from an incredible level of anxiety because of the quality of his cognitive activity. For example, whenever he is driving he envisions himself having a terrible accident and smashing himself all over the inside of the car. Bill might benefit from which of the following types of therapy?
(a) desensitization   (b) aversion   (c) thought-stopping   (d) time out

Chapter Review

1.   _____ is any psychological technique designed to facilitate positive changes in a person's _____, _____, or _____. There are many different kinds of therapy.

2. _____ therapies foster a deeper understanding of the assumptions, beliefs, emotions, and conflicts under-lying a problem. _____ therapies focus on directly changing troublesome habits and behavior. In _____ therapies, the therapist guides the client strongly, giving instructions, offering interpretations, posing solutions, and sometimes even making important decisions for the client.

3. _____ approaches place responsibility for the course of therapy on the client; it is up to the client to discover his or her own solutions. _____ therapies proceed on a one-to-one basis between client and therapist. In _____ therapy, individual problems are resolved by making use of the special characteristics of the group setting. _____-_____ therapy can be any of the previous therapies started with the expectation of limiting the number of sessions.

4. Therapy is not equally effective for all problems. Chances of improvement are fairly good for _____, low _____-_____, some _____ problems, and _____ complaints. People who enter therapy should not expect _____ results or changes.

5. During the Stone Age, spirits were released from the head by a process called _____, where a hole was bored, chipped, or bashed into the skull. During the Middle Ages, treatment for the mentally ill in Europe focused on _____ with the major technique being _____. Some psychotic-like behavior was probably caused by _____, the eating of bread made from grain infected with a fungus.

6. Finally, a more compassionate view of the mentally ill emerged after 1793 when _____ changed the Bicetre Asylum in Paris from a "mad house" to a mental hospital by personally _____ the inmates. The first true psychotherapy was developed around the turn of the century by _____.

7. Freud sought to understand and treat cases of _____, where physical symptoms like paralysis or numbness occur without known physical cause. Freud slowly became convinced that the symptoms of this disorder were caused by hidden _____ _____. Freud's form of therapy was called _____.

8. Freud relied on four basic techniques to uncover the unconscious roots of neurosis. One of these, _____ _____, required the patient to say whatever came to mind without regard for whether it made sense, was painful, or embarrassing.

9. The purpose of this technique was to lower _____ so that unconscious material could emerge. Another technique, _____ analysis, was considered by Freud to be an unusually good means of tapping the unconscious. He made a distinction between the obvious (_____) content and the hidden (_____) content of dreams. According to Freud, by interpreting one's _____ _____ one could reveal the latent meaning of dreams.

10. When free associating or describing dreams, the patient may _____ talking or thinking about certain topics. Such _____ are said to reveal particularly important unconscious conflicts. The individual undergoing psychoanalysis may also _____ feelings to the therapist that relate to important past relationships with others.

11. Because of the huge amounts of _____ and _____ required for psychoanalysis, this type of therapist has become relatively _____. In its place has come _____-_____ _____ therapy. Eysenck has suggested that psychoanalysis takes so long that patients improve due to the mere passage of time. This improvement is called _____ _____. Recent research reveals that _____ is better than no treatment at all.

12. The goal of Freudian therapy is _____. The humanistic therapies seek to help people make full use of their _____.

13. Carl Rogers has developed a therapy called _____-_____ therapy. Rogers believes that the psychoanalyst tends to take a position of _____ about what is wrong with the patient. He believes that the psychoanalyst's _____ of what is right or valuable may not be so for the client. Thus, Rogers uses a _____ approach in that the client determines what will be discussed during each session.

14. According to Rogers, the therapist's job is to create an "atmosphere of growth" by maintaining four basic conditions. First the therapist offers the client _____ _____ _____—the client is accepted totally. Second, the therapist attempts to achieve genuine _____ for the client by trying to view the world through the client's eyes.

15. As a third condition, the therapist strives to be _____ in his or her relationship with clients. Fourth, rather than making interpretations, posing solutions, or offering advice, the therapist _____ the client's thoughts and feelings.

16. _____ therapy focuses on problems of existence or "being in the world." Its goals are self-knowledge and self-actualization. This therapy emphasizes _____ _____, i.e., through _____ one can become the person he or she wants to be. An example of this therapy is _____ which is centered around _____.

17. Another approach called _____ therapy is built around the idea that perception or awareness becomes _____ and _____ in the maladjusted individual. The therapy developed by Perls emphasizes that emotional health comes from getting in touch with what you _____ to do—not what you should do, ought to do, or should want to do. The therapist seeks to help the individual rebuild thinking, feeling, and acting into connected _____. Above all else, the therapy emphasizes _____ experience.

18. In _____ therapy a person can act out or experience problems in addition to talking about them. Also support is provided by other members who share similar problems. This form of therapy helps form a _____ between therapy and real-life problems.

19. One of the first group approaches was developed by J. L. Moreno, who called his technique _____. Through this an individual role _____ (acts out) dramatic incidents resembling those that cause problems in real life. In these instances, therapists find that role _____ can also help in understanding the feelings of others.

20. The basic belief of _____ therapists is that problems are rarely limited to a _____ family member. Thus, family members work together to improve _____, to change destructive patterns, and to see themselves and each other in new ways.

21. _____ groups tend to be less confrontive than _____ groups. Participants in the former take part in experiences that gently enlarge_____ of oneself and others. The emphasis in the latter is on tearing down _____ and facades through discussion that can be brutally honest.

22. There has recently been a shift away from sensitivity and encounter groups to _____-_____ _____ training. Many people feel that all such groups are not really therapy-based, but that the derived benefits may simply result from a kind of _____ _____ effect.

23. Many people turn to _____ psychologists for help. There is much concern about this practice, but these psychologists defend themselves by saying that listeners learn from other people's problems and that their work is primarily _____, not _____. The APA takes the position that only problems of a _____ nature should be discussed and not a specific caller's problem.

24. Behavioral approaches include _____ _____ (the use of _____ principles to change behavior) and _____ _____ therapy (the use of learning principles to change upsetting _____ and _____).

25. Psychologists called _____ _____, who use behavior modification, believe that _____ or deep _____ of one's problems is unnecessary. Instead these therapists try to directly change _____. Behavior modification is based on one principal assumption: people have _____ to be the way they are. Consequently, they can _____ behavior, or _____ more appropriate habits.

26. Behavior modification is a term referring to any attempt to use the learning principles of _____ or _____ conditioning to change human behavior.

27. Behavior therapists may use the principles of classical conditioning to associate discomfort, called an _____, with a bad habit. Use of this technique is called _____ therapy and is one form of behavior modification. When an _____ is paired with a bad habit so that the habit no longer occurs or is replaced by a competing response, a _____ _____ has developed.

28. Psychologist Roger Vogler uses aversion therapy with alcoholics who have tried almost everything to stop drinking. Vogler associates painful, but non-injurious _____ with the intake of alcohol. This _____-_____ _____ takes the immediate pleasure out of drinking and causes the patient to develop a conditioned aversion to drinking. In this example, alcohol would be a _____ _____ and the aversion would be the _____ _____.

29. Similar aversion therapy can be done with smoking, but in this case the aversion is caused by _____ _____.

30. One problem with successful treatment is getting the conditioned aversion to _____ or _____ from the therapy situation to the real world. Another problem with the therapy is the fact that it is _____ to have to use on human beings.

31. A reduction in fear, brought about by gradually approaching a feared stimulus while maintaining complete relaxation, is called _____. An ordered set of steps called a _____ is used to allow the individual to adapt to gradual approximations of the end, desired behavior.

32. Desensitization is based on the principle of _____ _____, which means that one emotional state can _____ the occurrence of another. Desensitization is primarily used to help people unlearn _____ or strong _____.

33. Desensitization usually involves three steps. First, the patient and therapist construct a _____, a list of fear-provoking situations involving the phobia and ranging from the least disturbing to the most disturbing situation. Second, the patient is taught exercises that produce total _____. Once the patients are _____ they proceed to the third step by trying to perform the _____ disturbing item on their _____.

34. In situations where it is impractical for the patient to practice the steps, desensitization is accomplished when a patient vividly _____ each of the steps in the hierarchy. In some cases the problem can be handled by having clients observe models who are performing the feared behavior. This is known as _____ desensitization.

35. The principles of _____ conditioning have been developed by Skinner and his associates mostly through laboratory research with animals. There are seven principles most frequently used with humans: _____ reinforcement, nonreinforcement, _____, punishment, _____, stimulus control, and _____ _____.

36. Most frequently occurring human behaviors lead to some form of reward. An undesirable response can be eliminated by identifying and _____ the rewards which maintain it. Most of the rewards which maintain human behavior are more subtle than food, money, etc. Rather they include _____, _____, and _____.

37. This can be demonstrated in classroom situations where teachers give attention in various forms when misbehavior occurs. When attention takes the form of saying things such as "Sit down!" the frequency of misbehavior _____. Non-reward and extinction can eliminate many of these problem behaviors. For example, in the classroom example when misbehaving children are _____ and attention given to children not misbehaving, misbehavior _____.

38. A strategy used in institutions is called _____ _____, and involves refusing to reward maladaptive responses by refusing to play the attention game. Another form of this is to _____ an individual immediately from the setting in which an undesirable response occurs so that the response will not be _____.

39. A rapidly growing approach to therapy is based on the use of _____, symbolic rewards that can be exchanged for real rewards. So that incentives and rewards will have maximum impact, the therapist selects specific _____ _____ that could or should be improved.

40. Full-scale use of tokens in an institutional setting leads to the development of a _____ _____. The results of token economies have sometimes been dramatic. The effects can be a radical change in a patient's overall _____ and _____. Many "_____" retarded, mentally ill, and delinquent people have been returned to a productive life by means of token economies.

41. _____ _____ therapists are interested in thoughts as well as visible behavior. They try to help clients change _____ _____ that lead to trouble. This type of therapy has been especially effective in the treatment of _____.

42. According to Beck, depressed persons engage in many forms of negative thinking including _____ _____, _____, the tendency to _____ the importance of undesirable events, and _____ or _____ thinking. Cognitive therapists make a step-by-step effort to correct negative thoughts.

43. According to Ellis, people become unhappy and develop self-defeating habits because of unrealistic _____. His therapy is called _____-_____ therapy.

44. Ellis analyzes the situation like this: The person assumes the cause of the _____ consequence to be the _____ experience. In between the two is the client's unrealistic _____ which are the true cause of the difficulty.

45. Most irrational beliefs come from three unrealistic core ideas: I must perform well and be _____ of by significant others. You must _____ me fairly. _____ must be the way I want them to be.

46. In many studies of the effectiveness of psychotherapy, a modest but consistent _____ effect was found to exist. Half of the patients felt better in just _____ month(s).

47. All therapies have in common some combination of the following goals: _____, resolution of _____, an improved sense of _____, a change in unacceptable patterns of _____, better _____ relations, and an improved picture of _____ and the world.

48. To accomplish these goals, all psychotherapies offer four qualities. The first is a _____ _____ between client and therapist. Therapists also offer a _____ _____ in which emotional catharsis or release can take place. All therapies to some extent offer an _____ or _____ for the suffering the client has experienced and propose action which if followed will end this suffering. Therapy also provides patients with a new _____ about themselves and their situation.

49. Several points may help you when a friend wants to talk about a problem. First, you should practice _____ _____; a person with a problem needs to be heard. If you try to understand the person's problem, you may help him or her _____ it. By focusing on the person's _____ you can avoid making him or her defensive. This helps permit the free outpouring of emotion that is the basis for _____.

50. Avoid giving _____. It is not unreasonable to do so when asked but beware of the trap described by Eric Berne, "Why don't you? Yes, but." Accept the person's frame of _____. This will encourage freedom to examine and question his or her point of view objectively.

51. One of the most productive things you can do is to give feedback by simply _____ thoughts and feelings said by the person. You may find it helpful to be _____ so that the other person has plenty of opportunity to talk. To encourage free expression you should ask _____ questions. Your efforts to help should include maintaining _____. Avoid the temptation to gossip.

52. When a client and therapist come from different _____ backgrounds, _____ are common. A _____ skilled counselor is aware of his/her own biases and values, avoids thinking in _____, and sees minority cultural beliefs and values as different but not _____.

53. In _____ _____ disturbing or disgusting thoughts or images are associated with a behavior or habit to make a person less likely to want to do it. Therapists have found that upsetting or disturbing thoughts can be decreased by using a technique called _____- _____. The simplest technique uses mild _____ to suppress the thoughts.

54. Even though direct _____ is the most powerful way to alter behavior, covert or "_____" reinforcement can have similar effects.

55. The key to desensitization is _____. One way to learn this is to practice tightening different muscles for five seconds and then letting go.

56. In developing a _____, make a list of situations related to the fear that makes you anxious. If you can vividly imagine yourself in the first situation of your hierarchy without a noticeable increase in _____ _____ at least twice, proceed to the next card you have constructed.

57. Stop when you reach a card that you cannot visualize without _____ after three attempts. On each successive day, begin one or two cards before the one on which you stopped the previous day. Eventually you can learn to control the fear.

58. In determining when you should seek professional help, several guidelines can be suggested. The first is: if your level of psychological discomfort becomes comparable to a level of _____ discomfort that would cause you to see a dentist or physician. Another sign is the occurrence of _____ _____ in observable behavior.

59. If you find friends or relatives making suggestions that you seek professional help, they may be seeing things more _____ than you. Definitely seek help if you have persistent or disturbing _____ thoughts or impulses.

60. When looking for a therapist, one can be found through: the yellow pages, a community or county _____ _____ _____, the mental health _____, a local college or university (if you are a _____), and newspaper advertisements.

61. When choosing a therapist, remember that both psychologists and psychiatrists are trained to do _____. Whereas a _____ can administer somatic therapy, a _____ can work in conjunction with a physician for such services. If fees are a problem , many individual therapists charge on a _____ _____.

62. A balanced look at psychotherapies suggests that all _____ are about equally successful, but all _____ are not. With that in mind, the _____ between a client and therapist is the therapist's most basic tool.

ANSWER KEYS

Do You know the Information?

Multiple Choice

1. (b) obj. 1, p. 536
2. (d) obj. 2, p. 537
3. (b) obj. 2, p. 537
4. (e) obj. 2, p. 537
5. (a) obj. 2, p. 537
6. (c) obj. 3, pp. 536-537
7. (a) obj. 4, p. 538
8. (a) obj. 4, p. 538
9. (b) obj. 4, p. 538
10. (b) obj. 5, p. 539
11. (c) obj. 6, p. 541
12. (d) obj. 7, p. 541
13. (a) obj. 8, p. 542
14. (a) obj. 8, p. 543
15. (b) obj. 9, p. 543
16. (d) obj. 10, p. 544
17. (b) obj. 10, p. 544
18. (a) obj. 11, p. 544
19. (c) obj. 11, p. 545
20. (a) obj. 12, p. 546
21. (c) obj. 13, p. 546
22. (b) obj. 13, p. 547
23. (d) objs. 14-15, pp. 547-548
24. (b) obj. 16, p. 549
25. (b) obj. 17, p. 549
26. (a) obj. 18, p. 549
27. (d) obj. 19, p. 550
28. (d) obj. 20, p. 552
29. (d) obj. 20, p. 552

30. (b) obj. 20, p. 552
31. (c) obj. 21, p. 555
32. (a) obj. 22, p. 555
33. (a) obj. 23, p. 557
34. (c) obj. 24, p. 558
35. (c) obj. 24, pp. 558-559
36. (d) obj. 25, p. 559
37. (a) obj. 26, p. 560
38. (c) obj. 27, p. 561
39. (e) obj. 27, p. 562
40. (c) obj. 28, p. 563
41. (c) obj. 29, p. 563
42. (b) obj. 31, p. 565
43. (b) obj. 32, p. 567
44. (b) obj. 34, p. 568
45. (c) obj. 35, p. 569

True-False

1. F, obj. 2, p. 537
2. F, obj. 3, p. 536
3. T, obj. 4, p. 538
4. F, obj. 7, p. 541
5. T, obj. 7, p. 542
6. F, obj. 10, p. 544
7. T, obj. 13, p. 546
8. F, obj. 13, p. 546
9. T, obj. 13, p. 547
10. T, obj. 13, p. 547
11. T, obj. 19, p. 549
12. F, obj. 20, p. 552

13. T, obj. 22, p. 555
14. F, obj. 25, p. 559
15. T, obj. 25, p. 559
16. F, obj. 28, p. 563
17. T, obj. 30, p. 566
18. T, obj. 30, p. 566
19. F, obj. 33, p. 568
20. T, obj. 35, p. 569
21. F, obj. 35, p. 569

Can You Apply the Information?

1. (b) obj. 2, p. 537
2. (b) obj. 2, p. 537
3. (c) obj. 6, p. 541
4. (d) objs. 8-11, p. 543
5. (c) obj. 9, p. 543
6. (a) obj. 10, p. 544
7. (d) obj. 11, p. 545
8. (d) obj. 13, p. 546
9. (b) obj. 13, p. 547
10. (a) objs. 14-15, p. 547
11. (c) obj. 16, p. 549
12. (d) obj. 18, p. 550
13. (a) obj. 20, p. 552
14. (b) obj. 22, p. 555
15. (c) obj. 22, p. 556
16. (b) obj. 24, p. 558
17. (d) obj. 25, p. 559
18. (a) obj. 30, pp. 565-566
19. (c) obj. 30, p. 566

Chapter Review

1. Psychotherapy, personality, behavior, adjustment (p. 536)
2. Insight, Action, directive (p. 537)
3. Nondirective, Individual, group, Time-limited (p. 537)
4. phobias, self-esteem, sexual, marital, dramatic (p. 537)
5. trepanning, demonology, exorcism, ergotism (p. 538)
6. Pinel, unchaining (p. 538); Freud (p. 539)
7. hysteria, unconscious conflicts, psychoanalysis (p. 540)
8. free association (p. 540)
9. defenses, dream, manifest, latent, dream symbols (p. 540)
10. resist, resistances, transfer, game (p. 541)
11. time, money, rare, short-term dynamic, spontaneous remission, psychoanalysis (p. 541)
12. adjustment, potentials (p. 542)
13. client-centered, authority, interpretations, nondirective (p. 543)
14. unconditional positive regard, empathy (p. 543)
15. authentic, reflects (p. 543)
16. Existential, free will, choices, logotherapy, confrontation (p. 544)

17. Gestalt, disjointed, incomplete, want, wholes, present (p. 544)
18. group, bridge (p. 545)
19. psychodrama, plays, reversal (p. 546)
20. family, single, communication (p. 546)
21. Sensitivity, encounter, awareness, defenses (p. 547)
22. large-group awareness, therapy placebo (p. 547)
23. radio (media), educational, therapeutic, general (p. 548)
24. behavior modification, learning, cognitive behavior, thoughts, beliefs (p. 548)
25. behavior therapists, insight, understanding, behavior, learned, change (unlearn), relearn (p. 549)
26. classical, operant (p. 549)
27. aversion, aversion, aversion, conditioned aversion (p. 549)
28. shocks, response-contingent shock, conditioned stimulus, conditioned response (p. 550)
29. rapid smoking (p. 550)
30. transfer, generalize, unpleasant (p. 550)
31. desensitization, hierarchy (p. 551)
32. reciprocal inhibition, inhibit (prevent), phobias, anxieties (p. 552)
33. hierarchy, relaxation, relaxed, least, list (p. 552)
34. imagines, vicarious (p. 553)
35. operant, positive, extinction, shaping, time out (p. 554)
36. removing, attention, approval, concern (p. 555)
37. increases, ignored, decreases (p. 555)
38. time out, remove, rewarded (p. 556)
39. tokens, target behaviors (p. 556)
40. token economy, adjustment, morale, hopelessly (p. 557)
41. Cognitive behavior, thinking patterns, depression (p. 558)
42. selective perception, overgeneralization, magnify, all, nothing (p. 558)
43. beliefs, rational-emotive (p. 559)
44. emotional, activating, beliefs (p. 559)
45. approved, treat, Conditions (p. 560)
46. positive, two (p. 560)
47. insight, conflict, self, behavior, interpersonal, oneself (p. 561)
48. caring relationship (therapeutic relationship, emotional rapport), protected setting, explanation, rationale, perspective (p. 561)
49. active listening, clarify, feelings, catharsis (p. 562)
50. advice, reference (p. 563)
51. reflecting (restating) (p. 563); quiet, open, confidentiality (p. 564)
52. cultural, misundserstandings, culturally, stereotypes, inferior (p. 563)
53. covert sensitization (p. 565); thought-stopping, punishment (p. 566)
54. reinforcement, "visualized" (p. 566)
55. relaxation (p. 567)
56. hierarchy, muscular tension (p. 567)
57. tension (p. 567)
58. physical, significant changes (p. 567)
59. objectively, suicidal (p. 568)
60. mental health center, association, student (p. 568)
61. psychotherapy, psychiatrist, psychologist, sliding scale (p. 569)
62. techniques, therapists, relationship (p. 569)

chapter sixteen

Gender and Sexuality

primary and secondary sex characteristics
menarche, menopause
sex hormones
    estrogens, androgens, testosterone
gonads
dimensions of gender
    genetic sex, gonadal sex, hormonal sex,
    genital sex, gender identity
gender development
    androgen insensitivity, hermaphroditism
    androgenital syndrome, biological
    biasing effect
sex role, sex role socialization
    instrumental, expressive behavior
sex role stereotypes
androgyny
causes of sexual arousal

physical and emotional effects
sexual scripts
differences in sex drives
castration, sterilization
masturbation
homosexuality & lesbianism
    ego-dystonic
homophobia
    heredity and homosexuality
phases of sexual response
    excitement, plateau, orgasm, resolution
differences and similarities in male
    and female sexual response
ejaculation, refractory period
multiple orgasm
sexual revolution
double standard

sex role stereotyping
    acquaintance rape
sexually transmitted diseases
    AIDS
sexual problems
    desire disorders
        htpoactive sexual desire
        sexual aversion
    arousal disorders
        male erectile disorder
        female sexual arousal disorder
    orgasm disorder
        male orgasmic disorder
        female orgasmic disorder
        premature ejaculation
    sexual pain disorder
        dyspareunia, vaginismus
improving communication skills

LEARNING OBJECTIVES

To demonstrate mastery of this chapter you should be able to:

1. Differentiate primary from secondary sex characteristics and state (in general) what causes them.

2. Define or describe the following terms or concepts:

    a.   gonads

    b.   menarche

    c.   menopause

    d.   estrogens

    e.   androgens

    f.   testosterone

3.   List and describe the five dimensions of gender.

    a.

    b.

    c.

    d.

    e.

4.   Explain how a person's gender develops. Include in your discussion a description of these conditions:

    a.   androgen insensitivity

    b.   hermaphroditism

    c.   androgenital syndrome

    d.   biological biasing effect

5.   Describe the relationship between gender and intelligence.

6. Differentiate gender identity from sex role and explain how gender identity is formed.

7. Discuss whether or not there are inborn psychological differences between males and females.

8. Define "sex role stereotypes." Discuss how these stereotypes ignore the "diversity of humanity and human potential."

9. Describe the effects of socialization on sex roles and include a discussion of instrumental and expressive behaviors.

10. Discuss the concept of androgyny and its relationship to masculinity, femininity, and adaptability.

11. Describe the development of sexual behavior in humans and show how cultural norms influence that development.

12. Discuss the differences between males and females in their degree of arousal to erotic stimuli.

13. Explain what a sexual script is.

14. Explain what causes differences in sex drives in males and females.

15. Describe the effects of alcohol, castration, aging, and sterilization on the sex drive.

16. Discuss the frequency, importance, normality, and acceptablility of masturbation.

17. Discuss homosexuality in terms of incidence, acceptability, and psychological normality. Define the term ego-dystonic homosexuality.

18. Define the term homophobia and describe its significance to homosexuals. Briefly describe the influence of heredity on homo-sexuality.

19. List in order and briefly describe the four phases of sexual response in men and women.

Males	*Females*
a.	a.
b.	b.
c.	c.
d.	d.

20. Discuss the debate concerning possible differences between vaginal and clitoral orgasms and how has the issue been resolved?

21. Describe what is known concerning gender differences in sexual response styles in the following areas:

a. rate of passage through the sexual phases

b. sexual responsiveness

22 . List or describe four changes that have taken place in sexual attitudes or behavior that lead some people to label the differences a sexual revolution.

a.

b.

c.

d.

23. Summarize the current status of the sexual revolution. Explain how your answer reflects on the position of the double standard in our society.

24. Describe how the changing sexual attitudes and values of the society interact with one's personal freedom.

25. Describe the research demonstrating the relationship between sex role stereotyping and rape.

26. Briefly describe what is currently known about the factors affecting the spread of AIDS. Include in your answer a discussion of "at-risk" groups, risky behaviors, and the impact that AIDS has on sexual behavior.

The following objectives are related to the material in the "Applications" section of your text.

27.   Describe the following sexual problems including the nature, cause, and treatment of each:

   a.   hypoactive sexual desire

   b.   sexual aversion

   c.   male erectile disorder

   d.   female sexual arousal disorder

   e.   male orgasmic disorder

   f.   female orgasmic disorder

   g.   premature ejaculation

   h.   dyspareunia

   i.   vaginismus

28.   Explain what is meant by referring to sex as a form of communication within a relationship.

29.   List six techniques that can be used to encourage constructive disagreements.

a.

b.

c.

d.

e.

f.

SELF-QUIZZES

Do You Know the Information?

Multiple Choice

1.   In general, primary and secondary sex characteristics are caused by
(a) socialization.   (b) sexual activity.   (c) sex hormones.   (d) societal expectations.

2.   A female's gonads are the
(a) ovaries.   (b) clitoris.   (c) vagina.   (d) uterus.

3.   Male hormones secreted by the gonads are
(a) estrogens.   (b) androgens.   (c) adrenalins.   (d) progesterones.

4.   Which of the following is *not* a dimension of gender?
(a) sex role   (b) hormonal sex   (c) gender identity   (d) gonadal sex

5.   A learned, self-perception of one's maleness or femaleness is referred to as
(a) expressive behavior.   (b) instrumental behavior.   (c) sex-role socialization. (d) gender identity.

6.   Dual or ambiguous sexual anatomy may result from hormonal problems before birth. This is known as
(a) hermaphroditism.   (b) androgenital syndrome.   (c) general sexual dysfunction. (d) vaginismus.

7.   When a genetic abnormality causes the adrenal glands to secrete excess amounts of androgen, it can produce a condition known as _____ in which a female child has male genitals.
(a) gender misidentity   (b) androgenital syndrome   (c) primary sexual dysfunction (d) androgen insensitivity

8.   Which of the following statements is *incorrect*?
(a) Nature's primary impulse is to make a biological female.
(b) The balance of sex hormones before birth may "sex type" the brain.
(c) Gender identity is essentially formed at age two when the child has mastered the rudiments of language.
(d) Sex roles are public and observable while gender identity is a private inner feeling.

9.   Because of sex role socialization
(a) the female role appears to be definitely "not male."   (c) natural male or female behavior is universally adopted.
(b) girls are held less than boys at an early age.   (d) boys are encouraged to adopt instrumental behaviors.

10.   Sex role stereotypes are a major obstacle where _____ is concerned.
(a) dating   (b) college   (c) employment   (d) marriage

11. A man who is androgynous
    (a) would be more nurturant than a masculine man.
    (b) would have a higher feminine score than a masculine score on the BSRI.
    (c) would be less adaptable than other males.
    (d) would have a higher masculine score than a feminine score on the BSRI.

12. A capacity for sexual arousal
    (a) shows up during childhood.
    (b) begins at puberty.
    (c) occurs in females long before it occurs in males.
    (d) is apparent at birth or soon after.

13. When comparing the responses of males and females to erotic literature we find that
    (a) women are less aroused than men.
    (b) men are less aroused than women.
    (c) men and women are equally aroused.
    (d) men are more aroused by romance than are women.

14. In males and perhaps in females the strength of the sex drive is related to the amount of _____ secreted.
    (a) gonadin   (b) androgen   (c) estrogen   (d) testosterone

15. Castration leads to
    (a) a cessation of the sex drive in human males but not in females.
    (b) an immediate and drastic reduction of the female sex drive because of reduced estrogen levels.
    (c) a cessation of the sex drive in men over 85 years of age.
    (d) none of the above.

16. Which of the following statements about masturbation is *incorrect*?
    (a) Masturbation is considered a biologically healthy substitute for intercourse during adolescence.
    (b) A large percentage of people continue to masturbate after marriage.
    (c) Rhythmic self-stimulation has been observed in infants under one year of age.
    (d) Masturbation doesn't cause VD or insanity, but it can dull the pleasure of normal sexual intercourse after marriage.
    (e) There's nothing wrong with masturbation, you just don't meet a lot of nice people that way.

17. Which of the following statements about homosexuality is *incorrect*?
    (a) Ego-dystonic homosexuality is when the person feels lasting guilt and self-hate.
    (b) Although psychologically they are similar to heterosexuals, homosexuals show an overall poorer adjustment to life.
    (c) About 5.5 percent of all adults have had homosexual relationships.
    (d) Almost two-thirds of 76 cultures surveyed accept some form of homosexuality.

18. _____ is a term referring to the prejudice, fear, and dislike aimed at homosexuals.
    (a) Ego-dystonic homosexuality (b) Homophobia   (c) Homosexualism   (d) Sexual scripts

19. Which of the following statements concerning the origins of homosexuality is (are) *incorrect*?
    (a) If one identical twin is homosexual or bisexual, there is a 50 percent chance that the other twin is too.
    (b) Sexual orientation is from 50-70 percent genetic.
    (c) Genetic tendencies for homosexuality apparently are passed from fathers to their children via the X chromosome.
    (d) Heredity may shape areas of the brain which orchestrate sexual behavior.

20. The *correct* ordering of the stages of the human sexual response cycle are
    (a) excitement, plateau, orgasm, resolution.
    (b) plateau, resolution, excitement, orgasm.
    (c) resolution, excitement, plateau, orgasm.
    (d) excitement, resolution, orgasm, plateau.

21. With regard to female orgasm, Freud believed that
    (a) there was no difference in physical response regardless of what form of stimulation produces the orgasm.
    (b) since the clitoris is the female structure comparable to the penis, a clitoral orgasm was superior to a vaginal one.
    (c) a clitoral orgasm was an "immature" from of female response.
    (d) Masters and Johnson were on the right track.

22. As compared to the male sexual response cycle, females
   (a) are more capable of multiple orgasms.
   (b) usually go through the sexual phases more slowly than men.
   (c) are more similar to males than they are different.
   (d) are capable of all of the above.

23. Which of the following changes in sexual attitudes and/or behavior have taken place?
   (a) Attitudes have become more tolerant.
   (b) People are talking less about sex but doing it more.
   (c) There has been a marked increase in the sexual expression of males.
   (d) Contrary to popular belief, males are engaging in sexual behavior earlier and girls are delaying their first participation.

24. Which of the following statements concerning the results of the sexual revolution appears *correct*?
   (a) Sexual intercourse among unmarried couples is more common today.
   (b) The trend in liberalization of sexual standards represents a wholesale move toward sexual promiscuity.
   (c) Premarital sex and cohabitation are no longer viewed as preludes to marriage.
   (d) The association between sexuality and love remains weak for a majority of the population.

25. College males who scored _____ in sex role stereotyping were _____ aroused by rape stories when compared to stories of voluntary intercourse.
   (a) low; more   (b) high; more   (c) low; equally   (d) high; equally

26. Based on what we know about AIDS and how it is transmitted,
   (a) all sexually active persons are at risk.
   (b) only men who have had sex with other men are at risk.
   (c) heterosexuals are at relatively low risk.
   (d) having multiple partners is not a risk factor.

27. A primary erectile disorder refers to
   (a) males who have had active sex lives but who can no longer achieve an erection.
   (b) men who cannot achieve orgasm.
   (c) the inability to control orgasm.
   (d) men who have never been able to achieve or maintain an erection.

28. A major sexual therapy technique which involves nongenital physical contact is
   (a) sensate focus.   (b) squeeze technique.   (c) sex role socialization.   (d) orgasmic relearning.

29. Male orgasmic disorder refers to an inability to
   (a) sustain erection.   (b) feel physical pleasure.   (c) achieve orgasm.   (d) achieve erection promptly.

30. The technique of choice in treating premature ejaculation is
   (a) sensate focus.   (b) squeeze technique.   (c) sex role socialization.   (d) desensitization.

31. A condition in which muscle spasms make intercourse impossible for the female is known as
   (a) frigidity.   (b) androgenital syndrome.   (c) orgasmic dysfunction.   (d) vaginismus.

32. Expressing negative feelings as statements of one's own feelings rather than as statements of blame is characteristic of which guideline for a healthy emotional relationship?
   (a) intimacy and communication
   (b) be open about feelings
   (c) avoid gunnysacking
   (d) don't attack the other person's character

True-False

_____ 1. Nature's primary impulse is to make a male so as to assure abundant levels of sperm for procreation.

_____ 2. The biological biasing effect for females is caused by a prenatal exposure to androgen and results in an abnormal amount of masculine-type behaviors during childhood and adolescence only.

_____ 3. Working on an individual by individual basis, women can usually be expected to do better on skills that require math.

_____ 4. Acquiring a gender identity begins with the label "boy" or "girl" and thereafter is influenced by sex-role socialization.

_____ 5. There appear to be no "natural" male or female behaviors.

_____ 6. A person who is androgynous can be more adaptable and flexible according to what the situation demands.

_____ 7. Sexual scripts demonstrate the importance of the brain as an "erogenous" zone.

_____ 8. Attitudes toward sex, sexual experience, physical factors, and recency of sexual release are all important in determining a person's sex drive.

_____ 9. Alcohol (even in small doses) depresses sexual desire.

_____ 10. The critical factor for an extended sex life appears to be regularity.

_____ 11. Masters and Johnson provided extensive research support for Freud's contentions on the differences between vaginal and clitoral orgasms.

_____ 12. Following the sexual revolution, we find that choosing to be sexually inactive is unusual.

_____ 13. Male erectile disorder may be related to harsh religious training.

_____ 14. Rather than being a skill to be mastered, sex is a form of communication within a relationship.

_____ 15. Although it is not necessarily constructive, in order to resolve differences it is important for disagreement to be solved by having a winner.

Matching *(Use the letters on the right only once)*

_____ 1. primary sex characteristics
_____ 2. secondary sex characteristics
_____ 3. onset of menstruation
_____ 4. one of the androgens
_____ 5. hormonal sex
_____ 6. sex role
_____ 7. instrumental behaviors
_____ 8. genitals, mouth, breasts, ears, anus
_____ 9. sexual script
_____ 10. refractory period
_____ 11. secondary male erectile disorder
_____ 12. hypoactive sexual desire

A. estrogen
B. lack of sexual desire which is both persistent and troubling
C. no amount of continued stimulation will produce a second orgasm
D. "You know I like to make love in the dark."
E. goal-directed
F. menopause
G. body hair, development of breasts
H. plateau phase
I. predominance of androgen or estrogen
J. has previously performed successfully, but then became impotent
K. the pattern of behavior encouraged and expected of individuals on the basis of gender
L. retarded ejaculation
M. menarche
N. scrotum, ovaries
O. female orgasmic disorder
P. testosterone
Q. gender identity
R. primary male erectile disorder
S. erogenous zones

Can You Apply the Information?

1. Charles was born, and still is, a hermaphrodite, yet now at the age of 18 he has a very strong male gender identity. The most likely reason for his current self-perception is
    (a) strong male sex typing of the brain before birth.
    (b) the strong influence that genital sex has on gender identity.
    (c) the result of his inherited androgen insensitivity.
    (d) consistent male sex role socialization from infancy.

2. Bob is tough, ambitious, competitive, and creative at work. When he gets home he is tender and loving to his children and warm and affectionate to his wife. Together, these two situations indicate that
    (a) Bob is primarily showing instrumental behaviors.
    (b) Bob is primarily showing expressive behaviors.
    (c) Bob is androgynous.
    (d) Bob has a mixed-up gender identity.

3. If you were a mad scientist and wanted to permanently eradicate a man's sex drive, which of the following would you do?
    (a) Castrate him.
    (b) Give him estrogen shots.
    (c) Decrease his supply of androgen.
    (d) None of the above would likely be sufficient.

4. John has been married for 18 years and masturbates about once a week. His masturbation is an indication that he and his wife do not have a satisfying sex life.
    (a) True   (b) False

5. Bob and Melissa are seeing Dr. Budrionis, a noted sex therapist, because they are having trouble achieving simultaneous orgasm. The doctor most likely diagnoses the problem as
    (a) strictly an artificial concern on their part that may inhibit their sexual enjoyment.
    (b) caused by the relationship between penis size and male potency.
    (c) a lack of sexual responsiveness on Melissa's part.
    (d) related to Bob's passing through the sexual phases slower than Melissa.

6. Men are incapable of multiple orgasms.
    (a) True   (b) False

7. Bill has never had any sexual problems. However, shortly after he started his new job he has had trouble keeping his erection long enough to reach orgasm. Bill's problem would be diagnosed as
    (a) retarded ejaculation.   (b) premature ejaculation.   (c) primary erectile disorder.   (d) secondary erectile disorder.

8. Ron has been married for 23 years. He has not been able to have an orgasm for almost a year. Ron is most likely suffering from
    (a) hypoactive sexual desire.   (b) male erectile disorder.   (c) retarded ejaculation.   (d) premature ejaculation.

9. Janice is upset. She has never felt any response when her husband kisses and caresses her. Janice's problem would probably be diagnosed as
    (a) female orgasmic disorder.
    (b) vaginismus.
    (c) female impotence.
    (d) female sexual arousal disorder.

10. Sylvia was raped at age 13. After that experience she has been unable to have intercourse due to vaginismus. A therapist might suggest any of the following procedures *except*
    (a) desensitization of fears of intercourse.
    (b) progressive relaxation of the vaginal muscles.
    (c) masturbation.
    (d) sensate focus.

11. Bob and Betty have been married three years. They have about one explosive argument a month. This is the only time when Bob verbally releases his frustrations. This is an example of
    (a) gunnysacking.
    (b) attacking the other person's character.
    (c) being open about feelings.
    (d) winning a fight.

Chapter Review

1. Primary sexual characteristics refer to the _____ and _____
    organs of males and females. _____ sexual characteristics appear at puberty in response to
    hormonal signals from the pituitary gland. In females, they include development of the _____, the
    broadening of the _____, and other changes in body shape. For males, they include development of facial and body
    _____, and the deepening of the _____.

2. Secondary sex characteristics signal physical readiness for reproduction. This is especially evident in the female
    _____ (onset of menstruation). From then until _____,
    the end of regular monthly fertility cycles, women can potentially bear children.

3. Both primary and secondary sexual characteristics are closely related to the action of sex _____,
    chemical substances secreted by glands of the endocrine system. The _____ or sex glands affect sexual develop-
    ment by secreting hormones. These hormones include the female hormones (_____) and the male
    hormones (_____).

4. The gonads in the male are the _____ and in the female the _____. The
    _____ glands, located on top of the kidneys, also supply sex hormones in both males and females.

5. All individuals normally produce both _____ and _____, the
    balance of which influences sexual differences. The development of male or female genitals before birth is largely due to the
    presence or absence of _____, one of the _____.

6. The five dimensions of gender are _____ sex (chromosomes), _____ sex
    (ovaries or testes), _____ sex (androgens or estrogens), _____ sex
    (clitoris, vagina, penis, scrotum), and gender _____ (one's personal sense of maleness or
    femaleness).

7. _____ sex is determined at the instant of conception. In the absence of a Y chromosome, the
    embryo will develop female reproductive organs. Nature's primary impulse, then, is to make a
    _____.

8. A genetic male will fail to develop male _____ if insufficient testosterone is formed during
    prenatal growth. Even if testosterone is present, an inherited _____ _____
    may exist, again resulting in female development. Hormonal problems during early development may lead to
    _____ where dual or ambiguous sexual anatomy frequently occurs.

9. Masculinization of a female can result when normal amounts of estrogen are produced, but a genetic abnormality causes the
    adrenal glands to secrete excess amounts of androgen. This is called the _____ syndrome and can
    produce a female child with male genitals. In addition to determining genital development, the balance of sex hormones
    before birth may also permanently "sex-type" the _____, which may alter later chances of developing
    masculine or feminine characteristics.

10. However, although hormonal action is important in sexual development, psychologists believe that most sex-linked behavior
    is _____. Still, some researchers feel that prenatal exposure to androgens or estrogens exerts a biological
    _____ _____ on later psychosexual development in humans.

11. In the gender debate, it appears that males and females are more _____ than they are
    _____. Therefore, men and women do not differ in overall intelligence and no significant _____
    difference has been found.

12. One's personal, private sense of maleness or femaleness is referred to as _____
    _____ and appears to be a learned self-perception.

13. Gender identity begins with male-female labels and is then influenced by _____-_____ _____, that is the subtle pressure exerted by parents, peers, and cultural institutions that urge boys to "act like boys" and girls to "act like girls." In determining adult sexual behavior and sex-linked personality traits, _____ _____ are probably as important as chromosomal, genital or hormonal sex.

14. Sex role refers to the _____ of _____ that is encouraged and expected of individuals on the basis of gender. The naturalness of sex roles is _____ based on cross-cultural observations.

15. Sex role stereotypes are widely held _____ about what men and women are actually like. _____ _____ tend to dictate how men and women should act. whereas sex role stereotypes over-simplified _____ about the nature of men and women.

16. Learning sex roles begins immediately after birth. Overall, parents tend to encourage their sons to engage in _____ (goal-directed) behaviors, to control their _____, and to prepare for the world of work. Daughters are encouraged in _____ (emotion-oriented) behaviors and to a lesser degree for the _____ role.

17. Sandra Bem developed the Bem Sex Role Inventory (BSRI) to classify individuals as traditionally masculine, feminine, or _____ (literally meaning "man-woman"). If a person is in the latter category, he/she would be considered _____ with respect to sex roles and could act as the _____ requires.

18. A capacity for sexual arousal is apparent at _____ or soon after. Instances of orgasm (_____ _____) have been verified in boys as young as ____ months old and in girls as young as ___ months old. As a child matures, _____ _____ place restrictions on sexual activities. In adulthood, norms continue to shape sexual activity along _____ _____ lines. Generally, restrictions are somewhat _____. It can be said that any sexual act engaged in by consenting adults is "_____" if it does not hurt anyone.

19. Sexual arousal in humans is complex. It may be produced by direct _____ of the body's _____ zones which include the _____, _____, _____, ears, anus as well as the skin in general. In addition, a large _____ element is also involved in sexual arousal such that it may be triggered by mere _____.

20. Research suggests that women are _____ _____ physically aroused by erotic stimuli than are men. However, compared to men, women more often have a negative _____ response to pictures of explicit sex. It has been found that sexual _____ tend to guide our sexual _____ in terms of defining a plot, dialogue, and actions that take place.

21. The sex drive is influenced by _____ toward sex, sexual _____, _____ of sexual release, and the amount of _____ present (for both men and women).

22. Alcohol is a _____. As such it may lower _____ that would normally keep any prohibited behavior in check. However, it often has a _____ effect on sexual response.

23. In humans, the effects of male or female castration vary. Some individuals show a decline in sex drive, but many others experience no change. However, after several years almost all subjects report a(n) _____ in sex drive. Sterilization does not _____ the sex drive and in fact may _____ it.

24. Aging does not unavoidably end sexual activity. The crucial factor appears to be _____.

25. According to a recent national survey _____ percent of the women surveyed had masturbated at some time, and _____ percent of the males reported having masturbated. Through masturbation, people discover what is pleasing sexually and what their natural _____ and _____ are. For adolescents, _____ is an important part of psychosexual development.

26. It is estimated that _____ percent of all American adults have had homosexual or _____ relationships. A major survey of 76 cultures found that almost two-thirds _____ some form of homosexuality. Psychological testing consistently shows _____ _____ in personality or adjustment between homosexuals and heterosexuals. If homosexuals suffer lasting guilt or self-hate the homosexuality is described as _____-_____. Problems faced by gay men and lesbians are often the result of _____ (a powerful fear of homosexuality).

27. New evidence suggests that sexual orientation is from _____ to _____ percent hereditary. If one identical twin is homosexual or bisexual, there is a _____ percent chance that the other twin is too. Sexual orientation is influenced by a _____ found on the ____ chromosome. Thus, genetic tendencies for homosexuality apparently are passed from _____ to children.

28. Masters and Johnson have classified sexual response in both males and females into four phases: _____, _____, _____, and _____.

29. Sexual arousal in the male is signaled by _____ of the _____ during the excitement phase. In the mature male, orgasm is accompanied by _____ (release of seminal fluid) and is followed by a short _____ period during which no amount of continued stimulation will produce a second orgasm.

30. Although the timing and intensity of the phases vary considerably for individual women, the basic pattern of response is the same as that for men. During the excitement phase, a complex pattern of changes prepares the vagina for intercourse. After orgasm, many females return to the _____ phase and may be stimulated to orgasm again.

31. Masters and Johnson exploded the Freudian myth that clitoral orgasm is an immature form of female response. They showed there is _____ _____ in physical response no matter what form of stimulation produces orgasm. As a matter of fact, the _____ is relatively insensitive to touch. It is now apparent that sensations from many sources are responsible for the experience of _____ and that, for most women, those from the _____ are more important.

32. During love-making, _____ to _____ minutes are usually required for a woman to go from excitement to orgasm. Males may experience all four stages in as little as _____ minutes.

33. The _____ in the male and female sexual responses outweigh the _____. Women generally go through the phases more _____ than men, and men are not generally capable of _____ _____. Subjective feelings of pleasure and intensity of orgasm are not related to _____ _____. Attempting to reach sexual climax at the same time (_____ _____), is considered an _____ concern that may reduce sexual enjoyment.

34. _____ attitudes toward sexual expression, coupled with availability of effective _____, have significantly changed sexual _____. First, Lord recently found only _____ percent of people between the ages of 18 and 29 against premarital sex compared to _____ percent in 1959. Second, premarital intercourse rates continue to _____. Lastly, people are reporting earlier participation in sexual behavior (i.e., more teenagers are starting early). Yet, despite these changes and even though 1.5 percent of married people have _____ affairs, Americans live up to the norm of marital fidelity.

35.   A more comfortable acceptance of _____ _____ and the closing of the gap between male and female sexual patterns (_____ _____) are the positive side of changing sexual attitudes and values. However, not everyone is ready for, or interested in, greater _____ _____. Apparently, some people feel pressured into sexual behavior because it is "_____." During any given year, about 22 percent of adult Americans are sexually _____.

36.   The importance of respecting the right to say no is underscored by the recent dramatic increase in cases of _____ (or date) rape, the effects of which are no less devastating than _____ commit- ted by a stranger. _____ sex role stereotyping by males may be an important factor in cases of rape.

37.   The incidence of _____ _____ disease has been rising in the United States for the last 20 years. Although most STDs are treatable, _____ _____ _____ syndrome (AIDS) is almost always fatal. AIDS is caused by a _____, (with a long _____ period) that disables the immune system. AIDS can be spread by all forms of sexual intercourse because it is spread by _____ contact with _____ _____. Most AIDS transmission is now occurring during _____ sex.

38.   When lossw of sexual desire is both persistent and troubling, _____ sexual desire exists. If a person is repelled by sex and seeks to avoid it, that person suffers from sexual _____. There may be _____ causes such as _____ or _____, or _____ causes such as _____. The latter causes are generally treated through _____.

39.   Male _____ disorder refers to a male's inability to maintain an erection for sexual intercourse. This dysfunction is termed _____ if the man has never been able to produce or maintain an erection and _____ for those who have previously performed successfully, but then lose the ability. If this condition occurs occasionally, it is considered _____.

40.   Impotence resulting from physical causes is termed _____, and all other cases are called _____. _____ percent of the cases are in the former category. Most cases are related to highly restrictive _____ training, early sexual experience with a seductive _____, or other experiences leading to guilt, fear, and sexual inhibition. Medical treatments for impotence may employ _____ or _____.

41.   In _____ _____, a technique used in treating impotence and other sexual disorders, the couple is initially told to take turns stroking various parts of each other's bodies. Genital contact is avoided at first, with emphasis placed on giving pleasure and on signaling what is most gratifying.

42.   Women with female sexual _____ disorder respond with little or no physical _____ to sexual stimulation. The causes may be _____ or _____. Treatment may include _____ _____ or genital _____.

43.   A male's inability to reach orgasm (male _____ disorder also known as _____ ejaculation) may have many different causes. However, it too can be successfully treated using sensate focus, manual stimulation by the female, and work around personal conflicts and marital difficulties. In females this disorder is called female _____ disorder.

44.   Masters and Johnson define the problem of _____ _____ as one in which a man is unable to delay sexual climax long enough to satisfy his partner in at least one-half of their lovemaking attempts. The most common treatment for this problem is the _____ technique.

45.   Pain in the genitals before, during, or after sexual intercourse for either males or females is called _____. If muscle spasms in the vagina prevent intercourse, it is called _____. Treatment may include _____, _____, and _____.

46. When sexual problems arise in a relationship, partner's should be _____ to each other's needs at an _____ level and to recognize that all sexual problems are _____.

47. Several guidelines can be suggested to help facilitate communication. One of them is to avoid "_____," that is saving up feelings and complaints.

48. Another suggestion is to be open about _____. Happy couples not only talk more, they convey more personal feelings and show greater sensitivity to their partner's feelings. Don't attack the other person's _____. Expressions of negative feelings should be given as statements of one's own feelings, not as statements of _____.

49. Don't try to _____ a fight; instead try to resolve the differences without focusing on who is right or wrong. Recognize that _____ is appropriate. However, constructive fights require that couples fight fair by sticking to the real issues and not "hitting below the belt."

ANSWER KEYS

Do You Know the Information?

Multiple Choice

1. (c) obj. 1, p. 574
2. (a) obj. 2, p. 574
3. (b) obj. 2, p. 574
4. (a) obj. 3, p. 575
5. (d) objs. 3, 6, pp. 575, 577
6. (a) obj. 4, p. 576
7. (b) obj. 4, p. 576
8. (c) obj. 6, p. 577
9. (d) objs. 7, 9, pp. 578-580
10. (c) obj. 8, p. 579
11 (a) obj. 10, p. 581
12. (d) obj. 11, p. 583
13. (c) obj. 12, p. 583
14. (b) obj. 14, p. 584
15. (d) obj. 15, p. 585
16. (d) obj. 16, p. 586
17. (b) obj. 17, p. 587
18. (b) obj. 18, p. 587
19. (c) obj. 18, p. 588
20. (a) obj. 19, p. 588
21. (c) obj. 20, p. 590
22. (d) obj. 21, pp. 590-591
23. (a) obj. 22, p. 592
24. (a) obj. 23, p. 593
25. (b) obj. 25, p. 594
26. (a) obj. 26, pp. 594-596

27. (d) obj. 27, p. 598
28. (a) obj. 27, p. 598
29. (c) obj. 27, p. 599
30. (b) obj. 27, p. 600
31. (d) obj. 27, p. 600
32. (d) obj. 29, p. 601

True-False

1. F, obj. 4, p. 576
2. T, obj. 4, p. 576
3. F, obj. 5, p. 576
4. T, obj. 6, p. 577
5. T, obj. 7, p. 578
6. T, obj. 10, p. 581
7. T, obj. 13, p. 584
8. T, obj. 14, p. 584
9. F, obj. 15, p. 584
10. T, obj. 15, p. 585
11. F, obj. 20, p. 590
12. F, obj. 24, p. 592
13. T, obj. 27, p. 598
14. T, obj. 28, p. 600
15. F, obj. 29, p. 601

Matching

1. N, obj. 1, p. 574
2. G, obj. 1, p. 574
3. M, obj. 2, p. 574
4. P, obj. 2, p. 575
5. I, obj. 3, p. 575
6. K, obj. 6, p. 577
7. E, obj. 9, p. 580
8. S, obj. 12, p. 583
9. D, obj. 13, p. 584
10. C, obj. 19, p. 589
11. J, obj. 27, p. 598
12. B, obj. 27, p. 597

Can You Apply the Information?

1. (d) objs. 3, 4, 6, pp. 575-577
2. (c) objs. 9, 10, p. 581
3. (d) objs. 14-15, pp. 584-585
4. (b) obj. 16, p. 586
5. (a) obj. 21, p. 591
6. (b) obj. 21, p. 589
7. (d) obj. 27, p. 598
8. (c) obj. 27, p. 599
9. (d) obj. 27, p. 599
10. (d) obj. 27, p. 600
11. (a) obj. 29, p. 601

Chapter Review

1. sexual, reproductive, Secondary, breasts, hips, hair, voice (p. 574)
2. menarche, menopause (p. 574)
3. hormones, gonads, estrogens, androgens (p. 574)
4. testes, ovaries, adrenal (p. 574)
5. androgens, estrogens, testosterone, androgens (p. 574)
6. genetic, gonadal, hormonal, genital, identity (p. 575)
7. Genetic, female (p. 575)
8. genitals, androgen insensitivity, hermaphroditism (p. 576)
9. androgenital, brain (p. 576)
10. learned, biasing effect (p. 576)
11. alike, different, IQ (p. 577)
12. gender identity (p. 577)
13. sex-role socialization, sex roles (p. 578)
14. pattern, behavior, questionable (p. 578)
15. beliefs, sex roles, assumptions (p. 579)
16. instrumental, emotions, expressive, maternal (p. 579)
17. androgynous, flexible (adaptable), situation (p. 581)
18. birth, sexual climax, 5, 4, cultural norms, socially approved, arbitrary, "normal" (p. 583)
19. stimulation, erogenous, genitals, mouth, breasts, cognitive, thoughts (images) (p. 583)
20. no less, emotional (p. 583); scripts, behavior (p. 584)
21. attitudes, experience, recency, androgen (p. 584)
22. depressant, inhibitions, negative (p. 584)
23. decrease, decrease, increase (p. 585)
24. regularity (opportunity) (p. 585)
25. 89, 95, rhythms, preferences, masturbation (p. 586)
26. 22, bisexual, accept, no differences, ego-dystonic, homophobia (p. 587)
27. 50, 70, 50, gene, X, mother (p. 588)
28. excitement, plateau, orgasm, resolution (p. 588)
29. erection, penis, ejaculation, refractory (p. 589)
30. plateau (p. 590)
31. no difference, vagina, orgasm, clitoris (p. 590)
32. 10, 20, 4 (p. 590)
33. similarities, differences, slowly (p. 590); multiple orgasms, penis size, simultaneous orgasm, artificial (p. 591)
34. Liberalized, contraceptives, behaviors, 22, 88, increase (rise), extramarital (p. 592)
35. human sexuality, double standard, sexual freedom, expected, abstinent (p. 593)
36. acquaintance, rape, High (p. 593)
37. sexually transmitted, acquired immune deficiency, virus, incubation, direct, body fluids, heterosexual (p. 594)
38. hypoactive, aversion, physical, illness, fatigue (hormonal, pharmacological), psychological, depression (loss of control, conflict, etc.), psychotherapy (p. 597)
39. Erectile, primary, secondary, normal (p. 598)
40. organic, psychogenic, 40, religious, mother, drugs, surgery (p. 598)
41. sensate focus (p. 598)
42. arousal, arousal, medical, psychological, sensate focus, stimulation (p. 599)
43. orgasmic, retarded, orgasmic (p. 599)
44. premature ejaculation, squeeze (p. 600)
45. dyspareunia, vaginismus, extinction, desensitization, masturbation (p. 600)
46. responsive, emotional, mutual (p. 601)
47. gunnysacking (p. 601)
48. feelings, character, blame (p. 601)
49. win, anger (p. 601)

chapter seventeen

Social Behavior

social psychology
culture
groups – structure, cohesiveness
roles – ascribed, achieved,
   conflict, status
   effect of status on touching
norms
autokinetic effect
proxemics – personal space (zones)
   intimate, personal, social, public
attribution – internal, external,
   consistency, setting,
   discounting, distinctiveness,
   consensus
self-handicapping
fundamental attributional error

need to affiliate
   social comparison theory
   social exchange theory
interpersonal attraction –
   physical proximity, physical
   attraction, competence, similarity
self-disclosure
factors in selecting a mate
self-monitoring
social influence
conformity – Asch's experiment
groupthink
   group sanctions and unanimity
social power – reward, coercive,
   legitimate, referent, expert
obedience – Milgram's experiment

compliance
   foot-in-the-door effect
   door-in-the-face effect
   low-ball technique
passive compliance
attitudes – components and formation
why behavior sometimes does not
   reflect attitudes
attitude measurement
groups – reference, membership
persuasion and how to do it
cognitive dissonance theory
   & justification or reward
forced attitude change
   brainwashing and cults
assertiveness training – rehearsal,
   overlearning, broken record

LEARNING OBJECTIVES

To demonstrate mastery of this chapter you should be able to:

1.   Define social psychology.

2.   Define the following terms:

   a.   culture

   b.   role

c. ascribed role

d. achieved role

e. role conflict

f. status (and explain how status is related to touching)

g. group structure

h. group cohesiveness

i. norm

3. Explain how norms are formed using the idea of the autokinetic effect.

4. Define proxemics. List and describe the four basic interpersonal zones and describe the nature of the interactions which occur in each.

a.

b.

c.

d.

5.   Explain what attribution theory is, the difference between internal and external causes of behavior, and how the following factors are related to attribution:

    a.   consistency

    b.   distinctiveness

    c.   situational demands

        1.   actor

        2.   object

        3.   setting

        4.   discounting

    d.   consensus

6.   Explain what self-handicapping is and its purpose.

7.   Explain what the fundamental attributional error is.

8. Describe the research that indicates that humans have a need to affiliate.

9. Describe the social comparison theory.

10. Describe the social exchange theory as it relates to interpersonal relationships.

11. List and describe four factors that affect interpersonal attraction.

    a.

    b.

    c.

    d.

12. Explain how self-disclosure is important in the process of getting to know someone. Explain how overdisclosure can affect the same process.

13. Describe the similarities and differences in what men and women look for in a mate.

14.   Define the term self-monitoring and differentiate high self-monitoring behavior from low self-monitoring behavior. Explain the advantages and disadvantages of each.

15.   Describe the research demonstrating how human behavior comes under social influence.

16.   Describe Asch's experiment on conformity and list any personal factors that can influence it.

17.   Define groupthink and explain how it may contribute to poor decision-making. Describe four ways to prevent groupthink.

       a.

       b.

       c.

       d.

18.   Explain how group sanctions and unanimity affect conformity.

19.   List and describe the five sources of social power.

    a.

    b.

    c.

    d.

    e.

20.   Describe Milgram's study of obedience and identify the factors which affect the degree of obedience.

21.   Differentiate conformity, obedience, and compliance.

22.   Describe the following methods of compliance:

    a.   foot-in-the-door

    b.   door-in-the-face

    c.   low-ball technique

23.   Describe the research that deals with passive compliance.

24. Define attitude. Describe the belief, emotional, and action components of an attitude.

25. List, describe, and give examples of six ways in which attitudes are acquired.

    a.

    b.

    c.

    d.

    e.

    f.

26. Explain why people may exhibit discrepancies between attitudes and behavior.

27. Describe the following techniques for measuring attitudes:

    a. open-ended interview

    b. social distance scale

    c. attitude scale

28.   Differentiate between reference groups and membership groups.

29.   Define persuasion, and list nine principles of persuasion which can be applied to bring about attitude change.

a.

b.

c.

d.

e.

f.

g.

h.

i.

30.   Describe the activities and interests of a consumer psychologist.

31.   Present an overview of cognitive dissonance theory, indicate its influence on attitude formation, and describe the effect of reward or justification on dissonance.

32.   List two methods of forced attitude change.

a.

b.

33. Differentiate between brainwashing from other persuasive techniques.

34. Explain how beliefs may unfreeze, change, and refreeze, and indicate how permanent the attitude changes brought about by brainwashing are.

35. Describe how cults are able to recruit, convert, and retain their members.

The following objective is related to the material in the "Applications" section of your text.

36. Distinguish among assertive behavior, non-assertive behavior, and aggressive behavior. Describe how a person can learn to be more assertive using rehearsal, role playing, overlearning, and the broken record technique.

SELF-QUIZZES

Do You Know the Information?

Multiple Choice

1. The scientificstudy of how people behave, think, and feel in social situations is called
    (a) conformity.   (b) social psychology.   (c) groupthink.   (d) proxemics.

2. The ongoing pattern of life that is passed from one generation to the next is called
   (a) norms.   (b) roles.   (c) culture.   (d) group structure.

3. The Zimbardo prison experiment would seem to show that
   (a) ascribed roles conflict greatest with achieved roles.
   (b) group cohesiveness results after all role conflicts have ended.
   (c) position within a group is determined by one's status.
   (d) the source of many destructive relationships can be found in destructive roles.

4. The autokinetic effect
   (a) occurs when people experience role conflict.
   (b) demonstrates that when people interact, norms are formed and attitudes, beliefs, and behaviors tend to converge.
   (c) is subject to the presence of group sanctions.
   (d) is not affected by cultural stereotypes.

5. The study of the personal use of space is called
   (a) spaceology.   (b) kinesthetics.   (c) kinesics.   (d) proxemics.

6. The distance maintained in comfortable interactions with friends is called _____ distance.
   (a) personal   (b) public   (c) intimate   (d) social

7. Which of the following statements about attribution theory is *incorrect*?
   (a) If a person's behavior is distinctly different toward you, you may correctly assume that it has something to do with you or your behavior.
   (b) If someone's behavior is very consistent, we tend to assume that his/her behavior is externally caused.
   (c) A consensus in the behavior of a number of people implies that the behavior has an external cause.
   (d) If the situational demands are strong, we may know little about a person's motives.

8. When a person does not feel confident about succeeding or tries to protect a fragile self-image, he or she may engage in
   (a) discounting.   (b) proxemics.   (c) self-handicapping.   (d) consistency.

9. The fundamental attributional error
   (a) often leads to role conflict.
   (b) occurs when we attribute the actions of others to internal causes while attributing our own behavior to external causes.
   (c) results from the actor, the object, or the setting responding to situational demands.
   (d) is attributing the actions of others to situations while attributing our own behavior to internal causes.

10. When threatened with a series of painful electric shocks, women generally chose to
    (a) wait with calmer students not taking part in the experiment.   (c) wait with other shock subjects.
    (b) wait alone.   (d) wait with whomever was closest.

11. Often we must turn to others to evaluate our actions, feelings, or abilities. This idea is the basis for
    (a) self-disclosure.   (c) social exchange theory.
    (b) social comparison theory.   (d) Aronson's theory of social evaluation.

12. According to social exchange theory, a relationship must be _____ to endure.
    (a) meaningful   (b) reasonable   (c) profitable   (d) positive

13. Of the following, which are the factors identified by Aronson that determine interpersonal attraction between individuals?
    (a) physical proximity   (c) inherent goodness   (e) competence   (g) group status
    (b) physical attractiveness   (d) morality   (f) similarity   (h) cultural compatibility

14. It is apparent that self-disclosure
    (a) leads to reciprocity when the amount of self-disclosure is moderate.
    (b) is a major step toward friendship.
    (c) gives rise to suspicion and reduced attraction if it is excessive.
    (d) includes all of the above

15. In selecting a mate it has been found that
    (a) kindness and understanding are ranked first by almost all men and women.
    (b) people tend to choose someone who is different but complementary.
    (c) men rank a good earning capacity higher than women do.
    (d) women rank attractiveness higher than men do.

16. Which of the following characteristics would be *most* typical of low self-monitors? (You may choose more than one.)
    (a) keenly interested in the actions of others
    (b) tend to declare who they are by listing their roles and memberships
    (c) prefer jobs where their roles are very clearly defined
    (d) match their public behavior to their private attitudes, feelings, and beliefs

17. The research on social influence suggests that
    (a) everyday behavior is probably most influenced by group pressures for conformity.
    (b) simple suggestion can be used as social influence.
    (c) intensive indoctrination can be used as social influence.
    (d) all of the above are true.

18. In his experiment, Asch found that _____ percent of all subjects involved yielded to group judgment at least once.
    (a) 50   (b) 75   (c) 90   (d) 100

19. Decision making which becomes so compulsive in maintaining personal status and conformity that it minimizes critical thinking is called
    (a) proxcmics.   (b) obedience.   (c) role conflict.   (d) groupthink.

20. Having at least one person who agreed with the subject's judgment in Asch's experiment
    (a) greatly reduced the pressures to conform.
    (b) was not as influential as the number of people who disagreed with you.
    (c) often increased the group sanctions against the subject.
    (d) increased conformity but only in isolated situations.

21. Of the following, which are types of social power?
    (a) reward   (c) noble   (e) legitimate   (g) referent
    (b) coercive   (d) expert   (f) business   (h) group

22. In his original study of obedience to authority, Milgram found that _____ percent of those tested obeyed completely by going all the way up to the 450 volt shock level.
    (a) 25   (b) 50   (c) 65   (d) 75

23. Which of the following was *least* important in affecting the degree of compliance in Milgram's study?
    (a) the distance between the "learner" and the "teacher"
    (b) the opportunity to imitate two other teachers who resisted orders and walked out
    (c) the location of the experiment or the experimenter's appearance
    (d) the distance between the "teacher" and the "authority"

24. Which of the following statements is (are) *true*?
    (a) In conformity situations the pressure to get in line is usually indirect.
    (b) Compliance is when a person with little or no authority makes a direct request of another person.
    (c) Obedience is when a person of authority gives an order and the pressure is direct and difficult to resist.
    (d) All of the above statements are true.

25. If I get a person committed to act in a certain way and then make the terms of acting less desirable, this technique of compliance is called
    (a) passive compliance.   (c) the low-ball technique.
    (b) the door-in-the-face technique.   (d) the foot-in-the-door technique.

26. In Moriarty's experiment in which subjects were subjected to very loud music
  (a) many subjects were angry but only asked the culprit twice to turn off the music .
  (b) the accomplice was instructed to turn off the music at the first request, but no one made such a request.
  (c) about half of the subjects glared at first but only requested that the music be turned down when this did not work.
  (d) most subjects said nothing.

27. A(n) _____ is a learned predisposition to respond to people, objects, or institutions in a positive or negative way.
  (a) norm   (b) belief   (c) stereotype   (d) attitude

28. Assuming that a child's parents belong to the same political party, the chances are 2 out of 3 that the child will belong to the same party as an adult. This exemplifies the effect of _____ on attitude formation.
  (a) group membership   (b) child rearing   (c) direct contact   (d) interaction with others

29. Often there are large differences between attitudes and behavior. This occurs because
  (a) long-standing habits may take precedence.
  (b) the immediate consequences of our actions may be more important.
  (c) we may expect that others will negatively evaluate our actions.
  (d) of all of the above.

30. Which technique for measuring attitudes indicates a person's willingness to have contact with another person?
  (a) attitude scales   (b) open-ended interview   (c) liking/loving ratio   (d) social distance scale

31. Membership groups and reference groups differ in that
  (a) a person sees a reference group as holding values and attitudes relevant to his or her own.
  (b) to be a part of a membership group the membership need not be physical.
  (c) being part of membership group depends on who you identify with or care about.
  (d) none of the above are true.

32. Which of the following is *not* likely to be particularly persuasive?
  (a) The message is repeated as frequently as possible.
  (b) The message is presented rationally as opposed to appealing to the emotions.
  (c) The persuader appears to have nothing to gain if the message is accepted.
  (d) The message states clear-cut conclusions.

33. According to cognitive dissonance theory
  (a) there is usually an inconsistency between attitudes and behavior.
  (b) people tend to seek information which runs counter to previously established attitudes.
  (c) behavior which is inconsistent with attitudes may provoke attitude change.
  (d) a large reward will create more dissonance.

34. Persuasion resembles brainwashing except that the latter
  (a) is more effective.
  (b) is more effective for long-term attitude change.
  (c) requires a captive audience.
  (d) involves confession.

35. Which of the following statements concerning brainwashing is *true*?
  (a) The effects are relatively permanent.
  (b) It typically begins with praise for correct behavior.
  (c) The person being brainwashed goes through a cycle known as unfreezing, changing, refreezing.
  (d) The "target" is allowed to exist independent of his captors.

36. Cults
  (a) tend to create guilt and fear in their members.
  (b) isolate potential members from non cult members and try to wear down physical and emotional resistance.
  (c) try to catch potential converts at a time of need.
  (d) follow all of the above.

37. Which of the following statements is *correct* concerning assertion, aggression, and non-assertion?
    (a) People who are nonassertive are usually patient to a fault.
    (b) Assertion is exclusively self-serving.
    (c) Although very negative, aggression takes into account the other person's feelings.
    (d) Assertion usually leads to loss of self-respect.

38. Convincing yourself that you have the right to refuse, to request, and to right a wrong is a basic principle of
    (a) conformity.　　　　　(b) assertiveness training.　(c) groupthink.　　　　　(d) proxemics.

39. Learning to become more assertive by restating your request as many times and as many ways as necessary is called
    (a) overlearning.　　　　(b) broken record technique.　(c) challenging a wrong.　(d) rehearsal.

True-False

_____ 1. By virtue of their greater emotional expressiveness, women are more likely to touch men than vice versa.

_____ 2. A consensus among many people implies an external cause to some observed behavior.

_____ 3. In general, people consistently attribute the behavior of others to external causes.

_____ 4. Because of the halo effect, attractive people are also assumed to be intelligent.

_____ 5. People who are low in self-monitoring are unresponsive to the demands of different situations.

_____ 6. When directions come from an authority, people rationalize that they are not personally responsible for their actions.

_____ 7. A "mean" world view develops from direct contact and chance conditioning.

_____ 8. Marketing research is used by consumer psychologists to determine how people shop.

_____ 9. Brainwashing and cults are examples of persuasive attitude change.

Can You Apply the Information?

1. Which of the following is an ascribed role?
   (a) teacher　　　　　　(b) mother　　　　　　(c) daughter　　　　　(d) doctor

2. You are a college professor and your husband decides to enroll in your class. This could develop into an example of
   (a) role conflict.　　　(b) group cohesiveness.　　(c) ascribed roles.　　(d) attribution.

3. Vickie is a typical college student. In class she is quiet, attentive, and intelligent. In the college cafeteria she acts like the rest of her group. She can be rather loud, boisterous, and sometimes very lewd. The difference in her behavior can be attributed to
   (a) group structure.　　(b) obedience.　　　　(c) ascribed roles.　　(d) group norms.

4. At a cocktail party most people stand within touching distance while talking. What is this distance called?
   (a) public distance　　(b) personal distance　　(c) intimate distance　(d) social distance

5. Shortly after becoming a millionaire in the lottery, Bob got a call from an old sweetheart wanting to get together for "old times." When they split up two years ago she had said he was the dullest person she had ever met. Bob is now most likely to first
   (a) discount her current sincerity.
   (b) consider the distinctiveness of her request.
   (c) be aware of the situational demands of where they will get together.
   (d) wonder about the object of her request.

6. John has a drinking problem. For the past few months, he has appeared to be on a roller coaster. His life seems to hit rock bottom, and then he slowly seems to get better. His family and friends always seem to be willing to rescue him. They will even set him up with a new job, but every time he is supposed to show up for these really good jobs (considering John's present state), he gets drunk and "can't" show up. It appears that John is engaging in
   (a) the fundamental attributional error.
   (b) discounting.
   (c) self-handicapping.
   (d) social comparison theory.

7. Audrey and Lisa are looking at the grades posted outside of their class. They have both made a "D." Lisa says to herself that the reason her grade is so low is that she had to get a second job to make ends meet, but that Audrey just isn't as smart as her. This is an example of
   (a) social exchange theory.
   (b) the fundamental attributional error.
   (c) passive compliance.
   (d) group cohesiveness.

8. You have a chance to find out how much money your close friend makes. One reason you might want to find out could be because of
   (a) social exchange theory.   (b) social comparison theory. (c) proximity.   (d) the liking/loving dimension.

9. Bart and Bernice have been married for twelve years. From Bart's point of view Bernice is now overweight, a nag, and unstimulating. Bart believes that he is getting very little from the relationship even though he is still putting a lot into it. He wants a divorce. Bart's feelings can easily be explained from the point of view of
   (a) social comparison theory. (b) social influence.   (c) social exchange theory.   (d) conformity.

10. John and Jane are planning a June wedding. Their parents are thrilled because the parents have been best friends since high school and get together often. The original reason for John and Jane's relationship was probably
    (a) similarity.   (b) physical attraction.   (c) proximity.   (d) competence.

11. Sam is very reserved and quiet. He never tells others about himself or his feelings. It is likely that people respond to him by
    (a) asking a lot of questions.
    (b) telling him a lot about themselves.
    (c) comparing his possible feelings to their feelings.
    (d) disclosing little about themselves.
    (e) throwing sticks and stones at him.

12. People in your neighborhood feel that you should run for city council. You, however, are not sure it is a good idea. You are more likely to *agree* to run if
    (a) they send three representatives to talk with you.
    (b) you meet with all the neighbors, supporters and detractors alike, to hear both sides.
    (c) you can sit down and think it through logically.
    (d) the mayor calls you and asks you to think it over.

13. Although the speed limit now on major urban highways is 55, Ray remembers when it was 70. He figures it was safe then and it is safe now, so he ignores the 55 m.p.h. rule. His behavior shows a blatant disregard for
    (a) coercive power.   (b) legitimate power.   (c) referent power.   (d) reward power.

14. "Good evening Mr. Goodbar. How are you tonight? My name is Ralph and I'm calling to find out if you'd be willing to sponsor five underprivileged six-year-old children to the Shriner's Circus which will be visiting your city next week? Oh, I'm sorry you can't. Well, could you sponsor just one child then?" What compliance technique is Ralph using on you?
    (a) foot-in-the-door effect   (b) door-in-the-face effect   (c) low-ball technique   (d) passive compliance

15. Paul goes to the library with his Walkman turned so loud that it bothers other people. According to the findings from Moriarity's study, most people will probably
    (a) do nothing.
    (b) leave his vicinity.
    (c) ask him politely to turn it down.
    (d) ask someone in authority to speak to Paul about the noise.
    (e) use sign language to try to communicate with Paul.

16. Sally feels very strongly about uvulas and, in fact, went to the annual meeting of the National Uvula Foundation. Sally's attendance at that meeting was an example of the _____ component of her attitude.
    (a) emotional   (b) belief   (c) action   (d) none of these

17. Juanita owns and operates a small manufacturing company in Alaska. She doesn't pay her workers much money and constantly has trouble finding help. It seems that the only people she can find are down-and-out white men who tend to be alcoholics or drug abusers. As a result of this she has tended to take a rather negative attitude toward all white people. It could be said that her prejudice is a result of
    (a) group membership.
    (b) child rearing.
    (c) interaction with others with the same attitude.
    (d) direct contact.

18. Jane and Bob have recently moved and have joined a new recreation club. They spend a lot of their time at the new club because they had to quit the recreation club in their old neighborhood. They still feel closer to the members in the old club. Their new club is a(n) _____ group.
    (a) equal-status
    (b) reference
    (c) membership
    (d) identification

19. Phil will have a better chance convincing his nuclear physicist audience that nuclear energy is a threat to Earth if
    (a) he appeals to their emotions.
    (b) he presents both sides of the argument.
    (c) he tells them that he has recently sold his stock in coal and gas companies.
    (d) all of the above are done.

20. In which of the following situations will cognitive dissonance be *most* likely to occur?
    (a) Bill, a student, is asked to give a speech on why tuition at his college should be raised by $1000.
    (b) Bill has to give the same speech (as above) or get an "F" in his speech class.
    (c) Bill is paid $100 to give the speech.
    (d) Bill believes that tuition should be raised, and he wants to give the speech.

21. The Reverend Letus Fleecem has started a cult and currently has about 150 followers. He is successful in attracting new members because
    (a) he has learned how to unfreeze their former values quickly.
    (b) he showers potential converts with displays of understanding for their lonely and sad lives.
    (c) he pushes them to a breaking point that forces them to fear him.
    (d) he does not put each new member in a position of cognitive dissonance.

Chapter Review

1. _____ _____ is the study of how people behave in the presence (real or implied) of others. _____ is the ongoing _____ ____ _____ that is passed on from one generation to another.

2. In your day-to-day life your immediate social environment includes many _____ such as your family and your classmates. In each _____ you meet expectations associated with playing _____. Some of these are _____ _____ and you have no control over them. Others which you attain voluntarily are _____ _____. When actual behavior is not consistent with expected behavior you may be caught in a _____ _____.

3. Position in a group determines one's _____. In most groups, _____ status is associated with special privileges and respect and may lead such a person to _____ a person of lower status. The organization of roles, communications, pathways, and power in the group is _____ _____, and the degree of attraction among group members is _____ _____. The standards of conduct which indicate appropriate behavior are called _____.

4. Pressures toward conformity affect the perception of movement of a stationary pinpoint of light in a completely darkened room. This illusion is called the _____ effect.

5. People maintain and regulate personal _____ which forms an invisible spatial area around each individual. _____ is the study of rules for the personal use of space.

6. Hall has identified four basic zones which relate to comfortable or acceptable distances. The first, _____ distance, extends about _____ inches out from the skin. The second, _____ distance, is the distance maintained in comfortable interaction with friends. This extends from about _____ to _____ feet from the body. The third is _____ distance which includes impersonal business and casual social gatherings and covers a range of about _____ to _____ feet. Speeches and lectures are carried out at _____ distance when people are separated by more than 12 feet.

7. The process of making inferences about behavior is called _____. The cause of a behavior is deemed to be _____ if it lies outside a person and _____ if it lies within the person.

8. Two factors that greatly influence attribution are _____ and _____. We are also very sensitive to _____ demands (i.e., the behavior of the _____, the _____ of the action, and _____ in which the action occurs). In addition, when the situational demands are very strong, we are likely to _____ internal causes for a person's actions. If we have _____, it makes us feel much more assured about our inferences.

9. When a person does not feel confident about succeeding or to protect a fragile self-image, people sometimes arrange to be evaluated while engaging in _____-_____. That way, they can attribute the failure to the _____. One of the most popular and effective ways to do this is to use _____.

10. The fundamental attributional error is when we attribute the behavior of others to _____ causes and our own behavior to _____ causes.

11. The _____ to _____ helps people meet needs for approval, friendship, and support. Women waiting to be given painful _____ tended to want to wait with _____.

12. Group membership fills the need for _____ _____ which gives people a chance for self-evaluation. _____ _____ theory holds that a desire for self-evaluation determines what groups are joined. As relationships progress, they can be understood in terms of maximizing _____ while minimizing "_____." According to the _____ _____ theory we want to maximize profitable, rewarding relationships.

13. People also affiliate because of _____ _____ which is the basis for most voluntary social relationships. Attraction is influenced by physical _____ because it increases the frequency of contact between people. In addition physical _____, talent or _____, and _____ of backgrounds, interests and attitudes influence choice of friends.

14. Engaging in _____-_____ is a major step toward friendship. This process requires a degree of _____. There are definite _____ about when it is acceptable and when it is not. Moderate _____-_____ leads to _____. _____, however, gives rise to suspicion and reduced attraction.

15. People select a mate in a variety of ways. The thing which is most similar in married couples is _____. The two most important qualities picked by men and women were _____ and _____. However, physical attractiveness was ranked higher by _____ and earning capacity was ranked higher by _____.

16. When people observe or try to control the image of themselves that they display to others, this is called _____-_____. People who are high in this characteristic are flexible and adaptable and display different "_____" from situation to situation. In contrast, people who are low change very little from situation to situation and seek to match their public behavior to their private _____.

17. When people interact they almost always affect one another's behavior, a topic that social psychologists term _____ _____. It can range from simple suggestion to intensive indoctrination (_____). Everyday behavior is probably most influenced by group pressures for _____.

18. In Asch's experiment on conformity, subjects conformed to the group on about _____-_____ of the critical trials. Of those tested _____ percent yielded at least once.

19. A compulsion by decision-makers to maintain each other's approval even at the cost of critical thinking is called _____. The core of it is misguided group _____ where group members believe that there is more _____ and _____ than actually exists. To prevent it group leaders should _____ each group member's _____, avoid stating his or her own _____ in the beginning, state the problem _____, and make sure there is a _____ _____.

20. _____ _____ is the term given to the rewards for conformity or threats for nonconformity levied by groups. Negative sanctions (_____) for nonconformity may range from laughter to complete ostracism.

21. When judging the effects of group pressures to conform, more important than the size of the majority is its _____. Having at least _____ person(s) in your corner can greatly reduce pressures to conform.

22. _____ power differs from _____ power in that the first lies in the ability to punish whereas the second is based on respect. Of the three other types of social power, _____ power is based on acceptance of a person as a representative of an established social order, _____ power is based on the ability to reward compliance, and _____ power is based on knowledge or expertise.

23. Stanley Milgram studied _____ by investigating some of the factors which influenced whether or not an individual would administer _____ to a stranger in an experimental situation.

24. In Milgram's study _____ percent of those tested obeyed by going all the way to a 450-volt level. Obedience decreased when the victim was in the _____ _____, when the _____ and _____ were face-to-face, when the authority figure was _____ and when others refused to _____.

25. In _____ situations the pressure to get in line is usually indirect as opposed to when an authority commands _____. The term _____ is used to describe situations in which a person with little or no authority makes a direct request.

26. A person who agrees to a small request is later more likely to comply with a larger demand. This is called the _____-_____-_____-_____ effect. The _____-_____-_____-_____ effect is when a person agrees to a smaller request after having first denied a larger request. The _____-_____ technique consists of getting a person committed to act and then making the terms of acting less desirable.

27. In addition to excessive obedience, many people are surprisingly _____. This is demonstrated by _____ _____ to unreasonable requests and by failure to be assertive.

28. _____ are learned predispositions to respond in a certain way. They _____ past experience and _____ or direct future action. They have three major components, a _____ component, an _____ component, and an _____ component.

29. Attitudes are acquired in several basic ways, sometimes through _____ _____ with the object of the attitude, through _____ with others holding the same attitude, through _____ _____ in which one becomes like his/her parents, through _____ _____, through the _____ _____, and through _____ _____.

30. Many times there are discrepancies between our attitudes and our behavior because the _____ _____ of our actions weigh heavily on the choices we make. A second factor is our expectation of how others will _____ our actions. Finally, we must not overlook the effects of long-standing _____.

1. There are often large differences between _____ attitudes and _____ behavior. Barriers to action fall when a person holds an attitude with _____.

2. If you were asked, "How do you feel about drafting women?" you may be taking part in an _____ - _____ _____ designed to measure attitudes. Another approach to attitude measurement is the _____ _____ scale which measures the degree to which one person would be willing to associate with another. If you were asked to express agreement or disagreement with the concept of drafting women by using a five-point _____ ranging from "strongly agree" to "strongly disagree," you would be rated on an _____ _____.

3. A _____ group is one whose values and attitudes are seen by the individual as being relevant to his or her own. A _____ group is merely a group to which you belong.

4. A deliberate attempt to change attitudes by the transmission of _____ is called _____. Attitude change is most encouraged when (1) the communicator is _____; (2) the message appeals to _____; (3) the message presents a clear _____ _____; (4) the message states clear-cut _____; (5) the message is backed up by _____ and _____; (6) both sides of the argument are presented for a _____-informed audience; (7) one side of the argument is presented for a _____-informed audience; (8) the persuader appears to have nothing to _____; and (9) the message is presented _____.

5. _____ psychology is an applied field that focuses on how and why people buy and spend as they do. To that end, consumer behavior can be separated into: deciding to _____, selecting a _____, shopping, making the purchase, and evaluating the _____ in use.

6. People who engage in _____ _____ about a topic are more likely to change their opinions than people who merely hear a lecture about the topic. This phenomenon can be partially explained by _____ _____ theory which states that the maintenance and change of attitudes is closely related to needs for _____ in attitudes and action.

7. Studies have indicated that the amount of dissonance is inversely related to the amount of _____ or _____ for acting _____ to one's real beliefs.

8. Two methods of forced attitude change are _____, and _____.

9. One difference between persuasion and brainwashing is that brainwashing requires a _____ audience. The target of brainwashing is _____ from other people, is made _____ on his captors for satisfaction of needs, and the captors are in a position to _____ changes in attitudes or behavior. All of these techniques serve to _____, change, and then _____ the target's attitudes.

10. _____ use high-pressure indoctrination techniques similar to those used in brainwashing. Members stay because of _____ and _____ and because they are _____ on the group.

11. _____ is a direct, honest expression of feelings and desires and differs from _____ which is an attempt to get one's own way no matter what. In _____ _____ individuals learn that they have the right to stand up for their rights.

12. Assertiveness can be improved by _____ the behaviors that you will need to use is a situation. If possible, you should _____ _____ the scene with a friend. It may also help to use _____. The _____ _____ technique may prove helpful. To do this you simply _____ your request as many times and as many ways as necessary.

| ANSWER KEYS |

Do You Know the Information?

Multiple Choice

1. (b) obj. 1, p. 605
2. (c) obj. 2, p. 605
3. (d) obj. 2, p. 606
4. (b) obj. 3, p. 607
5. (d) obj. 4, p. 608
6. (a) obj. 4, p. 609
7. (b) obj. 5, p. 610
8. (c) obj. 6, p. 611
9. (b) obj. 7, p. 611
10. (c) obj. 8, p. 612
11. (b) obj. 9, p. 613
12. (c) obj. 10, p. 613
13. (a,b,e,f) obj. 11, pp. 614-615
14. (d) obj. 12, p. 615
15. (a) obj. 13, p. 616
16. (d) obj. 14, p. 618
17. (d) obj. 15, p. 618
18. (b) obj. 16, p. 619
19. (d) obj. 17, p. 620
20. (a) obj. 18, p. 620
21. (a,b,d,e,g) obj. 19, p. 621
22. (c) obj. 20, p. 622
23. (c) obj. 20, p. 623
24. (d) obj. 21, pp. 624-625

25. (c) obj. 22, p. 625
26. (d) obj. 23, p. 626
27. (d) obj. 24, p. 628
28. (b) obj. 25, p. 628
29. (d) obj. 26, p. 629
30. (d) obj. 27, p. 630
31. (a) obj. 28, p. 630
32. (b) obj. 29, p. 631
33. (c) obj. 31, pp. 632-633
34. (c) obj. 33, p. 634
35. (c) obj. 34, p. 634
36. (d) obj. 35, p. 635
37. (a) obj. 36, p. 638
38. (b) obj. 36, p. 638
39. (b) obj. 36, p. 639

True-False

1. F, obj. 2, p. 607
2. T, obj. 5, p. 611
3. F, obj. 7, p. 611
4. T, obj. 11, p. 614
5. T, obj. 14, p. 616
6. T, obj. 20, p. 623
7. F, obj. 25, p. 629
8. F, obj. 30, p. 632
9. F, obj. 32, p. 633

Can You Apply the Information?

1. (c) obj. 2, p. 605
2. (a) obj. 2, p. 605
3. (d) obj. 2, p. 607
4. (b) obj. 4, p. 609
5. (a) obj. 5, p. 610
6. (c) obj. 6, p. 611
7. (b) obj. 7, p. 611
8. (b) obj. 9, p. 613
9. (c) obj. 10, p. 613
10. (c) obj. 11, p. 614
11. (d) obj. 12, p. 615
12. (a) obj. 18, p. 620
13. (a) obj. 19, p. 621
14. (b) obj. 22, p. 625
15. (a) obj. 23, p. 626
16. (c) obj. 24, p. 628
17. (d) obj. 25, p. 628
18. (c) obj. 28, p. 630
19. (d) obj. 29, p. 631
20. (a) obj. 31, pp. 632-633
21. (b) obj. 35, p. 635

Chapter Review

1. Social psychology, Culture, pattern of life (p. 605)
2. groups, group, structure, roles, ascribed roles, achieved roles, role conflict (p. 605)
3. status, higher, touch, group structure, group cohesiveness, norms (p. 606)
4. autokinetic (p. 607)
5. space, Proxemics (p. 608)
6. intimate, 18 (p. 608); personal, 1 1/2, 4, social, 4, 12, public (p. 609)
7. attribution, external, internal (p. 610)
8. consistency, distinctiveness, situational, actor, object, setting, discount, consensus (p. 610)
9. self-handicapping, handicap, alcohol (p. 611)
10. internal, external (p. 611)
11. need, affiliate, shocks, others (p. 612)
12. social comparison, Social comparison, rewards, costs, social exchange (p. 613)
13. interpersonal attraction, proximity, attractiveness (p. 614); competence, similarity (p. 615)
14. self-disclosure, trust, norms, self-disclosure, reciprocity, Overdisclosure (p. 615)
15. attitudes (opinions), kindness, understanding, men, women (p. 616)
16. self-monitoring, "images" (behavior), beliefs (principles) (p. 616)
17. social influence, brainwashing, conformity (p. 617)
18. one-third, 75 (p. 619)
19. groupthink, loyalty, agreement, unanimity, define, role, preferences, factually, devil's advocate (p. 620)
20. Group sanctions, punishments (p. 619)

21. unanimity, one (p. 620)
22. Coercive, referent, legitimate, reward, expert (p. 621)
23. obedience, shocks (p. 622)
24. 65, same room, victim ("learner"), subject ("teacher"), distant (absent), obey (p. 622)
25. conformity, obedience, compliance (p. 624)
26. foot-in-the-door, door-in-the-face, low-ball (p. 625)
27. passive (compliant), passive compliance (p. 626)
28. Attitudes, summarize, predict, belief, emotional, action (p. 627)
29. direct contact, interaction, child rearing, group membership (p. 628); mass media, chance conditioning (p. 629)
30. immediate consequences, evaluate, habits (p. 629)
31. private, public, conviction (p. 630)
32. open-ended interview, social distance, scale, attitude scale (p. 630)
33. reference, membership (p. 630)
34. information, persuasion, likeable (trustworthy, expert, similar), emotions, course of action, conclusions, facts, statistics, well, poorly, gain, frequently (p. 631)
35. Consumer, spend, brand, product (p. 632)
36. role playing, cognitive dissonance, consistency (p. 632)
37. reward, justification, contrary (p. 633)
38. brainwashing, cults (p. 634)
39. captive, isolated, dependent, reward, unfreeze, refreeze (p. 634)
40. Cults, guilt, fear, dependent (p. 635)
41. Assertion, aggression, assertiveness training (p. 638)
42. rehearsing, role play, overlearning, broken record, restate (p. 638)

chapter eighteen

Applied Psychology and Human Relations

LEARNING OBJECTIVES

To demonstrate mastery of this chapter you should be able to:

1. Define the term applied psychology.

2. Describe the typical activities of an industrial/organizational psychologist.

3. Explain the concept of flexitime.

4. Describe the activities of personnel psychologists by defining or describing the following areas:

 a. job analysis

 b. biodata

 c. vocational interest test

 d. aptitude test

 e. assessment center

5. Differentiate scientific management styles (Theory X) from human relations approaches (Theory Y) to management. Be sure to contrast work efficiency versus psychological efficiency. Include the terms participative management, management by objectives, and quality circles.

6. List six factors which seem to contribute the most to job satisfaction.

 a.

 b.

 c.

 d.

 e.

7.   Explain what is done in job enrichment and what results from it.

8.   List and explain six ways to improve communication skills.

a.

b.

c.

d.

e.

f.

9.   List and describe six ways to be a good listener.

a.

b.

c.

d.

e.

f.

10.   Explain the thrust or interest of environmental psychology.

11.   Define the term territoriality.

12.   Discuss the results of animal experiments on the effects of overcrowding, and state the possible implications for humans.

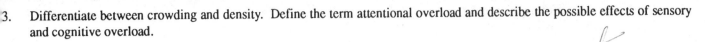

3. Differentiate between crowding and density. Define the term attentional overload and describe the possible effects of sensory and cognitive overload.

4. Explain how environmental assessment, architectural psychology, or even simple feedback can be used to solve environmental problems.

5. Explain what a social trap, a collective social trap, and the tragedy of the commons are. Explain how they can be avoided or escaped.

16. Describe Rubin's studies of romantic love. Discuss the differences between loving and liking and between male and female friendships. Include the term mutual absorption in your discussion.

17.   Briefly describe Sternberg's triangular theory of love including the three "ingredients" and a listing of the seven possible combinations of those ingredients.

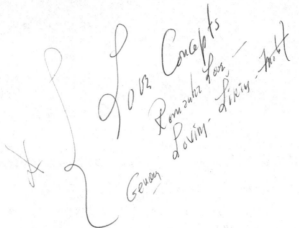

18.   Define and differentiate prejudice and discrimination.

19.   Explain how the following relate to the learning of prejudice:

a.   scapegoating

b.   direct experiences with members of the rejected group

c.   personal prejudice

d.   group prejudice

e.   personality characteristics-authoritarian personality

20.   Describe the characteristic beliefs (including ethnocentrism and dogmatism) and childhood experiences of the authoritarian personality.

21. Present the major characteristics of social stereotypes and indicate how they may lead to intergroup conflicts. Describe symbolic prejudice.

22. Explain how status inequalities may lead to the development of stereotypes and how equal-status contact may reduce intergroup tension. Give an example of each situation.

23. Describe Muzafer Sherif's camp study, and explain how superordinate goals can reduce conflict and hostility. Explain how a "jigsaw" classroom utilizes superordinate goals and helps reduce prejudice.

24. Describe the relationship between aggression and each of the following:

    a. instincts

(continued on page 366)

b. biology

c. frustration(-aggression hypothesis)

d. cues for aggression (include the weapons effect)

e. social learning

25. Describe the relationship between aggression and pornography.

26. With respect to the effects of violence on television:
    a. summarize the relationship between television violence and real life.

    b. explain how television violence may teach antisocial actions, disinhibit dangerous impulses, and desensitize a person to violence.

27. Describe how television could be used to promote prosocial behavior.

28.   Explain the basic principle of anger control.

29.   List six steps that parents can do to buffer the impact of television on their children.

a.

b.

c.

d.

e.

f.

30.   Give an example of bystander apathy, and indicate the major factor which determines whether or not help will be given.

31.   Trace the progress of an individual through the four decision points which must be passed before helping behavior is given. Indicate how the presence of other people can influence apathy.

The following objectives are related to the material in the "Applications" section of your text.

32.   Define the term multiculturalism.

33.   Discuss six ways in which a person can become more tolerant.

a.

b.

c.

(continued on page 368)

d.

e.

f.

34. Explain how a person can develop cultural awareness.

Do You Know the Information?

Multiple Choice

1. Which of the following *best* exemplifies the idea of flexitime?
    (a) Workers' hours are staggered and rotated.
    (b) Starting and quitting times are voluntarily adjustable within limits.
    (c) Days off are rotated and made flexible.
    (d) Twenty-five percent of the workers must arrive for the "core hours" during the day.

2. Which of the following statements about biodata is *false*?
    (a) Biodata is a good way to predict job success.
    (b) The idea behind biodata is that past behavior predicts future behavior.
    (c) Some useful items of biodata are past athletic interest, scientific interest, and religious activities.
    (d) Biodata is used to help screen out job candidates who seem to have serious psychological problems.

3. _____ are situations that an employee must be able to cope with if he or she is going to succeed in a particular job.
    (a) Critical incidents   (b) In-basket tests   (c) Personal interviews   (d) Aptitude tests

4. At an assessment center
    (a) one would be likely to receive vocational counseling.
    (b) one might be likely to receive an in-basket test.
    (c) candidates for assembly line positions would be screened and evaluated.
    (d) management strategies such as Theory X are evaluated.

5. Theory Y is most closely associated with which of the following terms?
    (a) scientific management   (b) work efficiency   (c) task analysis   (d) participative management

6. Which of the following factors is *not* closely associated with the highest job satisfaction?
    (a) relative freedom from close supervision   (c) pleasant working environment
    (b) allowed ordinary social contacts with others   (d) recognition for doing well

7. Which of the following principles is *not* associated with job enrichment strategies?
    (a) giving employees greater responsibility
    (b) allowing employees to do a complete cycle of work
    (c) giving workers feedback about their work through their immediate supervisor
    (d) encouraging workers to learn new and more difficult tasks

8. Which of the following *not* an effective way to improve communication?
    (a) speak slowly
    (b) avoid excessive use of jargon
    (c) don't overuse big words
    (d) state ideas clearly and decisively

9. Which of the following is *not* an effective way to improve listening skills?
    (a) try to identify the speaker's purpose
    (b) evaluate the information as you hear it so you can formulate an intelligent reply
    (c) pay attention to non-verbal messages
    (d) accept responsibility for effective communication

10. Environmental psychologists are most concerned with
    (a) physical environments.   (b) social environments.   (c) behavioral settings.   (d) all of the above.

11. With respect to crowding and density, it best to say that
    (a) crowding is a psychological condition separate from density.
    (b) density is a psychological condition separate from crowding.
    (c) crowding refers to subjective feeling of being over-stimulated by physical inputs.
    (d) density refers to a loss of privacy.

12. The term _____ refers to the number of people in a given space.
    (a) crowding   (b) discrimination   (c) overload   (d) density

13. Sensory and cognitive overload (according to Milgram) may result in
    (a) ignoring nonessential events.
    (b) brief, superficial interpersonal contacts.
    (c) callousness.
    (d) all of the above.

14. Which specialty would tend to work with people who design buildings?
    (a) industrial psychology   (b) organizational psychology   (c) architectural psychology   (d) personnel psychology

15. In general, any social situation that rewards actions that have undesirable effects in the long run is called a
    (a) social problem.   (b) tragedy of the commons.   (c) social trap.   (d) compliant behavior.

16. Rubin's study of romantic love revealed that
    (a) mutual absorption was important for both liking and romantic love.
    (b) mutual absorption almost always led to sexual intimacy.
    (c) dating couples liked and loved their partners but mostly liked their friends.
    (d) all of the above are true.

17. The three ingredients of Sternberg's triangular theory of love are
    (a) passion, commitment, and intimacy.
    (b) arousal, balance, and sharing.
    (c) affection, sharing, and communication.
    (d) respect, shared interests, and friendship.

18. _____ is the primary source of love's intensity.
    (a) Passion   (b) Commitment   (c) Intimacy   (d) Mutual absorption

19. Companionate love is characterized by
    (a) heightened arousal and mutual absorption.
    (b) liking someone.
    (c) a mixture of tenderness and sexuality, elation and pain, anxiety and relief.
    (d) affection and attachment built on shared interests and firm friendship.

20. The difference between prejudice and discrimination is
    (a) prejudice leads to discrimination, but discrimination doesn't lead to prejudice.
    (b) prejudice refers to behavior and discrimination doesn't.
    (c) discrimination is always negative and prejudice is not.
    (d) discrimination refers to behavior, prejudice refers to an attitude.

21. People who have an authoritarian personality
    (a) are happy but rather prejudiced.
    (b) were raised as children to be independent and achievement oriented.
    (c) have attitudes and values marked by rigidity, inhibition, and oversimplification.
    (d) are prejudiced against all in-groups.

22. Oversimplified images of people who fall into a particular category are called
    (a) social stereotypes.   (b) ethnocentrisms.   (c) group attitudes.   (d) status inequalities.

23. Which of the following statements is *incorrect*?
    (a) Status inequalities help to increase prejudice.
    (b) Superordinate goals are usually too difficult to reach and thus increase prejudice and discrimination.
    (c) Equal-status interaction between groups should reduce prejudice and stereotypes.
    (d) Prejudice and discrimination can be taught to children in as little as one day.

24. The social learning theory states that
    (a) when we become frustrated, we become aggressive.
    (b) there are certain areas of the brain responsible for triggering aggression.
    (c) aggression is an instinct.
    (d) we become aggressive by observing aggression in others.

25. Concerning aggression and pornography it has been found that
    (a) pornography causes aggression.
    (b) exposure to an aggressive film after becoming angry helps reduce a person's level of anger .
    (c) the mass media has not had an appreciable effect on sex-related crimes.
    (d) none of the above are true.

26. Which of the following statements *best* describes the effects of TV on children?
    (a) Violence on TV makes children more sensitive to aggressive acts in the real world.
    (b) Children who watch a great deal of televised violence will be more prone to behave aggressively.
    (c) TV has been shown to cause aggression in children.
    (d) Although found to be a tremendous source of entertainment, TV has not been found to have a definite positive or negative effect on children.

27. In helping to prevent aggression, social learning theorists suggest
    (a) avoiding violent TV programs around the age of 8 years old when a child would be most impressionable.
    (b) modeling prosocial behavior on TV.
    (c) giving a child a pet, such as a puppy.
    (d) none of the above.

28. To counteract the negative effects of television on children, parents (choose all that apply)
    (a) can limit total viewing time so that television does not dominate the child's view of the world.
    (b) can closely monitor what a child does watch.
    (c) should actively seek programs that model positive behavior and social attitudes.
    (d) need to help a child see the closeness between reality and TV fantasies.
    (e) can help children see how violence can apply in the real world.
    (f) can show by their own disapproval that violent TV heroes are not the ones to emulate.

29. A person will be likely to help someone when
    (a) there are few people around.
    (b) there is greater diffusion of responsibility.
    (c) there are many people around to provide emotional support.
    (d) status inequalities exist.

30. Multiculturalism
    (a) holds that some day there will be few cultural differences between people.
    (b) gives equal status to different ethnic, racial, and cultural groups.
    (c) supports racial integration because it encourages diversity.
    (d) includes all of the above.

31. Which of the following statements concerning multiculturalism is *incorrect*?
   (a) Just-world beliefs assume that all discrimination and prejudice will disappear in time.
   (b) Seeking individuating information helps to eliminate stereotypes.
   (c) People tend to act in accordance with other's expectations of them.
   (d) Social competition tends to foster a feeling of "we're better than all the rest" in every major ethnic group.

32. To develop cultural awarness one should
   (a) *not* fall prey to just-world beliefs.
   (b) be aware of self-fulfilling prophecies.
   (c) try to see those who are different from you as individuals.
   (d) do all of the above.

Matching (*Use the letters on the right only once.*)

____ 1. applied psychology
____ 2. industrial/organizational psychology
____ 3. personal interview
____ 4. concerned with work efficiency
____ 5. job enrichment
____ 6. environmental psychology
____ 7. protecting your space
____ 8. crowding
____ 9. how love and friendship differ
____ 10. behavior as opposed to attitude
____ 11. form of displaced aggression
____ 12. personal prejudice
____ 13. ethnocentric
____ 14. symbolic prejudice
____ 15. jigsaw classroom
____ 16. humans are naturally aggressive
____ 17. desensitization
____ 18. key to anger control
____ 19. define emergency

A. Theory Y
B. popular method to select people for jobs or promotions
C. how surroundings influence our behavior
D. a psychological condition from being overstimulated
E. use of psychological principles and research methods to solve practical problems
F. territoriality
G. Theory X
H. mutual absorption
I. studies the problems people face at work
J. removing some of the controls and restrictions promotes this
K. density
L. displaying prejudice in disguised forms
M. attentional overload
N. heightened arousal
O. job satisfaction
P. only members of own nationality, ethnic or religious group acceptable
Q. when members of another group represent a threat to individual security or comfort
R. a lowered sensitivity to violent acts
S. discrimination
T. instinct
U. see the upsetting situation as problem to solve
V. scapegoating
W. one of the decision points for helping behavior to occur
X. must cooperate in order to succeed
Y. group prejudice
Z. bystander intervention

Can You Apply the Information?

1. Company X needs to find out exactly who will best be able cope with the demands of a production line which uses robotics and other automation. In addition, for long periods there will be little social contact with co-workers. As a supervisor in this company, you would be most likely to employ the aid of a(n) _____ to help make this determination.
   (a) environmental psychologist
   (b) architectural psychologist
   (c) personnel psychologist
   (d) industrial/organizational psychologist

2. Marge is applying for an entry-level job in the complaint section at a local department store. She will be expected to handle the complaints of all customers, no matter how distasteful, with a smile on her face and the knowledge that patience is a virtue. Which of the following pieces of information about her background would be most helpful in her selection?
   (a) Marge was a model before she got married 22 years ago.
   (b) Marge was able to get an average score on the in-basket test.
   (c) Marge has raised four children who were constantly picking at each other, all without ever losing her cool.
   (d) Marge has taken and passed a CPR course.

3. At Hoof-Hearted Horseshoe Factory there are no private offices for management, everyone wears the same overalls, and there are daily meetings that everyone attends to air differences, talk about production, etc. Which type of management does this factory operate under?
    (a) Theory X   (b) scientific   (c) Theory Y   (d) work efficiency

4. Since buying the company, the employees of the Don't Step On Me Ladder Company meet regularly with their management representatives in order to achieve the maximum output at the lowest cost. These meetings resemble a
    (a) work efficiency management style.   (c) quality circle management style.
    (b) management by objectives style.   (d) participative management style.

5. You have been working on your taxes and have organized piles of receipts all over your dining room table. Your spouse enters and says, "Where did all this garbage come from?" thereby making what mistake of effective communication?
    (a) use of loaded words   (b) excessive use of slang   (c) overuse of big words   (d) not using your name

6. Linda works in a large office area where each person has his/her own desk, but their are no walls or other dividers. She brings a couple of plants from home and a picture or two. Linda is most likely engaging in
    (a) personal space.   (b) job satisfaction.   (c) job enrichment.   (d) territoriality.

7. Put eight people in a space the size of a hot tub, call it an elevator, and you'll probably find eight uncomfortable people. Put eight people in a hot tub and you'll probably find eight contented people. The difference is probably due to
    (a) density.   (b) images.   (c) psychic "noise."   (d) crowding.

8. The setting is the coast of Florida. It is August and the National Weather Service is predicting that a hurricane will strike Miami. There is plenty of food in the stores, but a minority of people go out and buy much more than they could possibly eat in a month. This creates a shortage for the rest of the population that has decided to stay and ride out the storm. This situation is called
    (a) a social problem.   (c) an environmental assessment.
    (b) the tragedy of the commons.   (d) heightened arousal.

9. Bill and Rita are each other's best friend and tell each other everything. They have been together for 43 years and seem to get closer every year. Although popular stereotypes contradict it, they also still have a passion which is unmatched by many younger couples. Which of the following statements about them is *true*?
    (a) They exhibit fatuous love.   (c) They exhibit companionate love.
    (b) They probably have more passion than commitment.   (d) They are a good example of consummate love.

10. Fred has a great distrust and suspicion of the Japanese. He always expects Japanese people to be cunning and wiley. This is an example of discrimination.
    (a) True   (b) False

11. It is likely that most members of the Ku Klux Klan possess a high level of (circle all that apply)
    (a) ethnocentrism.   (b) dogmatism.   (c) personal prejudice.   (d) group prejudice.

12. Fred is riding on a bus to a football game. The bus has a flat tire, and in order to get to the game Fred helps the Japanese bus driver change the tire. Fred's attitudes have mellowed toward Japanese people slightly as a result of the incident. This is an example of using a(n) _____ goal to reduce hostility.
    (a) overriding   (b) symbolic   (c) jigsaw   (d) superordinate

Chapter Review

1. The use of psychological principles to solve practical problems is called _____ psychology.

2. Industrial/_____ psychologists study the problems people face at work. Typically, they work in three major areas: testing and placement (_____ psychology); human relations at work; and, the design of machines and work environments (_____ _____).

3. The idea of _____ is that workers get to choose their starting and quitting times within limits. Benefits observed from this include increased job _____ and less _____.

4. Personnel psychologists try to match people with jobs. To do this they may do a _____ _____ to find out exactly what workers do. This can be done by interview, questionnaire, or observation. In addition, one can also identify the situations that an employee must be able to cope with if he or she is going to succeed in a particular job (_____ _____).

5. The methods most often used for evaluating job candidates include the collection of _____ , _____, standardized _____ _____ and the assessment center approach.

6. The idea behind collecting biodata is that _____ behavior is a good predictor of _____ behavior.

7. The personal _____ is a popular way to select people for jobs or promotions even though they may be subject to the _____ _____.

8. Along with intelligence and personality tests, personnel psychologists often use _____ _____ tests (to see if the applicant's interests match those of people already in the field) and _____ tests (to rate a person's potential to learn tasks used in various occupations).

9. In addition, _____ centers may be used to fill management and executive positions by doing in-depth evaluations of job candidates.

10. Managers who are concerned with improving work efficiency as opposed to worker autonomy and participation in management believe in Theory _____ (also known as _____ management). Theory ____ managers assume that workers enjoy independence and are willing to accept responsibility (as seen by the effective methods of _____ management and management by _____).

11. Theory Y workplaces may also involve the use of _____ _____ (voluntary discussion groups that meet regularly to solve business problems).

12. Job satisfaction appears to be closely related to the following factors: _____ contact with other workers, opportunity to use their own _____ and _____, recognition for doing well, chance to apply their _____, freedom from close _____, opportunity for _____ and _____.

13. Job enrichment involves removing some of the _____ and _____ on employees. As a result, there are usually lower production _____, increased job _____, reduced _____, and less _____.

14. Knowing how to communicate clearly can be very important. One should: state ideas _____ and decisively; not overuse _____ words; avoid excessive use of _____ or slang; avoid _____ words; use people's _____; and be polite and _____.

15. Being a good listener, on the other hand, requires paying _____, identifying the speaker's _____, suspending _____, checking your _____ of what is being said, looking out for _____-_____ messages, and accepting _____ for effective communication.

16. The speciality concerned with how our surroundings influence our behavior is called _____ psychology. This speciality is interested in _____ and _____ surroundings and _____ settings. A major finding of environmental research is that much of our behavior is controlled by the _____.

17. _____ refers to the tendency to identify a space as ours and to signal that "ownership" with obvious _____ _____.

18. Overpopulation is a serious problem today. However, distress is caused by factors in addition to the _____, the sheer number of people in a given space.

19. _____ refers to subjective feelings of being overstimulated by loss of privacy or increased social input. At a party, a high _____ may be experienced as pleasurable whereas in another situation it may lead to stress. A consequence of this is cognitive and sensory overload (also called _____ overload) which may lead to superficiality or callousness in interpersonal interactions.

20. The speciality concerned with the importance of designing buildings to maximize psychological comfort is called _____ psychology. This process may involve developing a picture of environments by the people who use them (an _____ _____). For example, such a process could be used to reduce _____ pollution, a major source of environmental stress.

21. A _____ _____ is any situation that rewards actions which have undesired effects in the long run. If this situation is one in which if many people act alike collective harm is done then it is called a collective _____ _____. If a number of people share a common resource and each individual acts in his or her own best interest which causes the resource to be depleted, this is called the _____ of the _____. Sometimes these situations can be avoided if the _____ and _____ can be rearranged.

22. Rubin has found that dating couples _____ and _____ their partners, but mostly _____ their friends. Women, however, were a little more "_____" toward their friends than were men. "Passionate" or romantic love is often associated with _____ _____.

23. Robert Sternberg has a _____ theory of love. He believes that love is made up of closeness (_____), heightened arousal (_____), and one's decision to love another person only (_____).

24. _____ is a negative attitude which may contribute to _____, behavior that prevents individuals from doing things they would like, such as buying a house or belonging to an organization.

25. Prejudice may represent itself as _____, a form of _____ aggression in which hostility and frustration cause aggression to be redirected to other targets. _____ prejudice occurs when an individual's comfort or security is threatened by members of another racial or ethnic group. _____ prejudice occurs through the individual's identifying with group norms.

26. One prejudice-prone personality is the _____ personality. _____ tend to be _____ or prejudiced against all _____-_____, that is, people who are not members of their own national, ethnic, or religious group. However, since authoritarian personalities can be found at both ends of the political spectrum, it may be more appropriate to label rigid and intolerant thinking as _____.

27. Prejudice may have its roots in positive or negative _____ _____ or oversimplified images of people who are in a particular category. This prejudice may become _____ if it is displayed in a disguised form since crude and obvious racism is considered socially unacceptable. In any event, stereotypes tend to be unusually _____.

28. Elliot demonstrated that prejudices were easy to develop when _____ _____ were present between two or more persons or groups.

29.   Increased _____-_____ interaction between groups in conflict should reduce prejudice and stereotyping. On the other hand, merely bringing people together may increase negative stereotyping unless _____ _____ force members of each group to cooperate for mutual gain. "_____" classrooms force this type of interaction by requiring cooperation for students to do well, by way of mutual _____, on tests.

30.   Some of the potential explanations for the occurrence of aggression include the theory of Konrad Lorenz, a prominent _____, who believes that aggression is an _____ behavior observed in all animals, including humans.

31.   Other researchers feel that there is a _____ basis for aggressive behavior. Certain _____ areas may be capable of triggering or ending aggressive behavior. In addition, there may be a relationship between aggression and _____, _____, specific _____ injuries and disorders, and between aggression and _____. Note that none of these conditions are a direct _____ of aggression. Instead they probably lower the _____ making hostile behavior more likely to occur.

32.   The _____-_____ hypothesis states that there is a close link between _____ and _____. However _____ does not always lead to _____, and _____ can occur in the absence of _____, such as instances in which such actions are committed by trick-or-treaters on Halloween even after they have received treats.

33.   The _____ _____ theory of aggression holds that we learn aggression by observing aggression in others. Among the most influential models for children were those observed on _____. Children may learn _____ in this way.

34.   Recent studies indicate that there is a link between _____ and _____. Exposure to mass media stimuli that have _____ and _____ content increases the audience's aggressive-sexual fantasies, beliefs in _____ myths, and _____ behavior. Experts warn that it is media _____ which is most damaging.

35.   All of the violence and aggression on television may be teaching our children new _____ actions, as well as _____ aggressive impulses viewers may already have, and _____ the viewers to the reality of violence.

36.   Since social learning theory implies that "_____ begets _____," the opposite should also be true. Specifically, television could be used to promote _____ behavior in the same way that it encourages aggression.

37.   _____ control can be taught. The key to it is the fact that people who respond calmly to upsetting situations tend to see them as _____ to be _____.

38.   One factor which leads to bystander _____ is the presence of other people. When many other people are present, personal responsibility for helping is spread thin. Before people decide to give help, they must _____ that something is happening, they must _____ the event as an emergency, they must take _____ and finally, they must _____ a course of action. Groups limit helping by causing a _____ of _____. Studies show that when we see someone in trouble, this tends to cause an increase in two types of arousal: _____ arousal and _____ arousal.

39.   Learning to respect and appreciate cultural differences is termed _____. To help ourselves become more culturally aware we can: (1) beware of _____; (2) seek _____ information; (3) be careful of _____-_____ beliefs as well as _____-_____ prophecies; (4) avoid unnecessary _____; and (5) look for _____.

ANSWER KEYS

Do You Know the Information?

Multiple Choice

1. (b) obj. 3, p. 644
2. (d) obj. 4, p. 644
3. (a) obj. 4, p. 644
4. (b) obj. 4, p. 646
5. (d) obj. 5, p. 647
6. (c) obj. 6, p. 649
7. (c) obj. 7, p. 649
8. (a) obj. 8, p. 650
9. (b) obj. 9, p. 651
10. (d) obj. 10, p. 652
11. (a) objs. 12-13, p. 654
12. (d) obj. 13, p. 654
13. (d) obj. 13, p. 655
14. (c) obj. 14, p. 656
15. (c) obj. 15, p. 658
16. (c) obj. 16, p. 659
17. (a) obj. 17, p. 660
18. (a) obj. 17, p. 660
19. (d) obj. 17, p. 661
20. (d) obj. 18, p. 662
21. (c) objs. 19-20, p. 663
22. (a) obj. 21, p. 664

23. (b) objs. 22-23, pp. 666-667
24. (d) obj. 24, p. 672
25. (d) obj. 25, p. 672
26. (b) obj. 26, p. 673
27. (b) obj. 27, p. 674
28. (a,b,c,f) obj. 29, p. 675
29. (a) objs. 30-31, p. 675
30. (b) obj. 32, p. 679
31. (a) objs. 32-33, pp. 679-680
32. (d) obj. 34, pp. 679-680

Matching

1. E, obj. 1, p. 643
2. I, obj. 2, p. 643
3. B, obj. 4, p. 644
4. G, obj. 5, p. 647
5. J, obj. 7, p. 649
6. C, obj. 10, p. 652
7. F, obj. 11, p. 653
8. D, obj. 13, p. 654
9. H, obj. 16, p. 660
10. S, obj. 18, p. 662

11. V, obj. 19, p. 662
12. Q, obj. 19, p. 663
13. P, obj. 20, p. 663
14. L, obj. 21, p. 665
15. X, obj. 23, p. 668
16. T, obj. 24, p. 670
17. R, obj. 26, p. 673
18. U, obj. 28, p. 674
19. W, obj. 31, p. 676

Can You Apply the Information?

1. (c) obj. 4, p. 644
2. (c) obj. 4, p. 646
3. (c) obj. 5, p. 647
4. (d) obj. 5, p. 648
5. (a) obj. 8, p. 650
6. (d) obj. 11, p. 653
7. (d) obj. 13, p. 654
8. (b) obj. 15, p. 658
9. (d) obj. 17, p. 661
10. (b) obj. 18, p. 662
11. (a,b,c,d) objs. 19-20, pp. 663-664
12. (d) obj. 23, p. 667

Chapter Review

1. applied (p. 643)
2. organizational, personnel, industrial engineering (p. 643)
3. flexitime, satisfaction, absenteeism (p. 644)
4. job analysis, critical incidents (p. 644)
5. biodata, interviews, psychological tests (p. 644)
6. past, future (p. 644)
7. interview, halo effect (p. 644)
8. vocational interest, aptitude (p. 645)
9. assessment (p. 646)
10. X, scientific, Y, participative, objectives (p. 647)
11. quality circles (p. 648)
12. social, judgment, intelligence, skills, supervision, promotion, advancement (p. 649)
13. controls, restrictions, costs, satisfaction, boredom, absenteeism (p. 649)
14. clearly, big, jargon, loaded, names, respectful (p. 650)
15. attention, purpose, evaluation, understanding, non-verbal, responsibility (p. 651)
16. environmental, physical, social, behavioral, environment (p. 652)
17. Territoriality, territorial markers (p. 653)
18. density (p. 654)
19. Crowding, density, attentional (p. 654)
20. architectural, environmental assessment, noise (p. 657)
21. social trap, social trap, tragedy, commons, rewards, costs (p. 658)
22. like, love, like, loving (p. 659); mutual absorption (p. 660)
23. triangular, intimacy, passion, commitment (p. 660)

24. Prejudice, discrimination (p. 662)
25. scapegoating, displaced, Personal, Group (p. 662)
26. authoritarian, Authoritarians, ethnocentric, out-groups, dogmatic (p. 663)
27. social stereotypes, symbolic, irrational (p. 665)
28. status inequalities (p. 664)
29. equal-status, superordinate goals, Jigsaw, interdependence (p. 666)
30. ethologist, instinctive (p. 670)
31. biological, brain, hypoglycemia, allergies, brain, drugs (alcohol), cause, threshold (p. 670)
32. frustration-aggression, frustration, aggression, frustration, aggression, aggression, frustration (p. 670)
33. social learning, television, aggression, television (p. 672)
34. aggression, pornography, violent, sexual, rape, aggressive, violence (p. 672)
35. aggressive (anti-social), disinhibiting, desensitizing (p. 673)
36. aggression, aggression, prosocial (p. 673)
37. Anger, problems, solved (p. 674)
38. apathy, notice, define, responsibility, select, diffusion, responsibility, general, empathic (p. 675)
39. multiculturalism, stereotypes, individuating, just-world, self-fulfilling, social competition, commonalities (p. 679)

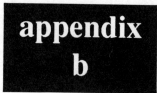

appendix b *Statistics*

descriptive statistics
  graphical statistics
    frequency distribution
    histogram
    frequency polygon
  measures of central tendency
    mean, median, mode
  measures of variability

range
standard deviation
  Z-scores
normal curve
inferential statistics
  sample vs. population
  representative, random

significant difference
correlation
  positive relationship
  zero relationship
  negative relationship
  prediction
variance
correlation vs. causation

LEARNING OBJECTIVES

To demonstrate mastery of this chapter you should be able to:

1. Distinguish between the purposes of descriptive and inferential statistics.

2. List the three basic techniques of descriptive statistics.

    a.

    b.

    c.

3. Explain the purpose of graphical statistics and give an example of a frequency distribution, a histogram, and a frequency polygon.

4. List and describe the three measures of central tendency. Explain why the mean is not always the best measure of central tendency.

    a.

    b.

    c.

5. Describe the use of the range, standard deviation, and z-score as measures of the variability of scores around the mean.

6. Describe the use of the normal curve and its relationship to the standard deviation (or z-score).

7. Explain the difference between a population and a sample.

8. Explain the importance of representativeness and randomness as they relate to a sample.

9. Explain the purpose of a test of statistical significance.

10. Describe how a correlation coefficient indicates the degree of relationship between two variables.

11. Give an example of the useful information that correlations can provide. Explain how correlation coefficients are used to make predictions.

12. Describe the limitations of correlation as it relates to causation.

SELF-QUIZZES

Do You Know the Information?

Multiple Choice

1. Which of the following statements is *incorrect*?
   (a) Inferential statistics are used for decision-making.
   (b) Inferential statistics are used for drawing conclusions.
   (c) Descriptive statistics are used for generalizing to the population-at-large from a small sample.
   (d) Inferential statistics allow us to generalize from the behavior of small groups of subjects to that of the larger groups they represent.

2. Which of the following is *not* one of the three basic techniques of descriptive statistics?
   (a) measures of central tendency   (c) measures of variability
   (b) measures of reliability   (d) graphical statistics

3. The graphic display of frequency distributions which uses bars to indicate the frequency of scores within class intervals is the
   (a) frequency polygon.   (b) histograph.   (c) histogram.   (d) frequency distribution.

4. Graphical statistics are used for the purpose of letting people "see" how a pattern of numbers looks.
   (a) True   (b) False

5. The measure of central tendency which is obtained by ranking scores from the highest to the lowest and selecting the middle score is the
   (a) mode.   (b) mean.   (c) standard deviation.   (d) median.

6. The mean is not always the best measure of central tendency because it
   (a) is difficult to compute.   (c) always distorts the population.
   (b) can't be used to help calculate a coefficient of correlation.   (d) is sensitive to extremely high or low scores in a distribution.

7. The measure of central tendency which expresses the most frequently occurring score in a distribution is the
   (a) mode.   (b) mean.   (c) standard deviation.   (d) median.

8. The number which represents the spread between the highest and the lowest score in a distribution is called the
   (a) range.   (b) standard deviation.   (c) z-score.   (d) normal score.

9. An advantage of the standard deviation is that it can be used to "standardize" scores to give them more meaning.
   (a) True   (b) False

10. A z-score is a number which shows the relationship among a person's score, the mean, and the standard deviation.
    (a) True   (b) False

11. Psychological traits or events (like chance events) tend to approximate a normal curve where some outcomes have very little probability but occur frequently.
    (a) True   (b) False

12. In a normal curve, 68 percent of all cases fall between 3 SD above and below the mean.
    (a) True   (b) False

13. A sample
    (a) is composed of the entire group about which you wish to make inferences.
    (b) should be representative of the composition and characteristics of the larger population.
    (c) provides an estimate of how often experimental results could have occurred by chance alone.
    (d) is an example of descriptive statistics.

14. Tests of statistical significance
    (a) relate the mean to the mode.
    (b) are predictive of the coefficient of correlation.
    (c) provide an estimate of how often experimental results could have occurred by chance alone.
    (d) are an example of descriptive statistics.

15. When two variables are not related, they have a
    (a) positive correlation.   (b) zero correlation.   (c) negative correlation.   (d) statistical significance.

16. If decreases in one measure (X) are matched by decreases in the other measure (Y), what we have is a
    (a) positive correlation.   (b) negative correlation.

17. If we know two measures are correlated, and we know a person's score on one measure,
    (a) we can predict his or her score on the other.   (c) the tests are probably causally related.
    (b) we can assume the tests are representative.   (d) all of the above answers are true.

Can You Apply the Information?

1. You are an average student, and you have a test in your psychology class. Your instructor decides to give a passing grade to everyone over a certain grade and a failing grade to everyone under that grade. There is a really brilliant student in your class who always aces every test. How would you rather have your instructor compute that dividing point?
    (a) Mean   (b) Median

2. Your instructor decides instead to report your score as a z-score. You get a +1.5. Are you happy with your score?
    (a) Yes   (b) No

3. Gordon wants to do an election prediction for Chicago. Should he get a sample or a population?
    (a) Sample   (b) Population

4. The first thing Gordon would do after polling everyone on his list would be to begin using _____ statistics.
    (a) descriptive   (b) inferential

5. As the temperature increases the activity level of dogs decreases. Which of the following coefficients of correlation best expresses this observation?
    (a) +.86   (b) -.30   (c) 0   (d) +.07

Chapter Review

1.   One of the two major types of statistical methods is _____ statistics. They are used to summarize large amounts of data. The second major type is used for decision-making, for _____ from _____ samples, and for drawing conclusions. This type is called _____ statistics.

2.   The three basic types of descriptive statistics are _____ statistics, measures of _____ _____, and measures of _____.

3.   One type of graphical statistics is the _____ distribution. It is formed by breaking down the entire range of possible scores into classes of equal size and then recording the number of scores falling in each class. This type of distribution is often expressed graphically using _____. An alternative way of graphing a distribution of scores is the more familiar _____ _____. Here, points are placed at the center of each class interval to indicate the number of cases. Then, the dots are connected by straight lines.

4.   A measure of _____ _____ is simply a number describing a "middle score" around which other scores fall. One familiar measure is the _____ or average. It is sensitive to extremely _____ or _____ scores in a distribution and, consequently, does not always give the best measure of _____ _____. In such cases the "middle score" in a group of scores, called the _____, is used instead.

5.   A final measure of central tendency is the _____. It simply represents the most frequently occurring score in a distribution.

6.   When we want to know if scores are clustered closely about the mean or scattered widely, we use measures of _____ to attach a numerical value to the "spread of scores." The simplest way to describe variability is to use the _____, which is the spread between the highest and lowest scores. A better measure of variability is the _____ _____.

7.   A particular advantage of the standard deviation is that it can be used to "standardize" scores in a way that gives them greater meaning. This is done using the _____-_____.

8.   When chance events are recorded and graphed, they resemble what is called a _____ _____. Measures of psychological variables tend to approximate this curve.

9.   A great deal is known about the mathematical properties of the normal curve. For example, there is a fixed relationship between the _____ _____ and the normal curve. The standard deviation measures off constant proportions of the curve above and below the mean. As an example of this principle, notice that _____ percent of all cases fall between one standard deviation above and below the mean. Similarly, _____ percent of all cases can be found between three standard deviations above and below the mean.

10.   _____ statistics, the other major division of statistical methods, includes techniques that allow us to _____ from the behavior of small groups of subjects to that of the larger groups they represent.

11.   In any scientific investigation, we would like to observe the entire set or _____ of subjects, objects, or events being studied. However, this is usually impossible. Instead, _____ or small cross sections of a population are selected, and observations of this group are used to draw conclusions about the entire group.

12.   The major requirement of any sample is that it be _____. It must truly reflect the composition and characteristics of the larger population. A very important aspect of representative samples is that their members are chosen at _____; that is, each member of the population must have an equal chance of being included in the sample.

13. When we compare results from different groups, we wish to know if they might have simply occurred by chance or if they represent a real difference. Tests of _____ _____ provide an estimate of how often experimental results could have occurred by chance alone.

14. The results of a test of statistical significance are stated as a probability, giving the odds that the observed difference was due to chance. In psychology, any experimental condition attributable to chance _____ times or less out of 100 is considered significant.

15. Many of the statements that psychologists make about behavior do not result from the use of experimental methods and are not analyzed using tests of statistical significance. Instead, they deal with the fact that two variables are _____-_____ (varying together in some orderly fashion).

16. We use _____ methods which give a number, called the _____ of _____, indicating the degree of relationship between two measures.

17. A _____ correlation occurs when there is no relationship between the two variables. With a _____ correlation, increases (decreases) in the scores of one variable are associated with increases (decreases) in the other. With a _____ correlation, increases (decreases) in the scores of one variable are associated with decreases (increases) in the other. The numerical value of a correlation coefficient may range from _____ for a perfect positive correlation to _____ for a perfect negative relationship.

18. Correlations often provide useful information. For instance, it is valuable to know that there is a correlation between _____ and lung cancer rates. Correlations are particularly valuable for making _____. If we know two measures are correlated, and we know a person's score on one measure, then we can predict the person's score on the other.

19. It is important to recognize that the existence of a correlation between two measures does not mean that one causes the other. This is expressed by the phrase, "_____ does not demonstrate _____."

ANSWER KEYS

Do You Know the Information?

Multiple Choice

1. (c) obj. 1, p. A7
2. (b) obj. 2, p. A7
3. (c) obj. 3, p. A8
4. (a) obj. 3, p. A8
5. (d) obj. 4, p. A10
6. (d) obj. 4, p. A9
7. (a) obj. 4, p. A10
8. (a) obj. 5, p. A10

9. (a) obj. 5, p. A10
10. (a) obj. 5, p. A10
11. (b) obj. 6, p. A11
12. (b) obj. 6, p. A12
13. (b) objs. 7-8, p. A13
14. (c) obj. 9, p. A14
15. (b) obj. 10, p. A14
16. (a) obj. 10, p. A14
17. (a) objs. 11-12, pp. A16-17

Can You Apply the Information?

1. (b) obj. 4, p. A9
2. (a) obj. 5-6, pp. A10, A12-A13
3. (a) obj. 7, p. A13
4. (a) obj. 1, p. A7
5. (b) obj. 10, pp. A14-A15

Chapter Review

1. descriptive, generalizing, small, inferential (p. A7)
2. graphical, central tendency, variability (p. A7)
3. frequency, histograms, frequency polygon (p. A8)
4. central tendency, mean (p. A8); high, low, central tendency, median (p. A9)
5. mode (p. A10)
6. variability, range, standard deviation (p. A10)
7. z-score (p. A10)

8. normal curve (p. A11)
9. standard deviation, 68, 99 (p. A12)
10. Inferential, generalize (p. A13)
11. population, samples (p. A13)
12. representative, random (p. A13)
13. statistical significance (p. A14)
14. five (p. A14)
15. co-relating (p. A14)
16. correlational, coefficient, correlation (p. A14)
17. zero, positive, negative, +1.00, -1.00 (p. A14)
18. smoking (p. A15); predictions (p. A16)
19. Correlation, causation (p. A17)